Truly and Falsely
JESUS
in the Bible

Saleh Ali as-Subayil

Copyright © 2023 Saleh Ali as-Subayil
All rights reserved
First Edition

NEWMAN SPRINGS PUBLISHING
320 Broad Street
Red Bank, NJ 07701

First originally published by Newman Springs Publishing 2023

ISBN 978-1-68498-406-0 (Paperback)
ISBN 978-1-68498-407-7 (Digital)

Printed in the United States of America

In the name of God, the Most Gracious, the Most Merciful

Contents

Preface xi

Introduction xiii
    Salvation, the goal xiii
    Why Jesus? xiii
    Faith in Jesus xiv
    Where is the truth about Jesus? xv
    The gospels xvi
    The author of the Gospel of Matthew xvii
    The author of the Gospel of Mark xviii
    The author of the Gospel of Luke xix
    The author of the Gospel of John xx

Chapter 1: Truly Jesus 1
    What did Jesus's contemporaries say? 8

Chapter 2: Jesus answers some conjectures and suspicions 11
    "I and my father are one" (John 10:30) 11
    Son of God 14
    The Trinity 19
    "The only begotten Son" (John 3:16) 28
    "Before Abraham was, I am" (John 8:58) 34
    "I am the way, the truth, and the life. No one comes to the Father except through me" (John 14:6) 37
    "He who has seen me has seen the Father" (John 14:9) 38
    Going to all nations 39

Chapter 3: Falsely Jesus 46
    The fake image of Jesus in the New Testament 46
    References of the fake image of Jesus 49
    Deconstructing the fake image of Jesus................................ 52

Chapter 4: Was Jesus really crucified? 61
    Preface.. 61
    Research 1: Was it a mission for Jesus to die for the
        forgiveness of sins?.. 63
    Research 2: Why did the Jews plot to put Jesus to death? 71
    Research 3: How did the Jews move to implement
        the plot of killing Jesus?.. 73
    Research 4: How did Jesus behave toward the Jewish
        conspiracy?... 74
    Research 5: Did the Jews find Jesus and arrest him
        when they seek him?... 77
    The plot to kill Jesus 80
    Preparing the Passover meal (the Last Supper) 82
    Jesus's prophecies at the Passover table (Last Supper) 82
    How did Jesus leave the garden to the place of hiding? 86
    When Jesus prophesied that the Jews would seek
        him and not find him, did he mean their last
        attempt with Judas? 87
    Did Jesus mean heaven for the place where he would go? 91
    Did Jesus mean the tomb for the place
        where he would go? 94
    What was the place of hiding that Jesus went
        to and where? 97
    Was Jesus hinting to the tomb with the term
        "the heart of the earth"? 100
    Research 6: Who was the crucified person? 102
    Peter was rescued too... 103
    Who was the substitute for Jesus? 104
    Other prophecies concerning saving Jesus in the
        book of Psalms 114

When and how did the substitution happen? 121
An abnormal event, at the most critical moment 123
What happened to Judas? 124
Who did deal with the body of Judas? 125
Did the Jews know that they had killed another person? 125
What did the Jews do to cover up the scandal? 126
What did the Jews do with the body of Judas? 130
Who were the persons near the tomb? 132
Why was Jesus not ascended before the coming of
   the troops? 137
How did Jesus come out of the place of hiding? 139
Research 7: Why did Jesus not give any details about
   the end of his life on earth? 141
Research 8: Did Jesus prophesy that he would be killed? 145
The prophecy that Jesus must suffer and be killed,
   and after three days he rises 146
The prophecy of pouring Jesus's blood for many for
   the remission of sins 150
The prophecy of lifting up the son of man (Jesus)
   by the Jews 153
The author of John inserts his own notion to the texts 156
Research 9: Did Jesus declare that he had passed
   through death and resurrection? 159
Research 10: How different are the authors'
   narrations of some events? 165
Summary of the topic of the crucifixion 171

Chapter 5: The Falsifier 175
   Who was Paul? 175
   Paul and the early followers of Jesus 176
   Stephen opened the door for Paul! 176
   Paul persecuted the followers of Jesus 179
   Suddenly Paul announced his conversion to the
      religion of Christ 182

Discrepancies in the narrations of the alleged conversion....188
Why did Paul change the religion of Christ?........................195
How did Paul carry out his plan to create his own
   new Christianity? 200
How did the disciples deal with Paul after he was
   exposed, and how was his end? 235

Chapter 6: The way to God after Jesus 240
Illusions and realities 240
How can we find the true way to salvation?.............................242
The prophet to come after Jesus 242
Who is this prophet? 252
Is religion important in man's life,
   and what is its name with God?...256
Christianity and Christians..269
Conditions of salvation 274
The true faith and its Six Pillars..274
Believing in Allah 275
Where is Allah? 278
Allah's names and attributes..279
Dealing with the attributes of Allah..280
Believing in angels...281
Believing in the books of Allah 283
Believing in Allah's messengers 285
Believing in the Last Day (the Hereafter).................................286
Believing in Fate (Predestination), the Good of It
   and the Bad of It 292
The human desire (wanting) and will 295
Man's life plan 296
The known aspect of fate (predestination) 298
The unknown aspect of fate (predestination)...........................300
Tape of life (movie of life) 300
Fate and causes 301

Examples of causes and destinies from life
  and the Quran 303
Questions in fate (predestination) 307
The benefit of understanding fate (predestination) 325
Testing of faith 330
The two pillars of accepting good deeds
  (devotional deeds) 331
The return of Jesus Christ to earth 333
Why and how will Jesus come back? 341
The messenger of mercy 343
How can you join the only way to salvation? 346

Chapter 7: Consideration and pondering over the gospels 347
  Putting gospels under microscope 347
  To the Christian reader 367

Conclusion 369

References 377

Preface

There is a biblical verse that clearly indicates that there was no unanimous agreement about Jesus, his reality and message, among those who went to preach about him after his ascension. Rather, there was substantial dispute among them to the point that one of those preachers announced his worry to his followers and warned them from the deception of the other preacher that may come to them and preach another Jesus other than Jesus that he had presented to them. This preacher described his counterpart as the devil who deceived Eve by his lies. So he was afraid that the minds of his followers may be corrupted and that they would gladly tolerate the one who comes to them and preaches another Jesus. This is in a clear text, thus,

> *I am afraid that your minds will be corrupted and that you will abandon your full and pure devotion to Christ—in the same way that Eve was deceived by the snake's clever lies. For you gladly tolerate anyone who comes to you and preaches a different Jesus, not the one we preached.* (2 Cor. 11:3–4)

This verse clearly speaks about two different images of Jesus were preached to people after his ascension. The pieces of the two different images of Jesus are already scattered into many chapters of the New Testaments. These two different depictions cannot, of course, both be concurrently authentic. But one must be for Truly Jesus, and the other one is for Falsely Jesus. Both images cannot meet in one heart. Surely, Jesus cannot be the source of both different images.

This book assembles all the parts of the two biblical images of Jesus that are scattered in the folds of the New Testament books and highlights them as two complete images, examines them, explores their differences, and answers the questions that may rise regarding them such as the following:

- What are the sources of Truly and Falsely Jesus?
- Why and how did Falsely Jesus appear?
- Does faith in Falsely Jesus benefit the one who believes in such Jesus?
- When does the truth come out and falseness come to an end?
- What title can be given to those who hang the image of Falsely Jesus in their hearts?
- What is the relation between salvation and Jesus?
- How can we find the true way to God, and how can we be sure of it?
- What are the conditions of Salvation?

Can we really grasp the genuine reality of Jesus? Surely. But with the spread of misinformation, there is a risk of facing the dangers of misguidance, unless we purify our intention and seek the proven truth. And at this point, God will not fail the one who seeks the truth, rather will guide him to it. Truly Jesus will remain as well as Falsely Jesus, until the second coming of Jesus, and then Truly Jesus is manifested, and the Falsely will be destroyed.

I pray to God to accept this effort as a sincere one and to provide the readers with both clarity of intention and the ability to distinguish between the two readings of Jesus as presented in this book.

Introduction

Salvation, the goal

People of all religious backgrounds throughout history who believe in an afterlife define salvation as a state of being saved from hell. And who would not want to attain this goal? Only on the day of resurrection shall we be paid our recompense in full. Whosoever is moved away from hell and admitted to paradise is indeed successful.

Our first life in this world is but the enjoyment of illusion and vanity, as for the Hereafter is the eternal life. Surely, there can be only one true formula that leads to salvation, but what is it? Is it a mystery, or is it obvious? The followers of every religion claim that the true formula of salvation is only within their religion. Surely, the only one, true formula of salvation can only be in one religion, which is the true religion, because it is the same formula that was brought by all the messengers of God since the first contact between heaven and earth. Therefore, it is necessary to rely on clear and conclusive proofs of the credibility of the salvation formula that we believe in before facing death.

Why Jesus?

Many people believe that Jesus is the key to their salvation as a savior. Surely, he was a unique being because of his miraculous birth, his ascension and second coming. However, significant disputes remain about his reality and mission.

The message of God to the human of earth about faith and salvation was always the same throughout history. It was always based on "submission" to the One and Only true God, by obedience with devotion. This message of God was revealed to Adam, who passed it to his children. Then it was confirmed by Noah and all the messengers and prophets of God who came after him throughout human history, to various societies and nations, whenever they needed guidance to the true path. So the religion of God that came with all the messengers always contains the same pillars of faith even if there were different legal systems and patterns of worship from one prophet or messenger to another—that is, until God chose to send the final revelation, with the final law and the final salvation's formula to all mankind for the remainder of human history.

Faith in Jesus

What is the reality about Jesus?

The disputes in faith concerning the reality about Jesus among the followers of different religions and sects are centered on the following points:

- Was Jesus God manifest in human form or merely a human?
- Was Jesus the only begotten son of God or merely a messenger, like all other messengers?
- Was Jesus the Word and the Knowledge of God manifest in a human form or one of the creatures of God?
- Was Jesus the only savior who came to take away the sins of humanity through his blood sacrifice on the cross, or was he killed as a normal human like the prophets who were killed, or was he not killed or crucified?
- Was his message a universal and forever or a local message addressed to a specific nation, people of Israel, and defined by a period of time?

These opposing beliefs about the reality of Jesus cannot be all true at the same time. They will remain until his second coming, and then his reality will be manifested to the man of that time. But for the man of today, whoever has based his faith in Jesus on clear and conclusive evidence is rightly guided or else he is in plain error. Who would want to be among those whose faith and deeds are wasted because of their misplaced understanding of the reality of Jesus? Who wants to be among those who will see their faith in Jesus on the day of judgment like a mirage in a desert, the thirsty one thinks it to be water, until he approaches and discovers nothing, but he will find God with him, who will pay him his due? They may also find Jesus himself to say to them, as the author of the Gospel of Matthew narrated, "*I never knew you; depart from me*" (Matt. 7:23).

I hope that this book can help to come to a conclusion of the correct salvation formula by recognizing the reality of Jesus with clear and conclusive evidence.

Where is the truth about Jesus?

A simple question that can be asked: did Jesus clearly revealed himself to people? The answer would be, surely, yes. Because one of his tasks was to reveal himself to the people. So the source of the truth about him should be Jesus himself, the speech he uttered. He already expressed himself to his people, the Israelites, through the gospel that he had preached. But where is the Gospel of Jesus that was written in his own language that he communicated with his people? Surely, there is no such gospel. In fact, there is no narration in the New Testament states that Jesus wrote down his gospel, or even instructed any of his followers to write one on his behalf. The available narrations tell us that Jesus simply carried out his mission. He went with his disciples from town to town in the land of Israel and to their synagogues, preaching his gospel that God had revealed to him through inspiration. "*Jesus came to Galilee, preaching the gospel of the kingdom of God, and saying, 'The time is fulfilled, and the kingdom of God is at hand. Repent, and believe in the gospel*" (Mark 1:14–15). The Jews were amazed, saying, "*How does this man know letters, having never studied?*" (John 7:15). The author of John narrated that Jesus asked his apostles to preserve his words, saying to them,

> *He who does not love me does not keep my words; and the word which you hear is not mine*

> *but the Father's who sent me. These things I have spoken to you while being present with you. But the helper, the Holy Spirit whom the father will send in my name, he will teach you all things, and bring to your remembrance all things that I said to you.*
> (John 14:24–26)

So according to this text, the disciples who continued preaching in the Jewish world after Jesus did not have any written record of the gospel of Jesus to teach people through it, but rather relying on their memories with the help of the Holy Spirit—as was claimed.

The gospels

So what about the gospels of Matthew, Mark, Luke, and John? Are they not authentic and reliable sources?

Well, historical evidence tells us that there were other many gospels and written materials that existed before these four gospels. The author of Luke says, *"Many people have done their best to write a report of the things that have taken place among us"* (Luke 1:1). But the four gospels were chosen in the fourth century to be included in the list of seventy-three books that were elected to compose the Bible. Christian researchers tell us that the Gospel of Mark was written first, around the year 65, more than thirty years after the ascension of Jesus. And the last gospel was John, around the year 96, more than sixty years after the ascension. Therefore, in order to determine these scriptures' authenticity and reliability, we need to carefully consider and ponder over them. The revealed Word of God cannot contain a single mistake. It is flawless and infallible precisely because it has been sent down by the All-Wise, the One worthy of all praise. A book that is containing many contradictions and mistakes cannot, by necessity, have come from God. Moreover, relying upon such a book for one's salvation would carry serious disastrous implications for one's Hereafter. But before making any consideration and pondering over the four gospels, we should better understand their authors first.

Let us imagine, for a moment, that we are able to somehow communicate directly with the authors of the four gospels. And let us start our conversation with Matthew.

The author of the Gospel of Matthew

Q: Sir Matthew; are you that Matthew, the disciple of Jesus?
MATTHEW: No, I am not.
Q: Who then are you?
MATTHEW: I am an anonymous author, merely carrying the same name as that disciple.
Q: How is this so? Would not the early Christian readers hearing the gospel ascribed to "Matthew" naturally associate it with the disciple of that name?
MATTHEW: Perhaps. Though the name was not uncommon during those times. The confusion between me and Matthew, the disciple, was the result of a very natural misunderstanding. But I must declare outright that never did I claim to be an eyewitness as a follower of Jesus, neither by the name of Matthew, the disciple, nor did I ever claim to be inspired by "the Holy Spirit." And if you read chapter 9 verse 9 of my gospel, you would see that the apostle Matthew and I are not the same person. *"Then as Jesus passed on from there, he saw a man named Matthew sitting at the tax office. And he said to him "follow me." And he arose and followed him"* (9:9).

Indeed, had Matthew the disciple been the author of the gospel, you would have read instead, *"He saw me sitting at the tax office. And he said to me 'follow me.' And I arose and followed him."*

Not only that, but it is well-known that the historical seniority is for Mark's gospel. And after ten years, I wrote my gospel. So it is not a secret anymore that most of my gospel was copied almost word-for-word from Mark's gospel, who was not a disciple either. So the disciple Matthew could not possibly have authored my gospel. After all, how could an apostle, an eyewitness of Jesus and his companion, as Matthew, have relied upon the effort of Mark, who was not himself a companion of Jesus? If the disciple Matthew was the real author of my gospel, the gospel attributed to him, he would have no need to rely upon or copy from Mark's gospel. Rather, he would have written his own account from his own memory and personal eyewitness.

Q: So you used Mark's gospel to produce your own gospel.
MATTHEW: Indeed, I did. It was common in our days to rely upon and copy from the written works of others. There was nothing untoward in doing so. Nor was there any concept of intellectual copyright infringement in those days.

So with the matter of Matthew's gospel having been cleared, let us now converse with Mark, so to speak.

The author of the Gospel of Mark

Q: Are you that Mark, the man who was also called John, whose surname was Mark, who is mentioned in the book, Acts of the Apostles (12:12), he who accompanied Peter?
MARK: No. I am not that Mark.
Q: So then, who are you?
MARK: I am an anonymous Christian. But as a result of pure speculation—on account of our sharing the same name—my gospel became associated with this John Mark. The truth of the matter is, that if John Mark had written a gospel that had been preached to him by the disciple Peter, he would have surely mentioned at least something about it. In other words, if there was any connection between Peter to this gospel, it would have been made when the gospel was written.

I did not identify myself in my gospel, nor did I give direct information about the time or the place in which my gospel was written, nor even any connection to any apostle. Furthermore, the oldest copies of my gospel end at chapter (16:8) while the manuscripts used by the translators of the later King James Version of the Bible had a much longer ending.

The author of the Gospel of Luke

Q: It cannot be stated conclusively that you are the author of the Gospel of Luke, especially since you do not identify yourself as such.

LUKE: Well, I was certainly not an eyewitness, nor for that matter was I a direct follower of the eyewitnesses of Jesus. I have only been described as a physician and a missionary companion of Paul, that Jewish who converted to Christianity after the ascension of Christ.

As to the purpose behind my writing a gospel, I was clear and direct from the outset: I wrote in dedication to Theophilus, who was a man of some considerable rank. I announced this clearly in chapter 1 wherein I wrote, *"It seemed good to me also, having had perfect understanding of all things from the very first, to write to you an orderly account, most excellent Theophilus."* (1:3). Also, I wrote another book, as another gift for Theophilus, which I called Acts of the Apostles, the disciples of Christ. It is about their work in spreading the religion of Christ after his ascension and what happened to them.

Q: I agree that you have not claimed to have been inspired by the Holy Spirit. In fact, you have made no claim at all. It was only that, as you said, *"Many people have done their best to write a report of the things that have taken place among us"* (1:1). So *"It seemed good to you also"* (1:3) to write just as wrote those who before you since you consider yourself as a man having had perfect understanding of all things from the very first. However, although your purpose in writing was clear, your written account itself was heavily borrowed from the Gospel of Mark.

LUKE: Yes, as Matthew had also done. The Gospel of Mark was too concise, so both Matthew and I made it longer.

And that is why these first three gospels discussed thus far are called the Synoptic Gospels. It is impossible to hold that they were completely independent from each other because of the literary interdependence.

The author of the Gospel of John

Q: What about you, John? Are you really John the son of Zebedee, the disciple of Jesus? And did the disciple John author a gospel?

JOHN: I will refer you to what Luke wrote about the disciple John in his book, Acts of the Apostles. He said, *"The members of the Council were amazed to see how bold Peter and John were and to learn that they were ordinary men of no education"* (Acts 4:13). Matthew, wrote telling us that John was a fisherman, like his companion, Peter (Matt. 4:18, 21) as well as Luke (5:10). And if the composition of the Gospel of John was in AD 96 or shortly thereafter, that makes the disciple John nearly one hundred years old. Can one really expect from such an aged, ordinary, uneducated Galilean fisherman like John, whose native language was almost certainly Aramaic, to have authored a gospel in elegant Greek and include within it advanced theological concepts?

Q: Surely not. So why do people insist upon the idea that the disciple John was the author of the Fourth Gospel?

JOHN: It was from the end of the second century that church tradition identified the disciple John as the actual author of the Fourth Gospel. This idea remained popular till the end of the eighteenth century, where after many biblical scholars finally acknowledged the lack of supporting solid historical evidence.

Q: But why did the church identify the disciple John as the author of the gospel for as long as it did? And if the disciple John, the aged, unschooled, ordinary Galilean fisherman, did not (and indeed could not) compose such a piece of writing, who then are you?

JOHN: This longstanding traditional position of the church was an attempt to solve the problem that the author himself raised in the gospel, when he addressed one disciple with this phrase: "The beloved disciple" or "the disciple whom Jesus loved," where he wrote, *"Now there was leaning on Jesus' bosom one of his disciples, whom Jesus loved"* (13:23). This phrase was mentioned no less than five times in this gospel. And the closing words of the gospel state explicitly concerning the beloved disciple, that he is the witness and writer of it. *"This is the disciple who testifies of these things and wrote these things"* (21:24).

The church provided a name for this "beloved disciple," and they chose the name of John specifically, based on an assumption thus: since the other three gospels suggested that the disciple John was close to the disciple Peter, and the Fourth Gospel described Peter as being close to the "beloved disciple." So the disciple John, son of Zebedee, was the "beloved disciple" and he who wrote the Fourth Gospel. In other words, there is no historical-evidence-based reason for the attribution of the Fourth Gospel to the disciple John, only a speculative one.

As for myself, the actual author of John's Gospel, I remain anonymous. And my true identity remains one of the biggest mysteries in biblical scholarship.

Q: Actually, some well-known facts raise more points than are answered, such as the following:

1. Why did the other three gospels not once mention this "beloved disciple"? Their silence on the matter only adds to the mystery.
2. Besides the admission that John was illiterate, as is stated in Acts (4:13), and about one hundred years old when the gospel was produced, he is not identified anywhere in the gospel as its author. The gospel itself does not even mention the disciple John by name anywhere, nor his brother, James, but rather mentions them by their father's name "sons of Zebedee." Surely, if John the disciple was the author of the gospel, he would have his name mentioned as an eyewitness about his association and his brother with Jesus.
3. The authors of the first three gospels narrated a strange incident happened to Jesus, where a change came over him on the mountain. The eyewitness for this transfiguration of Jesus were only three disciples: Peter; John; and his brother James, sons of Zebedee. *"Jesus took Peter, James, and John his*

brother, brought them up on a high mountain by themselves, and was transfigured before them. His face shone like the sun, and his clothes became as white as the light. And behold, Moses and Elijah appeared to them, talking with him"* (Matt. 17:1–3; Mark 9:2–4; Luke 9:28–30).

If the author of the Fourth Gospel is the disciple John, he would have reported in his gospel such profound event, which cannot be forgotten as the change of Christ's body, for he was one of the only three witnesses to that event; but the author of the Fourth Gospel did not report such incident in his gospel. This neglect is a clear proof that the eyewitness disciple of the event, John, son of Zebedee, was not the author of the Gospel of John.

4. The author of the Gospel of John, reported an incident that supports the opinion that the alleged beloved disciple and the apostle John, the son of Zebedee, are two different disciples. He reported about seven disciples were on a boat, including the two sons of Zebedee (John and James) and two unnamed disciples. He said, *"Simon Peter, Thomas, Nathanael, the sons of Zebedee, and two others of his disciples were together. Simon Peter said to them, 'I am going fishing.' They said to him, 'We are going with you also.' They went out and immediately got into the boat"* (John 21:2–3). Then the author narrated that the alleged beloved disciple was the first to recognize Jesus when he appeared to them on the seashore. *"Therefore, that disciple whom Jesus loved said to Peter, 'It is the lord'"* (John 21:7).

Here, the disciple John and his brother James are mentioned by their father's name (the sons of Zebedee) and, with them, two other unnamed disciples. And since the author never identifies himself as a witness to any event that he relates, so in this case, the one who recognized Jesus would not be John, the son of Zebedee, but one of the two unnamed disciples, who was supposed to be, in this case, the alleged beloved disciple.

5. If the church, merely by assumption, chose the disciple John to be the "beloved disciple" who were allegedly to be the author of the gospel, some biblical scholars chose Lazarus for this nickname rather than John, because of four separate instances in this gospel where the author reports that Jesus already loved Lazarus, who was not among the twelve chosen disciples but he was one of those who accompanied Jesus wherever he went. No one else has been specifically identified as having been loved by Jesus in such a way. Jesus said to his disciples, *"Our friend Lazarus sleeps"* (John 11:11). In addition, Lazarus's sister sent Jesus the message, *"Lord, behold, he whom you love is sick"* (John 11:3). The author further tells us again that Jesus loved Lazarus: *"Now Jesus loved Martha and her sister and Lazarus"* (John 11:5). The author further reported that Jesus went to the tomb to raise Lazarus from the death by God's permission, then, when he saw his body, he (Jesus) wept, causing the Jews to remark, *"See how he* (Jesus) *loved him"* (John 11:35–36).

    Others biblical scholars suggested the man, who in his house the Last Supper was prepared, to have been the beloved disciple; for they counted him as a secret disciple of Christ, because of fear of the Jews. Other scholars suggested Mary Magdalene to have be the beloved disciple.

6. A point of controversy created by the gospel's author himself, when he closed his Gospel with the following phrase, *"This is the disciple who testifies of these things and wrote these things; and we know that his testimony is true"* (John 21:24). With this verse, it is complex to identify a single person as an author of the gospel! This abrupt shift from the singular to the plural by use of the pronoun "we" makes it impossible to ascertain the identity of the gospel's author with any degree of certainty. Precisely because the "we" indicates a plurality of authors and not just one single "John," whichever that John was supposed to be!

    No one has ascertained who wrote the Fourth Gospel, nor if they were any eyewitness. But the internal evidence of the writing exposes the gospel as a work was formulated by an anonymous writer, who never met Jesus, and were so careful to mask their identity by this designation "the disciple whom Jesus loved" for pretending an apostolic authority for their ideas. The amazing thing is that the early church fathers, and millions of people who still read and studied this gospel, have missed the obvious references the author made of himself. And they just accept the traditional view that the disciple John, the son of Zebedee, was the beloved disciple who wrote the gospel.

This is the case of the authorship of the four gospels. The attributing of the two gospels of Matthew and John to disciples of the same names was pure speculation. The original authors were and remain anonymous, not eyewitnesses, and they did not claim divine inspiration. These four gospels do not represent the true gospel of Jesus that was preached in the Aramaic Galilee dialect. But they are biographical accounts of him, produced through purely human efforts, fallible endeavors that relied upon undocumented narrations, rumors and hearsay, copying from each other's works and the works of others.

CHAPTER 1

Truly Jesus

There is not any evidence that can assure us the ascription of the written sayings of Jesus in the gospels to him because of those circumstances surrounding the writing of the gospels and that the oldest existing copies of the gospels are written in a language other than the language of Jesus and his disciples but in Greek. Nevertheless, Christians consider the four gospels as the only available written records in the Bible containing the words of Jesus. So what do these gospels say about Jesus as he shows his reality to the nation to which he was sent?

A humble human prophet who did not come of himself, but was sent by God with a doctrine was not of his own making, but from God who sent him exclusively to the people of Israel; to confirm to them the true oneness of God, to show them the true path to salvation, to make their relation with God and him (Jesus) above all other familiar relations; to fulfill the law and to bring a better, more holistic understanding of the commandments; to preach the kingdom of God and to call the sinners to repentance. His miracles were performed by the will of God alone—not by his own power, for he can of himself do nothing, nor could he speak from his own authority, but God who sent him gave him a command, what he should say and what he should speak. So, what the people heard from Jesus were not his words, but the words of God Who sent him, for he never bears witness of himself, nor does he know about the unseen. He completed his mission and announced about another message to be brought by the final prophet who would come after him to guide people into all truth. He prophesied the plot of the Jews to kill him, and also prophesied that God would rescue him.

If you are surprised, reader, to see Jesus this way and began to wonder about the proofs. The proofs are as follows:

1. *Jesus's humility*

    When a Jewish ruler called him a good teacher, saying, *"Good teacher, what shall I do to inherit eternal life?"* Jesus objected to him before answering and said to him, *"Why do you call me good? No one is good but One, that is God"* (Luke 18:18–19). Also, Jesus said about himself, *"If I honor myself, my honor is nothing"* (John 8:54).

2. *His humanity*

    He said to the Jews, *"But now you seek to kill me, a man who has told you the truth which I heard from God. Abraham did not do this"* (John 8:40).

3. *A prophet*

    When Jesus had come to his own country (Nazareth), he taught them in their synagogue, so that they were astonished and said, *"Where did this man get this wisdom and these mighty works? Is this not the carpenter's son? Is not his* mother called Mary? And his brothers James, Joses, Simon, and Judas? And his sisters, are they not all with us? Where then did this man get all these things? So, they were offended at him. But Jesus said to them, "A prophet is not without honor except in his own country and in his own house" (Matt. 13:54–57). Luke reported this incident in another wording from Jesus: "Assuredly, I say to you, no prophet is accepted in his own country" (Luke 4:24).

4. *He did not come of himself but was sent by God.*

Some of the people of Jerusalem said, *"Is this not he whom they seek to kill? But look! He speaks boldly, and they say nothing to him. Do the rulers know indeed that this truly the Christ? However, we know where this man is from; but when the Christ comes, no one knows where he is from."* Then Jesus said to them in a loud voice, *"You both know me, and you know where I am from; and I have not come of myself, but He who sent me is true, whom you do not know"* (John 7:25–28).

5. *His doctrine was not of his own making but from God who sent him.*

About the middle of the feast, Jesus went up into the temple and taught. And the Jews marveled, saying, *"How does this man know so letters having never studied?"* Jesus answered them, *"My doctrine is not mine, but His who sent me"* (John 7:14–16).

6. *He was sent exclusively to the people of Israel (i.e., the Jews).*

He refused to heal a demon-possessed Canaanite girl, explaining to his disciples, *"I was not sent except to the lost sheep of the house of Israel"* (Matt. 15:24).

And when Jesus used to send his disciples to preach, he would give them the following instructions: *"Do not go into the way of the Gentile* (non-Jew), *and do not enter a city of the Samaritan. But go rather to the lost sheep of the house of Israel"* (Matt. 10:5–6).

7. *He came to the Jews to confirm to them the true oneness of God.*

One of the Jewish scribes who heard a discussion between Jesus and a group of the Jews, and saw that Jesus had given them a good answer, so he came to Jesus and asked him, *"Which is the first commandment of all?"* Jesus answered him, *"The first of all the commandments is: 'Hear, O Israel, the Lord our God, the Lord is one"* (Mark 12:28–29).

8. *He came to them to show them the true way to salvation.*

Jesus already explained to the Jews the way to salvation: that they must believe that there is only one true God and that Jesus is His messenger and to keep the commandments. He said, *"Most assuredly, I say to you, he who hears my word and believe in Him who sent me has everlasting life"* (John 5:24). Jesus also spoke these words, lifted up his eyes to heaven, and said, *"And this is eternal life, that they may know You, the only true God, and Jesus Christ, whom you have sent"* (John 17:3). And when a man asked him, *"Good Teacher, what good things shall I do that I may have eternal life?"* So, he said to him, *"Why do you call me good? No one is good but One, that is God. But if you want to enter into life keep the commandments."* (Matthew 19:16-17).

9. *He came to them to make their relationship with God and him above all other relations.*

Jesus declared that any Israeli who believes in him is not entitled to love those who did not believe from his family, where he said, *"Do not think that I came to bring peace on earth. I did not come to bring peace but a sword. For I have come to set a man against his father, a daughter against her mother, and a daughter-in-law against her mother-in-law. And a man's foes will be those of his own household. He who loves father or mother more than me is not worthy of me. And he who loves son or daughter more than me is not worthy of me"* (Matt. 10:34–37).

10. *He came to them to fulfill the law.*

    Jesus clarified about his message where he said, *"Do not think that I came to destroy the Law or the prophets. I did not come to destroy but to fulfill"* (Matt. 5:17).

11. *He came to them to bring a better, more holistic understanding of the commandments.*

    Jesus said, *"You have heard that it was said to those of old, 'You shall not commit adultery.' But I say to you that whoever looks at a woman to lust for her has already committed adultery with her in his heart. And if your right eye causes you to sin, pluck it out and cast it from you; for it is more profitable for you that one of your members perish, than for your whole body to be cast into hell"* (Matt. 5:27–29).

12. *He came to them to preach the kingdom of God.*

    Jesus said to the people who tried to keep him from leaving: *"I must preach the kingdom of God to the other cities also, because for this purpose I have been sent"* (Luke 4:43).

13. *He came to them to call the sinners to repentance.*

Jesus said, *"For I did not come to call the righteous but sinners, to repentance"* (Matt. 9:13).

14. His miracles were performed by the will of God alone, not by his own power.

   Jesus said to the Pharisees, *"But if I cast out demons by the spirit of God, surely the kingdom of God has come upon you"* (Matt. 12:28).
   When Jesus came to the tomb to raise his friend Lazarus from death, by God's permission, he wept and began to call God, not expressed in clear and audible words, but deep within himself with groaning, then asked them to take the stone away. When they moved the stone, Jesus lifted up his eyes, and with a loud voice, he glorified God and thanked Him for answering his call so that the attendees do not think that it is he the one who had raised Lazarus but God alone. He said, *"I thank you that you have heard me. And I know that you always hear me, but because of the people who are standing by I said this (i.e., thanking God aloud) that they may believe that you sent me"* (John 11:41–42).

15. For he can of himself do nothing.

   As all creatures of God, He is unable to act without the will of God. Jesus said, *"I can of myself do nothing. As I hear I judge; and my judgment is righteous, because I do not seek my own will but the will of the Father who sent me"* (John 5:30).

16. Nor could he speak from his own authority.

   But in fact, it was God Who commanded him what he should say and what he should speak. So what the people heard of Jesus was not his own words but the words of God who sent him. Jesus said, *"For I have not spoken on my own authority; but the Father who sent me gave me a command, what I should say and what I should speak"* (John 12:49).

And also, he said, *"He who does not love me does not keep my words; and the word which you hear is not mine but the Father who sent me"* (John 14:24).

17. *For he never bears witness of himself.*

    Rather, he said to the Jews, *"If I bear witness of myself, my witness is not true"* (John 5:31).

18. *Nor does he know about the unseen.*

    He said, *"But of that day and hour no one knows, neither the angels in heaven, nor the son, but only the father"* (Mark 13:32). One day Jesus was hungry, *"and seeing from afar a fig tree having leaves, he went to see if perhaps he would find something on it. And when he came to it, he found nothing but leaves, for it was not the season for figs. In response Jesus said to it, 'Let no one eat fruit from you ever again.' And his disciples heard it"* (Mark 11:13–14).

19. *He completed his mission.*

    He looked up toward heaven, saying, *"I have glorified You on earth. I have finished the work You have given me to do"* (John 17:4).

20. *And announced about another message to be brought by the final prophet who would come after him to guide people into all truth.*

    Jesus said, *"I still have many things to say to you, but you cannot bear them now. However, when he, the spirit of truth has come, he will guide you into all truth; for he will not speak on his own authority, but whatever he hears he will speak; and he will tell you things to come. He will glorify me"* (John 16:12–14).

And he also said, *"And I will pray the Father, and He will give you another helper, that he may abide with you forever"* (John 14:16). (More details in chapter 6.)

21. *He prophesied the plot of the Jews to kill him.*

Jesus said to the Jews, *"But you seek to kill me, because my word has no place in you"* (John 8:37). And he also said to them, *"But now you seek to kill me, a man who has told you the truth which I heard from God. Abraham did not do this"* (John 8:40). He questioned them, saying, *"Did not Moses give you the law, and yet none of you keeps the law? Why do you seek to kill me?"* (John 7:19).

22. *And also, he prophesied that God would rescue him in the end.*

Jesus informed the Jews that the remaining time for him with them is not very long, then he will ascend to heaven. And just prior to his ascension, they will seek him, but they will fail to arrest him because he will go to a place in which they cannot come to. He said to them, *"I shall be with you a little while longer, and then I go away to Him who sent me. You will seek me and not find me, and where I am you cannot come"* (John 7:33–34). (More details in chapter 4.)

What did Jesus's contemporaries say?

Who would understand Jesus better? The people around him or those who came many years after him? Surely, the people around Jesus would know him better. They believed in him as no more than a human prophet sent to the people of Israel with miracles performed by God through him. We can read this in the following texts:

The disciple Peter

Peter stood up with the eleven disciples, raised his voice, and said to the Jews, *"Men of Israel, listen to these words! Jesus of Nazareth was a man attested by God to you by miracles, wonders, and signs which God performed through him in your midst, as you yourselves also know"* (Acts 2:22).

Cleopas and his companion

They were followers of Jesus. They said, *"The things concerning Jesus of Nazareth who was a prophet mighty in deed and word before God and all the people"* (Luke 24:18–19).

Nicodemus

A Pharisee man who came to Jesus by night and said to him, *"Rabbi, we know that you are a teacher come from God; for no one can do these signs that you do unless God is with him"* (John 3:2).

The multitudes

When Jesus came into Jerusalem, all the city was moved, saying, "Who is this?" So the multitudes said, *"This is Jesus, the prophet from Nazareth of Galilee"* (Matt. 21:10–11). And when the chief priests and Pharisees heard Jesus's parables, they perceived that he was speaking of them. But when they sought to lay hands on him, *"they feared the multitudes, because they took him for a prophet"* (Matt. 21:45–46). And when they saw Jesus raising a dead man by God's will, fear came upon them, and they glorified God, saying, *"A great prophet has risen among us"* (Luke 7:16). Also, those who witnessed the miracle of Jesus's blessing the food declared, *"This is truly the prophet who is to come into the world"* (John 6:14). Also, when the multitudes saw Jesus healing the paralyzed man, *"they marveled and glorified God, who had given such power to men* (Jesus)*"* (Matt. 9:6–8).

This is Truly Jesus, and that is his genuine image and the reality of his mission. This is how he presented himself, and this is how he asked people to believe of him. And that is indeed the truth with which true believers had believed, those who followed the apostles' teachings after the ascension of Christ. But, unfortunately, this true, genuine image of Jesus did not last and did not persist. Rather, it was lost and was not explored in the narratives of those gospels. Instead, it was replaced by a fake image, one that was manufactured during the first century after his ascension and then spread all over the world. The aspects of this fake image are characterized in some books of the New Testament, but not in the four Gospels. However, none of the fake part of that fake image can be evidenced from Jesus's own words.

CHAPTER 2

Jesus answers some conjectures and suspicions

The most amazing thing is to see how people ignoring the clear-cut texts that were spoken by Jesus himself concerning his true nature and mission. Instead, they rely on other texts that were apparently of conjecture and suspicion, were also said by Jesus, to justify their holding to Jesus's fake image. So what is the truth about the texts of conjectures and suspicions that were ascribed to Jesus?

1. *"I and my father are one" (John 10:30)*

This verse is customarily quoted out of context. Therefore, there are three questions, and in their answers is the truth.

- To whom did Jesus address this phrase?
- Why did he say such phrase?
- What did Jesus say about the meaning of this phrase?

According to the story in John, Jesus addressed this phrase to the Jews in the temple, in the city of Jerusalem. While Jesus was walking in the temple, in Solomon's porch, the Jews surrounded him and said to him, *"How long do you keep us in doubt? If you are the Christ, tell us plainly." Jesus answered them, I told you, and you do not believe. The works that I do in my Father's name, they bear witness of me. But you do not believe, because you are not of my sheep, as I said to you. My sheep hear my voice, and I know them, and they follow me. And I give them eternal life, and they shall never perish; neither shall anyone snatch them out of my hand. My Father, who has given them to me, is greater than all; and no one is able to snatch them out of my Father's hand. I and my Father are one.* (John 10:23–30)

In this text, Jesus rebuked the Jews for not believing that he was the Christ, although the miracles that God performed through him were testifying that he was the Christ who did not come to them on his own but God sent him. Then he told them that they were not of his sheep because they did not listen to him while his sheep were those who listened to him from the commonalty Jews and followed him into the shed of his teachings. And therefore, they will have eternal life in the Hereafter, and they shall never perish. Neither shall anyone of those who had rejected him snatch them out of the shed of his teachings, nor can anyone snatch them out of the shed of God's religion, for the shed of Jesus's teachings is the shed of God's religion.

Jesus did not intend to say to the Jews that he and God are one person, one being, one God because God and Jesus are two different, distinct, and separate personages. God is above the universe, a separate and distinct being, while Jesus was another being entirely, a human, mortal messenger walking upon the earth. But obviously, Jesus meant to say to the Jews with this phrase, that whoever had believed in him is already protected within his shed, because it is the shed of God's religion. And so those commonalty Jews, who already with Jesus, are necessarily with God, because the word that they heard from him was not of him, but of God, Who sent him; for Jesus and God were one in what was required of the Jews. It is a unity of purpose between Jesus and God toward the Jews.

Let Jesus himself explain to us what he means with the phrase, "I and my Father are one." So what did he say?

The author of the Gospel of John reported that when Jesus was about to depart the earth, he prayed to God to cover all his disciples with His protection and keep them all to be one, as his unity is with

God. Jesus said, *"Now I am no longer in the world, but these* (the disciples) *are in the world, and I come to you. Holy father, keep through your name those whom you have given me, that they may be one as we are.* (One)*"* (John 17:11).

If Jesus and God were one person, one being, one God, so was Jesus asking God (himself) to make his disciples also into one person, one being, just as he and God are one? Or was Jesus calling on his Lord to unite his disciples after him and be one in their goal and purpose with God and Jesus, just in the same way that he was united with God in purpose toward the people of Israel?

The oneness in God and Jesus is not only for the disciples alone, but also Jesus has included all those who will believe in him through the disciples so that all be united with Jesus in God. Jesus said,

> *I do not pray for these* (disciples) *alone, but also for those who will believe in me through their word; that they all may be one, as you, Father are in me, and I in you; that they also may be one in us, that the world may believe that you sent me. And the glory which you gave me I have given them, that they may be one just as we are one.* (John 17:20–22)

It is oneness of purpose with God. Hence, if someone is prepared to believe that Jesus and God together constitute one existential being, then he must also be prepared to believe that the disciples and the believers also constitute component parts of the "One" divine being.

Furthermore, we read this text in the gospel of Mark: *"He was received up into heaven, and sat down at the right hand of God"* (Mark 16:19).

This text clearly speaks of two different, distinct personages, metaphysically separated from each other. Only one of the two is God.

Anyone who believes or claims that both of them are God no longer has one God but two!

2. Son of God

What about Jesus calling himself "son of God" and calling God "his father"?

Before Jesus himself explains this issue to us, here are some questions about it: Is sonship and fatherhood real or metaphorical? Is the term "Son of God" and the fatherhood exclusively for Jesus only? Had the term "Son of God" and the fatherhood been used before Jesus?

The term "son of God" is a translation of a Hebrew expression for honoring and high respect, not to meant to be taken literally. This term can be directed, in the Hebrew dialect, to a prophet sent by God or a righteous person close to God. The term "Father" is also a translation of a Hebrew expression that means "the Idol Lord." There is no real fatherhood with God, nor a physical kinship between Him and Jesus or any prophet or person. He begot none, nor was He begotten. It does not befit the divinity and the majesty of God that He should beget or sire a son.

God is not a father of any creature, and one must be disciplined with God and be careful not to underrate Him by describing Him with a mortal and earthly attribute, such as "father," even though a person may not intend it literally. And may the following incident, reported by the author of the Gospel of John, shows how the commonalty Israelis use the term "Son of God" for the person sent by God.

The author stated that Jesus at the beginning of his mission, when he was calling some young Israelis to be disciples accompany him, when *"Jesus wanted to go to Galilee, and he found Philip and said to him 'Follow me.' Philip found Nathanael and said to him 'We have found him of whom Moses in the law, and also the prophets, wrote, Jesus of Nazareth, the son of Joseph.' And Nathanael said to him, 'Can anything good come out of Nazareth?' Philip said to him, 'Come and see.' Jesus saw Nathanael coming toward him and said of him, 'Behold, an Israelite indeed, in whom is no guile!' Nathanael said to him, 'How do you know me?' Jesus answered and said to him, 'Before Philip called you, when you were under the fig tree, I saw you.' Nathanael answered and said to him, 'Rabbi, you are the son of God! You are the king of Israel!'"* (John 1:43–49).

This young Israeli Nathanael who did not follow Jesus yet did not mean that Jesus was a real son of God born of Him, but he used a prevalent term in their Hebrew language and in their religious books that describes the prophets as "Son of God," such as the following:

- *Solomon*
  The word of God came to David concerning his son Solomon, saying, *"He* (Solomon) *will build a temple for Me. He will be My son, and I will be his father"* (1 Chron. 22:6–10).
- *Israel (Jacob)*
  And the Lord said to Moses, *"Then you shall say to Pharaoh, thus says the Lord: 'Israel* (Jacob) *is My son, My first born'"* (Exod. 4:22).
- *Ephraim (the son of Joseph the son of Jacob)*
  "For I (God) *am a Father to Israel, and Ephraim is my first born"* (Jer. 31:9).

In numerous passages, we also find the Bible mentioning a plurality of sons of God: *"The sons of God saw the daughters of men"* (Gen. 6:2).

Even in the New Testament, such as *Adam*.

"Son of Seth, the son of Adam, the son of God" (Luke 3:38).

And in a plurality form, *"Blessed are the peacemakers, for they shall be called sons of God"* (Matt. 5:9).

And after the disciples followed Jesus, they continued to call him with that prevalent term in their Hebrew language, "Son of God," just as the ancient Israelis called their prophets. The disciple Simon Peter said to Jesus, *"Also we have come to believe and know that you are the Christ, the son of the living God"* (John 6:69).

Also, the term "Father" was not exclusively used by Jesus only, but also the Jews were using it. The Jews said to Jesus, *"We were not born of fornication; we have one Father-God." Jesus said to them, "If God were your Father, you would love me, for I proceeded forth and came from God; nor have I come of myself, but He sent me. Why do you not understand my speech? Because you are not able to listen to my word. You are of your father the devil, and the desires of your father you want to do... He who is of God hears God's words; therefore, you do not hear, because you are not of God"* (John 8:41–44, 47).

Even Jesus himself, as it reported in Matthew, was asking people to call God their father, as He was his.

> *But when you pray, do not use vain repetitions as the heathen do. for they think that they will be heard for their many words. Therefore, do not be like them. For your Father knows the things you have need of before you ask Him. In this manner, therefore, pray: Our Father in heaven, Hallowed be your name... For if you forgive men their trespasses, your heavenly Father will also forgive you.* (Matt. 6:7–9, 14)

While the author of John reported that Jesus said, *"I am ascending to my Father and your Father, to my God and your God"* (John 20:17).

Incidentally, in the Bible, there is another term for addressing a mortal, human being that is even greater than the term "son of God." This term is "God," as in Exodus: *"So the Lord said to Moses: see, I have made you as God to Pharaoh, and Aaron your brother shall be your prophet"* (Exod. 7:1).

Hence, if Jesus in the New Testament is called "son of God," Moses in the Old Testament is called with even a greater term, "God." Also, in the book of Psalms, the Israelite judges are called gods.

> *God stands in the congregation of the mighty; He judges among the gods... Defend the poor and fatherless; do justice to the afflicted and needy. Deliver the poor and needy; free them from the hand of the wicked.* (Ps. 82:1, 3–4)

Then He addresses the judges, saying, *"I said, 'You are gods, and all of you are the children of the most High'"* (Ps. 82:6).

Now let Jesus himself explain to us what did he mean by calling himself the "son of God." And also, the meaning of the term "gods" that was addressed to the Israelite judges in the book of Psalms. The author of the Gospel of John tells us that when Jesus was walking in the temple, in Solomon's porch, the Jews started to argue with him, then when he said to them the previous phrase, "I and my Father are one," *So, the Jews took up stones again to stone him. Jesus answered them, "Many good works* (miracles) *I have shown you from my Father. For which of those works do you stone me?" The Jews answered him, saying, "For a good work we do not stone you, but for blasphemy, and because you, being a man, make yourself God"* (John 10:31–33). (Because in his discussion with them, he said to them, "I do in my Father's name." Also, he said, "My father who has given them to me. No one is able to snatch them out of my Father's hand. I and my Father are one.")

The Jews are the first to know that the term "Son of God" is a Hebrew expression for honoring and high respect, not to meant to be taken literally, and they also know the meaning of the term "Father" because their books were replete with these terms that addressed to the prophets. They also know that in the book of Exodus, Moses is called "as God," and the Israelite judges were called "gods" in the book of Psalms, but they were simply being argumentative and fond of conspiring against Jesus whenever they saw him because of jealousy and envy. Actually, the author of John's Gospel states that the Jews sought all the more to kill Jesus because he said that, "God was his father." *"for this reason, the Jews persecuted Jesus and sought to kill him, because he had done these things on the Sabbath. But Jesus answered them, 'My Father has been working until now, and I have been working.' Therefore, the Jews sought all the more to kill him, because he not only broke the Sabbath, but also said that God was his father, making himself equal with God"* (John 5:16–18).

How did Jesus answer those Jews who accused him of blasphemy? It was a critical moment for Jesus to determine his real essence in front of those people, he to whom he was sent, whether he was a real son of God or merely a human messenger. It is more than reasonable to assume that Jesus, at that moment, would not hesitate nor be afraid or feel ashamed to declare his reality before them. Jesus would by no means willingly mislead or deceive the people by resorting to a false or politically expedient answer. Rather, his answer would be clear, comprehensive, and conclusive. And it would be a proof for the true faith in him through generations till the time of his second coming, when all the truth will be manifested to those people living then.

Jesus used the book of Psalms that was with the Jews and read to them the text describing the Israelite judges as "gods." *"I said, 'You are gods, and all of you are the children of the most High"* (Ps. 82:6). Rebuking them, how do they accuse him of blaspheming God and stone him because he used the metaphorical meaning of the famous Hebrew expression "son of God" while their book of Psalms says of the Israelite judges that they are "gods"?

> *Jesus answered them, "Is it not written in your law, 'I said, "You are gods"'?* (Ps. 82:6). *If He called them gods, to whom the word of God came (and the Scripture cannot broken), do you say of him whom the Father sanctified and sent into the world, "You are blaspheming," because I said, "I am the son of God"?* (John 10:34–36).

Jesus reminded those Jews about the figurative meaning of the term "son of God," that it referred to one who was sanctified by and sent from God. Even the term "god" could be used, in Hebrew language, free of any immortal connotations when referring to those to whom the message of God was given, such the Israelites judges. Although Jesus clearly stated the truth about the meaning of the term "Son of God" when he speaks of himself, and the word "god" when it is addressed to the human in Hebrew language, but in practice, there is partial acceptance of the two explanations. His explanation for the true meaning of the word "god" when it was addressed to the Israelite judges was accepted, but it is not his explanation of the true meaning of the term "Son of God" when he speaks of himself, as there are still many people who insist on calling Jesus the "son of God" and understanding it in a literal sense, and here is where the deviation from Jesus's own teaching lies.

Luke also reported about the angel who spoke to Mary, the mother of Jesus, saying, *"And behold, you will conceive in your womb and bring forth a son, and shall call his name Jesus. He will be great and will be called the Son of the Highest"* (Luke 1:31–32). Thus, it is. Jesus will be called the Son of the Highest (in Hebrew). That is, it is his nickname, not his reality.

Finally, if Jesus used to say clearly about himself that he was "the Son of Man." *"But Jesus answered them, saying, 'The hour has come that the Son of Man should be glorified'"* (John 12:23). And he meant the figurative meaning when he used the term "Son of God." So who then blaspheme? Is not he the one who considers Jesus a real son of God was begotten of him? And here is the risk of this faith and worst indeed is the destination!

3. *The Trinity*

Monotheism was the basis of the teaching of Jesus in the Israeli society and continued with his disciples after him. But suddenly, shortly after the ascension of Christ, a new brand of faith based on polytheism was proclaimed by a Jewish man who claimed to follow Jesus, even though he had never met him. This man already knew that he would not be able to market this brand of faith in the Israeli society, so he went to the neighboring pagan nations, who accepted his teaching and established there his own churches that falsely carry the name of Jesus Christ. He wrote epistles to these churches to urge them to adhere to his invented religion. Then in the fourth century, these epistles (fourteen epistles) were chosen to be included to the books of the New Testament (twenty-seven books) in the Bible.

The fathers of the churches of that innovator believed in the new doctrine, which he preached among his followers and wrote it down in his epistles, that Christ is God.

> *My brethren, my kinsmen according to the flesh, who are Israelites…and from whom, according to the flesh, Christ came, who is over all, the eternally blessed God.* (Rom. 9:3–5)

They also believed in the other doctrine that he also widely propagated among them and wrote it down in his epistles that Jesus is a real son of God.

> *The gospel of God which He promised before through his prophets in the holy Scriptures, concerning His son Jesus Christ our lord, who was born of the seed of David according to the flesh, and declared to be the Son of God with power, according to the spirit of holiness, by the resurrection from the dead.* (Rom. 1:1–4)

The following generations inherited this new faith in Jesus that he is God and a literal real son of God. And when the church fathers studied Jesus's biography from the available written materials, they find that the Holy Spirit was with Jesus guiding him where he should go. For example:

- *"Then Jesus, being filled with the Holy Spirit, returned from the Jordan and was led by the Spirit into the wilderness"* (Luke 4:1).
- *"Then Jesus returned in the power of the Spirit to Galilee"* (Luke 4:14).

Such these texts and others made the church fathers confused about the reality of this Holy Spirit, as it cannot be a creature since he was the one who use to guide and directed Jesus, the deity the son of the deity. Rather, he must also be a deity like them! Hence, the concept of the pagan Trinity began to be formed in the second century, after it was reformulated within the church's beliefs, which renders the One and Only Almighty God into a plurality of gods and portraying Him as an equilateral of Gods. The God with three hypostases. They are coequal, coeternal Gods. God the Father, God the Son, and God the Holy Spirit. Every one of them is a separate being or entity. Yet they are not three Gods but one God. It is three in one and one in three. None of them superseded the other, opposing logic and has no basis in any purported speech of God in any scripture.

Let us explore this concept of Trinity further. Had it been the true reality of God, surely, it would have been revealed to Adam in order that he may teach his children and humanity the truth about their God. The same holds true as regard to Noah, Abraham, Moses, and even Jesus. They would all do their best to expound the Trinity in clear terms so that people may truly know their God. Yet there is no statement nor any text attributed to any messenger or prophet of God in the Bible speaking of or explaining the dogma of the Trinity! Even Jesus himself, who is presented as one of the three "forms" of God, did not know of this dogma nor did he preach it. All of his words attributed to him in the four gospels combined do not refer to or symbolize Trinity. And all the true believers before Jesus and during his lifetime died believing in God as One and only One, not one in three and three in one, because there was no reference whatsoever for this concept. And if the Trinity truly explains the reality of the divine, why did it only appear among people many years after Jesus's ascension? Why did none of the previous messengers of God who came before Jesus ever speak of a Trinity? The Trinity is not just against the true and clear teachings of Jesus, but it is a false accusation against him. It is not supported or proven by Jesus's own statements.

Recently, some church fathers of some denominations have recognized the depth of the apparent problem with the pagan multigods of the Trinity and how it opposes logic. So they thought up a more acceptable formula and cover up the pagan multigods with a token veneer of monotheism. They came with this: Trinity is not three Gods—God, Jesus, and the Holy Spirit—but it is one God with three essential attributes, that God would not be existed without them. These three essential attributes of God are the existence (entity of the essence), the mind (knowledge, wisdom, and speaking) and the life (spirit). These three essential attributes were eternally existed with God without any beginning. It is impossible for God to be existed at any time without these three attributes. God is existed by his essence, speaks by his wisdom (his word), and lives by his spirit. He is one God: His Essence (person) is called the Father, His word and knowledge are called the Son (Jesus), and His spirit is called the Holy Spirit. The word "hypostasis" means an essential attribute associated with another, which is not separate from him.

In this new formula of the Trinity of certain denominations, which was painted with a layer of a gloss of monotheism, the fathers of their churches deny the existence of three distinct gods in the guise of God, Jesus, and the Holy Spirit. But they have chosen some essential attributes of God and divided them into three categories: The attribute of existence was directed to God's essence upon which they referred to Him as the Father. They combined the attribute of knowledge, wisdom, and speaking into the attribute of the mind and separated it from God's essence as a separate entity sharing the divinity with God and called it the Son and directed it to Jesus. They also separated the attribute of life from God's Essence as a separate entity, sharing also the divinity with God, and called it the Holy Spirit and directed it to Him. And in this way, the Holy Spirit is God Himself, and Jesus also is God Himself, but he was called Son because he came from God and was born of a human mother. Thus, with a token veneer of monotheism, the essential polytheism of the Trinity was masked. This new formula of the Trinity has not any supporting evidence from the words of God nor from any prophet, or even from Jesus's words.

What about the other essential attributes of God such as the attribute of omnipotence, power, majesty, greatness, etc.? Is it not impossible for God to exist at any time without all His essential attributes? Why were only three attributes chosen (existence, speaking, life) in deference to the rest, while all are equally essential?

God possesses the most perfect essence and attributes. None of God's messengers, Jesus included, ever described the knowledge, the word, or the life of God are separate and distinct divine personalities. His attributes are not separate entities of His essence, but they are inseparable from Him. There are numerous biblical passages that outrightly oppose the idea of a Trinity:

Mark narrated that Jesus said, *"But of that day and hour no one knows, neither the angels in heaven, nor the Son, but only the Father"* (Mark 13:32). How can it be that Jesus was the essential attribute of the knowledge of God, as the Trinity states, when in fact Jesus was negating his knowledge of the appointed day and hour to come? Was he then the knowledge of God without knowledge?

Mark also wrote,

> *Now the next day, when they* (Jesus and his disciples) *had come out from Bethany, he* (Jesus) *was hungry, and seeing from a far a fig tree having leaves, he went to see if perhaps he would find something on it. and when he came to it, he found nothing but leaves, for it was not the season for fig.* (Mark 11:12–13)

If Jesus was really the knowledge of God manifested in human form, surely, he would have known about the season of the figs! Had there been any divinity in him, he would not have troubled himself and walked all that distance to see if, perhaps, he could find some figs. Jesus's actions were distinctly human, utterly nondivine.

Matthew wrote,

> *Again the devil took him* (Jesus) *up on an exceedingly high mountain and showed him all the kingdoms of the world and their glory. And he said to him, "All these things I will give you if you will fall down and worship me."* (Matt. 4:8–9)

Was the creature Satan trying his Creator God? Was the devil offering God's kingdom to God himself if God would fall down and worship the devil?

John narrated that Jesus said, *"I am ascending to my Father and your Father, and to my God and your God"* (John 20:17). So if Jesus himself admitted that he had a God, why do people then make a God of him in the Trinity?

Another problem by that Jewish man who invented a divinity for Jesus and a real sonship for God, which made the church fathers to look for a solution in the Trinity, when he wrote,

> *If God is for us, who can be against us? Certainly not God, who did not even keep back His own Son, but offered him for us all.* (Rom. 8:32) *so that by his sacrificial death he should become the means by which people's sins are forgiven only through their faith in him* (Rom. 3:25–26) *and sins are forgiven only if blood is poured out.* (Heb. 9:22)

Did God kill His Son for atonement as a human or a God? If He had killed him as a human being, will then the sins of all people be forgiven by the blood of one of them? But if there is no forgiveness for all people by the blood of one of them, does this mean that God had killed Jesus as a God (a real son of God)? And if Jesus is God in the Trinity and his Father made him dead for three days, should not all the three also be dead since they were one? Was not there a God in that period? Or was there a God but without knowledge because His knowledge (Jesus) was dead? And if Matthew claimed that Jesus said on the cross, *"My God, my God why have you forsaken me?"* (Matt. 27:46), so if Jesus was God, a part of a Trinity, was God here complaining to Himself? Was God asking Himself some help in order to put Himself down from the cross? Glorified is God, the Lord of honor and power! He is free from what the polytheists attribute to Him.

In a clear and direct speech, Jesus declared how his people, the Israelites, would attain salvation in the Hereafter. He said, *"Most assuredly I say to you, he who hears my word and believe in Him who sent me has everlasting life"* (John 5:24). Jesus also spoke these words, lifted up his eyes to heaven, and said, *"And this is eternal life, that they may know you, the only true God, and Jesus Christ whom you have sent"* (John 17:3). And when a man asked Jesus, *"Good Teacher, what good things shall I do that I may have eternal life?"* So he said to him, *"Why do you call me good? No one is good but One, that is God. But if you want to enter into life, keep the commandments"* (Matt. 19:16–17). They were only required to believe in the true oneness of God and that Jesus is His messenger and to keep the commandments. It is uncompromising monotheism and a belief in Jesus, in full humanity, as God's messenger. No belief in Trinity is included here.

What about the third side of the "equilateral of Gods," the Holy Spirit? How could the Trinity make the life of God a separate and distinct person? While Luke narrated that Jesus said to his disciples, *"If you then, being evil, know how to give good gifts to your children, how much more will your heavenly Father give the Holy Spirit to those who ask him?"* (Luke 11:13), in this text, the Holy Spirit is something given by God to those who ask Him! So if the Holy Spirit is God in the Trinity, would God here give "Himself" or "His life" to those who ask Him? Or does God give a separate and distinct personality to those who ask Him? Or does God give the "life" and the third person according to the mythology of Trinity?

God is alive by His essence, not by another thing. And the life of God is one of His perfect essential attributes, belonging to Him and inseparable from Him. It cannot be given away nor it is to dwell in people. The "Holy Spirit" is not a name of God nor of His life because He neither called Himself the Holy Spirit nor did He describe His life with such terminology.

The Holy Spirit is, in reality, a name of one of God's creations: The Angel Gabriel, he who was entrusted by God to reveal God's words to His messengers and strengthen them. We also read and hear the terms "Spirit of God" or a "Spirit from God," but none of these terms were meant to describe God Himself. Rather, they also pertain to the Angel Gabriel or to what the righteous experience of feelings of tranquility, enlightenment, support, and such like. Also, God's inspiration to the prophets is a Spirit from Him. All the messengers of God, Jesus included, were supported by the Holy Spirit, Gabriel. None of them ever preached that the Holy Spirit was God Himself or His life. Surely, the Holy Spirit that God gives to those who ask Him, as Luke narrated, is the support of the Holy Spirit for those who God has permitted to be supported from the believers.

The only instance in the entire Bible in which Trinity is mentioned is in this text: *"For there are three who bear witness in heaven. The Father, the word, and the Holy Spirit; and these three are one"* (1 John 5:7). But this verse is no longer present in any of the revised versions of the Bible. It was omitted by scholars who recognized it as a deliberate interpolation: a forgery that does not occur in the oldest of manuscripts. Now this verse in the revised version reads like this: *"There are three witnesses. The spirit, the water, and the blood, and all three give the same testimony."*

What about the narration of Matthew about Jesus asking his disciples, when he appeared to them before his ascension, to go to people and *"baptizing them in the name of the Father, and of the Son, and of the Holy Spirit"* (Matt. 28:19)?

There is no text that says that the disciples baptized people after the ascension of Christ with the names of these three, but rather they were baptizing in the name of Jesus only. So were they ignoring the orders of Jesus's instructions? Certainly not. Or did Jesus not command them to baptize in the name of the Father, the Son, and the Holy Spirit? It certainly is, and the text was just an allegation from the anonymous writer. The Acts of the Apostles tells us how the disciples used to baptize people after the ascension of Christ in the name of Jesus only, thus:

The Jews said to Peter and the rest of the apostle, *"Men and brethren, what shall we do?"* Then Peter said to them, *"Repent, and let every one of you be baptized in the name of Jesus Christ"* (Acts 2:37–38). The followers of Christ who were scattered because of the persecution *"went everywhere preaching the word. Then Philip went down to the city of Samaria and preached Christ to them... But when they believed Philip as he preached the things concerning the kingdom of God and the name of Jesus Christ, both men and women were baptized... They had only been baptized in the name of the Lord Jesus"* (Acts 8:4–5, 12, 16). And when Peter went to Caesarea to meet Cornelius, a Roman commander, who with his household believed in God, and after Peter spoke to them, *"He commanded them to be baptized in the name of the Lord"* (Acts 10:48).

And even if Jesus had said, "Baptizing them in the name of the Father, and of the Son, and of the Holy Spirit," it does not prove the Trinity because the verse speaks about names of three different persons, each having his own share in the baptism: God Himself; the Son, which is the righteous chosen messenger, Jesus; and the Holy Spirit, the angel who brought the gospel from God to Jesus and supported him in his mission.

Still another verse in Mark presents more of problem to those who insist upon belief in the Trinity. *"He* (Jesus) *was received up into heaven and sat down at the right hand of God"* (Mark 16:19).

The verse shows two separate, distinct entities beside each other. What about the third person, the Holy Spirit? Where is he? Should He not be sitting on the other side? And if Jesus was the knowledge of God as the Trinity says, so was His knowledge sitting at His right hand? These contradictions are unavoidable for those who persist in believing corrupted concepts of God. They want to be monotheists, because monotheism is the natural belief in God as consistently taught throughout the scriptures. But at the same time, they want to keep to their inherited tradition of the polytheistic dogma exemplified in the Trinity. So when one thinks and speaks of the Trinity, one imagines three persons sitting beside each other. And when that Trinitarian wants to think or speak of monotheism, he has to merge the three into one God.

Yes, the Christ ascended to heaven, but the monotheistic belief prevents any perception or inclusion of Christ to be beside or equal to God. The right hand of God here does not mean equality, but only signifying the high rank of Christ in the sight of God. And since God is qualified with absolute transcendence (God is above the heavens and all creatures), none is above Him or beside Him, and He is distinct and separate from all creation. Christ is within heaven. God raised him to heaven, to free him permanently from his Jewish enemies and protect him, waiting for the time of his second coming to earth with another mission, as his return will be a sign for the coming of the hour of ending the life on the planet earth and then the end of the entire universe. At the time of the second coming of Christ Jesus, the imposter Christ (the Antichrist) will appear on earth with a false message, but the true Christ, Jesus, will kill that Antichrist. Jesus, of course, will return to earth because he is a pure human being, and he will live for some few years, then eventually die and be buried in the earth, and on the day of resurrection, he will be resurrected for judgment with all beings. Christ is now subject to heavenly laws, away from earthly time and laws. The two thousand years that have passed here on earth count as just a few days up in heaven.

4. "The only begotten Son" (John 3:16)

It can be said that this verse in the Gospel of John is the most famous verse in the New Testament and is on the tongues of all those who believe that God sent Jesus for a death mission so that whoever believes in him should not perish but have everlasting life. Therefore, they consider this verse to contain the central message of the gospel. The author of the gospel narrated that Jesus said, *"For God so loved the world that He gave His only begotten son, that whoever believes in him should not perish but have everlasting life"* (John 3:16). In context, there is actually nothing extraordinary about the verse, because the entire context of the story is a dialogue took place between Jesus and a Pharisee Jewish leader by the name of Nicodemus, but the problem is in directing of the understanding of the text to another meaning.

Let us review the entire dialogue between Jesus and Nicodemus, as it narrated in the Gospel of John. One night, Nicodemus came to Jesus and said to him, *"Rabbi, we know that you are a teacher come from God; for no one can do these signs that you do unless God is with him"* (John 3:2). Then Jesus answered him and said, *"Most assuredly, I say to you, unless one is born again* (born from above), *he cannot see the kingdom of God"* (John 3:3). Meaning, the faith of the human should be generated from a heavenly source, which is according to what God has sent, in order to see the kingdom of God. And any Israeli who believes that Jesus is a teacher has come from God and follows him as if he was born again.

Nicodemus did not understand Jesus's words. So he asked, *"How can a man be born when he is old? Can he enter a second time into his mother's womb and be born?"* (John 3:4). So Jesus explained that he did not mean a physical birth but a spiritual one. The human being becomes born again (spiritual birth) when he leaves the religion he inherited from his parents and enters into the religion of the prophet who is sent to them by God. So unless a person is spiritually reborn, he will not recognize the heavenly truth. The spiritual rebirth can be seen physically through its influence on a person's behavior and good deeds, just as the wind can be seen through the effect of its blowing and sound. Jesus said,

> *Most assuredly, I say to you, unless one is born of water and the Spirit, he cannot enter the kingdom of God. That which is born of the flesh is flesh, and that which is born of the Spirit is spirit. Do not marvel that I said to you, "You must be born again." The wind blows where it wishes, and you hear the sound of it, but cannot tell where it comes from and where it goes. So is everyone who is born of the Spirit.* (John 3:5–8)

But still Nicodemus did not comprehend Jesus's answers. He said, *"How can these be?"* (John 3:9). Jesus marveled at the lack of understanding of Nicodemus, although he was a teacher among the Jews. He said to him, *"Are You the teacher of Israel, and do not know these things?"* (John 3:10). Then Jesus criticized the Jews' ignorance and hardheartedness, saying,

> *Most assuredly, I say to you, we speak what we know and testify what we have seen, and you do not receive our witness. If I have told you earthly things and you do not believe, how will you believe if I tell you heavenly* (spiritual) *things?* (John 3:11–12).

Then Jesus indicated some of these heavenly things and began with his connection to heaven and his miraculous origin, which was not of an earthly father like all human beings, but God created him by His Word "Be" that was descended from heaven and cast to Mary by the Holy Spirit (Angel Gabriel). Also, he indicated his future ascension: *"No one has ascended to heaven but he who came down from heaven, that is the son of man who is in heaven"* (John 3:13).

Although Nicodemus had confessed to Jesus that he knew that he was a teacher came from God, for no one could do those signs that Jesus did unless God was with him, Jesus was aware of Nicodemus's difficulty in understanding heavenly things. Therefore, the story indicates that Jesus employed another technique to overcome this problem. He began to address Nicodemus with things that he already knew them, because they were written in the books of the Jews. He reminded Nicodemus about the story of the earlier Jews with Moses that is mentioned in the book of Numbers in the Old Testament.

The story says,

> *And the people spoke against God and against Moses: "Why have you brought us up out of Egypt to die in the wilderness? For there is no food and no water, and our soul loathes this worthless bread." So, the Lord sent fiery serpents among the people, and they bit the people; and many of the people of Israel died. Therefore, the people came to Moses and said, "We have sinned, for we have spoken against the Lord and against you; pray to the Lord that He take away the serpents from us." So, Moses prayed for the people.* (Num. 21:5–7)

The story continues, saying that God had mercy on them and gave to Moses the prescription of healing by faith.

> Then the Lord said to Moses, *"make a fiery serpent, and set it on a pole; and it shall be that everyone who is bitten, when he looks at it, shall*

live." So Moses made a bronze serpent, and put it on a pole;[1] *and so it was, if a serpent had bitten anyone, when he looked at the bronze serpent, he lived.* (Num. 21:8–9)

Jesus used this story as a means of explanation for Nicodemus, to explicate to him his mission with the Israelites of his time. Just as God had mercy on the ancient Israelites with the story of the bronze snake, so too He did with the later Israelites when He had sent the Christ to them, to get them out of the darkness to the light. Jesus explained to Nicodemus, *"As Moses lifted up the serpent in the wilderness, even so must the Son of man be lifted up"* (John 3:14).

What is the wisdom of raising a bronze snake on a pole in the wilderness as the story say? Surely, in order they can view, distinguish, and perceive it, and to remember wherever they go, that God already made their healing from the bites of snakes depend on the compliance with his command to look at the lifted bronze snake. Jesus, in his discussion with Nicodemus, used the story of the lifted bronze snake as a symbol of God's mercy for the ancient Israelites, to show him that he too is a lifted-up symbol of mercy in the later Israelites in order they can distinguish and know him, and always remember that God made their salvation depend on the compliance with his command to believe in Christ. *"That whoever* (of later Jews) *believes in him should not perish but have eternal life"* (John 3:15).

What did Jesus mean that he must be lifted up as the bronze snake was lifted up in the wilderness? What kind of lifting was Jesus talking about?

Certainly, the apparent meaning of the story of the bronze snake does not befit Jesus, that he would be lifted up physically among the later Israelites so that whoever believes in him should not perish. Rather, Jesus was explaining to Nicodemus that he too would be

---

[1] Although why God would instruct Moses to make a statue of a snake after He had revealed to that same prophet, "You do not sin by making for yourself a carved image in the form of any figure… Do not sin by making a carved image in the form of anything" (Deut. 4:16–18, 25). It is completely incomprehensible. But we deal with the story as narrated.

lifted up in a high spiritual rank among them, in terms of prophethood, honor, miracles, the gospel and the support of the Holy Spirit, and the light that he brought as proof of the truth of his prophethood. For God so had mercy on the Israelite world that He sent to them His Messiah to heal them from their straying and deviation from the teachings of Moses and the prophets and to get them out of darkness to the light, freeing them from their sins and wickedness and so that whoever believes in him should not perish but have everlasting life. (John 3:16). *For God wanted their salvation, not their condemnation* (John 3:17), *because His mercy precedes his wrath. But he* (of those Jews) *who does not believe is condemned already* (John 3:18).

So this verse, *"For God so loved the world that He gave His only begotten son, that whoever believes in him should not perish but have everlasting life"* (John 3:16), is a much misused and misunderstood verse. The "world" in this text is the Jewish world. Jesus never took his mission to other nations outside the Jewish community and nor did his faithful disciples. This can be seen in the following:

- *"And this is the condemnation, that the light* (Jesus) *has come into the world, and men* (the Jews who did not believe in him) *loved darkness rather than light, because their deeds were evil"* (John 3:19).
- *"Then those men, when they had seen the sign that Jesus did, said, "This is truly the prophet who is to come into the world""* (John 6:14). Meaning to us, the Jews.
- Jesus said to his brothers, *"The world cannot hate you, but it hates me because I testify of it that its works are evil"* (John 7:7). Who is this world that hated Jesus, and Jesus witnessed that their deeds were evil? Is it not the Jewish world?
- When the Pharisees saw how the people of the Jews received Jesus upon his last entry into Jerusalem, they said among themselves, *"You see that you are accomplishing nothing. Look, the world has gone after him"* (John 12:19).
- Jesus spoke these words, lifted up his eyes to heaven, *"I have manifested your name to the men whom you have given me out of the world"* (John 17:6), *"I pray for them* (the disci-

ples). *I do not pray for the world"* (John 17:9), *"Now I am no longer in the world, but these* (the disciples) *are in the world"* (John 17:11), *"While I was with them in the world, I kept them in your name"* (John 17:12).

Such restricted use of the word "world" is also mentioned in the Gospel of Luke: *"And it came to pass in those days that a decree went out from Caesar Augustus that all the world should be registered"* (Luke 2:1).

"All the world" here means all the Roman world, Roman Empire, not those peoples and lands beyond the authority of Rome.

Therefore, the "world" in John 3:16 never meant the entire world or all the nations of the world, but only a certain nation.

The word "gave" in John 3:16 means "sent." God also gave Noah, Abraham, and Moses to their nations before Jesus. Jesus, the Aramaic speaker, did not mean the sacrifice and killing. While "His son" means the chosen prophet, close to God. Jesus was never the only son of God, but he shared that title with several other prophets of God.

As for the word "begotten" in John 3:16, it was never spoken by Jesus and nor was written by the pen of the original author of the gospel. This is why this word is no longer found in the revised versions of the Bible. It was omitted upon revision by scholars who recognized it as a deliberate interpolation. It was a forgery not found in the earliest of manuscripts. It does not befit the divinity and the majesty of God that he should beget or sire a son like earthly creatures do.

The word "whoever believes in him" means whoever believe in Jesus from his nation, the Jews. Did he not say, *"I was not sent except to the lost sheep of the people of Israel"* (Matt. 15:24)? And was he not used to send his disciples with the following instructions: *"Do not go to any Gentile (non-Jew) territory or any Samaritan towns. Instead, you are to go to the lost sheep of the people of Israel"* (Matt. 10:5–6)?

5. "Before Abraham was, I am" (John 8:58)

Was Jesus an existing object with distinct entity and independent existence before Abraham? Surely not.

So how come that Jesus was before Abraham, when in fact that he came after him? Why did Jesus say such statement and what does that mean?

Well, this is only a text, but we should go through the whole context in order to know the real meaning of the statement.

It is a fact that the Jewish religious authorities did not accept Jesus as the true Christ. They gave him a hard time, and they argued with him whenever they saw him in the temple. The author of the Gospel of John recounts one of these arguments but with obvious confusion. The author wrote that when Jesus conversed with the Pharisees at the temple, many of the Jews who heard the conversation believed him. But the confusion and ambiguity by the author appeared when he recounted how Jesus spoke with those new believers. He said to them directly, "You do not believe me, because I tell the truth, and if I tell the truth, why do you not believe me? He who is of God hears God's words; therefore, you do not hear, because you are not of God." And he was trying to convince them that he had come to them from God and they should love him. Therefore, the conversation between Jesus and the new-believing Jews turned into a hot debate. Both parties began to insult each other.

How did Jesus address those new believers of the Jews as if he was addressing nonbelievers Jews? It is completely incomprehensible confusion and ambiguity by the author. But we deal with the story as it is received.

According to the story, the hot dialogue between Jesus and the new-believing Jews took place in the temple, after Jesus had a conversation with the Pharisees. *"In the treasury, as he taught in the temple"* (John 8:20). Then *"as he spoke these words, many believed in him"* (John 8:30). Then Jesus said to those Jews who believed him, *"If you abide in my words, you are my disciples indeed. And you shall know the truth, and the truth shall make you free"* (John 8:31–32). The new-believing Jews answered him, *"We are Abraham's descendants, and have never been in bondage to anyone. How can you say, 'You will be made free?'"* (John 8:33). Jesus answered them, *"Most assuredly, I say to you, whoever commits sin is a slave of sin. And a slave does not abide in the house forever, but a son abides forever. Therefore, if the son (Jesus) makes you free you shall be free indeed. I know that you are Abraham's descendants, but you seek to kill me because my word has no place in you. I speak what I have seen with my Father, and you do what you have seen with your father"* (John 8:34–38). They answered and said to him, *"Abraham is our father."* Jesus said to them, *"If you were Abraham's children, you would do the works of Abraham. But now you seek to kill me, a man who has told you the truth which I heard from God. Abraham did not do this. You do the deeds of your father"* (John 8:39–41). Then they said to him, *"We were not born of fornication; we have one father—God"* (John 8:41).

Then Jesus tried his best to prove to those Jews that he came to them from their God, not of himself, so they should love him. He said to them, *"If God were your father, you would love me, for I proceeded forth and came from God; nor have I come of myself, but he sent me"* (John 8:42).

Those Jews were just proud of their father Abraham and did not understand what Jesus had said to them because they were actually not listening to him. Jesus said to them, *"Why do you not understand my speech? Because you are not able to listen to my word"* (John 8:43).

The author of the Gospel of John recounts that Jesus was the one to start insulting those Jews. He said to them, *"You are of your father the devil, and the desires of your father you want to do… But because I tell you the truth, you do not believe me. Which of you convicts me of sin? And if I tell the truth, why do you not believe me? He who is of God hears God's words; therefore, you do not hear, because you are not of God"* (John 8:44–47). Then the Jews replied, insulting him, saying, *"Do we not say rightly that you are a Samaritan and have a demon?"* (John 8:48).

Jesus immediately cleared to them that he was glorifying God, not himself, and they should believe in his word in order to avoid spiritual death. He said to them, *"I do not have a demon; but I honor my Father, and you dishonor me. And I do not seek my own glory; there is One who seeks and judges. Most assuredly, I say to you, if anyone keeps my word, he shall never see death"* (John 8:49–51). But those Jews were ignorant. They understood the death literally, not as a spiritual death. They said to Jesus, *"Now we know that you have a demon! Abraham is dead, and the prophets; and you say, 'If anyone keeps my word, he shall never taste death'"* (John 8:52).

With this literal understanding about death, those Jews started to compare Jesus with Abraham. They asked Jesus if he thinks that he is greater than Abraham. They said to him, *"Are you greater than our father Abraham, who is dead? And the prophets are dead. Who do you make yourself out to be?"* (John 8:53).

Jesus immediately corrected them so that they may not misunderstand him that he was trying to make himself great. He said to them, *"If I honor myself, my honor is nothing. It is my Father who honors me, of whom you say that He is your God. Yet you have not known Him, but I know Him. And if I say, 'I do not know Him, I shall be a liar like you; but I do know Him and keep His word"* (John 8:54–55).

Then Jesus started to use their example, Abraham, to prove to them his case that he was sent to them by their God, Whom already had inspired their father Abraham, at his time, about the future and the coming of the Messiah to his descendants, the Jews. So Abraham became as if he saw already the day of the Messiah because he was sure it would happen since God had inspired him. Jesus said to them, *"Your father Abraham rejoiced to see my day, and he saw it and was glad"* (John 8:56).

Again, those Jews understood the words of Jesus literally, and they said to him, *"You are not yet fifty years old, and have you seen Abraham?"* (John 8:57). Then Jesus replied with an answer fitting their nonsense question to inform those ignorant Jews that his coming to them was already predestined there in the written knowledge of God before Abraham was even born. He said to them, *"Most assuredly, I say to you, before Abraham was, I am"* (John 8:58). In no way does the statement of Jesus means the preexist. Every creature was predestined in the written knowledge of God, even before the creation of heaven and earth, to come into existence on its appointed time.

6. *"I am the way, the truth, and the life. No one comes to the Father except through me" (John 14:6)*

Of course, in context, this verse makes perfect sense: in order for a person to go to his God, he needs a way for that. The ways to God are His prophets and messengers. So in order for that person to receive God's mercy and salvation, he needs first to obey and follow His designated prophet. And the prophet at that particular time for the Israelis was Jesus Christ.

The statement of Jesus was an answer from him to unexpected question from the disciple Thomas! The whole context was a dialogue that took place between Jesus and his disciples on his last night with them, at the Last Supper. The author narrated that Jesus asked his disciples, *"Let not your heart be troubled; you believe in God, believe also in me"* (John 14:1). Then Jesus started to talk in parables to them, *"In my father's house are many mansions; if it were not so, I would have told you. I go to prepare a place for you. And if I go and prepare a place for you, I will come again and receive you to myself; that where I am, there you may be also"* (John 14:2–3). Here, Jesus was encouraging his disciples to remain steadfast in faith so they can be with him in the Hereafter. Then he immediately continued saying to them, *"And where I go you know, and the way you know"* (John 14:4). Here he was reminding them of his imminent departure to heaven and that they know the way that leads to the paradise in heaven, through keeping their faith in him. *"You believe in God, believe also in me"* (John 14:1).

The disciple Thomas however did not understand Jesus's parable. He said to Jesus, *"Lord, we do not know where you are going, and how can we know the way?"* (John 14:5). So Jesus made it clear for him, saying, *"I am the way, the truth, and the life. No one goes to the Father except through me"* (John 14:6).

Meaning, their persistence in their belief in him after his departure is the way to God. Surely, Jesus was a way to God, not only for the disciples but also for the whole Jewish nation. The Jews who did not accept the way (i.e., Jesus), God would not accept their faith or their deeds because no Jew at that time could come to God except through the Messiah, Jesus. And those Jews who rejected Jesus, they were actually rejecting God who sent Jesus to them as a way to Him.

So this statement, *"I am the way, the truth, and the life. No one comes to the Father except through me,"* is appropriate for every messenger of God, not only Jesus. Every messenger was a way to God because He sent him to be followed and obeyed. Every messenger is the truth because God inspires him. Every messenger is the life, because all those of his people who believe in and follow him, they would attain good in this worldly life and in the Hereafter. Hence, no one from the people to whom God sent a messenger could come to God except through that messenger.

To put it clearer, this statement, *"I am the way, the truth, and the life. No one comes to the Father except through me,"* is yesterday's news, when Jesus was the way, appropriate and exclusive for the Jews of his time. Jesus did not address everyone with his statement, but only to his target audience, "the lost sheep of the house of Israel." Note that Jesus did not neglect to consider the later generations. He had announced another way to God to succeed him.

7. "He who has seen me has seen the Father" (John 14:9)

To know the true meaning of the statement, it is necessary to go through the whole context. The story started when Jesus said to his disciple Thomas, *"If you had known me, you would have known my Father also; and from now on you know Him and have seen Him."* Philip said to him, *"Lord, show us the Father, and it is sufficient for us."* Jesus said to him, *"Have I been with you so long, and yet you have not known me, Philip? He who has seen me has seen the Father; so how can you say, 'Show us the Father'?"* (John 14:7–9).

The teaching of Jesus about God in the presence of his disciples was thus: *"And the Father Himself, who sent me, has testified of me. You have neither heard His voice at any time, nor seen His form"* (John 5:37). But what about Jesus's statement to Thomas: *"And from now on you know Him and have seen Him"* (John 14:7)? What type of seeing is this? Certainly not a visual seeing, but a spiritual, because seeing God spiritually depended on knowing Him spiritually. And knowing Him spiritually depended on knowing the reality of Jesus, because the statement says, *"If you had known me, you would have known my Father also"* (John 14:7).

Back to the story of Philip and Jesus. It seems that Philip did not get (see) the point of Jesus in his teaching that no one could ever see God at any time, because Philip asked Jesus, saying, *"Lord, show us the Father, and it is sufficient for us"* (John 14:8). It was a very disappointing request for Jesus. How come a disciple, on the last night of the Messiah's mission, at the Last Supper, ask such a request? According to the story, Jesus was very wise and calm. He answered Philip with a very wise answer. He said to him, *"Have I been with you so long, and yet you have not known me, Philip?"* (John 14:9). Certainly, Jesus did not mean personal knowing, because Philip knew Jesus as a person, but spiritual knowing. Meaning that Philip did not understand the teaching of Jesus about God that no one can see Him at any time; otherwise, he would not have asked such stupid request. So he who has known Jesus spiritually has seen him spiritually, and he who has seen Jesus spiritually has seen God spiritually. In other words, he who has seen the point of Jesus in his teaching about God has known all about God and would not ask like the request of Philip.

Also, we read this: *"Then Jesus cried out and said, 'He who believes in me, believes not in me but in Him who sent me. And he who sees me sees Him who sent me'"* (John 12:44–45).

8. Going to all nations

Three authors of the gospels claimed that Jesus said to his disciples, before ascending to heaven, *"Go therefore and make disciples of all the nations"* (Matt. 28:19). And Mark narrated, *"Go into all the world and preach the gospel to every creature"* (Mark 16:15). And in Luke, *"And that repentance and remission of sins should be preached in his name to all nations, beginning at Jerusalem"* (Luke 24:47).

Is it not clear here that Christ's message should extend to all the nations, all the ethnic groups on the globe? Actually, this is but another example of the confusion that resulted from fallible human efforts to produce the gospels of Jesus's behalf, devoid of inspiration and personal eyewitness. Anonymous authors appeared thirty to sixty years after the ascension of Jesus, to put their words in his mouth, basing their testimony on uncertain narrations, rumors, and hearsay and copying from each other's and others' writings. The proofs for all of this are as follows:

a. Scholars doubt the authenticity of Mark 16:15 and all the additional verses that end the gospel, from Mark 16:9 to Mark 16:20 because both the syntax and style argue strongly that they were written by someone other than the original author. Besides their glaring absence in the earliest gospel manuscripts. The oldest copies of Mark's Gospel end at (16:8) while the manuscripts used by the King James translators had the much longer ending.
b. Every author claims that those words of Jesus were his last words to his disciples just before his ascension. But each author has reported a totally different statement.
c. The three authors have not even agreed about the place where Jesus has spoken his last words to his disciples nor the scene of his ascension. Matthew has reported that the disciples went to Galilee where Jesus had told them to go. And that Jesus spoke to them at the hill there. *"Then the eleven disciples went away into Galilee, to the mountain which Jesus had appointed for them"* (Matt. 28:16). And he reported nothing about Jesus's ascension. While the original author of Mark ended his gospel stating that a young man asked the women who came to the tomb to go and tell the disciples to go to Galilee to see Jesus there. But the women said nothing to anyone.

> *And entering the tomb, they saw a young man clothed in a long white robe sitting on the right said; and they were alarmed. But he said to them "Do not be alarmed. You seek Jesus of Nazareth, who was crucified. He is risen! He is not here… But go and*

tell his disciples and Peter that he is going before you into Galilee; there you will see him, as he said to you." And they went out quickly and fled from the tomb... And they said nothing to anyone, for they were afraid. (Mark 16:5–8)

And the author mentioned nothing about the meeting or the ascension. But the author who extended the gospel of Mark speaks as if the disciples remained at Jerusalem mourning and weeping, then Jesus appeared to them there as they sat at the table. And after he had talked with them, he ascended up to heaven, meaning they saw his ascension.

Now when he rose early on the first day of the week, he appeared first to Mary Magdalene... She went and told those who had been with him, as they mourned and wept.... Afterward he appeared to the eleven as they sat at the table; and he rebuked their unbelief and hardness of heart, because they did not believe those who had seen him after he had risen... So then, after the Lord had spoken to them, he was received up into heaven. (Mark 16:9–10, 14, 19)

As for Luke, he gave the scene of Jesus's alleged last speech to his disciples at Jerusalem.

So, they rose up that very hour and returned to Jerusalem and found the eleven and those who were with them gathered together... Now as they said these things, Jesus himself stood in the midst of them, and said to them, "Peace to you." (Luke 24:33, 36)

And he chose Bethany for the scene of the ascension, and the disciples saw that. Then after speaking with them in Jerusalem,

> *And he led them out as far as Bethany, and he lifted up his hands and blessed them. Now it came to pass, while he blessed them, that he was departed from them and carried up into heaven. And they worshiped him and returned to Jerusalem with great joy.* (Luke 24:50–52)

If the three authors have disagreed about one of the main facts in the first life of Jesus on earth, the ascension to heaven, and every one of them has written according to what he found of uncertain narrations regarding the location and the scene of the meeting and the ascension, it is no surprise also to see every author differing as to the scenario for Jesus's sending his disciples to all the nations just prior to his ascension.

On the other hand, we see the author of John has reported that Jesus said to his disciples, when he appeared to them on Sunday evening while they were gathered in Jerusalem, *"Peace to you! As the Father has sent me, I also send you"* (John 20:21). He did not state that to send them to all nations, as the three previous authors claim, but to send them only as God has sent him; and he was sent only to the people of Israel. *"I was not sent except to the lost sheep of the house of Israel"* (Matt. 15:24). Jesus did not go to any other neighboring nation, *"He came to his own, and his own did not receive him"* (John 1:11). Furthermore, the author of the gospel of John has not reported any thing about the ascension.

d. Luke, in his book Acts of the Apostles, contradicts himself in his gospel. He already confirmed in the Acts the idea that Jesus never asked his disciples to go to other nations. Actually, the disciples after Christ were committed to the

Jewish custom that it is unlawful for a Jewish man to keep company with or go to one of another nation. He reported about a man in Caesarea named Cornelius, a captain in the Roman army. He was a religious man. He and his whole family worshiped God instead of pagan idols as Romans were accustomed to do. He also did much to help the Jewish poor and was constantly praying to God. This man had a vision informing him that God was pleased with his prayers and charity and that he should send some men to bring the disciple Peter to his house to hear from him. Peter, on the other hand, also had a vision of something coming down from heaven that looked like a large sheet containing in it all kind of four-legged beasts as well as birds of the air. A voice instructed him to kill and eat the animals, but Peter said, *"Not so, Lord! For I have never eaten anything common or unclean."* And a voice spoke to him again the second time, *"What God has cleansed you must not call common."*

While Peter was still trying to understand what the vision meant, the spirit instructed him to get ready and to not hesitate to go with those men who were sent by Cornelius. The following day, Peter arrived in Caesarea where Cornelius was waiting for him together with relatives and close friends. Peter was welcomed, and as he entered the house, he said to the many people gathered, *"You know how unlawful it is for a Jewishman to keep company with or go to one of another nation. But God has shown me* (in a vision) *that I should not call any man common or unclean"* (Acts 10:1–28).

This is clear proof that the disciples had no intent in going to call other non-Jewish nations, nor did Jesus ever ask them to "go to all nations." Cornelius's case was a special one in so far as he, a righteous non-Jew worshiping God, alone he received guidance from God through a vision. But the exception only proves the rule. It was only this vision that convinced Peter to put aside the Jewish prejudice and speak to the Gentiles who were living among the Jews at the same territory.

e. Luke also reported in Acts that some of the followers of Jesus, *"those who were scattered after the persecution that arose over Stephen traveled as far as Phoenicia, Cyprus and Antioch, preaching the word to no one but the Jews only. But some of them were men from Cyprus and Cyrene, who, when they had come to Antioch, spoke to the Hellenists, preaching the Lord Jesus"* (Acts 11:19–20).

So the followers of Jesus at Antioch became divided into two camps: the majority who already knew the fact that the message of Jesus was not a universal one but a local one for the Jews only, and a minority (from Cyprus and Cyrene) who by their own authority and by their own will took it upon themselves to preach to both Jew and non-Jew.

As for the apostles at the original church in Jerusalem, they had remained steadfast in following of their master, Jesus, by limiting their teachings to their fellow Jews. For Jesus did not go to call the non-Israelites, even though they lived among his own community. He never conveyed his message to the nations that geographically surrounded with the peoples of Israel, such as the Romans, Persians, Greeks, Assyrians, and Arabs.

Therefore, when the news of Antioch reached the disciples at Jerusalem, they sent Barnabas to see what happened. When Barnabas arrived at Antioch, he saw how God had blessed the people, was gladdened, and urged them all to be faithful and true to Christ (Acts 11:22–23).

f. In the language of the gospels, "the world" does not mean the whole nations of the world, but the particular nation being spoken about, such: *"And it came to pass in those days that a decree went out from Caesar Augustus that all the world should be registered"* (Luke 2:1). "All the world" here means all the Roman world, Roman Empire, not those peoples and lands beyond the authority of Rome.

g. There are many passages that clearly delineate the ethnic boundaries of Jesus's mission, such as the following:

Jesus said to his disciples, *"I was not sent except to the lost sheep of the house of Israel."* (Matt. 15:24)

Also, he said to them, *"Do not go into the way of the Gentiles, and do not enter a city of the Samaritan. But go rather to the lost sheep of the house of Israel."* (Matt. 10:5–6)

Also, he said to them, *"But when they persecute you in this city, flee to another. For assuredly, I say to you, you will not have gone through the cities of Israel before the son of man comes."* (Matt. 10:23)

But you, Bethlehem, in the land of Judah, are not the least among the rulers of Judah; for out of you shall come a Ruler who will shepherd my people Israel. (Matt. 2:6)

And she will bring forth a son, and you shall call his name Jesus, for he will save his people (Israel) *from their sins.* (Matt. 1:21)

He came to his own, but his own did not receive him. (John 1:11)

CHAPTER 3

Falsely Jesus

The fake image of Jesus in the New Testament

In three years, through his words and actions, Jesus had painted a true picture of himself. And just as his life on earth began with controversy, a miraculous birth, so also ended in controversy, a miraculous ascension and an argument about the crucifixion. The Jews, due to their envy and jealousy, worked to discredit Jesus, and even plotted against him to kill him. They were afraid that their nation, their fellow Jews, may attach Jesus's true picture to their hearts (John 11:47–50).

After the ascension of Jesus, the disciples started calling people to repent and be baptized in the name of Jesus so that their sins will be forgiven (Acts 2:38). Then the high priest and all those who were with him became extremely jealous of the disciples, and they commanded them not to teach in Jesus's name. Bu the disciples continued preaching; so the high priest, the captain of the temple, and the chief priests called for them, beaten them, and commanded them again that they should not speak in the name of Jesus and let them go (Acts 5:40). But the disciples continued. *"Daily in the temple, and in every house, they did not cease teaching and preaching Jesus as the Christ"* (Acts 5:42), till the time that the church in Jerusalem began to suffer cruel persecution. Then all the believers, except the disciples, were scattered throughout the provinces of Judea and Samaria (Acts 8:1).

After Jesus's ascension, much has been written concerning Jesus's biography, but only four books, called Gospels, were selected in AD 325 to be included in the list of the books of the New Testament in the Bible (Matthew, Mark, Luke, and John). These gospels are merely biographical accounts of Jesus, written between AD 65 and 100. These gospels speak of Jesus in the context of his humanity, his prophethood, his miracles, his teaching, his relationship with the Jews, and about what has been spread among the people regarding his crucifixion. But the most dangerous of what has been written in that period were the fourteen books written during the first thirty years after the ascension of Christ and before the writing of these four gospels. They were written by a Jewish man who was studying the Jewish Law and a contemporary with Jesus, but he did not believe in him. Rather, he devoted himself to persecute his followers after his ascension. Then he suddenly declared his faith in Jesus and claimed that he had received a direct revelation from Jesus himself who is in heaven.

In his fourteen books, he never quoted a single sentence from Jesus because he knew nothing about Jesus's religion and biography. But he drew a false philosophical picture of Jesus that was totally different from the real picture that Jesus had made of himself and presented it specifically to the neighboring pagan nations with a new brand of faith that was completely different from the faith that was brought by all the messengers of God, including Moses and Jesus. His books were also chosen to be part of the books of the New Testament in the Bible, in which he painted a false philosophical picture of Jesus as follows:

> *My brethren, my kinsmen according to the flesh, who are Israelites…and from whom, according to the flesh, Christ came, who is over all, the eternally blessed God. Christ, who is the image of God, the image of the invisible God. Who, being in the form of God, did not consider it robbery to be equal with God, but made himself of no reputation, taking the form of a servant, and coming in the*

likeness of men. And being found in appearance as a man, he humbled himself and became obedient to the point of death. For there is one mediator between God and men, the man Christ Jesus, who was born of the seed of David according to the flesh and declared to be the son of God with power, according to the Spirit of holiness, by the resurrection from the dead. Christ was the spiritual rock that followed Moses and his people and drank of it. When the fullness of the time had come, God sent forth His own son, born of a woman, born under the law. God did not even keep back His own son but offered him for us all. to redeem those who were under the Law, that we might receive the adoption as sons. (Because) now God's way of putting people right with Himself has been revealed. It has nothing to do with Law. God puts people right through their faith in Jesus. He offered him, so that by his sacrificial death he should become the means by which people's sins are forgiven only through their faith in him. Knowing that a man is not justified by the works of the law but by faith in Jesus Christ. (For) if a person is put right with God through the Law, it means that Jesus died for nothing. Those who depend on obeying the Law live under a curse. Christ has redeemed us from the curse of the law, having become a curse for us, for it is written, "Cursed is everyone who hangs on a tree." Law was introduced in order to increase wrongdoing; but where sin increased, God's grace increased much more. So then, just as sin ruled by means of death, so also God's grace rules by means of righteousness, leading us to eternal life through Jesus Christ our Lord. Christ died for the wicked at the time that God chose. God demonstrates His own love toward us, in that while we were still sinners, Christ died for us. Not with the blood of goats and calves, but with his own blood he entered the most holy place once for all, having obtained eternal redemption, (because) *without shedding of blood there is no remission. Much more then, having now been justified by his blood, we shall be saved from wrath through him. For if when we were enemies we were reconciled to God through the death of His son. For as by one man's* (Adam) *disobedience many were made sinners, so also by one man's* (Jesus) *obedience many will be made righteous. That is, that God was in Christ reconciling the world to Himself, not imputing their trespasses to them, and has committed to us the word of reconciliation. And if Christ is not risen, then our preaching is vain, and your faith is also vain.* (And) *if in this life only we have hope in Christ, we are of all men the most pitiable.* (So) *if you confess with your mouth the lord Jesus and believe in your heart that God has raised him from the dead, you will be saved. There is no distinction between Jews and Greek, for the same Lord over all is rich to all who call upon Him. The Lord* (Jesus) *himself will descend from heaven with a shout, with the voice of an archangel, and with the trumpet of God. And the dead in Christ will rise first. Then we who are alive and remain shall be caught up together with them in the clouds to meet the Lord in the air. And thus, we shall always be with the Lord. Therefore comfort one another with these words.*

References of the fake image of Jesus

"*My brethren, my kinsmen according to the flesh, who are Israelites… and from whom, according to the flesh, Christ came, who is over all, the eternally blessed God*" (Rom. 9:3–5). "*Christ, who is the image of God*" (2 Cor. 4:4), "*the image of the invisible God*" (Col. 1:15). "*Who, being in the form of God, did not consider it robbery to be equal with God, but made himself of no reputation, taking the form of a servant, and coming in the likeness of men. And being found in appearance as a man, he humbled himself and became obedient to the point of death"* (Phil. 2:6–8). *"For there is one mediator between God and men, the man Christ Jesus"* (1 Tim. 2:5), *"who was born of the seed of David according to the flesh and declared to be the son of God with power, according to the Spirit of holiness, by the resurrection from the dead"* (Rom. 1:3–4). *"Christ was that spiritual rock that followed Moses and his people and drank of it"* (1 Cor. 10:4). *"When the fullness of the time had come, God sent forth His own son, born of a woman, born under the law"* (Gal. 4:4). *"God did not even keep back His own son, but offered him for us all"* (Rom. 8:32) *"to redeem those who were under the Law, that we might receive the adoption as sons"* (Gal. 4:5). *"Now God's way of putting people right with Himself has been revealed. It has nothing to do with Law. God puts people right through their faith in Jesus"* (Rom. 3:21–22). *"God offered him so that by his sacrificial death, he should become the means by which people's sins are forgiven through their faith in him"* (Rom. 3:25–26). *"Knowing that a man is not justified by the works of the law but by faith in Jesus Christ"* (Gal. 2:16). *"If a person is put right with God through the Law, it means that Christ died for nothing!"* (Gal. 2:21). *"Those who depend on obeying the Law live under a curse"* (Gal. 3:10). *Christ has redeemed us from the curse of the law, having become a curse for us, for it is written, 'Cursed is everyone who hangs on a tree'"* (Gal. 3:13). *"Law was introduced in order to increase wrongdoing, but where sin increased, God's grace increased much more. So then, just as sin ruled by means of death, so also God's grace rules by means of righteousness, leading us to eternal life through Jesus Christ our Lord"* (Rom. 5:20–21). *"Christ died for the wicked at the time that God chose"* (Rom. 5:6). *"God demonstrates His own love toward us, in that while we were still sinners, Christ died for us"* (Rom. 5:8). *"Not with the blood of goats and calves, but with his own blood he entered the most holy place once for all, having obtained eternal redemption"* (Heb. 9:12). *"And without shedding of blood there is no remission"* (Heb. 9:22). *"Much more then, having now been justified by his blood, we shall be saved from wrath through him. For if when we were enemies we were reconciled to God through the death of His son"*

(Rom. 5:9–10). *"For as by one man's (Adam) disobedience, many were made sinners, so also by one man's (Jesus) obedience many will be made righteous"* (Rom. 5:19). *"That is, that God was in Christ reconciling the world to Himself, not imputing their trespasses to them, and has committed to us the word of reconciliation"* (2 Cor. 5:19). *"And if Christ is not risen, then our preaching is vain, and your faith is also vain"* (1 Cor. 15:14). *"If in this life only we have hope in Christ, we are of all men the most pitiable"* (1 Cor. 15:19). *"That if you confess with your mouth, the Lord Jesus and believe in your heart that God has raised him from the dead, you will be saved. There is no distinction between Jews and Greek, for the same Lord over all is rich to all who call upon Him"* (Rom. 10:9, 12). *"The Lord (Jesus) himself will descend from heaven with a shout, with the voice of an archangel, and with the trumpet of God. And the dead in Christ will rise first. Then we who are alive and remain shall be caught up together with them in the clouds to meet the Lord in the air. And thus, we shall always be with the Lord. Therefore, comfort one another with these words"* (1 Thess. 4:16–18).

Yes, the falsifier is Paul, the founder of the world Pauline Christianity. The genuine message of Jesus was directed to the Israelite only, and his main role was to bring them out of the darkness into the light. Jesus said,

> The light (Jesus) has come into the world, and men (the Jews who did not believe in him) loved darkness rather than light, because their deeds were evil. For everyone practices evil hates the light and does not come to the light, lest his deeds should be exposed. But he who does the truth comes to the light, that his deeds may be clearly seen, that they have been done in God. (John 3:19–21)

In his role to bring the Jews out of the darkness into the light, Jesus worked on them for more than three years, moving from town to town, preaching the true Gospel in their temple and their synagogues to confirm to them the true oneness of God (Mark 12:28–29), to fulfill the law (Matt. 5:17), to call the sinners to repentance

(Matt. 9:13), and to show them the true path of salvation that is by faith in God and believing in Jesus as a messenger (John 5:24, 17:3), as well as by keeping the commandments (faith alongside with deeds) (Matt. 19:16–17).

Then this falsifier came and replaced the genuine message of Jesus and its direction with another, polytheist, Gentile-wide, and a pagan role for Jesus and addressed it to the neighboring pagan world to the Jews. He introduced them to a mixture of heavenly scriptures with satanic, earthly inspiration, then mixed together with the alleged blood of Jesus. Truth, law, and encouragement to do good deeds were not ingredients in this mixture. They were removed because they cannot be combined in a mixture of falsehood. So before knowing the truth about Paul, we first analyze the fake image of Jesus painted by him.

Deconstructing the fake image of Jesus

By a personal initiative and an invented lie, Satan has helped Paul at it. Paul, the falsifier, has painted that fake image of Jesus. It gives a horrible conception of both God and Jesus. It shocks anyone with an innate sound mind and sound heart. The attributes of God in the epistles of Paul are contrasting to the attributes of God in the Old Testament and His attributes in the four gospels, in addition to Jesus also being distorted into a paganized mold. However, upon careful examination for this fake image of Jesus that does not contain even one word of Jesus at all, we notice the following:

1. Paul was the first corrupter of the reality of Jesus. He even showed him in a mix of different images such as, *"He is over all, the eternally blessed God. He is the image of God, the image of the invisible God." Who, being in the form of God, did not consider it robbery to be equal with God; but made himself of no reputation, taking the form of a servant, and coming in the likeness of men. And being found in appearance as a man, he humbled himself and became obedient to the point of death. For there is one mediator between God and*

men: the man Christ Jesus, who was born of the seed of David according to the flesh and declared to be the son of God with power, according to the Spirit of holiness, by the resurrection from the dead. All these different images of Jesus were new inventions. They were originated by Paul himself. He also corrupted the Hebrew figurative meaning of the term "Son of God" from the one who was sanctified by and sent from God, as Jesus himself explained, *"Do you say of him whom the Father sanctified and sent into the world, 'You are blaspheming, because I said, 'I am the son of God'?"* (John 10:36), to a distinct deity alongside God, just as a real father and a real son sitting beside one another. This conception of Jesus raises several inescapable questions: How many Gods are there? Is it one, for the sake of monotheism, or two Gods, One a greater Father God and the other is God the Son, who has the nature of his Father and sits beside him?

Is this really what is in the mind of a common Christian, just as with a common pagan idolater? It is just a confused dogma that can more accurately be coined as mono-polytheism. Jesus was not responsible for such a confused dogma. He never preached such polytheistic pagan-like mythology. Jesus himself, his disciples, the original followers of Jesus, and the successors to the apostles of Jesus—none of them ever preached a heavenly divine Jesus. None of the words of Jesus that were recorded in the four gospels spell out divinity for him in any way, shape, or form. Rather, Jesus's words that attributed to him only portrayed him as purely human messenger to the house of Israel.

So Jesus was betrayed twice. The first time by his disciple Judas, who was inspired by Satan to betray his teacher and to lead the Jews to arrest him. The second was by Paul, who was also inspired by Satan to betray the original teaching of Jesus. He succeeded to present of a fake Jesus and lead the non-Jews away from the truth in the true Jesus into his own false theology. So if the painting of Jesus that you are hanging in your heart is the fake one of Paul, you already have associated Jesus with God in His divinity. And this is the worst sin that God never forgives if you die upon it. So please start to seek truly Jesus. It will lead you to the way to salvation.

2. Another deceiving mythology invented by Paul was the theology of the atonement and redemption. It is the idea of a sacrificed savior and the blood of a transformed savior washing away sins and granting eternal life. This mythology was originated neither from Jesus nor from his disciples, but from Paul himself. It was entirely his own invention. Never was it based upon any divine revelation. It is an idea derived from the ancient pagan religions in the Roman city Tarsus, where Paul was born.

In the city of his birth, Tarsus, Mithraism was the most popular ancient pagan religions of the Roman Empire in the first century, where the pagans Romans believed that Mithras was the son of the pagan god who saved the world by sacrificing a bull, and through its blood, the world was purified. He was called a mediator. And since the news about Jesus being crucified and resurrected was widespread among the people at that time, Paul, therefore, borrowed the idea of purification by blood from Mithraism and made it the backbone for his philosophy and then applied it to his own Christianity, claiming that there is no remission without shedding of blood. Not the blood of goats and calves, but the blood of the son of God for obtaining eternal redemption. Paul took Mithraism up a step, from a sacrificial bull to a sacrificial man-God, representing a real son for God. This son was the exact likeness of God and had God's nature and called by him a mediator too. Not only that, he said that God the father was a cruel father. He did not have compassion for His own son, because in order to have mercy on humanity and save the world, He sacrificed His son without mercy. And Paul marketed all of this to the neighboring pagan nations to the Jews. With this pagan thought, Paul brought to Christianity the following problems:

How many Gods are there in the thought of Paul? Is it only one God? If so, did He just kill Himself (suicide)? This mythology suggests that Almighty God committed suicide in order to correct the error of Adam's disobedience after He chose to descend to earth to offer Himself to be killed on the cross and taste death. Glory be to God above all what they ascribe to Him.

Or were there more than one God in the thought of Paul, just as the pagans believe? Father and His son, the one to be sacrificed for the sake of humanity, as is Mithras, the son of the pagan god who had killed a bull to save the world! It is a great disaster from any angle you look at it. If it is one God, His death on the cross is considered suicide. If two Gods, it is a pagan polytheistic belief. If Jesus was just a human prophet, how can the death of just one human wash away the sins of all human and grant them eternal life?

3. Was Jesus a curse? And does the law of God bring curses upon its followers? This is precisely what Paul had suggested. *"Christ has redeemed us from the curse of the law, having become a curse for us, for it is written, 'Cursed is everyone who hangs on a tree'"* (Gal. 3:13). Paul's own distorted philosophy was thus: as Jesus was hanged upon a tree, he must have been cursed because the scripture says, *"He who is hanged is accursed of God"* (Deut. 21:23).

What the scripture actually says is this: *"If a man has committed a sin worthy of death, and he is put to death, and you hang him on a tree, his body shall not remain overnight on the tree, but you shall surely bury him that day…for he who is hanged is accursed of God"* (Deut. 21:22–23).

What if an innocent man was unjustly hanged to death on tree, would he be cursed? Surely not. Because the scripture talks about the criminal man who committed a sin worthy of death. It has nothing to do with what Paul is trying to impute to Jesus when he manipulated the scripture out of context to fit his false claim of the curse of Jesus and the curse of the law. And even if Jesus had been hanged on a tree, was he hanged as criminal who committed a sin worthy of death and curse?

Paul exploited the spread of the news of the death and resurrection of Jesus among the people and manufactured a paganized teaching for Christianity: one is the gift of salvation by faith alone without any behavioral requirement or legal obligation. *"Now God's way of putting people right with Himself has been revealed. It has nothing to do with Law. God puts people right through their faith in Jesus"* (Rom. 3:21–22). *"God offered him, so that by his sacrificial death he should become the means by which people's sins are forgiven through their faith in him"* (Rom. 3:25–26). *"Knowing that a man is not justified by the works of the law but by faith in Jesus Christ"* (Gal. 2:16). And he claimed that the law of God, which He had sent to man as a pattern of worship, was introduced in order to increase wrongdoing. To the extent that it would bring a curse to those who act depend on it. *"Those who depend on obeying the law live under a curse"* (Gal. 3:10). *"Law was introduced in order to increase wrongdoing"* (Rom. 5:20). Surely, this is not true. God did not introduce His law to increase wrongdoing but to establish the system of worshipping God through faith and deeds. God had created humanity different from angels. The human being is by nature subject to erring. But the best of those who commit sins are those who repent because they realize their mistake and grieve of over them. They turn to God in order that He may forgive them; for God is the most forgiving, most gracious, most merciful. It is not befitting God to have a son and to sacrifice him in order to wash away the sins of man with his blood, as the pagan believe that their gods do so.

Paul opposed God, the One gave the law, and opposed Jesus, the one who had said, *"Do not think that I came to destroy the Law or the Prophets. I did not come to destroy but to fulfill. For assuredly, I say to you, till heaven and earth pass away, one jot or one title by no means pass from the law till all is fulfilled"* (Matt. 5:17–18). And he also opposed the disciple James, who said, *"But do you want to know, O foolish man, that faith without works is dead? Do you see that faith was working together with his works, and by works faith was made perfect? You see then that a man is justified by works, and not by faith only"* (James 2:20, 22, 24).

4. Paul fraudulently claimed that all of mankind were God's enemies! That newborn babies were born sinners as a result of the disobedience of Adam. And because of this, the innocent baby is born contaminated by that sin. *"Sin came into the world through one man* (Adam), *and his sin brought death with it. As a result, death has spread to the whole human race because everyone has sinned"* (Rom. 5:12). Then only some two thousand years ago, God found a solution to stop this enmity between Him and mankind, and He reconciled with us by sacrificing His son for our sake! So as a result of Jesus's obedience by accepting the death mission, God and man were reconciled through Jesus. *"For if when we were enemies we were reconciled to God through the death of His son"* (Rom. 5:10). *"For as by one man's* (Adam) *disobedience many were made sinners, so also by one man's* (Jesus) *obedience many will be made righteous"* (Rom. 5:19). Paul was the first one to introduce the concept of original sin (Adam's sin) and the inheritance of that sin. These concepts raise many questions, such as the following:

When God created man, did He know that man would commit sins due to the free will that He already granted him? If the answer is yes, that He indeed knew that Adam would sin (because Adam was not created as an angel without will), then what, during all those thousands of years between Adam and the time of Jesus, was the solution to the problem of the alleged inherited sin? Was God all those years trying to convince His alleged son to sacrifice himself to cover up this expected sin; but then, in the end, God felt compelled not to show compassion for His own alleged son, as Paul claimed? Is not God always all-pardoning, all-forgiving, the most gracious, and the most merciful? Cannot God forgive a sin without harming anyone? What Paul says about millions of people before Jesus all over the world and those who never heard about the alleged savior and never believed in his mythology?

Or God, glory to Him, did not know that Adam would sin; so He tried to cover up this human defect with the blood of His alleged son? Glory be to God! He is free from all that Paul and those who believe him had ascribed to Him. Many other questions remain, such as "Why are you, reader, responsible for the sin of Adam? How can one be considered guilty for something that he knows nothing of and is not involved in? And how is a person put right with God through a sacrifice that was done by another person, millions of people did not feel it, and did not interact with it psychologically and practically?"

In any civilized law, people are not supposed to be punished for something they have no control over. So is man more just than God who allows the inheritance of the alleged original sin? If Satan already succeeded to mislead many people during previous centuries with pagan creeds, how is it that the people of this later century who are more literate and educated find it acceptable to inherit and believe in such heresies and mythology that underrate the might of the true God? Nowhere in the words of God can we find such a concept of an inherited original sin. The sin of Adam and Eve was forgiven immediately as soon as they both realized their mistake and immediately repented. God was in no need to wait until the time of Jesus to forgive the sin of Adam. And there was no need for blood to forgive such sin since He is the most forgiving. He never inspired any of His messengers, Jesus included, as regards any notion of an original sin. Even the words of Jesus himself never spilled out such a creed. The teaching of God as regards sins has always remained consistent: everyone is responsible for his own sin. There is no inheritance in sins between father and son, mother and daughter. In the book of Ezekiel in the Old Testament, we read, *"The soul who sins shall die. The son shall not bear the guilt of the father, nor the father bear the guilt of the son"* (Ezek. 18:20). And in Jeremiah, it similarly reads, *"But everyone shall die for his own iniquity"* (Jer. 31:30).

5. Paul had become convinced that Jesus would return back while Paul was still alive. He prophesied that Jesus would descend from heaven with a shout, with the voice of the archangel, and with the trumpet of God. Those who have died believing in Jesus will rise to life first. Then Paul and his followers, who were still alive and remain, would be caught up together with them in the clouds to meet Jesus in the air.

> *The Lord* (Jesus) *himself will descend from heaven with a shout, with the voice of an archangel, and with the trumpet of God. And the dead in Christ will rise first. Then we who are alive and remain shall be caught up together with them in the clouds to meet the Lord in the air. And thus, we shall always be with the Lord. Therefore comfort one another with these words.* (1 Thess. 4:16–18)

Now, more than two thousand years have passed since the prophecy, but nothing happened as Paul had prophesied. But his soul is facing upon the effects of his false teaching, and at judgment day, he will be called to account for deceiving the nations.

6. Finally, Paul did not write anything that gave the actual teaching of Christ. Instead, he plotted to spread his own philosophy and his own brand of pagan Christianity outside the Jewish world. Paul knew what to do to spread his teaching among the neighboring gentiles to the Jews. He

made his teaching all the more attractive because it is devoid of "the burden of the law," without any accountability due to sins. He claimed that entering into paradise requires no more than acknowledging that Christ is Lord raised by God from death and accepting of the alleged son of God as one's personal savior who has washed away sins with his blood and resurrection. *"If you confess with your mouth the Lord Jesus and believe in your heart that God has raised him from the dead, you will be saved"* (Rom. 10:9). Rebranding of Jesus's message with such pagan creed explains why it spread so rapidly and superficially.

Paul announced that the whole function of Jesus is centered on his death and resurrection. Thus, he placed all his eggs in one basket, gambling with his credibility by making his own version of Christianity totally dependent upon faith in the crucifixion. This announcement puts more focus on Paul's philosophy that the Christians have nothing to preach about and have nothing to believe in except the death and resurrection of Jesus. *"And if Christ is not risen, then our preaching is vain, and your faith is also vain"* (1 Cor. 15:14).

So it is easy for anyone who really has the intention in his heart to seek the truth to shortcut to it by knowing the true answer to this question: Was Jesus really crucified? This is the subject of the next chapter.

CHAPTER 4

Was Jesus really crucified?

Preface

Any prophet can be killed if God has destined murder to be a cause for his death as the Jews did with some prophets. Jesus said, *"O Jerusalem, Jerusalem, the one who kills prophets and stones those who are sent to her!"* (Matt. 23:37). And he said, pointing to the Jewish scribes and Pharisees, *"Therefore, you are witnesses against yourselves that you are the sons of those who murdered the prophets"* (Matt. 23:31).

In principle, there is no problem to add Jesus to be among those murdered prophets, but was he really among them? The account of the crucifixion that was reported to have occurred in a place called Golgotha is a certain historical fact, but has it really happened to Jesus himself? The four gospels, of course, recount the events of the crucifixion as facts, occurred to Jesus himself. It ended with his death on the cross. Then on the third day, he rose from the dead, went out of the tomb, met his disciples and then ascended to heaven. Some narrations in the gospels even say that Jesus himself had prophesied during his life on earth that he would be killed and after three days, he would rise from death.

There are those who wrote that the events of the crucifixion occurred to Jesus himself, as mentioned in the Gospels, but he did not die; rather, he was unconscious, then he was taken down from the cross and put into the tomb. After he woke up, he came out of the tomb. It was not a resurrection but a resuscitation. While others wrote that the crucifixion did not occur to Jesus himself but to another person, but without proofs, without details, and many questions unanswered.

Why was Jesus the only one who has a disputed end? Was it because of the sources? There is no written record by Jesus himself that we can refer to about the mysterious final part of his life on earth. The only available records from early Christians for this final part of Jesus's life are the four gospels, which are merely biographical accounts of Jesus and were produced through purely human efforts, fallible endeavors that was neither inspiration involved nor eyewitnesses when they were written by anonymous authors that came thirty to sixty years after the ascension. And each author came with his own collection of rumors and uncertain narrations that conflict with the other's narrations about the crucifixion and the resurrection. But the matter became serious when a new doctrine came out after the ascension of Christ that ascribes a main mission for Jesus that God had sent him for the mission of a sacrificial death to become the means by which people's sins would be forgiven and to obtain eternal salvation. Therefore, the case now is a matter of immortal destiny in paradise or in hell, based on the credibility of ascribing a death mission for Jesus as a key to salvation.

Was Jesus hanged on the cross and died? Or was he hanged on the cross but did not die? Or was he not hanged on the cross at all? This study is a new analytical study, which to deconstruct the texts deeply with pondering over them, to explore some fundamental traces within the texts that may lead us to some internal facts from which we can imagine the scenario of the events of the last days of Jesus on earth and answer the previous questions and many other questions raised by the events contained in those texts.

This study contains ten researches that may help, after pondering over them, to reach to a conclusion for the main question: Was Jesus really crucified? These researches begin with this fundamental point: was it a mission for Jesus to die for the forgiveness of sins? Then it goes on like this: Why did the Jews plot to put Jesus to death? How did the Jews move to implement the plot of killing Jesus? How did Jesus behave toward the Jewish conspiracy? Did the Jews find

Jesus and arrest him when they sought him? Who was the crucified person? Why did Jesus not give any details about the end of his life on earth? Did Jesus prophesy that he would be killed? Did Jesus declare that he had passed through death and resurrection? How different are the authors' accounts of some events?

Research 1
Was it a mission for Jesus to die for the forgiveness of sins?

All those who believe that Jesus was crucified, then he rose from death and ascended to heaven also believe that this death was his main mission, which God had sent him for it, to redeem the sins of everyone who believes in him.

If God had really sent Jesus for pouring out his blood for the forgiveness of sins and to preach such mission to the people, surely Jesus will not mislead people by keeping silence about such main mission but will seek with all the strength and statement to confirm this belief in the hearts of those who had believed in him from the Jews, using clear words that signify of this belief. And the disciples after him would also be keen to highlight the doctrine of atonement and redemption.

Therefore, since the issue is now relating to the immortal destiny of people in paradise or in hell, depending on the credibility or falsity of Jesus's death for eternal salvation, the simple question that can be addressed to anyone who attributes his religion to Christ is thus, Is there any stated clearly evidence from the words that were ascribed to Jesus in the four gospels, declaring that he came to die for the salvation of the people?

Those who believe that Jesus died for the forgiveness of sins will not hesitate to use, as a proof for their belief, what has been written by Mark, wherein Jesus had said, *"This is my blood of the new covenant, which is shed for many"* (Mark 14:24); and also, what Matthew wrote, *"This is my blood of the new covenant, which is shed for many for the remission of sins"* (Matt. 26:28); as well as what Luke did: *"This cup is the new covenant in my blood, which is shed for you"* (Luke 22:20).

While on the other hand, we find that Jesus had already clearly declared to the Jews how to attain salvation in the Hereafter, without any mention or an indication to faith in the blood of a savior. Jesus said, *"Most assuredly I say to you, he who hears my word and believe in Him who sent me has everlasting life"* (John 5:24). Jesus also spoke these words, lifting up his eyes to heaven: *"And this is eternal life, that they may know you, the only true God, and Jesus Christ whom you have sent"* (John 17:3). And when a man asked Jesus, *"Good Teacher, what good things shall I do that I may have eternal life?"* he said to him, *"Why do you call me good? No one is good but One, that is God. But if you want to enter into life keep the commandments"* (Matt. 19:16–17). They were required only to believe in the true Oneness of God, that Jesus is a messenger of God, and to keep the commandments. They we're not required to believe in the doctrine of atonement and redemption.

Not only that, but he challenged the Jews and told them that in the end of his mission with them, and before he ascended to heaven, they will fail to find him when they seek him. *"I shall be with you a little while longer, and then I go to Him who sent me. You will seek me and not find me, and where I am you cannot come"* (John 7:33–34).

What were the requirements for the salvation in the Hereafter, proclaimed by Jesus to his people? Was it a faith in the oneness of God, that Jesus is His servant and messenger, and keeping the commandments? Or was it a faith in the death of Jesus as a savior, whose blood would be poured out for many for the forgiveness of sins? Can Jesus announce the mission of pouring out his blood for the remission of sins and at the same time challenging the Jews that they would not find him when they seek him to kill him? Where is the truth in the previous texts?

The truth is that we really need more effort in research, clarification, comparisons, and texts analysis to know the truth. The other fact is that after the ascension of Christ, a new brand of faith was announced in the neighboring pagan nations of the Jews, completely different from the faith that was brought by all the previous messengers of God, including Jesus himself. A faith that was coated in the blood of Christ to imitate the philosophy of purification by blood in some pagan religions. This new brand of faith was introduced by Paul after the ascension of Christ, claiming that it is more advance than what Jesus preached during his lifetime, and it was not his own but had come to him by personal inspiration from Jesus himself, even though he had never met him.

Paul claimed that Jesus's death mission was God's secret wisdom, which He had kept it hidden from humanity, for if He had announced it, the Jewish leaders would have known and they would not have crucified Jesus. Not only that, but he made himself the only authorized person to declare God's secret wisdom in Jesus's death. In fact, he thought himself to be the great interpreter of Jesus's mission, having explained it in a way that Jesus himself never did. Paul said,

> *The wisdom I proclaim is God's secret wisdom, which is hidden from mankind, but which He had already chosen for our glory even before the world was made. None of the rulers of this world knew this wisdom. If they had known it, they would not have crucified the Lord of glory.* (1 Cor. 2:7–8)

Paul asked the pagan nations to believe that God had sent Jesus for the mission of the sacrificial death to become the means by which people's sins would be forgiven and to obtain eternal salvation. Paul said, "*God did not even keep back His own son but offered him for us all*" (Rom. 8:32). "*(Jesus) made himself of no reputation, taking the form of a servant, and coming in the likeness of men. And being found in appearance as a man, he humbled himself and became obedient to the point of death, even the death of the cross*" (Phil. 2:6–8). "*To redeem those who were under the Law*" (Gal. 4:5). "*Now God's way of putting people right with Himself has been revealed. It has nothing to do with Law. God puts people right through their faith in Jesus*" (Rom. 3:21–22). "*God offered him, so that by his sacrificial death he should become the means by which people's sins are forgiven only through their faith in him*" (Rom. 3:25–26). "*Christ died for the wicked at the time that God chose*" (Rom. 5:6). "*Not with the blood of goats and calves, but* with his own blood he entered the most holy place once for all, having obtained eternal redemption, because without shedding of blood there is no remission" (Heb. 9:12, 22). *God demonstrates His own love toward us, in that while we were still sinners, Christ died for us* (Rom. 5:8). *"Much more then, having now been justified by his blood, we shall be saved from wrath through him. For if when we were enemies we were reconciled to God through the death of His son"* (Rom. 5:9–10). *"That is, that God was in Christ reconciling the world to Himself, not imputing their trespasses to them, and has committed to us the word of reconciliation"* (2 Cor. 5:19).

Paul clothed his own thoughts with religious attire and hallmarked them with the pagan mark of quality in order to do an effective marketing for himself and imposes his illusion as an apostle pertaining to the Gentile to gain religious leadership, but it was a leadership at the expense of the truth that was in the true religion of Jesus. He replaced the genuine Christianity that was addressed to the Jews with another polytheist, Gentile-wide and gave a pagan meaning to the rumor of the death and resurrection of Jesus. He presented Jesus to the Gentile as a heavenly being, claiming that he was a real Son of God who did not have compassion for His own son and sacrificed him on the cross to wash out, by his blood, the original sin that was committed by Adam, because of that sin, people were made sinners. *"Sin came into the world through one man (Adam), and his sin brought death with it. As a result, death has spread to the whole human race because everyone has sinned"* (Rom. 5:12), *"for as in Adam all die, even so in Christ all shall be made alive"* (1 Cor. 15:22), *"and sins are forgiven only if blood is poured out"* (Heb. 9:22).

But on the other hand, if we look in the four gospels as a record of the biography of Jesus and his words, we will find many evidences prove that there is not a mission of death for Jesus as a savior, as follows:

1. Jesus clearly declared to the Jews the way to salvation in the Hereafter, which is to believe in the oneness of God and that Jesus is His messenger—*"Most assuredly I say to

you, he who hears my word and believe in Him who sent me has everlasting life" (John 5:24). Also, he said, *"And this is eternal life, that they may know you, the only true God, and Jesus Christ whom you have sent"* (John 17:3)—and to keep the commandments. *"If you want to enter into life, keep the commandments"* (Matt. 19:17). There is no mention or an indication to have faith in the blood of a savior.

2. Jesus challenged the Jews and told them that in the end of his mission with them, and before he ascended to heaven, they will fail to find him when they seek him. *"I shall be with you a little while longer, and then I go to Him who sent me. You will seek me and not find me, and where I am you cannot come"* (John 7:33–34). If his mission was to die for the forgiveness of sins, would he then challenge those who wanted to kill him that they would not find him and would not arrest him?

3. The author of John narrated that Jesus rebuked the Jews for seeking to kill him. *"But you seek to kill me, because my word has no place in you"* (John 8:37).

   If God had sent Jesus to be killed, would Jesus then rebuke the Jews for seeking to kill him?

4. He also rebuked them again. *"But now you seek to kill me, a man who has told you the truth which I heard from God. Abraham did not do this"* (John 8:40).

5. He questioned the Jews for seeking to kill him. *"Did not Moses give you the law, and yet none of you keeps the law? Why do you seek to kill me?"* (John 7:19).

   If the mission of Jesus was to die, would he then question the Jews why do they seek to kill him?

6. He used to avoid those who wanted to kill him. *"Jesus walked in Galilee; for he did not want to walk in Judea, because the Jews sought to kill him"* (John 7:1). Also, the author wrote, *"Then from that day on they plotted to put him to death. Therefore, Jesus no longer walked openly among the Jews, but went from there into the country near the wilderness, to a city called Ephraim, and there remained with his*

disciples" (John 11:53–54). Also, the author of Matthew wrote, *"Then the Pharisees went out and took counsel against him, how they might destroy him. But when Jesus knew it, he withdrew from there"* (Matt. 12:14–15).

7. Paul claimed that the mission of Jesus's death to save mankind was not announced to the Jewish leaders, for had they known about it, they would not have crucified Jesus. *"None of the rulers of this world knew this wisdom. If they had known it, they would not have crucified the Lord of glory"* (1 Cor. 2:8). While Mark, Matthew, and Luke claimed that Jesus had announced to his disciples that his blood is poured out for many for the remission of sins. *"This is my blood of the new covenant, which is shed for many"* (Mark 14:24; Matt. 26:28; Luke 22:20).

    Anyway, if Jesus had announced such mission to his disciples, as the three authors claimed, surely the devil would hear about it and be aware of such mission. So the question now is, Is it expected from the devil to participate in a mission that free people from their sins?

    Certainly no one says that the devil works for the benefit of man and seeks to have his sins forgiven but rather works hard to increase them and keeps man a prisoner of them. The author of John and Luke wrote that the devil was behind the arrangement of Judas's betrayal of Jesus to be arrested. *"And supper being ended, the devil having already put it into the heart of Judas Iscariot, Simon's son, to betray him"* (John 13:2). *"Now after the piece of bread, Satan entered him"* (John 13:27). *"Then Satan entered Judas"* (Luke 22:3).

    The involvement of the devil in the betrayal of Judas to deliver Jesus to the Jews, proves that Jesus never declared the mission of pouring out his blood for many to forgive sins; otherwise, the devil would not have put into the heart of Judas the thought of betraying Jesus.

8. Jesus warned Judas and predicted a terrible end for him. The author of Matthew narrated that when evening had come, Jesus sat down with the twelve. And as they were

eating, he said to them, *"Assuredly, I say to you, one of you will betray me... The Son of Man goes as it is written of him, but woe* (how terrible) *to that man by whom the Son of Man is betrayed! It would have been good for that man if he had not been born"* (Matt. 26:21, 24).

If what's written about Jesus *"the Son of Man goes as it is written of him"* was to mean the mission of pouring out his blood for the forgiveness of sin, it would be fair to reward Judas and consider him one of the great heroes for participating in accomplishing such a mission, not to threaten him with a terrible end.

9. In the most critical moments, Jesus separated from his disciples and knelt down then fell on his face and prayed to God to remove the cup of adversity from him. *"And he was withdrawn from them about a stone's throw, and he knelt down and prayed"* (Luke 22:41). *"He went a little farther and fell on his face, and prayed, saying, 'O my Father, if it is possible, let this cup pass from me; nevertheless, not as I will, but as you will'"* (Matt. 26:39).

10. If the mission of Jesus was to have his blood poured out for many for the remission of sins, so his appearance to his disciples after the event of the crucifixion and before he ascended to heaven would be a great opportunity for him to teach them the doctrine of atonement and redemption that he had come for, and he would have asked his disciples to preach it among the people, but there was nothing like that at all!

All the authors of the four gospels have not reported a word from Jesus about the mission of saving mankind through death when he appeared to his disciples in his last chance with them before he ascended to heaven. All what they reported was that, before Jesus departed from this earth, he wanted them to make people his disciples, baptize them, obey his commands, and preach the Gospel and the message of how to repent and forgive their sins (Matt. 28:19–20; Mark 16:15; Luke 24:47; John 20:23).

Not mentioning about the mission of a sacrificial death proves that there was no such a mission.

11. All those who believe that Jesus came to die in order to redeem from sins anyone who believes in him must also believe that Jesus tried to escape with his disciples at the last moment, when Judas came with the troops to arrest him, because Matthew wrote that Jesus said to his disciples, *"Rise, let us be going, see, he who betrays me is at hand"* (Matt. 26:46). How did Jesus come for the mission of death, then tried to escape at the last moment?

12. How can he who believes that God sent Jesus in order to be killed and at the same time believes that the one who delivered Jesus to the Roman governor Pilate to have him crucified has the greater sin? The author of the Gospel of John claims that Jesus said to Pilate, *"Therefore, the one who delivered me to you has the greater sin"* (John 19:11).

13. Also, all those who believe that God sent Jesus in order to be killed must also believe that Jesus was blaming God for letting him die, for Matthew wrote that Jesus said on the cross, *"My God, My God, why have you forsaken me?"* (Matt. 27:46; Mark 15:34). Or did Jesus come for a death mission but did not know anything about it?

14. The authors of the Gospels wrote that Jesus was humiliated when Pilate had him whipped. Then his soldiers took him and stripped him and put on him a purple robe. Then they made a crown of thorns, and put it on his head, and put a stick in his right hand. Then they knelt before him and made fun of him. They spat at him and took the stick and hit him over the head and led him away to be crucified (Matt. 27:26–31; John 19:1–3). So the question now is for anyone who believes that Jesus is a real son of God, who sent him to be killed for the remission of sins: Does the remission of sins also require humiliating and insulting Jesus and injuring his dignity and pride in front of the people?

The doctrine of atonement and redemption is an invented belief, never based upon any divine revelation. It is an old pagan philosophy based on the idea of a sacrificed savior and the blood of a savior washing away sins and granting eternal life. It was borrowed and formulated by Paul and made it the rock foundation where he had laid it upon the edge of a sand-cliff and built his fake church!

Research 2
Why did the Jews plot to put Jesus to death?

Jesus was the Messiah who was sent to the Israelites with wisdom, wonders, and clear signs to confirm to them the true oneness of God, to preach the gospel, and to fulfill the law. So he carried the teaching to their cities and towns, and he entered their synagogues and showed to the multitude his signs. Also, he used to go to Jerusalem at the feasts of the Jews and teach in the temple there. He did not keep silent in his first visit to Jerusalem when he saw how the Jews were using the house of God as a market.

> *And he found in the temple those who sold oxen and sheep and doves, and the money changers doing business. When he had made a whip from cords, he drove them all out of the temple, with the sheep and the oxen, and poured out the changers' money and overturned the tables. And he said to those who sold doves, "Take these things away! Do not make my father's house a house of merchandise!"* (John 2:14–16)

The Jewish religious authorities in Jerusalem did not believe in him. And at the same time, due to his activities, they were worried about their fellow Jews may accept him. So they sought to destroy him while he was daily teaching in the temple. But they were unable to do anything as all the people were very attentive to hear him.

And he was teaching daily in the temple. But the chief priests, the scribes, and the leaders of the people sought to destroy him and were unable to do anything; for all the people were very attentive to hear him. (Luke 19:47–48)

Then they watched him and sent spies, who pretended to be righteous, that they might seize on his words in order to deliver him to the power and the authority of the governor (Luke 20:20). And the more Jesus surprised them with his knowledge and wisdom, the more they besmirch his reputation, that he had a demon and is mad (John 7:20).

The Jews' envy toward Jesus became more when many of the Jews believed in him after they had seen him in the town of Bethany, near Jerusalem, raising his friend Lazarus from the dead, by God permission, in his late days on earth. And because of that, the chief priests and Pharisees gathered a council (John 11:45–47). And they said, *"What shall we do? For this man works many signs. If we let him alone like this, everyone will believe in him, and the Romans will come and take away both our place and nation"* (John 11:47–48).

The decrees that came out from that meeting and other following meeting were as follows:

1. It is better that one man (Jesus) should die for the people and not that the whole nation should perish (by following Jesus and then absolute control of the Romans). *"And one of them, Caiaphas, being high priest that year, said to them, 'You know nothing at all, nor do you consider that it is expedient for us that one man should die for the people, and not that the whole nation should perish'"* (John 11:49–50).
2. Jesus must be put to death from that day. *"Then from that day on they plotted to put him to death"* (John 11:53).
3. They gave a command, if anyone knew where Jesus is when he comes to Jerusalem, he should report it, that they might seize him. *"Now both the chief priests and the pharisees had*

given a command, that if anyone knew where he was, he should report it, that they might seize him" (John 11:57).
4. Lazarus should be also put to death, because on his account, many of the Jews went away and believed in Jesus. *"But the chief priests took counsel that they might also put Lazarus to death, because on account of him many of the Jews went away and believed in Jesus"* (John 12:10–11).

So it was because of envy that the Jews plotted to kill him (Matt. 27:18; Mark 15:10).

Research 3
How did the Jews move to implement the plot of killing Jesus?

After the suggestion of Caiaphas, the high priest, to kill Jesus, the chief priests and Pharisees waited Jesus to come to Jerusalem for the feast of the Passover, which was very near. And they had issued a command that if anyone knew where he was, he should report it, that they might seize him. (John 11:57). Then when Jesus entered Jerusalem, as his last visit, *"all the city was moved, saying, 'Who is this?' So, the multitudes said, 'This is Jesus, the prophet from Nazareth of Galilee.' Then Jesus went into the temple of God and drove out all those who bought and sold in the temple and overturned the tables of money-changers and the seats of those who sold doves. And he said to them, 'It is written My house shall be called a house of prayer, but you have made it a den of thieves'"* (Matt. 21:10–13). He also performed some miracles there. And during his stay in Jerusalem, waiting the feast, he was teaching there. And the chief priests and Pharisees saw him teaching in the temple and heard him telling some parables against them. So they reacted when they saw all this, as follows:

1. They became angry and indignant when they saw the wonderful things that Jesus did, and the children cried out in the temple, saying, *"Hosanna to the son of David"* (Matt. 21:15).

2. The Pharisees then said among themselves, *"You see that you are accomplishing nothing. Look, the world has gone after him"* (John 12:19).
3. They sought to lay hands on him because they knew that he was talking about them with his parables. But they were afraid of the crowds, who considered Jesus to be a prophet. *"But when they sought to lay hands on him, they feared the multitudes, because they took him for a prophet"* (Matt. 21:46).
4. They met together in the palace of Caiaphas, the high priest, and plotted to take Jesus by trickery and kill him. But they said, *"Not during the feast, lest there be an uproar among the people"* (Matt. 26:3–5).
5. While the chief priests and the scribes were trying to find a way of putting Jesus to death secretly, because they were afraid of the people (Luke 22:2), the betrayer disciple, Judas, came and spoke with the chief priests and captains how he might betray Jesus to them. *"And they were glad and agreed to give him money"* (Luke 22:4–5).
6. They provided Judas with a detachment of troops and officers with lanterns, torches, and weapons to arrest Jesus. *"Then Judas having received a detachment of troops, and officers from the chief priests and Pharisees, came there with lanterns, torches, and weapons"* (John 18:3).

Research 4
How did Jesus behave toward the Jewish conspiracy?

Jesus had a mission, which was to call all Jews to God through the gospel that God had revealed to him. He already expected the troubles from the chief priests and the Pharisees, and he knew (through inspiration) that they were conspiring against him because of envy. Therefore, Jesus based his behavior toward the Jews' conspiring on two things: faith and action.

As for faith, Jesus had total dependence on God that He would not leave him alone in facing the Jews' conspiring to kill him. This was demonstrated as follows:

1. The total dependence of Jesus on God gave him the power to challenge the Jews when the Pharisees and the chief priests sent some officers to arrest him during one of his early visits to Jerusalem. He told them that the remaining time for him with them is not very long, then he will ascend to heaven. And just prior to his ascension, they will seek him, but they will fail to arrest him because they will not find him. He said to them, *"I shall be with you a little while longer, and then I go to Him who sent me. You will seek me and not find me, and where I am you cannot come"* (John 7:33–34).
2. He already told the Jews that God was already with him and He had not left him alone. *"And He who sent me is with me. The Father has not left me alone, for I always do those things that please Him"* (John 8:29).
3. One day, the Jews sought to take him while he was teaching in the temple, but no one laid a hand on him (John 7:30, 44).
4. When the Jews took up stones to throw at him, Jesus hid himself and went out of the temple, going through the midst of them and so passed by. *"Then they took up stones to throw at him; but Jesus hid himself and went out of the temple, going through the midst of them, and so passed by"* (John 8:59).
5. In his last visit to Jerusalem, Jesus already had full trust that God would thwart the Jewish murder conspiracy and knew that He would raise him up to heaven. *"Now before the feast of the Passover, when Jesus knew that his hour had come that he should depart from this world to the Father"* (John 13:1).
6. And in his last visit to Jerusalem, he also had full trust that God would not enable the Jews to see him. Jesus said to his disciples at the Passover table (Last Supper), *"A little while longer and the world* (the Jews) *will see me no more"* (John

14:19). And two days before the feast, Jesus was speaking to the multitudes and to his disciples in the temple, and at the end, he addressed the scribes and Pharisees, saying, *"See! Your house is left to you desolate; for I say to you, you shall see me no more till you say, 'Blessed is he who comes in the name of the Lord!'"* (Matt. 23:38–39).
7. He also told his disciples that he would never be alone, even if they all scattered and leave him, because God will be with him. *"Indeed, the hour is coming, yes has now come, that you will be scattered, each to his own, and will leave me alone. But I am not really alone, because the father is with me"* (John 16:32).
8. While he was praying to God for help in the garden, before the coming of Judas and the troops to arrest him, an angel appeared to him from heaven, strengthening him. *"Then an angel appeared to him from heaven, strengthening him"* (Luke 22:43).

And as for the action, Jesus took some steps to defend himself against the Jewish conspiracy, such as follows:

1. Avoiding the Jewish conspirators: *"After these things Jesus walked in Galilee; for he did not want to walk in Judea, because the Jews sought to kill him"* (John 7:1). And he was no longer walking openly among them: *"Therefore, Jesus no longer walked openly among the Jews, but went from there into the country near the wilderness, to a city called Ephraim, and there remained with his disciples"* (John 11:54).
2. Withdrawing from the place where there is danger for him: *"Then the Pharisees went out and took counsel against him, how they might destroy him. But when Jesus knew it, he withdrew from there"* (Matt. 12:14–15).
3. He was questioning the Jews: *"Did not Moses give you the law, and yet none of you keeps the law? Why do you seek to kill me?"* (John 7:19).

4. He was rebuking them: *"I know that you are Abraham's descendants, but you seek to kill me, because my word has no place in you"* (John 8:37). Also, he said, *"But now you seek to kill me, a man who has told you the truth which I heard from God. Abraham did not do this"* (John 8:40).
5. Jesus and his disciples left the upper room, where they had the Last Supper, and went to a garden in the Mount of Olives after the traitor Judas had gone out to bring the troops to arrest him. *"And when they had sung a hymn, they went out to the Mount of Olives"* (Matt. 26:30) *"to a place called Gethsemane"* (Matt. 26:36) *"over the Brook Kidron, where there was a garden, which he and his disciples entered. And Judas, who betrayed him, also knew the place; for Jesus often met there with his disciples"* (John 18:1–2).
6. At the most critical moment in the garden, a prior of the coming of Judas and the troops, Jesus prayed to his Lord not to drink the cup of death from the hand of his enemy. *"He went a little farther and fell on his face, and prayed, saying, 'O my Father, if it is possible, let this cup pass from me; nevertheless, not as I will, but as you will'"* (Matt. 26:39).
7. After Jesus had prayed to his Lord in the garden, and while his disciples were in a deep sleep. He left the garden and went to a safe place to hide where the Jews cannot come.

Research 5
Did the Jews find Jesus and arrest him when they seek him?

There are two answers for the above question. One is by Jesus himself. He said no. *"You will seek me and not find me"* (John 7:34).

The other answer is by the people who still say, yes, they found him, arrested him, then crucified him.

Are not they contradicted answers?

Should not Jesus be the one who tells the truth?

Is it not a strange to work to prove that Jesus was telling the truth?

Was Jesus, who said no, and the people, who said yes, referring to the same arresting attempt?

What is the evidence that Jesus meant the last attempt by the Jews in which his traitorous disciple Judas was involved?

To end this controversy and the truth manifests, we start where the story starts, as it been narrated in the Gospel of John as follows:

Because of envy, the Jewish religious authorities did not believe in Jesus, and they were not pleased with his activities in Jerusalem whenever he comes there at their feasts. At the beginning of his mission, Jesus went to Jerusalem for a religious festival. Then it happened that he healed a man who had been sick, by God permission, and that day was the Sabbath. *"For this reason, the Jews persecuted Jesus, and sought to kill him, because he had done these things on the Sabbath. But Jesus answered them, 'My Father has been working until now, and I have been working.' Therefore, the Jews sought all the more to kill him, because he not only broke the Sabbath, but also said that God was his father, making himself equal with God"* (John 5:16–18).

After this, Jesus went across Lake Galilee (or Lake Tiberias, as it is also called). Then a large crowed followed him. He went up on a mountain and sat there with his disciples. The time for the Passover, a feast of the Jews, was near (John 6:1–4). The following day they were in the land of Capernaum (John 6:17, 21–22). Jesus taught in the synagogue in Capernaum (John 6:59). Then after this, *"He walked in Galilee; for he did not want to walk in Judea, because the Jews sought to kill him"* (John 7:1).

The time for the Feast of Tabernacles was near. His brothers therefore suggested that he should go to Judea, but he said to them, *"My time has not yet come, but your time is always ready. The world* (the Jews) *cannot hate you, but it hates me, because I testify of it that its works are evil. You go up to this feast. I am not yet going up to this feast, for my time has not yet fully come. When he had said these things to them, he remained in Galilee. But when his brothers had gone up, then he also went up to the feast, not openly, but as it were in secret. Then the Jews sought him at the feast and said, 'Where is he?'* (John 7:6–11).

"Now about the middle of the feast Jesus went up into the temple and taught. And the Jews marveled, saying, 'How does this man know

letters, having never studied?' Jesus answered them and said, 'My doctrine is not mine, but His who sent me'" (John 7:14–16). Then he asked them, *"'Did not Moses give you the law, and yet none of you keeps the law? Why do you seek to kill me?' The people answered and said, 'You have a demon. Who is seeking to kill you?' Jesus answered and said to them, 'I did one work, and you all marvel. Moses therefore gave you circumcision (not that it is from Moses, but from the fathers), and you circumcise a man on the Sabbath. If a man receives circumcised on the Sabbath, so that the law of Moses should not be broken, are you angry with me because I made a man completely well on the Sabbath?'"* (John 7:19–23). Then they tried to seize him, but no one laid a hand on him. And many of the people believed in him (John 7:30–31).

The Pharisees heard the crowd murmuring about Jesus. Then the Pharisees and the chief priests sent some officers to arrest him. Then Jesus told them that the remaining time for him with them is not very long, then he will ascend to heaven. And just prior to his ascension, they will seek him, but they will fail to arrest him because they will not find him. He said to them, *"I shall be with you a little while longer, and then I go to Him who sent me. You will seek me and not find me, and where I am you cannot come"* (John 7:33–34).

On the last and most important day of the feast, Jesus stood up and started to teach. Then many of the crowd when they heard his teaching said, *"Truly this is the prophet." Other said, "This is the Christ"* (John 7:40–41). *"Some of them wanted to take him, but no one laid hands on him"* (John 7:44). When the officers went back, the chief priests and Pharisees asked them, *"Why have you not brought him?"* (John 7:45). The officers answered, *"No man ever spoke like this man!" Then the Pharisees answered them, "Are you also deceived? Have any of the rulers or the Pharisee believed in him? But this crowed that does not know the law is accursed"* (John 7:46–49). *"And everyone went to his own house"* (John 7:53). *"But Jesus went to the mount of Olives"* (John 8:1).

Early the next morning, Jesus came again into the temple, and all the people came to him, and he sat down and taught them. The scribes and Pharisees came as well. Then after he had discussed with them, he assured them what he said yesterday, that they would not find him in the place where they would come to arrest him, for he would have gone elsewhere, and where he goes, they cannot come. He said, *"I am going away, and you will seek me, and will die in your sin. Where I go you cannot come"* (John 8:21).

(1/5) The plot to kill Jesus

Jesus continued carrying his teaching to the Jewish cities and towns and showing the multitude of his signs. Also, he continued going to Jerusalem at the feasts of the Jews and teaching in the temple there.

Bethany was a town less than two miles from Jerusalem. In this town, there was a sick man named Lazarus. He had two sisters, who sent a message to Jesus informing him about the sickness of their brother, as Jesus loved Lazarus and his sisters. Then after two days, Jesus went to Bethany to see Lazarus. When he arrived there, he found that Lazarus had already been in the tomb for four days.

Many of the Jews had come to the two sisters to comfort them about the death of their brother. At the tomb, which was a cave with a stone placed at the entrance, Jesus wept and began to call God, not expressed in clear and audible words, but deep within himself with groaning. Then he asked them to take the stone away. When they moved the stone, Jesus looked up and with a loud voice. He glorified God and thanked Him for answering his call so that the attendees do not think that it is he was the one who had raised Lazarus but God alone. He said, *"I thank you that you have heard me. And I know that you always hear me, but because of the people who are standing by I said this* (i.e., thanking God aloud) *that they may believe that you sent me"* (John 11:41–42). Then he cried with a loud voice, *"Lazarus, come forth!" And he who had died came out bound hand and foot with graveclothes, and his face was wrapped with a cloth. Jesus said to them, "Loose him, and let him go"* (John 11:43–44).

After this, *"Many of the Jews who had seen the things Jesus did, believed in him. But some of them went away to the Pharisees and told them the things Jesus did. Then the chief priests and the Pharisees gath-*

ered a council and said, "What shall we do? For this man works many signs. If we let him alone like this, everyone will believe in him, and the Roman will come and take away both our place and nation" (John 11:45–48). Caiaphas, being high priest that year, said to them, *"You know nothing at all, nor do you consider that it is expedient for us that one man should die for the people, and not that the whole nation should perish"* (John 11:49–50). So the main decree that came out of that council was this: Jesus must be put to death. *"Then from that day on they plotted to put him to death"* (John 11:53).

This decree of killing Jesus was issued while he was still in Bethany, the home of Lazarus. Therefore, *"He no longer walked openly among the Jews, but went from there into the country near the wilderness, to a city called Ephraim, and there remained with his disciples"* (John 11:54), awaiting the time to go to Jerusalem for the last visit and to celebrate his last Passover feast, which it was near (John 11:55), before he leaves this world and go to heaven. Both the chief priests and the Pharisees had given a command that if anyone knew where he is when he comes to Jerusalem, he should report it, that they might seize him (John 11:57).

Six days before the Passover feast, Jesus returned from the city of Ephraim to Bethany, the home of Lazarus, in his way to Jerusalem. (John 12:1). Then a great many of the Jews knew that he was there; and they came, not for Jesus's sake only but that they might also see his friend Lazarus, whom he had raised from the dead, by God permission (John 12:9). *"But the chief priests took counsel that they might also put Lazarus to death, because on account of him many of the Jews went away and believed in Jesus"* (John 12:10–11).

"The next day a great multitude that had come to the feast, when they heard that Jesus was coming to Jerusalem, took branches of palm trees and went out to meet him, and cried out: 'Hosanna! Blessed is he who comes in the name of the Lord! The King of Israel!'" (John12:12–13). Then Jesus found a young donkey and rode on it, on his way to Jerusalem to celebrate his last Passover feast with his disciples, for he later will be ascended to heaven. Then when the Pharisees saw how the crowed met Jesus, they said among themselves, *"You see that you*

are accomplishing nothing. Look, the world has gone after him!" (John 12:19).

Then the chief priests and scribes met and while they were trying to find a way of putting Jesus to death secretly, *"For they feared the people"* (Luke 22:2), came to them was Judas Iscariot, one of Jesus's disciples to whom the devil had already put into his heart the thought of betraying his teacher Jesus. *"Then Satan entered Judas, surnamed Iscariot, who was numbered among the twelve. So, he went his way and conferred with the chief priests and captains, how he might betray him to them"* (Luke 22:3–4). Judas said to them, *"What are you willing to give me if I deliver him to you?"* (Matt. 26:15). *"And they were glad and agreed to give him money. Then he promised"* (Luke 22:5–6). *"And they counted out to him thirty pieces of silver. So, from that time he sought opportunity to betray him"* (Matt. 26:15–16).

(2/5) Preparing the Passover meal (the Last Supper)

It was now the day before the Passover feast. Jesus knew that the hour had come for him to leave this world and go to heaven (John 13:1). He sent two of his disciples into the city of Jerusalem to meet a man who would guide them to the place where they can prepare the Passover. So they went and prepared the Passover. The place was a large furnished upper room (Luke 22:8–13). When it was evening, Jesus and his disciples sat down to eat (Matt. 26:20).

(3/5) Jesus's prophecies at the Passover table (Last Supper)

Jesus rose from supper, took off his outer garment, and tied a towel around his waist (John 13:4). Then he began to predict to his disciples about some of the events that will happen on that same night after the Last Supper. Jesus prophesied six prophecies in one session at the Passover table. They are as follows:

1. The first prophecy was about Judas. God inspired Jesus about Judas's intentions and his secret contact with the Jewish chief priests. Jesus said to his disciples, *"You are*

clean, but not all of you. For he knew who would betray him; therefore, he said, "You are not all clean" (John 13:10–11). And also said, *"Most assuredly, I say to you, one of you will betray me"* (John 13:21). "Then when a disciple asked him, 'Who is it?' Jesus answered, *'It is he to whom I shall give a piece of bread when I have dipped it.'* And having dipped the bread, he gave it to Judas Iscariot, the son of Simon. Now after the piece of bread, Satan entered him… Having received the piece of bread, he then went out immediately. And it was night" (John 13:26–27, 30).

2. The second prophecy was after Judas had left the room to arrange with the Jews how to arrest Jesus. He told his disciples that shortly after supper, he would disappear from them and go to the place of which he had previously told the Jews about it, when he said to them, *"And where I am you cannot come"* (John 7:34), and he also said, *"Where I go you cannot come"* (John 8:21). He also told the disciples that they too would seek him, after discovering his disappearance, but that they also cannot come to the place where he would go, just like the Jews. Jesus said, *"Little children, I shall be with you a little while longer. You will seek me; and as I said to the Jews, 'Where I am going, you cannot come,' so now I say to you"* (John 13:33). Then he continued to deliver commandments and lessons to his disciples at the Passover table in the upper room.

3. The third prophecy was when Jesus wanted to reassure his disciples that his absence in the place of hiding would be a temporary absence because soon, he would come to them and they will see him. But the Jews will never be able to see him anymore. He said to his disciples, *"I will not leave you orphans; I will come to you. A little while longer and the world* (the Jews) *will see me no more, but you will see me"* (John 14:18–19). Then he continued to give his disciples some commandments and teachings before leaving this world.

4. The fourth prophecy was when Jesus once again wanted to reassure his disciples that his absence would be just for

a very short time, for he would leave the place of hiding to ascend to heaven and then they would see him. He said to them, *"A little while, and you will not see me; and again, a little while, and you will see me, because I go to the father"* (John 16:16).

5. The fifth prophecy was when Jesus knew that the disciples desired to ask him about what is this little while that he was talking about.

> *Then some of his disciples said among themselves, "What is this that he says to us, 'A little while, and you will not see me; and again, a little while, and you will see me; and because I go to the Father?'" They said therefore, "What is this that he says, 'A little while'? We do not know what he is saying." Now Jesus knew that they desired to ask him.*
> (John 16:17–19)

Then he told them that they would weep and lament and they would be sorrowful, thinking that he was the one who was killed, while the Jews would rejoice. But their sorrow will be turned into joy when Jesus leaves the place of hiding and comes to them and they see him alive. Jesus said,

> *Are you inquiring among yourselves about what I said, "A little while, and you will not see me; and again, a little while, and you will see me"? Most assuredly, I say to you that you will weep and lament, but the world (the Jews) will rejoice; and you will be sorrowful, but your sorrow will be turned into joy... I will see you again and your hearts will rejoice.*
> (John 16:19–20, 22)

6. The sixth prophecy was before Jesus left the upper room with his disciples to go to the Mount of Olives. Perhaps

Jesus was expecting Judas and the Jewish soldiers would come to the upper room to arrest him. So he wanted to leave the room with his disciples and go to a garden at the Mount of Olives because it is more appropriate than the room to deal with such situation. In this prophecy, Jesus was describing the inner feeling of the disciples in the most fearful moments and how their reaction would be when the Jewish troops arrive at the garden. He said to his disciples, *"Indeed the hour is coming, yes has now come, that you will be scattered, each to his own, and will leave me alone"* (John 16:32). Then he commanded them to unite in his name to get peace because the Jews will make them suffer after he leaves this world. He also asked them to trust that he had defeated the Jews. Jesus said, *"I have told you this so that you will have peace by being united to me. The world will make you suffer. But be brave! I have defeated the world (the Jews)!"* (John 16:33).

He then closed his session in the upper room, by glorifying God and praying for the disciples that God would keep them through His name after his ascension (John 17:11). After this, Jesus left the upper room and went at night with his disciples to a garden in the Mount of Olives. *"Over the Brook Kidron, where there was a garden, which he and his disciples entered"* (John 18:1).

Judas, after leaving the room, went to the chief priests and the Pharisees to receive a detachment of troops and officers to arrest Jesus. Perhaps Judas went first to the upper room where he left Jesus and the disciples there. When he did not find them, he went to the garden on the Mount of Olives as he knew this place, for Jesus often met there with his disciples. *"And Judas, who betrayed him, also knew the place; for Jesus often met there with his disciples"* (John 18:2). He came there with *"a detachment of troops, and officers from the chief priests and Pharisees, and with lanterns, torches, and weapons"* (John 18:3).

(4/5) How did Jesus leave the garden to the place of hiding?

After Jesus and his disciples had reached the garden in the Mount of Olives, he separated from them to pray to God for help. *"He was withdrawn from them about a stone's throw, and he knelt down and prayed"* (Luke 22:41). On the other hand, a strange situation had happened with the disciples. Their eyes became heavy and an irresistible sleep came upon all of them, although it was a fear hour! *"And he came and found them asleep again, for their eyes were heavy"* (Matt. 26:43).

God answered the prayer of Jesus and supported him with the Holy Spirit (Angel Gabriel). *"Then an angel appeared to him from heaven strengthening him"* (Luke 22:43). After Jesus had finished praying, he came to his disciples in the midst of the darkness and found them still sleeping. Then he sneaked out of the garden without their awareness and was led by the angel to the place of hiding, fulfilling his prophecies to his disciples when he said to them in the upper room, at the supper table, *"Little children, I shall be with you a little while longer. You will seek me; and as I said to the Jews, 'Where I am going, you cannot come,' so now I say to you"* (John 13:33). Also, he said, *"A little while, and you will not see me"* (John 16:16).

Now Jesus was no longer in the garden while Judas and the troops were on their way to the garden. The disciples were still sleeping. The question now is that when would the prophecy of seeking Jesus by his disciples *"You will seek me"* be fulfilled? This prophecy had to be fulfilled before the arrival of Judas and the troops to the garden. It was a night of fear and darkness inside the garden. But any disciple who hung between sleeping and waking would worry about his teacher, who was praying separately from them, and would seek him around the place where he was praying in that dark garden to make sure he is safe and then would inform the rest of the disciples in order to seek Jesus. But because of the irresistible sleep, they would back to sleep. Therefore, the two prophecies concerning seeking Jesus by the Jews (John 7:34) and by the disciples (John 13:33) were fulfilled on the same night, at the same place, and at a very close time.

(5/5) When Jesus prophesied that the Jews would seek him and not find him, did he mean their last attempt with Judas?

Jesus said to the Jews, *"You will seek me and not find me"* (John 7:34). Then the next day he confirmed it to them and said, *"I am going away, and you will seek me, and will die in your sin. Where I go you cannot come"* (John 8:21). So did Jesus mean with this prophecy their last attempt with Judas to arrest him?

If the answer is yes, the discussion is over. Because it means that Jesus was not arrested nor he was crucified. But those who believe that Jesus was crucified, their answer would be no. Jesus did not mean the arresting attempt by the Jewish troops with Judas. Therefore, they try to find a way out to avoid interpreting of the obvious challenge in the text, *"You will seek me and not find me, and where I am you cannot come"* (John 7:34), using the method of indirect and unclear explanation of the text and avoiding mentioning about the attempt by the Jewish troops with Judas specifically.

But the evidence says, yes, that Jesus was specifically referring to the failure of the Jewish attempt with his disciple Judas arresting him, as follows:

1. Jesus explained to the Jews why their conspiracy of arresting him would fail, because he would not be in the place where they would seek him. *"You will seek me and not find me."* Rather, he would be in another place, to which they cannot come. *"And where I am you cannot come."* Not only that, but even his disciples cannot come either. *"Little children, I shall be with you a little while longer. You will seek me; and as I said to the Jews, 'Where I am going, you cannot come,' so now I say to you"* (John 13:33).

Is there any narration in any gospel saying that the Jews sought Jesus to arrest him and did not find him because he had gone to unknown place? Certainly not. All the narrations of the attempts of the Jewish religious authorities to conspire against Jesus consisted of working against him, wanting to harass him, even wanting to kill him; but they didn't move to do anything because they were afraid of the crowds or that the people may riot. And in the first place, no decree was issued yet to kill him.

At first, they tried to seize on his words in order to deliver him to the power and the authority of the governor (Luke 20:20–22). Also, they were even afraid of the crowds, if they sought to lay hands on him, because the crowds considered Jesus to be a prophet (Matt. 21:46). And if they sought to destroy him while he was daily teaching in the temple, they were unable to do anything, for all the people were very attentive to hear him (Luke 19:47–48). And even when they plotted to take Jesus by trickery and kill him, they said, *"Not during the feast, or the people will riot"* (Matt. 26:3–5). At the same time, Jesus was present in all these events and did not separate from his disciples and did not go yet to any place, where neither the Jews or the disciples could come, because he had not yet finished his mission.

If there is no narration in any gospel saying that the Jews sought Jesus and did not find him because he had left the place before they came and went to another place as Jesus had prophesied, so was the prophecy of Jesus false or not fulfilled? Certainly not.

If this prophecy was not false but must be fulfilled, then what is this Jewish attempt in which we can see the fulfillment of the prophecy of Jesus' challenge to the Jews? And if all the previous narrations of the attempts of the conspiring against Jesus mention that the Jews did not practically move to arrest and kill Jesus, because they were afraid of the crowds who might revolt, and in the first place, Jesus was present and did not separate from his disciples in all the narrations of the previous conspiring attempts. Also, until that time, no decree was issued to kill him. So, the only remaining is the last narration of the only serious and practical attempt by the Jews to arrest and kill Jesus, when they went with the traitorous Judas to the garden to arrest him, but they certainly did not find him, as Jesus had prophesied, and as it ought to happen.

The attempt by the Jews, accompanied with Judas, to arrest Jesus is the only attempt in which a decree was issued by the Jewish authorities to kill him, when the Pharisees and the High Priests gathered a council to discuss what they shall do with Jesus, after many people believed in him when they saw the miracle of raising Lazarus from death. *"Then from that day on they plotted to put him to death"* (John 11:53).

This was in his late days with them, and he already knew that the hour had come for him to leave this world and go to heaven (John 13:1), for he had finished his mission with the Jews: *"I have finished the work which you have given me to do"* (John 17:4). After his arrival to Jerusalem and while the chief priests and scribes were seeking how they might kill him secretly for they feared the people (Luke 22:2), the traitor Judas came to them and spoke with them, how he might betray Jesus to them. And they were glad and agreed to give him money (Luke 22:4–5; Matt. 26:14–16).

Therefore, the solid fact is that there was one decree, one serious conspiracy, and one arrangement with one traitorous disciple, Judas, to arrest Jesus and kill him. Jesus already prophesied this conspiracy and said to the Jews, *"You will seek me."* Also, he prophesied the failure of this conspiracy and said, *"And not find me, and where I am you cannot come"* (John 7:34).

2. On his last night with the disciples, the night of the Last Supper, Jesus himself announced about the time of the fulfillment of his challenging prophecy to the Jews, *"You will seek me and not find me,"* which would be that same night, shortly after dinner. This is an evidential fact that appears clearly in the statement of Jesus to his disciples, after Judas had left the upper room to bring the Jews to arrest him. For in order the prophecy be fulfilled and the Jews would not find him, Jesus told the disciples that he would be with them on that night a little while longer, then he would go to the place he had previously told the Jews that they could not come to and told them that they too would seek him when they discovered his absence but they would be like the Jews, they will not be able to come to that place to which he is going, because they and the Jews do not know where that is. Jesus said, *"Little children, I shall be with you*

a little while longer. You will seek me; and as I said to the Jews, 'Where I am going, you cannot come,' so now I say to you" (John 13:33).

3. After dinner, Jesus assured the disciples that after a little while, he would hide from their eyesight. *"A little while, and you will not see me"* (John 16:16). Then Jesus and his disciples left the upper room and went to a garden at the Mount of Olives. After they arrived, God made the disciples sleep deeply, then Jesus left the garden without their awareness, going to the hiding place so that Judas and the troop would not find him when they come to arrest him. And this is what happened. When Judas and the troops came to the garden seeking Jesus, they did not find him, as the prophecy states, but they arrested another person instead. Therefore, Jesus's prophecy, *"You will seek me and not find me,"* was fulfilled only with the last attempt of the Jews with Judas.

Jesus remained in the place of hiding until the arrested person was killed. He then left the place to be ascended to heaven. Only the disciples saw him before his ascension, but the Jews never saw him. *"A little while, and you will not see me. And again, a little while, and you will see me, because I go to the father"* (John 16:16). *"I will not leave you orphans; I will come to you. A little while longer and the world* (the Jews) *will see me no more, but you will see me. Because I live, you will live also"* (John 14:18–19). *"And he led them out as far as Bethany, and he lifted up his hands and blessed them. Now it came to pass, while he blessed them, that he was parted from them and carried up into heaven"* (Luke 24:50–51).

So if one believes that Judas and the troops already found and arrested Jesus, then one must also believe that Jesus was talking nonsense and his prophecy, *"You will seek me and not find me"* (John 7:34), was false and unfulfilled! But if one believes that Jesus was telling the truth in that prophecy, then that person must also believe that Jesus was not found and was not arrested. One cannot have it both ways.

Here are two questions that must be searched and answered:

a. What is that place where Jesus went, to which neither the Jews, nor the disciples can come, and where? *"Where I am going, you cannot come"* (John 13:33).
b. If Judas and the troops did not find Jesus in the garden, then who was that person they had arrested instead? And how did he take the place of Jesus in the sight of the people? And before that, how did this matter escape his Jewish enemies' notice

(6/5) Did Jesus mean heaven for the place where he would go?

Why won't the Jews find Jesus when they come to his place to arrest him? *"You will seek me and not find me."* Because he left the place that was known to Judas, and went to another unknown place, where neither the Jews nor the disciples could come there. *"I am going away, and you will seek me… "Where I go you cannot come."* (John 8:21). *"As I said to the Jews, 'Where I am going, you cannot come,' so now I say to you."* (John 13:33). So, What was that place where Jesus went, and where?

The majority of those who believe that Jesus was arrested by the troops with Judas and then crucified say that Jesus hinted at heaven for that place, because heaven is an inaccessible place. But if Jesus meant heaven, as they say, this contradicts their belief that Jesus was arrested and killed because Jesus announced that he would go first to that place and then afterward the Jews would seek him: *"I am going away, and you will seek me"* (John 8:21). Therefore, their insistence that the place is heaven simply means that Jesus ascended to heaven before Judas and the troops came to arrest him. And at the same time, it is an acknowledgment of the failure of Judas's mission because it was the only Jewish attempt before the ascension of Jesus. Note that there is not any narration in any gospel that says the Jews were seeking Jesus after his ascension. And why should they do so?

Anyway, according to the texts of the prophesies, Jesus did not mean heaven at all, rather a place of hiding on earth. He had already left the garden to go to hide there before Judas and the troops come to the garden to arrest him. The evidence are as follows:

1. Jesus himself told of the sequence of events as thus: first, he goes to that place *"I am going away,"* and then the Jews seek him *"You will seek me"* at the place that they had expected him to be (the garden), but they would not find him, *"And not find me."* And they would not be able to come to the place where he went, *"Where I go you cannot come."* Anyone says that Jesus hinted at heaven for the place where he would go, he must acknowledge of the failure of arresting him. Jesus left the garden, not to heaven but to somewhere else to hide for a little while: *"A little while, and you will not see me; and again, a little while, and you will see me."* The ascension to heaven was later, after he had left the place of hiding, where only the disciples could see him: *"And again, a little while, and you will see me, because I go to the father"* while the Jews would never see him. *"A little while longer and the world* (the Jews) *will see me no more"* (John 14:19). The Jews were not in need to seek Jesus again after his ascension, and they had never done. And why should they do so?
2. Jesus himself told his disciples that he would go to a place on earth before the journey to heaven. At first, he told them at the gathering of Passover meal (the Last Supper) that he would go to the place that he had already told the Jews about it. *"As I said to the Jews, 'Where I am going, you cannot come,' so now I say to you"* (John 13:33). Then at the same gathering, he told his disciples that he would not forget about them but would come to them from where he went: *"I will not leave you orphans; I will come to you"* (John 14:18). Finally, he told them at the same gathering that his absence in the place of hiding would be just for a little while and then they will see him because he would walk out of that place to ascend to heaven: *"A little while, and you will not see me; and again, a little while, and you will*

see me, because I go to the father" (John 16:16). Therefore, heaven is not the place where Jesus hinted, he was going to. Heaven would be another stage after that place.

3. If the night of the Last Supper was Jesus's last night with his disciples and he said to them as they were eating the Last Supper, *"Little children, I shall be with you a little while longer. You will seek me"* (John 13:33), so when will this prophecy of seeking Jesus by his disciples be fulfilled?

   Certainly, Jesus did not mean that they would seek him after he was in heaven, because the disciples were not naive to seek him after they have already seen him ascend to heaven, as Luke has stated: *"And he led them out as far as Bethany, and he lifted up his hands and blessed them. Now it came to pass, while he blessed them, that he was parted from them and carried up into heaven"* (Luke 24:50–51). *"Now when he had spoken these things, while they watched, he was taken up, and a cloud received him out of their sight"* (Acts 1:9). But Jesus intended that they would seek him when they notice his absence from them in the garden, going to the place of hiding on earth, before the coming of Judas and the troops there.

4. Jesus reassured his disciples that his absence from them on that night to go to the place where they cannot come, *"A little while, and you will not see me,"* will be a temporary absence because he will come to them and they will see him before he ascends to heaven: *"And again, a little while, and you will see me, because I go to the father."* Certainly, Jesus did not mean that he would come to his disciples descending from heaven, then appear to them and they see him, and then ascend again to heaven, but he would come to them coming out of a place of hiding on earth.

5. And even the Jews themselves did not understand that the place where they cannot come was heaven, rather a place on earth. They said among themselves, *"Where does he intend to go that we shall not find him? Does he intend to go to the Dispersion among the Greeks and teach the Greeks? What is*

this thing that he said, 'You will seek me and not find me, and where I am you cannot come'?" (John 7:35–36).

(7/5) Did Jesus mean the tomb for the place where he would go?

There is a minority who has seriously considered the sequence of events in this prophecy, *"I am going away, and you will seek me... Where I go you cannot come"* (John 8:21), and realized that Jesus should go away first, then later the Jews would seek him. Also in this prophecy, *"You will seek me and not find me. And where I am you cannot come"* (John 7:34), Jesus should go away first, then later the Jews would seek him, but of course, they would not find him. This minority already realized the biggest problem of the majority who say that Jesus was hinting to heaven for the place where he would go away because if he had gone away to heaven first, this means the Jews had failed to arrest him.

So those minority tried to think of a place on earth that does not conflict with the belief of arresting Jesus and killing him and to escape the problem of heaven. They thought about the tomb where the body of the crucified person was placed to be the answer to the question of the place that Jesus has hinted to go to; but in fact, they fell into a worse problem on earth, because the tomb is a well-known place for the Jews and disciples. They can come to it whenever they want while the place that Jesus had hinted to, they cannot come to it.

What made this minority to say that the tomb is the place that Jesus had hinted he was going to? It was merely a desperate attempt to avoid admitting the failure of arresting Jesus by Judas and the forces. They made use of, in a tricky way, the challenge prophecy of Jesus that was addressed only to the Jews who were seeking Jesus to kill him, *"You will seek me and not find me,"* and addressed it to the two disciples who went to the tomb on Sunday morning, claiming that it was the fulfillment of the prophecy of Jesus, as the two disciples did not find Jesus in the tomb but only the linen cloths.

Peter therefore went out, and the other disciple, and were going to the tomb. So, they both ran

> *together, and the other disciple outran Peter and came to the tomb first. And he, stooping down and looking in, saw the linen cloths lying there; yet he did not go in. Then Peter came, following him, and went into the tomb; and he saw the linen cloths lying there.* (John 20:3–6)

Whereas the truth of the matter is that when Jesus said to the disciples, *"You will seek me,"* he did not say to them, "And not find me." Rather, he said to them, *"You will seek me; and as I said to the Jews, where I am going, you cannot come, so now I say to you"* (John 13:33), because the purpose of the disciples seeking Jesus in the garden, after noticing his absence from them, was to ensure his safety. So Jesus reassured them and hinted to them that they should not worry if they miss him later that night because he would be somewhere else but they cannot come to it.

Choosing the tomb to be an answer to the question of where Jesus hinted to go to is no less invalid than choosing heaven, for the following reasons:

1. In the first place, if Jesus already prophesied and challenged the Jews, saying, *"You will seek me and not find me"* (John 7:34), and informed them, saying, *"And where I am you cannot come,"* so could the Jews then be able to find Jesus in the garden and arrest him, then kill him and put him in a tomb? Surely not.

2. It was an impossibility for the Jews to come to the place where Jesus had gone: *"And where I am you cannot come"* (John 7:34) and *"Where I go you cannot come"* (John 8:21). While the tomb was under the control of the Jews, the Roman governor Pilate gave them full authority over it when he said to the chief priests and the Pharisees, *"You have a guard; go your way, make the tomb as secure as you know how"* (Matt. 27:65).

3. Also, it was an impossibility for the disciples to come to where Jesus had gone, *"'Where I am going, you cannot come,'*

so now I say to you" (John 13:33), while two disciples (Peter and the other disciple) already went to the empty tomb.
4. The reason why the Jews and the disciples could not come to the place where Jesus had gone was because it was unknown to them while the tomb was publicly known place.
5. If the absence of Jesus, away from the eyesight of the Jews and the disciples, took place just after a little while of informing his disciples, at the Last Supper, Thursday night, till his first appearance, Sunday morning, and if Jesus already announced that no disciple or Jew could see him during the whole of this period, *"A little while, and you will not see me"* (John 16:16), so this period of absence proves that he was not the one who was crucified and put into the tomb, because the one who was arrested instead of Jesus was seen Thursday night and all day of Friday.
6. Jesus said to the disciples, *"Little children, I shall be with you a little while longer. You will seek me"* (John 13:33). Would then they seek him if they already knew that he is dead and put in the tomb? Surely not. And when Peter went to the tomb, it was not for seeking Jesus but to check if what the women had said about the empty tomb was true, because the disciples thought that what the women said was nonsense and they did not believe them.

> *Then they returned from the tomb and told all these things to the eleven and to all the rest... And their words seemed to them like idle tales, and they did not believe them. But Peter arose and ran to the tomb; and stooping down, he saw the linen cloths lying by themselves; and he departed, marveling to himself at what had happened.* (Luke 24:9, 11–12)

Also, John narrated that only Peter and the other disciple who went to the tomb, not to seek Jesus but to check if what Mary Magdalene said about the empty tomb was true, because after that, they did not seek Jesus, but they *"went away again to their own homes"* (John 20:10).

7. Here are some questions to those who say that Jesus meant the tomb for the place where he had gone, *"I am going away, and you will seek me… Where I go you cannot come"*:

    - Were the Jews in need to seek Jesus in the tomb, if they had killed him?
    - Were the Jews in need to seek a corpse? And before that, was Jesus challenging the Jews that they cannot come to the tomb that they already had full authority over it?

8. Jesus was talking about a place that he would go to by himself, *"I am going away… Where I go you cannot come"* (John 8:21) and *"Where I am going, you cannot come"* (John 13:33), while the tomb is a place for the dead to be taken by others and carried to be put inside it.

(8/5) What was the place of hiding that Jesus went to and where?

The following facts are the backbone for the way how this prophecy was fulfilled, *"You will seek me and not find me, and where I am you cannot come"* (John 7:34):

1. In the last days of Jesus on earth, the chief priests and the Pharisees gathered a council and issued a decree to put Jesus to death. *"Then from that day on they plotted to put him to death"* (John 11:53). And while they were trying to find a way of putting Jesus to death secretly (Luke 22:2), Judas came and spoke with them, how he might betray Jesus to them. They were glad and agreed to give him money (Luke 22:4–5).
2. Until the time of the Last Supper in the upper room with Judas, Jesus's challenge prophecy to the Jews, *"You will seek me and not find me,"* was not yet fulfilled. Because Jesus

has not yet gone to the place he had hinted that he would go to, *"I am going away, and you will seek me... Where I go you cannot come,"* and the Jews have not yet moved to seek Jesus.

3. The prophecy of seeking Jesus by the Jews had to be fulfilled at any moment of the night of the Last Supper, after Jesus and his disciples reached the garden at the Mount of Olives. But before that, Jesus must secretly leave the garden and go to the place he hinted that he was going to so that the troop of the Jews accompanying Judas would not find him when they seek him in the garden.
4. After Jesus had left the garden, Judas and the troops came to the garden seeking Jesus, but of course, they did not find him.
5. With full confidence and victory, the troops had arrested, bound, and led someone to the place of the high priest.
6. If the place that Jesus hinted that he was going to can by no means to be heaven nor the tomb, then there is no escape from this conclusion that the place where Jesus went was on earth. He took refuge, and there he hid for a little while, away from the eyesight of the Jews and the disciples, until they killed the person they had arrested.

This place of hiding seems, and God knows best, is the place that Jesus already hinted to it as "the heart of the earth," in his answer to the Jews, who asked him to see a sign (miracle) from him.

> *Then some of the scribes and Pharisees answered, saying, "Teacher, we want to see a sign from you." But he answered and said to them "An evil and adulterous generation seeks after a sign, and no sign will be given to it except the sign of the prophet Jonah. For as Jonah was three days and three nights in the belly of the great fish, so will the son of man be three days and three nights in the heart of the earth."* (Matt. 12:38–40)

Jesus was not alone in that place of hiding, but God was with him. *"But I am not really alone, because the father is with me"* (John 16:32). The narration of Matthew indicates that Jesus would stay in the heart of the earth, three days and three nights, safe from all the dangers that surrounded him, just as prophet Jonah remained safe from all dangers that surrounded him in the belly of the great fish.

Luke reported this incident in a different way:

> *And while the crowds were thickly gathered together, he began to say, "This is an evil generation. It seeks a sign, and no sign will be given to it except the sign of Jonah the prophet. For as Jonah became a sign to the Ninevites, so also the son of man will be to this generation."* (Luke 11:29–30)

What was the thing that made Jonah a sign to the Ninevites? The answer is in the book of Jonah, in the Old Testament: *"Jonah prayed to the Lord God from the fish's belly"* (Jon. 2:1). *"So, the Lord spoke to the fish, and it vomited Jonah onto dry land"* (Jon. 2:10). This was the miracle of Jonah. He was thrown to the deadly sea, but God rescued him. Then he became by this miraculous rescue a sign to the Ninevites. So, in the same way, Jesus prophesied that he too would be rescued by God like Jonah. Then he would become by the miraculous rescue a sign for the people of his generation.

Jesus already hinted to the location of the place of hiding. It was in the heart of the Jewish land (such as a cave in a mountain or any other place of refuge in the middle of their territory). It was not in the Greek cities, as the Jews thought.

> *Where does he intend to go that we shall not find him? Does he intend to go to the Dispersion among the Greeks and teach the Greeks?* *"What is this thing that he said, 'You will seek me and not find me, and where I am you cannot come'?"* (John 7:35–36)

(9/5) Was Jesus hinting to the tomb with the term "the heart of the earth"?

Those who still believe that Jesus was arrested and crucified interpreted the term "the heart of the earth" as the tomb. But surely, "the heart of the earth" by no means it signifies the tomb where the body of the crucified person was laid. But rather, it means, in the Jewish territory's heartland, for the following evidences:

1. If Jesus already prophesied and said to the Jews, *"You will seek me and not find me, and where I am you cannot come"* (John 7:34), surely, Jesus would not then hint to a tomb since the Jews would not be able to find him when they seek him.
2. When the Jews asked Jesus to see a sign from him (miracle), proving to them that he was the Messiah, the author of Matthew narrated that Jesus answered them, *"No sign will be given to it except the sign of the prophet Jonah"* (Matt. 12:39). The sign of the prophet Jonah was the rescue miracle from death in the belly of the great fish after he was thrown into the deadly sea. Jesus informed the Jews that the rescue miracle from death that had happened with the prophet Jonah would also happen with him. And it happened when the Jews came to arrest him, they did not find him because he was already safe in the place of hiding in their territory's heartland (the heart of the earth), as Jonah was in the belly of the great fish, not exposed to danger or risk and not likely to be harmed, for the Jews could not come to him. *"And where I am you cannot come"* (John 7:34). The disciples did not know his place as well, lest the news leaked to the Jews. And as Jonah came out safely from the belly of the great fish, so came Jesus out of the place of hiding in the Jewish territory's heartland (the heart of the earth). This repeated sign with Jesus is the proof that he was the Christ.

> *No sign will be given to it* (to prove to them that he was the Christ) *except the sign of the prophet Jonah. For as Jonah was three days and three nights in the belly of the great fish, so will the son of man be three days and three nights in the heart of the earth.* (Matt. 12:39–40)

If Jesus had been the dead person in the tomb, he would not have been like Jonah, who was alive and safe in the belly of the great fish, and his answer to the Jews that the sign of Jonah would also happen to him would be false. Therefore, Jesus did not hint to the tomb with the term "the heart of the earth," but rather the place of hiding in the Jewish territory's heartland.

3. According to Luke's narration (Luke 11:29–30), Jesus rebuked those Jews that asked him a sign (miracle) proving to them that he was the Messiah and gave them the sign of the rescue miracle that made Jonah a sign for the people of Ninevites and told them that the same miracle would happen to him as well, which it would make him a sign for the people of his generation. Therefore, the tomb was not the heart of the earth because there was not any rescue miracle with the dead person who was put in the tomb that would make him a sign for his generation.
4. If the body was put in the tomb about sunset on Friday, when the Sabbath was about to begin (Luke 23:54), then it remained in the tomb for only one day, Saturday, and two nights (Friday night and Saturday night), which is not close enough to concur with Jonah's three days and three nights in the belly of the great fish. On the other hand, Jesus went to the place of hiding in the Jewish heartland, "the heart of the earth," during the night of the Last Supper, Thursday night, till Sunday morning. This would make him approach the period of Jonah in the great fish.
5. There is no similarity between the containing of the belly of the great fish for the prophet Jonah, who was surrounded

with a miracle (sign) of staying alive and safe in it for three days, and the containing of the tomb for the body of the crucified person, in which there was not any miracle (sign) with his condition; but rather, he was a dead body placed in the tomb for one day and two nights. Therefore, it is very clear that Jesus was not hinting to the tomb with the term "the heart of the earth." Rather, he intended his place of hiding in the heart of the Jewish land.

6. The tomb was dug out of solid rock in a garden (Mark 15:46; John 19:41). It was as a cave with a stone placed at the entrance. It was not a hole in the ground where the dead is buried with soil. A sculpted cave in a rock inside a garden is not expressed by the heart of the earth.

7. Finally, the word "earth" is mentioned in the gospels and refers to a specific land, not the globe, such what is written in Luke, *"There was darkness over all the earth"* (Luke 23:44). While in Matthew, it is written, *"There was darkness over all the land"* (Matt. 27:45)—that is, the Jewish land.

Research 6
Who was the crucified person?

Before answering this question, we need to agree that Jesus said what he meant and meant what he said. If Jesus had said to the Jews that *"you will seek me and not find me, and where I am you cannot come"* (John 7:34), we should believe that the Jews did not find him because he did not speak of his own desire. It was only a revelation revealed. And if he had rebuked the Jews for asking him a miracle, then told them that the only miracle that they would be given to prove that he was the Christ is the miracle of the prophet Jonah, so we should believe in such miracle had happened also with him. And if Jesus had said to his disciples, *"But I am not alone, because the father is with me"* (John 16:32), so we should believe that God did not let him down. And if he also said to his disciples, *"Be of good cheer, I have defeated the world* (the Jews) *"* (John 16:33), so we should believe that the Jews did not gain a victory over him.

Surely, there was someone who was arrested and judged, then hung on a cross, then was killed and put in a tomb. If we believe that this person was Jesus, surely, we will disbelieve in all the texts that determine his rescue. And if we believe that this person was not Jesus, we will believe in the texts' rescue, but who will rescue us from the barrage of questions? Such as who was the crucified person? How was he a substitute for Jesus? What was his guilt? And before that, how did this matter escape his Jewish murderers' notice?

Are we commissioned to specify that person or the way how Jesus was rescued? Surely not, because nothing from the inspiration reveals the details of that event. But how were the Jews convinced that the arrested person was Jesus? Simply, it was a miracle from God that He made the substitute person appear in the eyes of the Jews and utter before them as if he was Jesus. Also, this substitute was not an innocent person but a criminal who deserved a punishment.

(1/6) Peter was rescued too

The author Luke in his book the Acts of the Apostles tells us about a miraculous rescue that saved the disciple Peter from death. It says,

> *King Herod began to persecute members of the church. He had James put to death by the sword. When he saw that this pleased the Jews, he went ahead and had Peter arrested. Peter was put in Jail, where he was handed over to be guarded by four groups of four soldiers each. Herod planned to put him on trial in public after Pass over. So, Peter was kept in jail, but the people of the church were praying to God for him. The night before Herod was going to bring him out to the people, Peter was sleeping between two guards. He was tied with two chains, and there were guards on duty at the prison gate. Suddenly an angel stood there, and a light shone in the cell. The angel shook Peter by the*

> *shoulder, woke him up, and said "Hurry! Get up!" At once the chains fell off Peter's hands. Then the angel said, "Tight your belt and put on your sandals." Peter did so, and the angel said, "Put your cloak around you and come with me." Peter followed him out of the prison, not knowing, however, if what the angel was doing was real; he thought he was seeing a vision. They passed by the first guard station and then the second and came at last to the iron gate. The gate opened for them by itself, and they went out. They walked down a street, and suddenly the angel left Peter.* (Acts 12:1–10)

If such things had happened to rescue a disciple of Jesus, the more so would be with Jesus himself, who made his prayers and requests with loud cries and tears to God to save him from death. He separated from his disciples in the garden and knelt down and prayed (Luke 22:41). Then he went a little farther and fell on his face and prayed to his God if it is possible to let this cup of difficulty pass from him (Matt. 26:39). Then an angel appeared to him from heaven, strengthening him (Luke 22:43).

(2/6) Who was the substitute for Jesus?

If Jesus had already predicted the impossibility of being arrested by the Jews, so who was the criminal who deserved to be cast on him the likeness of Christ so that he can be killed and disgraced with his murderers? And if the Old Testament contains many prophecies concerning Jesus, what about the substitute for Jesus? Shouldn't he also be included in some of these prophesies? Surely, yes.

So let us start searching for him in the Bible. We may find a clue that points to him. Let us start from the operations room, the upper room in Jerusalem, where the disciples used gathered frequently to pray as group. It was a few days after the ascension of Jesus when Peter stood up in the midst of the disciples and said,

> *Men and brethren, this Scripture had to be fulfilled, which the Holy Spirit spoke before by the mouth of David concerning Judas, who became a guide to those who arrested Jesus; for he was numbered with us and obtained a part in this ministry. (Now this man purchased a field with the wages of iniquity, and falling headlong, he burst open in the middle and all his entrails gushed out. And it became known to all those dwelling in Jerusalem, so that field is called in their own language, Akel Dama—that is, Field of Blood.) For it is written in the book of Psalms: "Let their habitation be desolate and let no one live in it' and 'Let another take his office."* (Acts 1:16–20)

So the disciples proposed two men—Joseph, who was called Barsabas, and Matthias—to take the place of Judas of service. Then the disciples drew lots to choose between the two men, and the one chosen was Matthias (Acts 1:23–26).

Let us read the Psalms and begin with Psalm 109 from which Peter quoted this passage: *"Let another take his office,"* which the Holy Spirit spoke before by the mouth of David concerning Judas. This Psalm 109 prophesies about Jesus's supplications and prayers against the traitor disciple, Judas, who sold his teacher Jesus for a low price, thirty silver coins, and became the guide for those who came to arrest Jesus to kill him. The prophecy says,

> *Choose some corrupt judge to try my enemy, and let one of his own enemies accuse him. When he is judged, let him be found guilty and let his prayer become sin. May his life soon be ended; may another man take his job! May his children become orphans, and his wife, a widow. May his children be homeless*

beggars; may they be driven from the ruins they live in! May his creditors take away all his property, and may strangers get everything he worked for. May no one ever be kind to him, or care for the orphans he leaves behind. May all his descendants die, and may his name be forgotten... Because he did not remember to show mercy, but persecuted the poor and needy man, that he might even slay the broken in heart. As he loved cursing, so let it come to him; as he did not delight in blessing, so let it be far from him. As he clothed himself with cursing as with his garment, so let it enter his body like water, and like oil into his bones. Let it be to him like the garment which covers him, and always be around him like a belt. Let this be the Lord's reward to my accusers, and to those who speak evil against my person. But you, O God the Lord, deal with me for your name's sake; because your mercy is Good, deliver me... Help me, O Lord my God! Oh, save me according to Your mercy, that they may know that this is Your hand that You, Lord, have done it! Let them curse, but you bless; when they arise, let them be ashamed, but let your servant (Jesus) *rejoice. Let my accusers be clothed with shame and let them cover themselves with their own disgrace as with a mantle. I will greatly praise the Lord with my mouth; yes, I will praise Him among the multitude. For He shall stand at the right hand of the poor, to saves him from those who condemn him.* (Ps. 109:6–13, 16–21, 26–31)

Thanks, Apostle Peter, for answering the above question. If this psalm was a prediction about Judas, as the apostle Peter declared, so who was the second party that was supplicating to his Lord against Judas and praying for himself that God rescue him, help him, and save him? There is no other than Jesus. In this prophecy, supplications and prayers against Judas, that he may found guilty when he is judged so that his days would be few and another man (Matthias) would take his job in the service because he worked against Jesus to slay him. Also, in this prophecy, Jesus prayed to God that as Judas loved cursing, so let it come to him, and as he did not find delight in the blessing of the ministry and apostleship, so let it be far from him. This curse would be God's reward to Judas and to those Jews who spoke evil against Jesus. God would disgrace them and clothe them with shame, especially when they realize that it was God Himself who had done this to them.

What about Jesus, according to this prophecy? What would happen to him? He also prayed that God deal with him for His name's sake and to rescue him, help him, and save him according to God's mercy and to let him rejoice. Finally, he would greatly praise the Lord openly for standing with him and saving him from those who condemned him to death.

Again, if this prophecy was a prediction about Judas, as the apostle Peter declared, and the second party, who prayed to his Lord to rescue him, help him was Jesus, so there are then three simple questions can be asked:

1. Who among these two should have been killed and deserved the curse and shame?
2. Who among these two should have been saved and rejoice?
3. Can this prophecy be fulfilled in reverse?

The answers have already been confirmed by Jesus's tongue in the book of Matthew. It says,

> Now when evening had come, he sat down with the twelve. Now as they were eating, he said, "Assuredly, I say to you, one of you will betray me… The son of man goes as it is written of him but woe (how terrible) for that man by whom the son of man is betrayed! It would have been good for that man if he had not been born." (Matt. 26:20–21, 24)

In this text, Jesus predicted four events, and all were fulfilled:

1. The crime of betraying Jesus by one of his disciples: *"One of you will betray me."* Judas went to the garden, taking with him a group of Roman soldiers and some temple guards, after he had received thirty pieces of silver.
2. Jesus would go as it is written of him in Psalms: *"I shall not die, but live, and declare the works of the Lord. The Lord has chastened me severely, but he has not given me over to death… I will praise you, for you have answered me, and have become my salvation. The stone which the builders rejected has become the chief cornerstone"* (Ps. 118:17–18, 21–22). And in other psalms.
3. Failure of the attempt of arresting Jesus because he *"goes as it is written of him"* that the Lord has not given him over to death (Ps. 118:18). He left the garden and went to the place of hiding in the Jewish heartland, "the heart of the earth," before Judas and the troops arrived in the garden. *"You will seek me and not find me"* (John 7:34).

    If the thing that was written of Jesus, *"The Son of Man goes as it is written of him,"* means the mission of shedding his blood for the forgiveness of sin, so it is fair to reward Judas and consider him one of the great heroes for participating in such a mission, not to threaten him with a terrible end.
4. Woe, torment, and pain fall on the traitor Judas after they arrested him. They whipped him and spat on him, took a stick and hit him on the head, made him carry the cross, then hung him on it with nails penetrating his hands; and on the cross, he bled then died. *"But woe* (how terrible) *for that man by whom the son of man is betrayed."*

What about Psalm 69?

The disciple Peter quoted from the Psalm 109 a prophecy about Judas. *He said, "This Scripture had to be fulfilled, which the Holy Spirit spoke before by the mouth of David concerning Judas"* (Acts 1:16). He also quoted from the Psalm (69:25) another prophecy about Judas, where he said, *"For it is written in the book of Psalms: 'Let their habitation be desolate and let no one live in it"* (Acts 1:20). Let us read Psalm 69, which the disciple Peter said about that it is talking about Judas, to know who the crucified person was? Was he the righteous Jesus or the wicked Judas?

Psalm 69 speaks about Judas that he began to scream and seeking God's help.

> *Save me, O God! For the waters have come up to my neck. I sink in deep mire, where there is no standing; I have come into deep waters, where the floods overflow me. I am weary with my crying; my throat is dry; my eyes fail while I wait for my God. Those who hate me without a cause are more than the hairs of my head; they are mighty who would destroy me, being my enemies wrongfully; thought I have stolen nothing, I still must restore it.* (Ps. 69:1–4)

Judas marveled of the friends of yesterday, the Jews, which because of them, he had betrayed Jesus. Then they became enemies today. They hate him and kill him for no reason! But he admits his sin and his folly. He said,

> *O God, you know my foolishness; and my sins are not hidden from you… Shame has covered my face. I have become a stranger to my brothers, and an alien to my mother's children.* (Ps. 69:5, 7–8)

Elsewhere, he said,

> *You know my reproach, my shame, and my dishonor; my adversaries are all before you. Reproach has broken my heart, and I am full of heaviness; I looked for someone to take pity, but there was none;*

and for comforters, but I found none. They also gave me gall for my food, and for my thirst they gave me vinegar to drink. (Ps. 69:19–21)

Who was this pariah and fool who was stained with stigma, disgrace, and shame and was given vinegar to drink for his thirst? Judas or Jesus? The author of the Gospel of John also quoted this passage from the Psalm: *"They also gave me gall for my food, and for my thirst they gave me vinegar to drink"* (Ps. 69:21). And he emphasized that in order for the scripture (Ps. 69) be fulfilled, the crucified person said, *"I thirst!" "Now a vessel full of sour wine was sitting there; and they filled a sponge with sour wine, put it on hyssop, and put it to his mouth"* (John 19:28–29).

Psalm 69 indicates that Judas regretted and sought refuge in God, calling him to invoke his mercy, hoping that God would listen to him because of his previous good deeds with Christ, referring to those deeds.

Because zeal for your house has eaten me up, and the reproaches of those of those who reproach you have fallen on me. When I wept and chastened my soul with fasting, that became my reproach. I also made sackcloth my garment; I became a byword to them. Those who sit in the gate speak against me, and I am the song of the drunkards. But as for me, my prayer is to you, O Lord, in the acceptable time; O God, in the multitude of your mercy, hear me in the truth of your salvation. Deliver me out of the mire and let me not sink; let me be delivered from those who hate me, and out of the deep waters. Let not the floodwater overflow me, nor let the deep swallow me up; and let not the pit shut its mouth on me. Hear me O Lord, for your lovingkindness is good; turn to me according to the multitude of your tender mercies. And do not hide your face from your servant, for I am in trouble; hear me speedily. Draw near to my soul and redeem it; deliver me because of my enemies You know my reproach, my shame, and my dishonor; my adversaries are all before you. (Ps. 69:9–19)

What was the result of the prayer of Judas and his hoping an intercession of his previous good deeds? Peter said that the scripture had to be fulfilled, which the Holy Spirit spoke before by the mouth of David concerning Judas. *"For it is written in the book of Psalms, 'Let their habitation be desolate, and let no one live in it'"* (Acts 1:20). He was quoting this from Psalm 69. It says,

Let their table become a snare before them, and their well-being a trap. Let their eyes be darkened, so that they do not see; and make their loins shake continually. Pour out your indignation upon them, and let your wrathful anger take hold of them. Let their habitation be desolate; let no one dwell in their tents. For they persecute him whom you have struck and talk of the grief of those you have wounded. Add iniquity to their iniquity and let them not come into your righteousness. Let them be blotted out of the book of the living, and not be written with the righteous. (Ps. 69:22–28)

This is Judas. His habitation became desolate, and he was blotted out of the Book of the Living. At the end, when God did not respond to him, he cried on the cross-questioning God, saying, *"My God, my God why have you forsaken me?"* (Matt. 27:46). The author of Luke added that, at the most hopeless moment on the cross, the crucified person asked his Lord, *"Forgive them, for they do not know what they do"* (They crucified him, not knowing that he was not Jesus.) (Luke 23:34). Surely, this crucified person was not Jesus, for Jesus would not ask God to forgive those Jews who rejected him and sought to kill him. Jesus already said his word about them and their destiny in the Hereafter:

> *And you do not keep God's message in your hearts, for you do not believe in the one whom he sent. You study the Scriptures, because you think that in them you will find eternal life. And these very Scriptures speak about me! Yet you are not willing to come to me in order to have life.* (John 5:38–40)
>
> *I am going away, and you will seek me, and will die in your sin… Therefore I said to you that you will die in your sins; for if you do not believe that I am he, you will die in your sins… If God were your father you would love me, for I proceeded forth and came from God; nor have I come of myself, but he sent me. Why do you not understand my speech? Because you are not able to listen to my word. You are of your father the devil, and the desires of your father you want to do… He who is of God hears God's words; therefore, you do not hear, because you are not of God.* (John 8:21, 24, 42–44, 47)
>
> *Even though Jesus had performed all these miracles in their presence, they did not believe in him… And so they were not able to believe, because Isaiah also said, "God has blinded their eyes and closed their minds, so that their eyes would not see, and their minds would not understand, and they would not turn to me, says God, for me to heal them."… Even then, many Jewish authorities believed in Jesus; but because of the Pharisees they did not confess him, so as not to be expelled from the synagogue. They loved the approval of man rather than the approval of God.* (John 12:37, 39–40, 42, 43)

> *If I had not come and spoken to them, they would have no sin, but now they have no excuse for their sin. He who hates me hates my father also. If I had not done among them the works which no one else did, they would have no sin; but now they have seen and also hated both me and my father. But this happened that the word might be fulfilled which is written in their law, "They hated me without a cause."* (John 15:22–25)

> *So you actually admit that you are the descendants of those who murdered the prophets! Go on, then, and finish up what your ancestors started! You snakes and sons of snakes! How do you expect to escape from being condemned to hell? And so, I tell you that I will send you prophets and wise men and teachers; you will kill some of them, crucify others, and whip others in the synagogues and chase them from town to town. As a result, the punishment for the murder of all innocent men will fall on you, from the murder of innocent Abel to the murder of Zechariah son of Berechiah, whom you murdered between the Temple and the altar. I tell you indeed: the punishment for all these murders will fall on the people of this day.* (Matt. 23:31–36)

What about Jesus? What does Psalm 69 says about him?

> *But I am poor and sorrowful; lift me up, O God, and save me. I will praise the name of God with a song and will magnify Him with thanksgiving. This also shall please the Lord better than an ox or bull, which has horns and hooves. The humble shall see this and be glad; and you who seek God, your hearts shall live. For the Lord hears the poor and does not despise His prisoners.* (Ps. 69:29–33)

God already listened to Jesus. He saved him and raised him up, and the humble saw this and was rejoiced.

> *Because he has set his love upon Me, therefore I will deliver him; I will set him on high, because he has known My name. He shall call upon Me, and I will answer him; I will be with him in trouble; I will deliver him and honor him.* (Ps. 91:14–15)

(3/6) Other prophecies concerning saving Jesus in the book of Psalms

There are many quotations of prophecies, from the book of Psalms, by the authors of the gospels, concerning the Christ, Judas, and the Jews:

1. Luke, in his book Acts of the Apostles, narrated,

> (The disciples) *Raised their voice to God with one accord and said: "Lord you are God, who made heaven and earth and the sea, and all that is in them, who by the mouth of your servant David have said: 'Why did the nations rage, and the people plot vain things? The kings of the earth took their stand, and the rulers were gathered together against the Lord and against his Christ.' For truly against your holy servant Jesus, whom you anointed, both Herod and Pontius Pilate, with the Gentiles and the people of Israel, were gathered together."* (Acts 4:24–27)

The previous words, which were in the mouth of David, are from Psalm 2. Thus,

> *Why do the nations rage, and the people plot a vain thing? The kings of the earth set themselves, and the rulers take counsel together against the Lord*

and against his Anointed, saying, "Let us break their bonds in pieces and cast away their cords from us." He who sits in the heavens shall laugh; the Lord shall hold them in derision. Then He shall speak to them in His wrath and distress them in his deep displeasure. (Ps. 2:1–5)

Was the Lord laughing at the conspirators and scoffing at them because they killed his Anointed or because he had saved him from their plotting?

2. The author of John narrated that Jesus said,

If I had not done among them the works which no one else did, they would have no sin; but now they have seen and also hated both me and my Father. But this happened that the word might be fulfilled which is written in their law, "They hated me without a cause." (John 15:24–25)

Where is it written in the law of the Jews "They hated me without a cause"? It is written in Psalm 35 of David, speaking thus about Christ.

Oppose those who oppose me, Lord, and fight those who fight against me! Take your shield and armor and come to my rescue. Lift up your spear and war ax against those who pursue me. promise that you will save me. May those who try to kill me be defeated and disgraced! May those who plot against me be turned back and confused! May they be like straw blown by the wind as the angel of the Lord pursues them! May their path be dark and slippery while the angel of the Lord strikes them down! For without cause they have hidden their net for me in a pit, which they have dug without cause for my life. Let destruction come upon him unexpectedly and let his net that he has hidden catch himself; into that very destruction let him fall. Then I will be glad because of the Lord; I will be happy because he saved me... Let them not rejoice over me who are wrongfully my enemies; nor let them wink with the eye who hate me without a cause... You are righteous, O Lord, so declare me innocent; do not let my enemies gloat over me. Do not let them say to themselves, "We are rid of him! That is just what we wanted!" May those who gloat over my suffering be completely defeated and confused; may those who claim to be better than I am be covered with shame and disgrace. May those who want to see me acquitted shout for joy and say again and again, "How great is the Lord! He is pleased with the success of his servant." Then I will proclaim your righteousness, and I will praise you all day long. (Ps. 35:1–9, 19, 24–28)

And in Psalm 40, it says,

Save me, Lord! Help me now! May those who try to kill me be completely defeated and confused. May those who are happy because of my troubles be turned back and disgraced. (Ps. 40:13–14)

Thus, Christ called upon his Lord to save him. And he prayed against Judas, that destruction come upon him unexpectedly and his net that he had hidden catch himself and into that same destruction to fall, but Jesus's soul shall be joyful in the Lord and be happy in his saving. And in Psalm 9, we see that God answered the supplication of His Messiah. He already put those who try to kill Jesus into shame and brought them to dishonor. And he made Judas to fall into the evil of his work, and the destruction came upon him unexpectedly, and his own foot was caught in the net that he hid, and he fell into that same destruction. The psalm says,

> *Have mercy on me, O Lord! Consider my trouble from those who hate me. You who lift me up from the gates of death, that I may tell of all your praise in the gates of the daughter of Zion. I will rejoice in your salvation. The nations have sunk down in the pit which they made; in the net which they hid, their own foot is caught. The Lord is known by the judgment He executes; the wicked is snared in the work of his own hands.* (Ps. 9:13–16)

Also, Psalm 91 says:

> *Because he has set his love upon Me, therefore I will save him; I will set him on high, because he has known My name. He shall call upon Me, and I will answer him; I will be with him in trouble; I will rescue him and honor him.* (Ps. 91:14–15)

Does anyone, after all those calls and supplications that Christ directed to his Lord to save him and disgrace his enemies, believe what Paul claims that Jesus came to die?!

3. The author of Matthew narrated that when Jesus saw the multitudes, he went up on a mountain, and when he was seated, his disciples came to him. Then he opened his mouth and taught them. In his teaching, he said, *"Blessed are the meek, for they shall inherit the earth"* (Matt. 5:1–2, 5). Jesus was alluding to Psalm 37 where David spoke, predicting the safety of Jesus, and the coming of the day of Judas, and the failure of the attempt of the Jews.

> *For yet a little while and the wicked shall be no more; indeed, you will look diligently for his place, but it shall be no more. But the meek shall inherit the earth and shall delight themselves in the abundance of peace. The wicked plots against the just, and gnashes at him with his teeth. The Lord laughs at him, for He sees that his day is coming. The wicked have drawn the sword and have bent their bow, to cast down the poor and needy, to slay those who are of upright conduct. Their sword shall enter their own heart, and their bows shall be broken.* (Ps. 37:10–15)

And Psalm 34 says about Christ:

> *I sought the Lord, and He heard me, and delivered me from all my fears… Evil shall slay the wicked, and those hate the righteous shall be condemned.* (Ps. 34:4, 21)

The Lord laughed at Judas, for He saw his day was coming and the sword of the Jews had entered their own hearts because He has saved his anointed one and they killed the one who betrayed his teacher and conspired with them.

4. The author of John narrated that Jesus said to his disciples, at the Last Supper in the upper room, about the traitor Judas:

> *If you know these things, happy are you if you do them. I do not speak concerning all of you. I know whom I have chosen; but that the Scripture may be fulfilled, "He who eats bread with me has lifted up his heel against me."* (John 13:17–18)

What is this scripture that speak about Jesus and his traitor disciple, Judas, who ate bread with him and lifted up his heel against him? This is stated in psalm of David, Psalm 41, speaking about the survival of Christ from the hand of Judas and the Jews.

Blessed is who considers the poor; the Lord will deliver (save.) *him in time of trouble. The Lord will preserve him and keep him alive, and he will be blessed on the earth; You will not deliver him to the will of his enemies… All who hate me whisper together against me; against me they devise my hurt. "An evil disease," they say, "clings to him. And now that he lies down, he will rise up no more." Even my own familiar friend in whom I trusted, who ate my bread, has lifted up his heel against me.* (Ps. 41:1–2, 7–9)

5. The author of Matthew and Luke narrated that the devil took Jesus up into the holy city; set him on the pinnacle of the temple; and tempted him, saying to him,

If you are the son of God, throw yourself down. For it is written: "He shall give his angels charge concerning you, and in their hands, they shall bear you up, lest you dash your foot against a stone." (Matt. 4:5–6; Luke 4:9–10)

Where is it written about Christ that angels would have charge concerning him? This is written in Psalm 91 of David, prophesying about Christ, who calls upon God who answered him. God was with him in distress and saved him. The psalm says about Christ:

You will look and see how the wicked are punished. You have made the Lord your defender, the

Most High your protector, and so no disaster will strike you, no violence will come near your home. God will put his angels in charge of you to protect you wherever you go. They will hold you up with their hands to keep you from hurting your feet on the stones. You shall tread upon the lion and the cobra. The young lion and the serpent you shall trample underfoot. Because he has set his love upon Me, therefore I will deliver him; I will set him on high, because he has known My name. He shall call upon Me, and I will answer him; I will be with him in trouble; I will deliver him and honor him. With long life I will satisfy him and show him My salvation. (Ps. 91:8–16)

6. Luke, in his book Acts of the Apostles, narrated that the disciple Peter was speaking about Jesus in the midst of the rulers, elders, and scribes. He said about Jesus, *"This is the stone, which was rejected by you builders, which has become the chief cornerstone"* (Acts 4:11). Where did Peter come to this description of Jesus? He was quoting from Psalm 118. What does this psalm say about Jesus?

I called on the Lord in distress; the Lord answered me and set me in a broad place. The Lord is on my side; I will not fear. What can man do to me? The Lord is for me among those who help me; therefore, I shall see my desire on those who hate me. It is better to trust in the Lord than to put confidence in man. It is better to trust in the Lord than to put confidence in princes. All nations surrounded me, but in the name of the Lord I will destroy them. They surrounded me, yes, they surrounded me; but in the name of the Lord I will destroy them... You pushed me violently, that I might fall, but the Lord helped me. The Lord is my strength and song, and

> *He has become my salvation. The voice of rejoicing and salvation is in the tents of the righteous; the right hand of the Lord does valiantly. The right hand of the Lord is exalted; the right hand of the Lord does valiantly. I shall not die, but live, and declare the works of the Lord. The Lord has chastened me severely, but he has not given me over to death. Open to me the gates of righteousness; I will go through them, and I will praise the Lord. This is the gate of the Lord, through which the righteous shall enter. I will praise you, for you have answered me, and have become my salvation. The stone which the builders rejected has become the chief cornerstone. This was the Lord's doing; it is marvelous in our eyes. This is the day which the Lord has made; we will rejoice and be glad in it. Save now, I pray, O Lord; O Lord, I pray, send now prosperity. Blessed is he who comes in the name of the Lord!* (Ps. 118:5–11, 13–26)

Any clearer evidence than this for the survival of Christ, who already put trust in the Lord, Who answered him and helped him in distress and extinguished the fire of his enemies and thwarted their conspiracy. He did not deliver him to death but saved him. Therefore, he praises Him because He answered him; and on the day of his deliverance, which the Lord made, he rejoiced and was glad.

(4/6) When and how did the substitution happen?

At first, Judas sneaked into the garden, the place of Jesus and his disciples; but Jesus did not give him the chance to carry out his plan because he had already left the garden while his disciples were already in deep sleep. Then while Judas was looking for Jesus in the midst of the sleeping disciples, a great miracle had happened in the place. God made Judas appear in the eyes of people in the likeness of Jesus, even his voice and his clothes. The sleeping disciples did not notice what had happened around them. But when they heard the noise of the troops and saw them, then all of them fled and scattered, each to his own, thinking that the standing Judas was Jesus. *"Indeed, the hour is coming, yes has now come, that you will be scattered, each to his own, and will leave me alone"* (John 16:32). Judas, who appeared as though he was Jesus, remained standing there, then was arrested by the troops.

A question may be asked as thus: if Jesus already had left the garden before the coming of the troops with Judas, *"You will seek me and not find me,"* how will the disciples be scattered and leave Jesus alone, if he was already not there? *"You will be scattered, each to his own, and will leave me alone"* (John 16:32).

Well, in John 16:32, Jesus was describing the inner feeling of his disciples at the most fearful moment when the troops arrive to the garden. Each disciple will run away, worrying only about himself and is not thinking about the Christ Jesus. All of them at that moment will decide within themselves to forget all about Jesus, who they thought was the one who is standing there (it was Judas who appeared as though he was Jesus), leaving him alone to face the troops. But in fact, Jesus was not in the garden anymore, and he was not alone at that moment. He was already protected by the angels of God, on his way to the place of hiding in the heart of the earth, the Jewish country's heartland. Neither the Jews nor the disciples could come there because he would be surrounded with God's care as was prophet Jonah in the belly of the great fish and waiting his hour to depart this world.

Similar to this is the prophecy of Jesus about Peter that he will deny him three times: *"Jesus said to Peter, 'Assuredly, I say to you that this night, before the rooster crows, you will deny me three times'"* (Matt. 26:34). Then when the troops led Judas to the house of the high priest, Peter followed them at a distance, thinking that Judas was Jesus. Then when the servants pointed to Peter three times that he knew Jesus, he denied him every time. So the one who was seen by Peter was Judas, who appeared as though he was Jesus, but the one whom Peter denied is not the visible person but the person or the name Jesus, who was at that moment in the place of hiding.

(5/6) An abnormal event, at the most critical moment

The author of John narrated about an event that indicates an abnormal happening at the critical moment of the attempt of arresting Jesus. This event is in John only. It says,

> *Then Judas having received a detachment of troops, and officers from the chief priests and the Pharisees, came there with lanterns, torches, and weapons. Jesus, therefore, knowing all things that would come upon him, went forward and said to them, "Whom are you seeking?" They answered him "Jesus of Nazareth." Jesus said to them, "I am he." And Judas, who betrayed him, also stood with them. Then when he said to them, "I am he," they drew back and fell to the ground. Then he asked them again, "Whom are you seeking?" And they said, "Jesus of Nazareth."* (John 18:3–7)

What scared those armed soldiers and guards? Did the armless Jesus scare them? The author did not bother himself to investigate why did those armed soldiers and guards fell to the ground.

If this event really happened, it means that they met Jesus in his way out of the garden to go to the place of hiding, then there was something abnormal had happened in front of them and scared them. This could be the moment of the coming of the forces of God, the angels, to rescue Jesus and a moment of preparation for the miraculous event, the moment of the formation of Judas to appear in the eyes of the people in the likeness of Jesus in all aspects. Verily, this event, the disciples' heavy eyes and the irresistible sleep that came upon all of them at that most critical hour (Matt. 26:43)—all of that were the starting of the first phase of the scenario of rescuing Jesus.

(6/6) What happened to Judas?

After arresting Judas, who appeared as though he was Jesus, the troops did not ask about Judas, because they were completely engrossed in the attempt of arresting Jesus. Also, they already knew that his mission would end by his directing to Jesus's place. And there was not any sign that would make them to have doubt about him. So they thought that Judas, after his mission, left the garden, during the escape of the disciples in the midst of the darkness of that night.

Naturally, Judas who was arrested, would try to defense himself. But either he was not able to speak, for God made him under the effect of the shock of the miracle, or he was able to speak but no one listened to him because they thought that he was Jesus, pretending madness to avoid punishment. They led him away to be judged at the place of the high priest, where the scribes and the elders were assembled, thinking that they were dealing with Jesus, while the real Jesus was spending the night in the place of hiding in the Jewish heartland, the heart of the earth. Neither the Jews nor the disciples could come there. He was surrounded with God's care, as was Jonah in the belly of the great fish and waiting his hour to depart this world.

On the next morning, Judas was led away and delivered to Pilate, the governor, who whipped him and delivered him to be crucified. Then the soldiers stripped off his clothes and put a purple robe on him. Then they made a crown out of thorny branches and placed it on his head and put a stick in his right hand. Then they knelt before him and made fun of him. They spat on him and took the stick and hit him over the head and led him away to be crucified. On the cross with nails penetrating his hands, Judas shouted, hopeless, *"My God, my God why have you forsaken me?"* (Matt. 27:46). He fell into the very destruction and fell into the pit that he had dug and was caught by the net that he hid. *"He has fallen into the ditch which he made"* (Ps. 7:15). *"The wicked is snared in the work of his own hands"* (Ps. 9:16). *"Let destruction come upon him unexpectedly and let his net that he has hidden catch himself; into that very destruction let him fall"* (Ps. 35:8). So the scripture about Judas was fulfilled, as Jesus said, *"While I was with them* (the disciples) *in the world, I kept them in your name. Those whom you gave me I have kept; and none of them is lost except the son of perdition* (Judas), *that the Scripture might be fulfilled"* (John 17:12).

(7/6) Who did deal with the body of Judas?

Matthew and John tell us that there was a rich man named Joseph who was a disciple of Jesus but secretly, for fear of the Jews. This man went Friday evening to Pilate and asked for the body, and Pilate gave him permission. So he took the body, wrapped it in a clean linen cloth, and laid it in his own tomb, which he had just recently dug out of solid rock. Then he rolled a large stone against the door of the tomb and departed. The tomb was in a garden near where the crucifixion took place. (See Matthew 27:57–60 and John 19:38–42.)

(8/6) Did the Jews know that they had killed another person?

It seems, and God knows best. Yes, they knew that, for of the following reasons:

1. In the prophecy of Psalm 109, Jesus asked God, *"Help me, O Lord my God; because of your constant love, save me! Make my enemies know that you, Lord, have done it!"* (Ps. 109:26–27). Also, Jesus asked his Lord in the same prophecy, saying, *"Let them curse, but you bless; when they arise, let them be ashamed. But let your servant* (Jesus) *rejoice. let my accusers clothed with shame and let them cover themselves with their own disgrace as with a mantle"* (Ps. 109:28–29). So God mocked at those Jews. He covered them with disgrace when they realized that it was the hand of God that made Judas appear in their eyes in the likeness of Jesus and they killed him instead of Jesus. If those Jews were certain of themselves that they had killed Jesus, they would not feel shame and scandal and wear their shame like a robe.

2. The Jews were eager to obtain an official decree from the Roman governor Pilate to guard the tomb containing the body of Judas. If they were sure that the crucified person was Jesus himself, they will not care about guarding his body in the tomb, after killing him, and they will not care if the disciples come and enter the tomb. But, in fact, they were worried that Jesus, who was still alive, may appear to people. Then it would be a big scandal for them, and so more people would believe in him.
3. The defamation of Jesus before Pilate after the event of the crucifixion, in order to obtain his consent to guard the tomb, and their dubious dealing with the tomb's guards, prove that they already knew that the crucified person was not Jesus and that they were facing a scandal.
4. The obscurity of Judas's end, for there is no certainty with the people till now about his end.

(9/6) *What did the Jews do to cover up the scandal?*

Well, those Jews realized how big the problem was that they were facing, because they did not know to where Jesus had gone, so they could go to him and kill him. *"And where I am, you cannot come"* (John 7:34). They were worried that he might appear to people at any time, while the crucified Judas still in the tomb. It would be a big scandal for them if the people knew later that the crucified person was not Jesus and the body in the tomb did not belong to him. They will be shown defeated in front of their people, and then another trial may occur, as more people may start believing in Jesus. And what would they say if Jesus appears to people?

They thought about the matter. No backing down from saying that Jesus himself was the crucified, but what can they say to people if Jesus appears? They had only one solution: to fabricate of the idea of his resurrection, since the people at that time believed in the resurrection of the dead. In fact, many of them already had seen Lazarus, whom Jesus raised from the dead by God's permission. Therefore, they had two bad choices: the spread of their defeat and that they had been deceived by killing someone rather than Jesus or the spread of the killing of Jesus but he was resurrected, as an answer to his appearance to people. They chose the lesser harm of the two bad choices, the second option, and agreed on the following:

1. Keep saying in boast that they succeeded in killing Jesus, because the people already saw the one who resembled Jesus being led openly to be crucified.
2. Make the guarding of Judas's tomb the most important priority, until they can get rid of his body, in order to ensure that the disciples do not come there, remove the stone from the door, enter the tomb, and then discover the truth.
3. Slandering Jesus again before the Roman governor that he was deceiving and misleading the people so that he may sympathize with their request to guard the tomb. The first slander: when they lied to Pilate and claimed that Jesus deceives people and misleads them, as he claims that he is the king of the Jews, and they threatened Pilate that if he does not kill Jesus, he would not be Caesar's friend, because whoever makes himself a king speaks against Caesar. And they said to Pilate, *"We have no king but Caesar"* (John 19:12,15). As for the second slander against Jesus in front of Pilate, it was after the event of the crucifixion, when they fabricated a false story about Jesus and said that he had claimed that he would be resurrected three days later. They described this as another deception and misleading of the people, which is worse than the first deception (that he is the king of the Jews).
4. Never admit that they were defeated and deceived in killing someone else instead of Jesus, since the person who was arrested and crucified appeared to people as though he was Jesus.

How did the Jews implement their plan?

The next day, Saturday, the chief priests and the Pharisees met with Pilate and said to him,

> *Sir, we remember, while he* (Jesus) *was still alive, how that deceiver said, "After three days I will rise." Therefore, command that the tomb be made secure until the third day, lest his disciples come by night and steal him away, and say to the people, "He has risen from dead." So the last deception will be worse than the first.* (Matt. 27:63–64)

Surely, this was not true. How come such saying was ascribed to Jesus although he himself already had challenged the Jews, saying to them, *"You will seek me and not find me, and where I am you cannot come"*? Also, there is not any narration in any gospel that Jesus said to the leaders of the Jews or to the common people, *"After three days I will rise."* (More details about this in "Research 8.") Pilate gave the Jews more than what they asked for, by giving them full authority over the tomb. He said to them, *"You have a guard; go your way, make it as secure as you know how"* (Matt. 27:65).

With this authority from Pilate, the tomb became under the Jews' control. Now they can get rid of Judas's body and leave the door opened to spread the resurrection rumor of Jesus, if he appears to people. They went there with their own selected guards. *"They went there and made the tomb secure, sealing the stone and setting the guard"* (Matt. 27:66).

From the context of the story in Matthew, it seems that late at night, before the dawn of Sunday, the Jews went to the garden where the tomb is located and then sneaked into the tomb's area and rolled the stone from the door of the tomb. There was no difficulty in rolling the stone because Matthew tells us that the disciple Joseph, who laid the body into the tomb, he by himself alone who rolled the stone against the door of the tomb. *"And he rolled a large stone against the door of the tomb and departed"* (Matt. 27:60). And it seems that the rolling of the stone made a sound that alerted the guards, but also it seems that the Jews were ready for any surprise. One of them was wearing very white clothes and was sitting on the stone, so the guards thought it was an angel who descended from heaven and was the one who rolled the stone, so they got afraid of him. Matthew says, *"And the guards shook for fear of him and became like dead men"* (Matt. 28:4). The Jews took the body of Judas and left the door of the tomb open to spread the resurrection rumor, if Jesus appears. Mark says about the time of the first visit to the tomb: *"Very early in the morning, on the first day of the week* (Sunday) *they came (*the women*) to the tomb when the sun had risen"* (Mark 16:2).

After the guards had woken up, some of them went to the city on Sunday morning and informed the chief priests about what had happened and the empty tomb (Matt. 28:11). But since the chief priests and the elders were the ones who planed that matter, they surprised the guards with a calm reaction to what had happened. Not only that, but they made a deal with them. Matthew says, *"The chief priests met with the elders and made their plan"* (Matt. 28:12). At the meeting, they agreed to make a deal with the guards as follows:

1. Tempting the guards with money, in exchange of accusing the disciples of Jesus of stealing the body while they were asleep.
2. Reassure the guards and make them secure by defending them in case the news comes to the governor's ears and appease him.

"They gave a large sum of money to the soldiers (the guards) *saying, 'Tell them, "His disciples came at night and stole him away while we slept." And if this comes to the governor's ears, we will appease him and make you secure.' So, they took the money and did as they were instructed"* (Matt. 28:12–15).

Why did the high priests ask the guards to lie and say that the disciples stole the body while they were sleeping instead of spreading the story of the angel who descended from heaven and rolled the stone from the door of the tomb and sat on it?

Because the chief priests themselves were the first to know, the invented fable, in the story of the angel who scared the guards and made them like dead. And if the pagan Pilate heard this fable, they would not be able to appease him to the guards. And perhaps, this invented fable may let him know the truth that condemns them. While spreading the story of stealing of the body at night, by the disciples while the guards were sleeping, will make them take away any doubt that may revolve around them. The author of Matthew tells us that the bribing of the guards with a large sum of money succeeded in spreading the rumor of the stealing story of the body by the disciples, to the day the author wrote his Gospel. *"So, they took the money and did as they were instructed; and this saying is commonly reported among the Jews until this day"* (Matt. 28:15).

It may be said that the chief priests resorted to the fabrication of the stealing story of the body by the disciples so as not to spread among the people that an angel was descended from heaven and moved the stone away from the door of the tomb, because this will be an evidence that Jesus was sent from God and He raised him from death, and this would increase those who believe in him. This is not true. The chief priests know that the descent of an angel from heaven is not more powerful than the miracles that people saw by the hands of Jesus, and because of these miracles, many people believed in him. Rather, the rulers of the Jews themselves acknowledge within themselves that Jesus was sent by God. Didn't Nicodemus, who was a ruler of the Jews, came to Jesus at night and said to him, *"Rabbi, we know that you are a teacher come from God; for no one can do these signs that you do unless God is with him"* (John 3:1–2)? They aimed from inventing the stealing of the corpse by the disciples to remove any doubt or suspicion around them. This fabrication does not contradict the rumor of the rising from the dead, which they were forced to accept its spreading rather than the spreading of the fact of killing Judas instead of Jesus.

(10/6) What did the Jews do with the body of Judas?

Three gospels were silent about Judas himself. There is no mention about him since the moment of his coming with the troops to arrest Jesus. He already disappeared from the theatre of the events.

The Fourth Gospel, Matthew, has a narration that Judas had committed suicide! It says,

> *Then Judas, his betrayer, seeing that he (Jesus) had been condemned, was remorseful and brought back the thirty pieces of silver to the chief priests and elders, saying, "I have sinned by betraying innocent blood to death!" And they said, "What is that to us? You see to it!" Then he threw down the pieces of silver in the temple and departed and went and hanged himself. But the chief priests took the silver pieces and said, "It is not lawful to put them into the treasury, because they are the price of blood." And they took counsel and bought with them the Potter's field, to burry strangers in. Therefore, that field has been called the Field of Blood to this day.* (Matt. 27:3–8)

The evidence of the Jews' success in disposing of Judas's corpse and making a mysterious end for him is that there is no certainty with the people till today about Judas's end! The author of Acts, narrated from Peter, as we saw before, another different end for Judas. He said about him,

> *Now this man purchased a field with the wages of iniquity; and falling headlong, he burst open in the middle and all his entrails gushed out. And it became known to all those dwelling in Jerusalem; so that field is called in their own language, Akel Dama, that is, Field of Blood.* (Acts 1:18–19)

Was this a result of falling from the tenth floor or an attempt to distort the body by the Jews to hide its out shape before burial and fabricating a death scenario for Judas to spread among people? Peter said about the spread of this scenario, *"It became known to all those dwelling in Jerusalem; so that field is called in their own language, Akel*

Dama, that is, Field of Blood." But even though hanging himself, or even falling to his death, are not strong enough to be considered as a fulfillment for the promised terrible end for Judas by Jesus: *"The son of man goes as it is written of him but woe* (how terrible) *for that man by whom the son of man is betrayed! It would have been good for that man if he had not been born"* (Matt. 26:24). The promised terrible end for Judas was fulfilled when he could not defend himself. But they stripped him, mocked him, spat on him, struck him on the head with a reed, then he was hung on the cross with nails penetrating his hands, to have a long death.

Anyway, the Jews succeeded in making a fuzzy picture of Judas's end to this day. Was Judas remorseful? *"Then Judas, his betrayer, seeing that he* (Jesus) *had been condemned, was remorseful"* (Matt. 27:3). Or not? Did Judas return back the thirty silver coins to the chief priests and elders, and they were the one who bought the field? *"And brought back the thirty pieces of silver to the chief priests and elders... And they took counsel and bought with them the Potter's field, to bury strangers in"* (Matt. 27:3, 7). Or did he not return them, and he himself the one who bought the field with the wages of iniquity? *"Now this man* (Judas) *purchased a field with the wages of iniquity"* (Acts 1:18). Did Judas commit suicide by hanging himself? *"And went and hanged himself"* (Matt. 27:5). Or did he fall on his face and split from the middle and all his bowels spill out? *"Falling headlong, he burst open in the middle and all his entrails gushed out"* (Acts 1:18). Was the field called the Field of Blood because its price was the price of Jesus's blood. *"It is not lawful to put them into the treasury, because they are the price of blood"* (Matt. 27:6). Or is it because Judas's corpse required false blood to be spilled out on the field? *"Falling headlong, he burst open in the middle and all his entrails gushed out... So that field is called in their own language, Akel Dama, that is, Field of Blood"* (Acts 1:18–19). Thus is the fuzzy picture of the end of Judas.

(11/6) Who were the persons near the tomb?

The gospels talk of persons in white clothes that were inside the tomb early Sunday morning. The authors of the gospels did not agree on the identity of those persons, their number, their places, their talk, and to whom they talk and their number. Although man cannot see angels unless they manifest in human form for example, but some authors (Matthew) suspected that it was an angel sitting on the stone outside the tomb and spoke to two women came to the tomb. While (John) suspected that they were two angels sitting inside the tomb talking to Mary Magdalene, who came alone to the tomb. And while (Mark) mentioned that he was a young man sitting inside the tomb, speaking to three women who had come to the tomb. The author (Luke) mentioned that they were two men standing inside the tomb, talking to several women who came to the tomb.

The narrations about the task of these persons came as follows:

In Matthew and Mark, the task was to spread the rumor of Jesus's resurrection and to locate the place of the meeting of Jesus with his disciples, in Galilee. In Luke, the task was to spread the rumor of Jesus's resurrection only, without locating any meeting place. As for John, the author mentioned that they only asked Mary Magdalene why she was crying.

The reactions of the women who visited the tomb, after those persons near the tomb had talked with them, were as follow, according to the authors' narrations:

1. The two women (in Matthew) came out of the tomb quickly to tell the disciples. Then Jesus met them on the way and asked them to tell the disciples about the meeting place, Galilee. So they went.

> *For an angel of the lord descended from heaven and came and rolled back the stone from the door and sat on it... And the guards shook for fear of him and became like dead men. But the angel answered and said to the women, "Do not be afraid, for I know that you seek Jesus who was crucified... Go quickly and tell his disciples that he is risen from the dead, and indeed he is going before you into Galilee; there you will see him... So, they departed*

quickly from the tomb and ran to bring his disciples word. And as they went to tell his disciples, behold, Jesus met them. Then he said to them, "Go and tell my brethren to go to Galilee, and there they will see me." (Matt. 28:2, 4–5, 7–10)

2. The three women (in Mark), after the person inside the tomb had asked them to tell the disciples, came out quickly and fled from the tomb and said nothing to anyone because they were afraid.

> *Now when the Sabbath was past, Mary Magdalene, Mary the mother of James, and Salome bought spices, that they might come and anoint him. Very early in the morning on the first day of the week, they came to the tomb when the sun had risen... But when they looked up, they saw that the stone had been rolled away—for it was very large. And entering the tomb, they saw a young man clothed in a long white robe sitting on the right side; and they were alarmed. But he said to them, "Do not be alarmed. You seek Jesus of Nazareth, who was crucified. He is risen! He is not here... But go and tell his disciples and Peter that he is going before you into Galilee; there you will see him, as he said to you." And they went out quickly and fled from the tomb, for they trembled and were amazed. And they said nothing to anyone, for they were afraid.* (Mark 16:1–2, 4–8)

3. The several women (in Luke) came from the tomb and told the disciples.

> *And the women who had come with him from Galilee followed after, and they observed the tomb... And they rested on the Sabbath according*

to the commandment. Now on the first day of the week, very early in the morning, they came to the tomb... But they found the stone rolled away from the tomb. Then they went in and did not find the body of Jesus. And it happened, as they were greatly perplexed about this, that behold, two men stood by them in shining garments... They said to them, "Why do you seek the living among the dead? He is not here but is risen!"... Then they returned from the tomb and told all these things to the eleven and to all the rest. It was Mary Magdalene, Joanna, Mary the mother of James, and the other women with them, who told these things to the apostles. (Luke 23:55–56, 24:1–6, 9–10)

4. Mary Magdalene (in John) came to the tomb and saw that the stone had been taken away from the tomb. Then she ran and told the disciple Peter and another disciple. The two ran to the tomb and entered inside, but they did not see anyone, so they went away again to their own homes. But Mary stood outside weeping, and as she wept, she stooped down and looked into the tomb. She then saw the two persons inside. They did not ask her to tell the disciples. But the one who asked her to tell the disciples was Jesus himself, when she saw him at the tomb, so she went and told the disciples.

On the first day of the week Mary Magdalen came to the tomb and saw that the stone had been taken away from the tomb. Then she ran and came to Simon Peter, and to the other disciple and said to them, "They have taken away the Lord out of the tomb, and we do not know where they have laid him." So, they both ran together and came to the tomb... Then Simon Peter went into the tomb... Then the other disciple went in also... Then the dis-

> *ciples went away again to their homes. But Mary stood outside by the tomb weeping, and as she wept, she stooped down and looked into the tomb. And she saw two angels in white sitting. Then they said to her, "Women, why are you weeping?" She said to them, "Because they have taken away my lord, and I do not know where they have laid him." Now when she had said this, she turned around and saw Jesus standing there, and did not know that it was Jesus… Jesus said to her, go to my brethren and say to them "I am ascending to my father and your father, and to my God and your God." Mary Magdalene came and told the disciples that she had seen the Lord, and that he had spoken these things to her.* (John 20:1–3, 6, 8, 10–14, 17–18)

The author of Matthew is the only one who took the person out of the tomb and made him sit on the rolled stone of the door because he added another task for him, to scare the guards until they became like dead men, so the tomb can be evacuated. While the tomb in the narrations of the other three was unguarded and available to all, so the persons in their narrations were inside the tomb. It also seems that those persons talk only to women and avoid appearing and talking to men. The author of John made the two persons disappear when Peter and the other disciple came to the tomb. But when the two disciples had left, the two persons went into the tomb and Mary Magdalene saw them.

The differences in the narrations of the four authors are obvious and expected, for those anonymous authors came thirty to sixty years after the ascension to write books of the biography of Christ based on fallible human effort, devoid of inspiration, and personal eyewitness but on the author's own notion, assumptions, rumors, hearsay, and copying from each other. Therefore, each one of the four authors of the four gospels came with his own collection of uncertain narrations that conflict with other's narrations. So we do not know for sure about the fact of the person, or persons, whom the authors claimed that they were inside the tomb and who assigned them there to appear and talk only to women. Were they working in the favor of the Jews to spread the news of Jesus's alleged resurrection to cover up the stolen of Judas's body and as an answer for the empty tomb? Or were they working in the favor of Jesus to give a message to his disciples, through the women, to go to the place where they can meet him? The authors of the gospels themselves are not sure!

(12/6) Why was Jesus not ascended before the coming of the troops?

Yes, if the purpose of Jesus's ascension was to protect him from the evil plots of the Jews, then why did he not ascend to heaven just before the arrival of Judas and the troops to the garden to arrest him? What is the wisdom behind his going to a place in the Jewish heartland to hide there for three days, then walk out thereafter and make an appearance to his disciples, then ascending to heaven?

First, the person who believes that Jesus is a pure human being also believes that the purpose of his ascension was nothing more than to protect him from the Jews, for there is no benefit of his ascension if he has already been killed. But the one who still believes that Jesus was arrested and killed, this belief would lead him to another false belief, that Jesus was not a pure human being but a divine being. Because if he was a human being, there is no benefit of his ascension since he was already killed. But the fact is that, ascending Jesus to heaven does not conflict with his pure humanity. But it was a great saving miracle by God for Jesus, to purify him of those who kill the prophets and to protect him in heaven from the Jewish conspiracies. Therefore, the Jews did not find him and saw him no more. *"A little while longer and the world* (the Jews) *will see me no more"* (John 14:19).

If Jesus was already killed, then resurrected and ascended to heaven, it means the Jews already succeeded with their plot against him. But saving Jesus in the place of hiding, then saving him by his ascension, would clothe the Jews with shame, especially when they realized that it was God Himself who had done this to them. Jesus will stay a few days up, according to the heavenly time, then he will come back to planet earth with another mission, as his return will be a sign for the coming of the hour of ending the life on the planet earth and then the end of the entire universe. The Christ Jesus will come back at the time that the imposter Christ (the Antichrist) will appear on earth with a false message, but the true Christ, Jesus, will kill that Antichrist. Jesus will return to earth because he is a pure human being, where he dies at his appointed time, then to be buried, and then he will be resurrected alive with all the human beings for judgment in the next life.

Regarding the previous question: if the purpose of his ascension was to protect him, then why did he not ascend to heaven directly, before the coming of Judas and the troops to arrest him? What was the wisdom of going first to a place in the heart of the Jewish land to hide for three days, then walk out of that place and appear to his disciples, and then ascend to heaven? The answer can be summarized as follows:

1. Yes, the purpose was to protect Jesus and kill the traitor Judas. Therefore, if Jesus had ascended to heaven before the coming of Judas and the troops to arrest him, perhaps by a way or another, the disciples might know about it; and then they would realize that the person who was arrested was not Jesus but someone who resemble him, which will be none other but Judas, and may the news reach to the Jews, then they will not kill the traitor Judas, or may not the disciples know about Jesus's ascension, then it will be certain to them and the people that the crucified person was Jesus. But the biding of Jesus on earth, hiding in the heart of the land of the Jews during the crucifixion of Judas, then appearing after the event of the crucifixion, declaring that he had not yet ascended to heaven but he will, *"I have not yet ascended to my father, but go to my brethren and say to them 'I am ascending to my father and your father, and to my God and your God'"* (John 20:17), made those who differed in the matter of the crucifixion full of doubts. They had no certain knowledge. They followed nothing but conjecture.

2. To fulfill his prophecy to the Jews, and later to his disciples, that he would go to a place, which both cannot come to it and at the same time to fulfill his prophecy, that to be like the prophet Jonah. As Jonah was surrounded with God's care in the belly of the great fish for three days, so Jesus was also surrounded with God's care in the place of hiding in the Jewish heartland, the heart of the earth, hiding there for three days (Matt. 12:40). And as Jonah was by his miraculous rescue a sign to the Ninevites, in the same way, Jesus would also become by his miraculous rescue a sign for the people of his generation (Luke 11:39–40).
3. To fulfill the prophecy of Psalm 109:26–29, when God had disgraced the Jews and clothed them with shame when they acknowledged that it was God who had saved Jesus and made them kill Judas, who became a guide to them.
4. For Jesus to live through the moments of victory over his enemies, the Jews, and his betrayer, Judas, while still on earth, and before becoming subjected to the heavenly laws. *"When they arise, let them be ashamed, but let your servant* (Jesus) *rejoice"* (Ps. 109:28).

(13/6) How did Jesus come out of the place of hiding?

After crucifying Judas, and after the Sabbath, early Sunday morning, Jesus came out of that place of hiding, which seems not far from the garden where the tomb is located, to see his disciples first, then to go to heaven, as he already promised them, *"A little while, and you will see me, because I go to the father"* (John 16:16). And it seems, and God knows best, that when Jesus came out of that place for the first time, he was disguising. This can be understood from the narration in John, where he stated that the first appearance of Christ was in a face-to-face conversation between him and Mary Magdalene early Sunday morning in the garden, near the tomb. Mary was talking to him and supposing him to be the gardener! Why could not she recognize either the shape or the voice of her teacher, the Christ? Why did she suppose him to be the gardener? The only answer, if that really happened, is that he was not resurrected in the first place but that he was perfectly disguised in voice and appearance as a gardener. If Jesus had already been the crucified person, Mary Magdalene would have known him of the effect of the nails in his hands. Then, after giving Mary cause to believe that he was as a stranger man, Jesus spoke to her with his normal voice, calling her by her name, whereupon she recognized him. So she ran toward him to express her excitement and happiness at seeing him, but he stopped her.

> *Now when she had said this, she turned around and saw Jesus standing there, and did not know that it was Jesus. He said to her "Woman, why are you weeping? Whom are you seeking?" She, supposing him to be the gardener said to him, "Sir, if you have carried him away, tell me where you have laid him, and I will take him away." Jesus said to her, "Mary!" She turned and said to him, "Rabboni!"* (which is to say, teacher). *Jesus said to her, "Do not cling to me, for I have not yet ascended to my father, but go to my brethren and say to them 'I am ascending to my father and your father, and to my God and your God."* (John 20:14–17)

Luke also reported that on that same day, Sunday evening, Jesus appeared to two of his followers who were traveling on the road to a village called Emmaus. They were talking together about the things that had happened as Jesus drew himself near to them and began to accompany them. But somehow they did not recognize him. Then Jesus asked them about their conversation, and one of them answered him and said, *"Are you the only stranger in Jerusalem, and have you not known the things which happened there in these days?"* And he said to them, *"What things?"* And they said to him, *"The things concerning Jesus of Nazareth,"* and they talked to him about the crucifixion. Then Jesus put some comments to their answer. Approaching the village, Jesus, still unrecognized by his two followers, indicated that he would keep traveling farther. However, the two men invited him for dinner since it was late and it is getting dark. So Jesus went in to stay with them. He sat down to eat with them, took the bread, and said the blessing; then he broke the bread and gave it to them. It was at that precise moment that his two followers recognized him, but he disappeared from their sight (Luke 24:13–31).

Why did they not recognize their teacher all the way while they were conversing with him? Because he was perfectly disguised, neither his shape nor his voice was familiar. The author of Mark had put it this way: *"After that, he appeared in another form to two of them as they walked and went into the country"* (Mark 16:12). Jesus's followers only recognized him when he blessed the bread as he was previously known to do. If Jesus had already been the crucified person, the two followers would have known him of the effect of the nails in his hands.

Research 7
Why did Jesus not give any details about the end of his life on earth?

It was God's wisdom to destine an unusual end for the first life of Jesus on earth. This end was a part of God's plan against the conspiracy of the Jews and the betrayal of Judas. Therefore, Jesus did not give any details about that, not even to his disciples. He only gave some outlines and parables as clues to the events that will happen.

For security reasons, Jesus left the garden sneakily, after God has made the disciples into a deep sleep that made them not to notice his leaving, and went in the darkness of the night to the place of hiding. Also, for the same security reasons, the disciples would not know where Jesus has gone and will not be able to come there. *"Where I am going, you cannot come,' so now I say to you"* (John 13:33). But he hinted to them that his absence there would be just for a little while. He said to them, *"A little while, and you will not see me; and again, a little while, and you will see me, because I go to the father"* (John 16:16). Then some of his disciples asked among themselves, *"What is this that he says to us, 'A little while, and you will not see me; and again a little while, and you will see me'; and 'because I go to the father'? They said therefore, "What is this that he says, 'A little while'? We do not know what he is saying"* (John 16:17–18). Jesus knew that they desired to ask him, and he said to them, *"Are you asking among yourselves about what I said, 'A little while, and you will not see me; and again, a little while, and you will see me?'"* (John 16:19).

Jesus was not that naive to give his disciples any details about the reason of his absence or where he will go because it was a part of his rescue and killing of Judas. And the disciples may weaken because of the fear of the oppression of the Jews, then the news may reach them. He already prophesied that his disciple Peter will deny him three times because of the fear of the Jews (Matt. 26:34). And he also prophesied that due to the fear of the Jews, all his disciples will forget all about him and run away, worrying only about themselves and not thinking about their teacher (John 16:32).

This "little while," and God knows best, is the time when the plan of God was fulfilled. It is while the Jews were thinking that Jesus was arrested and being crucified, Jesus was during that "little while," sheltered by God in a place of hiding, somewhere in the Jewish heartland. The Jews and also the disciples could not go to that place where he awaited his hour of departure from this world.

What did Jesus answer his disciples about this "little while"? He answered them with parables.

> He said, *"Most assuredly, I say to you that you will weep and lament, but the world will rejoice; and you will be sorrowful, but your sorrow will be turned into joy. A woman, when she is in labor, has sorrow because her hour has come; but as soon as she has given birth to the child, she no longer remembers the anguish, for joy that a human being has been born into the world. Therefore, you now have sorrow; but I will see you again and your hearts will rejoice, and your joy no one will take from you."* (John 16:20–22)

Again, Jesus was not that naive to tell his disciples that God will make Judas appear in the eyes of the people in his likeness and then he would be arrested and killed instead of him. But rather, he let them weep, lament, and feel sad in front of the Jews, as if he was the one being crucified so that the Jews would not doubt. The world (Jews) would rejoice, thinking that they had arrested Jesus.

In his parable to his disciples, Jesus emphasized that he would not be the one who would suffer and feel sad but that they would cry, weep, and suffer. Then he would see them after leaving the place of hiding, and their hearts would rejoice, as the woman who is about to give birth: she is sad, but as soon as she sees the child, she no longer remembers the anguish for joy. Jesus said, *"But I will see you again and your hearts will rejoice"* (John 16:22). He did not say, "I will be resurrected." At the end of his conversation with his disciples, Jesus emphasized that as if he was now obliged to talk to them with parables and not plain words so that the news would not reach the Jews. He said, *"These things I have spoken to you in figurative language; but the time is coming when I will no longer speak to you in figurative language, but I will tell you plainly about the Father"* (John 16:25). Then the disciples said, *"Now we are sure that you know all things and have no need that anyone should question you. By this we believe that you came forth from God"* (John 16:30). Jesus answered them and said, *"Do you now believe?"* (John 16:31). He even gave them a clue about the one who will be killed instead of him! *"The son of man goes as it is written of him but woe (how terrible) for that man by whom the son of man is betrayed! It would have been good for that man if he had not been born"* (Matt. 26:24). But what is going to happen at the end? Jesus told them, *"Indeed the hour is coming, yes has now come, that you will be scattered, each to his own, and will leave me alone. And yet, I am not alone, because the father is with me"* (John 16:32). So if God was already with Jesus, how would the end be going? Jesus said to his disciples, *"Be of good cheer, I have defeated the world* (the Jews)*"* (John 16:33). How could Jesus defeat the Jews if he was the one arrested, stripped off his clothes, spat, beaten, and crucified? He defeated the Jews because God saved him, and they killed the traitor Judas thinking that he was Jesus.

At the end, the disciples did as Jesus prophesied. When they saw the troops who had come with Judas, they all fled and scattered, each to his own. *"Then all the disciples forsook him and fled"* (Matt. 26:56), and they followed conjecture and hearsay and mourned and cried. *"She went and told his companions. They were mourning and crying"* (Mark 16:10). But their initial reaction when they heard that Jesus was alive was *"They did not believe"* (Mark 16:11). Then when they saw Jesus, as he prophesied, *"They were terrified and frightened, and supposed they had seen a spirit"* (Luke 24:37). So they accepted the rumor that he raised from the dead. They had no certain knowledge and followed nothing but conjecture because Jesus did not give them any details about what had happened to him. He only tried to prove to them and said, *"It is I myself"* (Luke 24:39). Then their sadness turned into gladness, as Jesus also prophesied.

This was the hypothetical picture in the minds of the early Christians. They just added Jesus to the list of the previous murdered prophets by the Jews, but he was different from them because of his alleged resurrection, then his ascension. And despite the early Christians' belief that Jesus had been crucified, they never believed or preached that he died for atonement and redemption. In fact, they used to blame the Jews for that.

Jesus already declared to his disciples that only them would be able to see him after his disappearance for a little while in the heart of the earth, the Jewish country's heartland. But for the security of Jesus, the Jews would see him no more, since he was speaking to the multitudes and to his disciples in the temple two days before the Passover, and he said, pointing to the Jewish scribes and Pharisees, *"See! Your house is left to you desolate; for I say to you, you shall see me no more"* (Matt. 23:38–39). And the ban continued till he ascended to heaven. He clearly informed his disciples, after finishing supper on his last night with them, that he would appear after his disappearance and he would come to them and they will see him because he was alive, not resurrected. As for the Jews, they will not be able to see him during his appearance. Jesus said to his disciples: *"I will not leave you orphans; I will come to you. A little while longer and the world* (the Jews) *will see me no more, but you will see me. Because I live, you will live also"* (John 14:18–19). Also, for Jesus's security, he went out of the place of hiding disguised as a gardener, as he seemed to Mary Magdalene. *"She turned around and saw Jesus standing there and did not know that it was Jesus. He said to her, 'Woman, why are you weeping? Whom are you seeking?' She was supposing him to be the gardener"* (John 20:14–15). And in the evening, he appeared to two of his followers, also disguised. *"After that, he appeared in another form to two of them as they walked and went into the country"* (Mark 16:12). He walked and talked with them, but they could not recognize their teacher all the way, seven miles. Then for a security purpose, he right away disappeared from their sight, when they recognized him, after he had taken bread, blessed, and broke it as he used to doing before with his disciples (Luke 24:30–31). And while Jesus was waiting his hour to be ascended to heaven, he was the one to surprise his disciples with his appearance to them because no one can go to his place. So the reason of not giving any details about the mysterious final part of his life on earth appears to have been for security reasons until he departs from this world.

Research 8
Did Jesus prophesy that he would be killed?

Did Jesus predict that he would be killed as he predicted that God would save him? Certainly, he did not predict. But what about these alleged prophecies about his hanging on the cross, the pouring of his blood, and his resurrection from death? Could it be true? When we find such things in the gospels, it should not surprise us. Because each author of the four gospels came with his own collection of uncertain stories that conflict with other's stories and to put his own words in the mouth of Jesus to produce the gospel of Jesus's behalf, devoid of inspiration and personal eyewitness. Here are some of these alleged prophecies:

(1/8) The prophecy that Jesus must suffer and be killed, and after three days he rises

The author of Mark wrote that Jesus began to teach his disciples, saying, *"The son of man must suffer many things, and be rejected by the elders and chief priests and scribes, and be killed, and after three days rise again. He spoke this word openly"* (Mark 8:31–32). Then later, it was copied by Matthew (16:21). Then Luke did the same (9:22). Matthew also said that Jesus had told his disciples that he would be delivered up to be crucified: *"You know that after two days is the Passover, and the son of man will be delivered up to be crucified"* (Matt. 26:2). Mark also said that Jesus told his disciples that he would have been raised: *"But after I have been raised, I will go before you to Galilee"* (Mark 14:28). Then it was also copied by Matthew (Matt. 26:32).

Jesus may have said to his disciples that he *"will be rejected by the elders and chief priests and scribes."* And that had happened to him. But surely, he had never said, *"He must suffer many things, and be killed, and after three days rise again."* But this was a result of the fallible human efforts, which was based on uncertain narrations, rumors and hearsay, and the imaginary personal belief of the author. The proofs for all of this are as follows:

1. By no means Jesus would say, *"He must be killed, and after three days rise again"* (Mark 8:31), while he is the one who already had challenged those who worked to kill him that they would not find him when they seek him and cannot come to his place. *"You will seek me and not find me, and where I am you cannot come"* (John 7:34).
2. Mark claimed that the declaration of Jesus that he would be killed and after three days rise again was very clear to his disciples. *"He spoke this word openly"* (Mark 8:32), and they fully understood his words, to the point that the reaction of Peter toward the declaration of his teacher was very

strong. *"He took Jesus aside and began to rebuke him!"* (Mark 8:32). But when Jesus had turned around and looked at his disciples, he rebuked Peter, saying, *"Go behind me, Satan!"* (Mark 8:33).

But after six days of this event, Mark narrated about another event indicates that Jesus had never told his disciples that he would be killed and after three days rise again! He wrote, *"Now after six days Jesus took Peter, James and John and led them up on a high mountain apart by themselves; and he was transfigured before them"* (Mark 9:2). Then Mark continued writing:

> *Now as they came down from the mountain, he commanded them that they should tell no one the things they had seen, till the son of man had risen from the dead. So, they kept the word to themselves, questioning what the rising from the dead meant?* (Mark 9:9–10)

Surely, if Jesus had openly said six days before to his disciples, *"He must be killed, and after three days rise again,"* and then a strong argument had happened between Jesus and Peter because of this declaration; so the six days were not a long time to make the three disciples forget Jesus's declaration about death, resurrection, and all about the argument, to the point that they kept his word to themselves, questioning what the rising from the dead meant? But this was the confusion that resulted from fallible human efforts that was devoid of inspiration and personal eyewitness. It was no more than the author relying upon narrations, rumors, hearsay, and the author's own notion, trying to put his own words in Jesus's mouth.

The author of John already blew up the narration of Mark, who claimed that Jesus had told his disciples that he would be killed and after three days rise again, as well as the narration of Matthew and Luke. After Mary Magdalene came to the disciple Peter and another disciple and told them that she did not find Jesus in the tomb, as she said to them, *"They have taken the lord from the tomb, and we do not know where they have put him!"* (John 20:2); *so Peter and the other disciple both ran together to the empty tomb, entered into it, and looked at its contents* (John 20:3–8). The author of John explained why the two disciples ran to the empty tomb and entered it, because the disciples did not yet know the scripture that Jesus must rise again from the dead. He said, *"For as yet they did not know the Scripture, that he must rise again from the dead"* (John 20:9). Meaning, that Jesus had never told his disciples that he would be killed and after three days rise again, as Mark claims as well as Matthew and Luke. And if Jesus had really said to his disciples, *"He must be killed, and after three days rise again,"* Peter and the other disciple would have calmed Mary and tell her that Jesus already had prophesied to them about his resurrection.

3. When Jesus appeared in disguise and went with two of his followers, who were traveling on the road to a village called Emmaus, the followers told him clearly, not knowing that he was Jesus, the disciples were astonished when the women told them about the empty tomb. Meaning that Jesus never declared to his disciples that he would pass into a stage of death and resurrection. *"Besides all this, today is the third day since these things happened. Yes, and certain women of our company, who arrived at the tomb early, astonished us; when they did not find his body"* (Luke 24:21–23).

4. The reaction of the disciples after they heard that Jesus alive and when they saw him was as follows:

   a. Luke wrote that when some women came to the disciples and told them that Jesus was alive, they thought that what the women said was nonsense, and they did not believe in such a thing.

   The women were Mary Magdalene, Joanna, and Mary the mother of James; they and the other women with them told these things to the apostles. But the apostles thought that what the women said was nonsense, and they did not believe them. (Luke 24:10–11)

Not only that, rather, Peter arose and ran to the tomb; looked inside; and departed, marveling to himself at the empty tomb.

But Peter arose and ran to the tomb; and stooping down, he saw the linen cloths lying by themselves; and he departed, marveling to himself at what had happened. (Luke 24:12)

b. Mark wrote that when Mary Magdalene came to the disciples and told them that she had seen Jesus and he was alive, they did not believe. And also, when two of Jesus's followers told the disciples that Jesus had appeared to them on the road, they did not believe them either.

And when they heard that he was alive and had been seen by her, they did not believe. After that, he appeared in another form to two of them as they walked and went into the country. And they went and told it to the rest, but they did not believe them either. (Mark 16:11–13)

c. Matthew wrote that when the disciples saw Jesus, some doubted. *"And when they saw him, they worshiped him. But some doubted"* (Matt. 28:17).
d. Luke wrote that when Jesus himself stood in the midst of them, while they were gathered together, that they were terrified and frightened, thinking that they were looking at a ghost. *"But they were terrified and frightened, and supposed they had seen a spirit"* (Luke 24:37). This caused Jesus to ask them and said, *"Why are you troubled? And why do doubts arise in your hearts? Behold*

my hands and my feet, that it is I myself. Handle me and see, for a spirit does not have flesh and bones as you see I have" (Luke 24:38–39), and to the point that *"he showed them his hands and his feet"* (Luke 24:40), and asked them, *"Have any food here? So, they gave him a piece of a broiled fish and some honeycomb. And he took it and ate in their presence"* (Luke 24:41–43) to prove to them that he was the live Jesus, not a ghost.

The thinking of the disciples that what the women had said was nonsense and they did not believe them; and when Peter marveled in himself about the empty tomb; and the disbelief of the disciples to Mary Magdalene when she told them that she had seen Jesus and he was alive; also, the disbelief of the disciples in what the two followers said about the appearance of Jesus to them; and the terrifying and frightfulness of the disciples when they saw Jesus, thinking that they were looking at a ghost—all of these are an evidence that Jesus had never told his disciples that *"He must be killed, and after three days rise again."* Otherwise, the disciples would have just waited expectantly for him on the third day with joy.

(2/8) The prophecy of pouring Jesus's blood for many for the remission of sins

The following narration started by the anonymous Mark, who came after thirty years from the ascension, accusing Jesus of a false narration that he pointed to the cup and said, *"This is my blood of the new covenant, which is poured for many"* (Mark 14:24). Then after ten years, the anonymous Matthew came without scrutiny and copied this narration. *"This is my blood of the new covenant, which is poured for many for the remission of sins"* (Matt. 26:28). Luke as well did the same after another ten years. *"This cup is the new covenant in my blood, which is poured for you"* (Luke 22:20).

How does one believe that Jesus has declared that his blood is poured for many for the remission of sins and at the same time believe that Jesus has told the Jews that they will not find him when they seek him and cannot come to where he will go, as John narrates? *"You will seek me and not find me, and where I am you cannot come"* (John 7:34).

And how can a person believe that Jesus has declared that his blood is poured for many for the remission of sins and at the same time believe that Jesus has rebuked the Jews for seeking to kill him, as John narrates? *"But you seek to kill me, because my word has no place in you"* (John 8:37). *"But now you seek to kill me, a man who has told you the truth which I heard from God. Abraham did not do this"* (John 8:40). He also believes that Jesus was questioning the Jews for seeking to kill him, as John also narrates? *"Did not Moses give you the law, and yet none of you keeps the law? Why do you seek to kill me?"* (John 7:19). And believes that Jesus was avoiding the Jews who wanted to kill him, as John narrates? *"Jesus walked in Galilee; for he did not want to walk in Judea, because the Jews sought to kill him"* (John 7:1). *"Then from that day on they plotted to put him to death. Therefore, Jesus no longer walked openly among the Jews but went from there into the country near the wilderness to a city called Ephraim, and there remained with his disciples"* (John 11:53–54), and as Matthew narrates, *"Then the Pharisees went out and took counsel against him, how they might destroy him. But when Jesus knew it, he withdrew from there"* (Matt. 12:14–15).

And how can a person believe that Jesus has declared to his disciples that his blood is poured for many for the remission of sins, which make the devil hear about this mission and be aware of it, and at the same time believes that the devil was involved in the betrayal of Judas to deliver Jesus to the Jews in order to kill him, as John narrates? *"And supper being ended, the devil having already put it into the heart of Judas Iscariot' son, to betray Jesus"* (John 13:2). *"Now after the piece of bread, Satan entered Judas" (John 13:27)*, as well as Luke, *"Then Satan entered Judas"* (Luke 22:3). Does the devil work for the benefit of man and seeks to have his sins forgiven? Does not he work hard in order for man to add sins and remain a prisoner of them?

The involvement of the devil in the betrayal of Judas to deliver Jesus to the Jews proves that Jesus never declared the mission of shedding his blood for many to forgive sins, because originally, there is no such a mission.

And how can a person believe that Jesus has declared that his blood is poured out for many for the remission of sins and at the same time believes that Jesus has threatened Judas and prophesied a terrible end for him, for he would contribute in accomplishing of the mission of pouring out his blood, as Matthew narrates? *"But woe (how terrible) for that man by whom the son of man is betrayed! It would have been good for that man if he had not been born"* (Matt, 26:24). Should not Judas be rewarded instead and considered as one of the great heroes for participating in the mission of pouring Jesus's blood?

And how come a person believe that Jesus has declared that his blood is poured for many for the remission of sins and at the same time believes that Jesus did not want to shed his blood, because he tried to flee with his disciples at the last moment when Judas came with the troops to arrest him, as Matthew narrates? Jesus said to his disciples, *"Rise, let us be going, see, he who betrays me is at hand"* (Matt. 26:46).

And how come a person believe that Jesus has declared that his blood is poured for many for the remission of sins and at the same time believes that Jesus was complaining to God why has He forsaken him and let his blood pour out? As Matthew narrates that Jesus said on the cross, *"My God, My God, why have you forsaken me?"* (Matt 27:46), as well as Mark (Mark 15:34).

Finally, if the blood of Jesus would be poured out for many for the forgiveness of sins, then why did not he ask his disciples to preach such a mission to people when he appeared to them before his ascension? Neither Jesus nor the disciples after him ever preached such creed. The omission should in reality come as no surprise because there was no death, no resurrection, no atonement and redemption. Nothing of that sort at all.

(3/8) The prophecy of lifting up the son of man (Jesus) by the Jews

The author of John narrated that Jesus said to the Jews,

> *When you lift up the son of man, then you will know that I am he* (the Messiah) *and that I do nothing of myself; but as my father taught me, I speak these things. And He who sent me is with me, the father has not left me alone, for I always do those things that please Him.* (John 8:28–29)

Did the Jews lift up Jesus?
To answer this question, we need to start from the beginning of the story. After Jesus had challenged the Jews in the Temple (John 7:32–34), he went to the Mount of Olives. Then early the next morning, Jesus came again into the temple, and all the people came to him, and he sat down and taught them (John 8:2). The scribes and Pharisees came as well. Then after he had discussed with them, he confirmed to them the challenging prophecy of yesterday and told them that they cannot come to him in his place of hiding. He said, *"I am going away, and you will seek me and will die in your sin. Where I go you cannot come"* (John 8:21). Then Jesus explained to the Jews about what he meant by *"will die in your sin."* He said to them,

> *Therefore I said to you that you will die in your sins; for if you do not believe that I am he* (the Messiah) *you will die in your sins. Then they said to him, "Who are you?" And Jesus said to them, "Just what I have been saying to you from the beginning."* (John 8:24–25)

When would the Jews know that Jesus was the Messiah and he did nothing of himself but as God taught him he spoke? Well, Jesus himself had answered this question. He said to the Jews,

> *When you lift up the son of man, then you will know that I am he* (the Messiah) *and that I do nothing of myself; but as my father taught me, I speak these things. And He who sent me is with me, the father has not left me alone, for I always do those things that please Him.* (John 8:28–29)

What is this lifting up that would make the Jews to know that Jesus is the Messiah? This lifting up have specifications that Jesus himself defined as follows:

1. It is an abnormal lifting up. It is a powerful and miraculously lifting up that makes the Jews know that Jesus was the Messiah. However, they would die in their sin because they knew but they insisted in not believing in him. *"When you lift up the son of man, then you will know that I am he."*
2. It was God Himself who informed Jesus about this lifting up. *"But as my father taught me, I speak these things."*
3. This lifting up would happen because God was with Jesus, to save him from the conspiracy of murder by the Jews, not to forsake him and let him be lifted up on a wood to die. *"And He who sent me is with me, the father has not left me alone."*

Elsewhere, Jesus identified this lifting up and said, *"And I, if I am lifted up from the earth"* (John 12:32). It is the powerful miraculous lifting up, from the earth to heaven, and not just a few meters on a cross, as what the author of John falsely hinted when he inserted his own notion to the texts. He wrote, *"In saying this he indicated the kind of death he was going to suffer"* (John 12:33). By no means could Jesus have intended a lifting up on a cross for the following evidence:

1. Jesus himself stated that it is lifting up from the earth, *"And I, if I am lifted up from the earth,"* while lifting up on a cross is still on earth.
2. There is no miracle in the hanging on a cross and the killing that makes the Jews know that Jesus was the Messiah.
3. Jesus answered the Jews who asked him to see a sign from him, confirming that he was the Messiah, and said to them: "It would be as the sign of the Prophet Jonah." Lifting up on a cross and death will nullify the similarity with the sign of the prophet Jonah.
4. Jesus challenged the Jews that they would not find him when they seek him and they could not come to him where he would go. Lifting up on the cross and killing makes the challenge just nonsense.
5. Even the Jews themselves already understood this "lifting up from earth" as a departing from earth, not hanged to death. They said to Jesus, *"We have heard from the law that the Christ remains forever. And how can you say, 'The son of man must be lifted up'?"* (John 12:34). Therefore, Jesus asked the Jews to believe in him before he departed from earth. He said to them, *"A little while longer the light* (Jesus) *is with you. Walk while you have the light, lest darkness overtake you; he who walks in darkness does not know where he is going. While you have the light* (Jesus), *believe in the light that you may become sons of lights"* (John 12:35–36). But the Jews would die in their sins because they were not able to believe in Jesus as the Messiah. *"And so, they were not able to believe"* (John 12:39).
6. All the previous narrations that were made up, for Jesus prophesying his crucifixion and resurrection, do not stand and resist in front of the storm of the narrations of the prophecies of his rescue: Prophecy, *"You will seek me and not find me, and where I am you cannot come"* (John 7:34). Prophecy, *"But I am not alone, because the father is with me"* (John 16:32). Prophecy, *"Be of good cheer, I have defeated the world* (the Jews)*"* (John 16:33). Prophecy, *"The sign of

the prophet Jonah" (Matt. 12:38–40; Luke 11:29–30). And prophecies of Psalms. Simply because one cannot have it both ways (true prophecies for his crucifixion and true prophecies for his rescue).

But why did Jesus ascribe his lifting up from the earth to the Jews? *"When you lift up the son of man."* In actual fact, while Jesus was discussing with the Jews in the Temple, he already knew that they sought to kill him. He said to them, rebuking them, *"But you seek to kill me, because my word has no place in you"* (John 8:37). Also, he said, *"But now you seek to kill me, a man who has told you the truth which I heard from God"* (John 8:40). So the seeking of the Jews to kill Jesus was the cause of lifting him up from the earth to heaven, as a great saving miracle for Jesus, to be safeguarded in heaven and purified him of those who tried to kill him. Then by this great saving miracle, the Jews would know that he was he (the Messiah) but they insisted, not believed. If the Jews did not seek to kill Jesus, he would remain on earth until his death. Therefore, their seeking to kill him became as if it was their seeking to lift him up to heaven, and so, the lifting was ascribed to them.

(4/8) The author of John inserts his own notion to the texts

1. In one of his early visits to Jerusalem, Jesus was discussing with the scribes and Pharisees in the treasury, as he taught in the temple (John 8:20), then he had hinted to them that their conspiracy would make him ascend from earth to heaven, and only then they will know that he is the Christ. In his dialogue with them, Jesus used the term "Son of Man." *"When you lift up the Son of Man, then you will know that I am He"* (John 8:28).

And in his last visit to Jerusalem, there was a gathering of people who stood by. Jesus talked to them, referring to his miraculous lifting up, from the earth to heaven. He said, *"And I, if I am lifted up from the earth, will draw all people to myself"* (John 12:32). Here Jesus did not use the term "Son of Man." He precisely said, *"I, if I am lifted up from the earth."* But the author of the Gospel of John inserted into the texts his own personal notion for the lifting up: to be hanged on a cross! He wrote in the following verse, *"In saying this he indicated the kind of death he was going to suffer"* (John 12:33). Not only that, but in the other following verse, the author exposed the manner in which his gospel was produced. He wrote that the people who stood by answered Jesus, saying, *"We have heard from the law that the Christ remains forever and how can you say, 'The son of man must be lifted up'? Who is this son of man?"* (John 12:34).

Did Jesus use the term "Son of Man" in his dialogue with those people who were standing? Surely not. It was never mentioned in that dialogue as it clear in the text! Rather, he said, *"And I, if I am lifted up."* But the author himself mixed up between two dialogues, between them a period more than one year. He mixed up the dialogue of Jesus in his early visit to Jerusalem with the scribes and Pharisees, in the treasury in the temple, when he used with them the term "Son of Man," with his dialogue on his last visit to Jerusalem with the people who were standing there, in which he did not use the term "Son of Man" and made those people talking and asking about the Son of Man. *"How can you say, 'The son of man must be lifted up'? Who is this son of man?"* even though Jesus had not mentioned this term with them at all. This confusion is one of the results of the human's fallible endeavors!

2. Another example of the human's fallible endeavors that relies upon the author's own notion: the author of John also narrated about the council that was gathered by the chief priests and Pharisees and they said,

> *What shall we do? For this man (Jesus) works many signs. If we let him alone like this, everyone will believe in him, and the Romans will come and take away both our place and nation. And one of them, Caiaphas, being high priest that year, said to them, "You know nothing at all, nor do you consider*

> *that it is expedient for us that one man should die for the people, and not that the whole nation should perish."* (John 11:47–50)

Then in the following verse, the author of John exposed the manner in which his gospel was produced when he inserted his own notion to the texts, trying to justify why the high priest, Caiaphas, suggested the killing of Jesus. He falsely wrote,

> *Now this he* (Caiaphas) *did not say on his own authority; but being high priest that year he was prophesied that Jesus would die for the nation,* (Jewish people) *and not for that nation only, but also that he would gather to gather in one the children of God who were scattered abroad.* (John 11:51–52)

If the Jewish Caiaphas had the ability to prophesy that Jesus would die for his nation, surely, he would be then the first one to believe that Jesus was sent from God for this mission. Also, if Caiaphas was prophesying that Jesus was going to die for his nation, as the author falsely justifying, so why then the same Caiaphas with the chief priests took another counsel that they might also put Lazarus to death? Was there any connection between killing this poor Lazarus and the death of Jesus for his nation? But the fact was that Caiaphas suggested killing Jesus to stop his nation of going away and believing in him. And for this reason, he also made plans to kill Lazarus too because on account of him many of the Jews went away and believed in Jesus. The author wrote,

> *Then a great many of the Jews knew that he was there; and they came, not for Jesus' sake only, but that they might also see Lazarus, whom he had raised from the dead. But the chief priests took counsel that they might also put Lazarus to death, because*

on account of him many of the Jews went away and believed in Jesus. (John 12:9–11)

Finally, two opposing false personal notions can be seen with two authors. This is the author of the Gospel of John, who claims that Caiaphas suggested the killing of Jesus because he knew by being high priest that year that *"Jesus would die for the nation"* (John 11:51). Paul claimed that the chief priests did not know that Jesus had come to die for the salvation of people because *"if they had known it, they would not have crucified the Lord of glory"* (1 Cor. 2:8).

Research 9
Did Jesus declare that he had passed through death and resurrection?

There are no such things by Jesus himself in Matthew, Mark, and John. Only Luke, who wrote that Jesus said to his disciples when he met with them after his appearance, *"Thus it is written, and thus it was necessary for the Christ to suffer and to rise from the dead the third day"* (Luke 24:46). But the fact is this, there is nothing of that at all. The evidence for this is in the following discussion:

Luke reported about Jesus appearing to two of his followers that were traveling to a village called Emmaus on the same Sunday that Jesus first appeared. They were talking together about the event of the crucifixion. And while they conversed, that Jesus himself drew near and went with them, but they did not know him. He asked them about their conversation, and one of them answered, telling the things that he thought had happened to Jesus. And he also said, *"Besides all this, today is the third day since these things happened. Yes, and certain women of our company, who arrived at the tomb early, astonished us, when they did not find his body, they came saying that they had also seen a vision of angels who said he was alive. And certain of those who were with us went to the tomb and found it just as the women had said, but him they did not see"* (Luke 24:21–24).

Then Jesus said to them, *"O foolish ones, and slow of heart to believe in all that the prophets have spoken! Ought not the Christ to have suffer these things and to enter his glory?"* (Luke 24:25–26). Then the author claimed that he explained to them what was said about Jesus in all the scriptures, beginning with the book of Moses and the writings of all the prophets (Luke 24:27). Then the author continued his narration that those two followers went back to Jerusalem and found the eleven disciples with the others gathered together, saying, *"The Lord is risen indeed, and has appeared to Simon!"* (Luke 24:34). The two then explained to them what had happened on the road and how Jesus was known to them in the breaking of bread (Luke 24:35).

If Simon (Peter) already had seen Jesus (24:34) and if the rest of the disciples also already believed that Jesus was risen, because they were together, saying, *"The Lord is risen indeed"* (24:34); and also, if the two followers of Jesus already had seen him and they even held him back, saying, *"Abide with us, for it is toward evening, and the day is far spent"* and he went in to stay with them. Now it came to pass, as he sat at the table with them, that he took bread, blessed, broke it, and gave it to them, then their eyes were opened and they knew him and he vanished from their sight"* (Luke 24:29–31); and they explained all of that to the disciples, so, surely, Peter, the two followers and the rest of the disciples would expect and wait to see Jesus at any moment.

But the confusion in Luke's narration is in the following narration. He narrated that while the disciples were still talking, Jesus himself came to them and stood in the midst of them.

> *Now as they said these things, Jesus himself stood in the midst of them and said to them, "Peace to you." But they were terrified and frightened, and supposed they had seen a spirit.* (Luke 24:36–37)

The confusion here is that the author included Peter, who already had met Jesus in the afternoon, and the two followers, who also had met him in the evening, to be also terrified and frightened with the rest of the disciples when they saw Jesus at night, although they knew of the appearance of Jesus and expected to see him at any moment. They were not frightened because of the way Jesus entered the room, for they were familiar with all his miracles, just as he did with the Jews when he hid and went out of the temple, going through the midst of them (John 8:59), but because they were thinking that they were seeing a ghost, which caused Jesus to ask them, *"Why are you troubled? And why do doubts arise in your hearts? Behold my hands and my feet, that it is I myself. Handle me and see, for a spirit does not have flesh and bones as you see I have"* (Luke 24:38–39) and to the point that *"He showed them his hands and his feet"* (Luke 24:40). But they still did not believe, so he asked them, *"Have any food here? So, they gave him a piece of a broiled fish and some honeycomb. And he took it and ate in their presence"* (Luke 24:41–43) to prove to them that he was the alive Jesus, not a ghost. The author tried to justify their insisting not to believe because of *"joy, and marveled"* (Luke 24:41).

How did Peter and the two followers believe that he was Jesus himself when they saw him for the first time in the afternoon, but when they saw him again at night, they did not believe because of joy and wonder? Was there not any joy and wonder when Peter met Jesus for the first time in the afternoon? What about the two followers who even had invited Jesus for a diner in the evening and sat down to eat with them, was there not any joy and wonder when they had recognized him?

The author continued his writing, claiming that Jesus said to his disciples, *"These are the words which I spoke to you while I was still with you, that all things must be fulfilled which were written in the law of Moses and the prophets and the Psalms concerning me." And he opened their understanding that they might comprehend the scriptures. Then he said to them, "Thus it is written, and thus it was necessary for the Christ to suffer and to rise from the dead the third day"* (Luke 24:44–46).

This narration in the gospel of Luke raises many questions such as the following:

1. No way that Jesus would say, *"Thus, it is written, and thus it was necessary for the Christ to suffer and to rise from the dead the third day"* (Luke 24:46), while he was the one who already challenged his enemy, the Jews, that they would not find him when they seek him? *"You will seek me and not find me, and where I am you cannot come"* (John 7:34).

And he said about them, *"Be of good cheer, I have defeated the world* (the Jews)*"* (John 16:33).

2. No way that Jesus would say, *"It was necessary for the Christ to suffer and to rise from the dead the third day,"* while he had previously told the Jews that he would have a rescue sign as the rescue sign of prophet Jonah, confirming that he is the Christ?

3. No way that Jesus would say, *"It was necessary for the Christ to suffer and to rise the third day,"* while he was the one who already informed the Jews that God had not left him alone: *"And He who sent me is with me. The Father has not left me alone, for I always do those things that please Him"* (John 8:29)? Also, he informed his disciples that he would never be alone because God would be with him: *"But I am not alone, because the father is with me"* (John 16:32).

4. Why did the two of Jesus followers not recognize their teacher? Neither his shape nor his voice was familiar all the way while they were conversing with him. And also, why did he disappear from them when they recognized him after he had sat down to eat with them? The author did not bother himself to find out why they did not recognize him and why the mark of the nails did not appear on his hands if he had really been crucified and the reason for his disappearance.

5. Luke wrote, claiming that Jesus said to the two followers on the road, *"O foolish ones, and slow of heart to believe in all that the prophets have spoken! Ought not the Christ to have suffer these things and to enter his glory?"* (Luke 24:25–26). He also claimed that Jesus said to the disciples, when he appeared to them in their gathering, *"These are the words which I spoke to you while I was still with you, that all things must be fulfilled which were written in the law of Moses and the prophets and the Psalms concerning me."* And he opened their understanding that they might comprehend the scriptures. Then he said to them, *"Thus it is written, and thus it was necessary for the Christ to suffer and to rise*

from the dead the third day" (Luke 24:44–46). Where are the words of the prophets written, regarding the necessity that the Christ should suffer death, and thus entering his glory? Where is it written in the Law of Moses, the Books of the Prophets, and the Psalms, about the necessity for the Christ to suffer and to rise from the dead the third day? Why was there no quotation of any text of the Law of Moses, the Books of the Prophets, and the Psalms that Luke claims that Jesus opened the disciples' understanding, that they might comprehend the Scriptures about the necessity for the Christ to suffer and to rise from the dead the third day? Did Jesus not quote Psalm 82:6 to prove to the Jews that he was not a real son of God, as in John 10:34–36? Indeed, thus, it is written in the Psalms, and thus it was necessary for the Christ should neither suffer nor taste death, as follows:

- *"But you, O God the Lord, deal with me for your name's sake; because your mercy is Good, deliver me"* (Ps. 109:21).
- *"Help me, O Lord my God! Oh, save me according to your mercy"* (Ps. 109:26).
- *"I will greatly praise the Lord with my mouth; yes, I will praise Him among the multitude. For He shall stand at the right hand of the poor, to saves him from those who condemn him"* (Ps. 109:30–31).
- *"Blessed is who considers the poor; the Lord will deliver (save) him in time of trouble. The Lord will preserve him and keep him alive, and he will be blessed on the earth; You will not deliver him to the will of his enemies"* (Ps. 41:1–2).
- *"I sought the Lord, and He heard me, and delivered me from all my fears"* (Ps. 34:4).
- *"Because he has set his love upon Me, therefore I will deliver him; I will set him on high, because he has known My name. He shall call upon Me, and I will answer him;*

I will be with him in trouble; I will deliver him and honor him" (Ps. 91:14–15).

- *"I shall not die, but live, and declare the works of the Lord. The Lord has chastened me severely, but he has not given me over to death... I will praise you, for you have answered me, and have become my salvation. The stone which the builders rejected has become the chief cornerstone"* (Ps. 118:17–18, 21–22).
- As for Judas, the psalms say that he fell into the very destruction and fell into the pit that he had dug and was caught by the net that he hid, and the evil shall slay the wicked, and those hate the righteous shall be condemned.
- *"He made a pit and dug it out and has fallen into the ditch which he made"* (Ps. 7:15).
- *"The wicked is snared in the work of his own hands"* (Ps. 9:16).
- *"The wicked plots against the just, and gnashes at him with his teeth. The Lord laughs at him, for He sees that his day is coming"* (Ps. 37:12–13).
- *"For without cause they have hidden their net for me in a pit, which they have dug without cause for my life. Let destruction come upon him unexpectedly and let his net that he has hidden catch himself; into that very destruction let him fall. Then I will be glad because of the Lord; I will be happy because he saved me"* (Ps. 35:7–9).
- *"Evil shall slay the wicked, and those hate the righteous shall be condemned"* (Ps. 34:21).

6. If Jesus, as Luke only claimed, already said to those two followers on the road, *"Ought not the Christ to have suffer these things and to enter his glory?"* (Luke 24:26). He also claimed that Jesus said to his disciples when he appeared to them in their gathering that, *"it was necessary for the Christ to suffer and to rise from the dead the third day"* (Luke 24:46), then why did he not declare to them at his last moment with them about the purpose of his alleged death and res-

urrection that to save humanity through the doctrine of atonement and redemption? And why did he not ask them to inform the people of the necessity to believe in him as a savior in order to attain eternal salvation?

The answer is this: there was no death, no resurrection, no mission, and no creed. But there were instructions from him to his disciples, at his last moment with them, to encourage people to repent so that their sins may be forgiven by baptizing in his name (joining his religion). He said to them, *"Repentance and remission of sins should be preached in his name"* (Luke 24:47).

Surely, the one who already had challenged the Jews (John 7:34) and had defeated them (John 16:33) and told that God has not left him alone (John 8:29) and a rescue miracle had happened to him like the rescue miracle of the prophet Jonah (Matt. 12:40; Luke 11:30) cannot be the one who was arrested by the Jews, then stripped him, mocked him, spat on him, struck him on the head with a reed, and crucified him. But this obvious confusion in Luke's narration should not surprise us because Luke was one of those authors who came after thirty to sixty years from the event of the crucifixion, and each author came with his own collection of rumors and uncertain narrations, but rather conflict with other's narrations, they put their own words in the mouth of Jesus to produce the gospel of Jesus's behalf devoid of inspiration and personal eyewitness.

Research 10
How different are the authors' narrations of some events?

1. The disciples' question about the name of the traitor.

Mark: All of them asked Jesus, one by one. *"And they began to be sorrowful, and to say to him one by one, 'Is it I?' And another said, 'Is it I?'"* (14:19).
Matthew: They all asked Jesus directly. *"And they were exceedingly sorrowful, and each of them began to say to him, 'Lord, is it I?'"* (26:22).

Luke: They questioned among themselves. *"Then they began to question among themselves, which of them it was who would do this thing"* (22:23).

John: They looked at each other and wondered about whom he spoke. Then only one disciple asked Jesus. *"Then the disciples looked at one another, perplexed about whom he spoke. now there was leaning on Jesus' bosom one of his disciple, whom Jesus loved. Simon Peter therefore motioned to him to ask who it was of whom he spoke. Then, leaning back on Jesus' breast, he said to him, "Lord, who is it?"* (13:22–25).

2. What did Jesus say to identify the disciple who would betray him?

Mark: *"It is one of the twelve, who dips with me in the dish"* (14:20).
Matthew: *"He who dipped his hand with me in the dish will betray me"* (26:23).
Luke: There is no answer, because the disciples did not ask Jesus but asked among themselves.
John: *"It is he to whom I shall give a piece of bread when I have dipped it"* (13:26).

3. What did Jesus do as soon as he arrived at the garden?

Mark: He separated from them to pray, taking three disciples with him. *"He said to his disciples, 'Sit here while I pray.' And he took Peter, James, and John with him"* (14:32–33).
Matthew: Copied from Mark (26:36–37).
Luke: He separated from them all and took no one with him. *"And he was withdrawn from them about a stone's throw and he knelt down and prayed"* (22:41).
John: He did not separate nor did he pray.

4. What happened to the troops and officers who came to arrest Jesus?

Mark: Nothing.

Matthew: Nothing.
Luke: Nothing.
John: *"They drew back and fell to the ground"* (18:6).

5. With whom was Peter when he denied Jesus three times?

Mark: With a servant girl two times, then with those who stood by (14:66–71).
Matthew: With a servant girl, then with another servant girl, then with those who stood by (26:69–74).
Luke: With a servant girl, then with a man, then with another man (22:56–60).
John: With a servant girl, then with those who stood by, then with one of the servants men (18:17–26).

6. Who carried the cross?

Mark: Simon, a Cyrenian (15:21).
Matthew: Simon, a Cyrenian (27:32).
Luke: Simon, a Cyrenian (23:26).
John: Jesus himself (19:17).

7. What are the last words of the substitute for Jesus?

Mark: *"Eloi, Eloi, lama sabachthani? Means My God, My God why have you forsaken me?"* (15:34).
Matthew: Copied from Mark (27:46).
Luke: *"Father, into your hands I commend my spirit"* (23:46).
John: *"It is finished"* (19:30).

8. What happened after the death of the substitute for Jesus?

Mark: *"Then the veil of the temple was torn in two from top to bottom"* (15:38).
Matthew: *"And behold, the veil of the temple was torn in two from top to bottom; and the earth quaked, and the rocks were split, and*

the graves were opened; and many bodies of the saints who had fallen asleep were raised; and coming out of the graves after his resurrection, they went into the holy city and appeared to many" (27:51–53).

Luke: He says that the following events occurred before he breathed his soul. *"And there was darkness over all the earth until the ninth hour. Then the sun was darkened, and the veil of the temple was torn in two"* (23:44–46).

John: Nothing happened.

Was the earthquake, split of rocks, the open graves, coming out of the dead, the darkness over all the earth, the darkened sun, and the torn of the veil of the Temple all of these are heavenly wrath for killing the Christ?

If the answer is yes, this contradicts the alleged death mission of Jesus. Or was it as a celebration of the success of the alleged death mission?

The author of the gospel of Matthew overstated the wrath/celebration! He even brought the dead out of the graves and made them enter the city! Did they walk naked?

Although the sources of the Gospels of Matthew, Luke, and Mark claimed that there were earthquakes, splitting of rocks, opening of graves and coming out of the dead, darkness over all the earth, darkness of the sun, and tearing of the veil of the temple, John's source did not feel anything of that!

9. Who of the two crucified thieves with the substitute of Jesus insulted him?

Mark: Both. *"And the two who were crucified with Jesus insulted him also"* (15:32).
Matthew: Both. *"Even the bandits who had been crucified with him insulted him in the same way"* (27:44).
Luke: Only one. *"One of the criminals hanging there hurled insults at him: 'Are not you the Messiah? Save yourself and us!' The other one, however, rebuked him, saying, 'Do not you fear God? You received the same sentence he did.'"* (23:39–40).

John: No one has insulted him. *"And they also crucified two other men, one on each side"* (19:18).

10. Who went to the tomb first, early Sunday morning?

Mark: Three women—Mary Magdalene; Mary, the mother of James; and Salome (16:1).
Matthew: Two women—Mary Magdalene and the other Mary (28:1).
Luke: Many women—Mary Magdalene; Joanna; Mary, the mother of James; and the other women with them (24:10).
John: Only one woman—Mary Magdalene (20:1).

11. Who were the persons near the tomb?

Mark: A young man was sitting inside the tomb (16:5).
Matthew: An angel was sitting outside the tomb (28:2).
Luke: Two men were standing inside the tomb (24:4).
John: Two angels were sitting inside the tomb (20:12).

12. To whom did Jesus appear first?

Mark: To Mary Magdalene (16:9).
Matthew: To Mary Magdalene and the other Mary (28:9).
Luke: To two of his followers (24:15).
John: To Mary Magdalene (20:14).

13. Did the disciples believe the two followers when they told them about the appearance of Jesus to them on the road?

Mark: They did not believe them. *"And they went and told it to the rest, but they did not believe them either"* (16:13).
Matthew: No narration about them.
Luke: They believed them, and even supported them, because they found the disciples, saying, "Jesus is risen indeed, and has appeared to Simon!" *So they rose up that very hour and returned to Jerusalem and found the eleven and those who were with them*

gathered together, saying, "The lord is risen indeed, and has appeared to Simon!" And they told about the things that had happened on the road (24:33–35).

John: No narration about them.

14. When and where the appearance of Jesus and for how long was it?

Mark: Although there was a message from Jesus to his disciples, carried by Mary Magdalene that they should go to Galilee to see him there (16:7), they did not believe her (16:11). They remained in Jerusalem. The evidence is that the two disciples, who went into the country and saw Jesus on the road before the sun set on Sunday, returned back evening to Jerusalem and told the rest of the disciples, but they did not believe them either (16:12–13) Finally, he appeared to the disciples in Jerusalem as they sat at the table, Sunday night. He rebuked them for not believing (16:14). And then after he had spoken to them, he ascended into heaven (16:19). This means that he stayed on earth after his appearance less than twenty-four hours. He then ascended from Jerusalem.

Matthew: The disciples complied with Jesus's request and went to Galilee. *"Then the eleven disciples went away into Galilee, to the mountain which Jesus had appointed for them"* (28:16). Then Jesus came and spoke to them. The author did not say anything about the ascension.

Luke: On the same day that Jesus first appeared, Sunday, *"two (followers) of them were traveling that same day* (Sunday) *to a village called Emmaus... Jesus himself drew near and went with them. But their eyes were restrained, so that they did not know him"* (24:13–16). When it was toward evening, they asked Jesus, *"Abide with us, for it is toward evening, and the day is far spent." And he went in to stay with them"* (24:28–29). At the moment that Jesus start to bless and break the bread, *"their eyes were opened, and they knew him; and he vanished from their sight... So they rose up that very hour and returned to Jerusalem, and found the eleven and those who were with them gathered together... And they told about the things that had happened on the road... Now as they said these things, Jesus himself stood in the midst of them and said to them, "Peace to you"* (24:30–36). After Jesus spoke to them at that meeting (Sunday night), *"He led them out as far as Bethany, and he lifted his hands and blessed them. Now it came to pass, while he blessed them, that he was parted from them and carried up into heaven"* (24:50–51).

According to the previous texts, all these events, from the first appearance of Jesus until his ascension, occurred in one day, Sunday. This means that Jesus stayed on earth less than twenty-four hours. Then he ascended from Bethany.

But Luke, in his other book Acts of the Apostles, wrote in the introduction that Jesus stayed on earth from his first appearance until his ascension forty days, appearing to his disciples and speaking of the things pertaining to the kingdom of God. *"To whom he also presented himself alive after his suffering by many infallible proofs, being seen by them during forty days and speaking of the things pertaining to the Kingdom of God"* (Acts 1:3).

John: On the same day, Sunday at evening, being the first day of the week, Jesus came where the disciples were together in Jerusalem (20:19), *"And after eight days his disciples were again inside, and Thomas with them. Jesus came, the doors being shut, and stood in the midst, and said, 'Peace to you'"* (20:26). *"After these things Jesus showed himself again to the disciples at the sea of Tiberias"* (21:1) That is, he stayed on earth after his first appearance more than eight days. But the author had not collected any narration about the most important event in Jesus's life, the ascension, because he wrote nothing about it!

Summary of the topic of the crucifixion

God appointed the Christ Jesus to the house of Israel only (Matt. 15:24). He supported him in his mission with the Holy Spirit and with great signs. But because of envy, the Jewish religious authorities did not accept him. They even gathered a council to discuss what they shall do with him, for he worked many signs. And if they let him alone like this, everyone would believe in him, and the Romans will come and take away both their place and nation (John 11:47–48). The result that came out of that meeting was that Jesus must be put to death from that day, and they plotted for that. God too plotted, but to save Jesus and kill the traitor disciple, Judas. It was in three phases, as follows:

1. During his mission in carrying his teaching to their cities, towns, the temple and their synagogues, God was with him in all the ways that he did to defend himself.
2. At the end of his mission, when the Jews issued the decree to put him to death (John 11:53), God also was with Jesus. So He restrained the Jews of seeing Jesus two days before the Passover until he ascended into heaven. *"See! Your house is left to you desolate; for I say to you, you shall see me no more"* (Matt. 23:38–39). *"A little while longer and the world (the Jews) will see me no more"* (John 14:19).

Then while the chief priests and the scribes were trying to find a way to put Jesus to death secretly, Judas came and made a deal with them to hand Jesus over to them without the people knowing about it (Luke 22:2–6). God did not give Judas and the Jews the chance to carry out their plot. He sent the Holy Spirit to led Jesus away to the place of hiding to save him on earth for a while, while the Jews were deceived by arresting and killing Judas, who had appeared to them as though he was Jesus.

3. After crucifying Judas, Jesus left the place of hiding on Sunday and appeared to his disciples. Then God raised him to heaven, to free him permanently from his Jewish enemies and protect him, away from earthly time and laws, waiting for the time of his second coming to earth with another mission, as his return will be a sign for the coming of the hour of ending the life on the planet earth, and then the end of the entire universe. At the time of the second coming of Christ Jesus, the imposter Christ (the Antichrist) will

appear on earth with a false message, but the true Christ, Jesus, will kill that Antichrist. Jesus, of course, will return to earth because he is a pure human being who dies and is buried at his fixed appointed time.

The Jews said in boast, "We killed Jesus." Then, because of the exact likeness of the substitute, Judas, with Jesus in all aspects and the escaping of all the disciples for fear of the Jews, the rumor of crucifying Jesus spread among people and the disciples too; but in fact, they killed him not, nor crucified him. But it appeared so to them. And those who differed in the matter of the killing were in doubt. They had no certain knowledge. They followed nothing but conjecture. The thing that supported the rumor to spread was that the people had already seen the person who resembled Jesus led publicly to be crucified and not knowing that the real Jesus was indeed safe somewhere else. Jesus did not give his disciples any details about how God would rescue him in order to stop the news reaching his enemies, the Jews. But he did give them some allusions to his survival. Therefore, the hypothetical picture in the minds of the early Christians was thus: they just added Jesus to the list of the previous murdered prophets by the Jews, but he was different from them because he was resurrected, then ascended to heaven.

Going back to the main question, "Was Jesus really crucified?" The answer is in the following verse: *"In his life on earth, Jesus made his prayers and requests with loud cries and tears to God, who was able to save him from death and was heard because of his godly fears."*

Is this verse in the Bible? Absolutely! Did God answer the prayers, the requests, the loud cries, and the tears of Jesus? The verse says that Jesus was heard by God. Did God save Jesus from death? The verse states clearly without any doubt that God had already saved Jesus from death. Who wrote this verse and where? The one who said, *"And if Christ is not risen, then our preaching is vain, and your faith is also vain"* (1 Cor. 15:14) is the one who had said, *"God was able to save Jesus from death"* (Heb. 5:7).

Yes, it is Paul himself! What confusion is this? It is as if the one who placed all his eggs in one basket broke them! Did not Paul lay the foundations of his fake church on the edge of a sand-cliff? God already struck at the foundation of his church, and then the roof fell down upon him so that it crumbled to pieces with him. So who is this Paul?

CHAPTER 5

The Falsifier

Who was Paul?

We know about Paul not only from his own letters, but also from the book of Acts, which was written by Luke, the admirer and missionary companion of Paul, who was also the author of the Gospel. But the information given by Paul about himself needs to be cautiously looked at because everyone has strong reasons for portraying himself in the best light possible. While the author of the book of Acts was clear and direct with his purpose and reason of writing the book, it was also a dedication to the same man, Theophilus. Meaning, it was not an inspired book, but a historical book, littered with a pure human effort. It cannot be a source of belief. Although Luke had accompanied Paul on two missionary trips, he did not present Paul in the same light Paul presented himself in his letters.

Paul at first was called Saul of Tarsus (Acts 9:11). He gave information about himself as follows: *I am a Jew from Tarsus, in Cilicia, a citizen of no mean city"* (Acts 21:39). *"I am an Israelite, of the seed of Abraham, of the tribe of Benjamin"* (Rom. 11:1), *"circumcised the eighth day, of the stock of Israel, of the tribe of Benjamin, a Hebrew of the Hebrews; concerning the law, a Pharisee* (Phil. 3:5).

The young Saul left Tarsus and came to the land of Israel. He said about himself, *"I am indeed a Jew, born in Tarsus of Cilicia, but brought up in this city* (Jerusalem) *at the feet of Gamaliel, taught accord-*

ing to the strictness of our fathers' law, and was zealous toward God as you all are today" (Acts 22:3).

Therefore, on the basis of origin and religion, Paul was an Israelite Jew. As for citizenship, he was a Roman citizen from Tarsus. He was even called Saul of Tarsus, and this indicates that he moved to Jerusalem as a young man, not a child. *"But Paul said to the police officers, 'We were not found guilty of any crime, yet they whipped us in public—and we are Roman citizens!'"* (Acts 16:37). *"And as they bound him with thongs, Paul said to the centurion who stop by, 'Is it lawful for you to scourge a man who is a Roman, and uncondemned?' When the centurion heard that, he went and told the commander, saying, 'Take care what you do, for this man is a Roman.' Then the commander came and said to him, 'Tell me, are you a Roman?' He said, 'Yes.' And the commander answered, 'With a large sum I obtained this citizenship.' And Paul said, 'But I was born a citizen'"* (Acts 22:25–28).

Paul and the early followers of Jesus

Jesus and Paul never met. They did not know each other. Paul started to appear in the picture with the disciples and followers of Jesus after the ascension to heaven. Luke reported in his book, the Acts, many incidents regarding the relation between Paul and the early followers of Jesus as well as Paul himself did in his letters. All these narrations by the two require research and analysis. The first appearance of the name Saul (who later became Paul) in the book of Acts was in chapter 7. He was involved, to some extent, in the death of Stephen, one member of the groups who worked with the disciples.

Stephen opened the door for Paul!

Luke wrote in his book the Acts, *"And Stephen, full of faith and power, did great wonders and signs among the people"* (Acts 6:8). Then there arose some Jews, who were members of the synagogue of the freedmen that had Jews from different locations, disputing with Stephen. But they were not able to resist the wisdom and the spirit by which he spoke. Then they secretly induced men to say, "We have heard him speaking against Moses and God." In this way, they stirred up the people, the elders, and the teachers; and they came upon him, seized him, and brought him to the Council. They also set up false witnesses to tell lies about him. They said, *"This man does not cease to speak blasphemous words against this holy place and the law; for we have heard him say that this Jesus of Nazareth will destroy this place and change the customs which Moses delivered to us." And all who sat in the council, looking steadfastly at him, saw his face as the face of an angel!"* (Acts 6:9–15).

Then the high priest asked Stephen, "Are these things so?" Stephen answered with a long speech. He started talking about Abraham, Moses, David, and Solomon; and then he said to them, *"You stiff-necked and uncircumcised in heart and ears! You always resist the Holy Spirit; as your fathers did, so do you. Which of the prophet did your fathers not persecute? And they killed those who foretold the coming of the just one* (Jesus), *of whom you now become the betrayers and murderers, who have received the law by the direction of angels and have not kept it"* (Acts 7:1–53).

Here comes the shock in the rest of the narration!

"As the members of the Council listened to Stephen, they became furious and ground their teeth at him in anger. But Stephen, full of the Holy Spirit, looked up to heaven and saw God's glory and Jesus standing at the right hand of God. And said, 'Look, I see heaven opened and the son of man standing at the right hand of God.' With a loud cry the Council members covered their ears with their hands. Then they all rushed at him at once, threw him out of the city, and stoned him. The witnesses laid down their clothes at the feet of a young man named Saul. They kept on stoning Stephen as he called out to the Lord, 'Lord Jesus, receive my spirit.' He knelt down and cried out in a loud voice, 'Lord! Do not charge them with this sin.' He said this and died" (Acts 7:54–60). *"Now Saul was consenting to his death"* (Acts 8:1).

We cannot confirm the validity of all the details of this narration, because some of the details contradict the fundamentals of true faith brought by all the messengers of God. All the prophets and the messengers including Jesus Himself did not have the same alleged opportunity of Stephen, to see heaven open and the glory of God. Was Stephen more righteous than Jesus and the prophets? If the author Luke says that Stephen saw Jesus standing at the right hand of God, it is a claim of seeing two distinct personages next to each other. That means he already individualized each one with his own limited magnitude, space, and direction.

This narration of Luke creates many problems for the Pauline Christian, such as what about the third God of the Trinity? Where was He? And how was it possible for Jesus to have been "standing on the right hand of God" if they (God and Jesus) are one and the same entity? Paul says, *"When He raised him from the dead and seated him at his right hand in the heavenly place"* (Eph. 1:20). And in Mark we read, *"So then after the Lord had spoken to them, he was received up into heaven, and sat down at the right hand of God"* (Mark 16:19). While Luke in his book the Acts says that Stephen saw Jesus standing at the right hand of God rather than sitting. Did he want to prove that Jesus is not always sitting at the right hand of God? Anyway, Stephen would deserve the stoning as far as the Jews might be concerned, for claiming to have seen heaven open and the glory of God and a distinct personage was standing at the right hand of God. And also, he deserves the stoning from the Trinitarian's perspective due to his acknowledging only two personages rather than three. Exalted is God above all that they attribute to Him.

Another problem with Luke and Stephen: Luke at first presented Stephen, "Full of faith and power." And in the end, he presented him as a polytheistic person, neglecting the true God and, therefore, calling only upon the servant Jesus, saying, *"Lord Jesus, receive my spirit." He knelt down and cried out in a loud voice, "Lord! Do not charge them with this sin"* (Acts 7:59–60). In his speech, Stephen considered Jesus as a righteous servant, but when the stoning began, he called upon him as a deity, ascribing him with God's divinity.

Young Paul, who was standing there, guarding the clothes at his feet while stoning Stephen, seemed to think of Stephen being able to see Jesus standing at the right hand of God (trillions to a large power of light-years) and hearing him calling Jesus. Paul kept this within himself, until the time came that it opened for him the door into Jesus.

Paul persecuted the followers of Jesus

Luke says in the book of Acts, *"Now Saul was consenting to his death* (Stephen's death). *At that time a great persecution arose against the church which was at Jerusalem; and they were all scattered throughout the regions of Judea and Samaria, except the apostles"* (Acts 8:1–2). Luke reported in the book of Acts four stories of Paul's persecution of the followers of Christ following the death of Stephen:

The first narration

In chapter 8, as the author Luke continued to narrate thus: *"Saul tried to destroy the Church; going from house to house, he dragged out the believers, both men and women, and threw them into prison"* (Acts 8:3). If Paul was consenting to the death of Stephen, surely this young man was not just a guard on the clothes of those who stoned Stephen and he could not havoc of the church, enter every house, and drag off men and women to commit them to prison on his own, unless he had an authority. Paul said, *"That is what I did in Jerusalem. I received authority from the chief priests and put many of God's people in prison; and when they were sentenced to death, I also voted against them"* (Acts 26:10).

The second narration

In chapter 9, where Luke narrates about the connection between Paul and the high priest, he said, *"Then Saul, still breathing threats and murder against the disciples of the Lord, went to the high priest and asked letters from him to the synagogues of Damascus, so that if he found any who were of the Way, whether men or women, he might bring them bound to Jerusalem"* (Acts 9:1–2).

The third narration

In chapter 22, Luke records here Paul's account of his experience in persecution of the followers of Christ, as he was addressing a large group of angry Jews who seized Paul and dragged him out of the temple and beat him, because of his teachings that opposing their law. And as they were seeking to kill him, the news came to the Roman commander, who came with soldiers and took Paul into the barracks, and the multitude of the people followed after. And as Paul was about to be led into the barracks, he asked for permission to speak to the multitude. So, when he was given permission, Paul stood on the stairs and addressed them, saying, after he had introduced himself, *"I was just dedicated to God as are all of you who are here today. I persecuted to death the people who followed this way. I arrested men and women and threw them into prison. The high priest and the whole Council can prove that I am telling the truth. I received from them letters written to fellow Jews in Damascus, so I went there to arrest these people and bring them back in chains to Jerusalem to be punished"* (Acts 22:3–5).

The fourth narration

Luke wrote that while Paul was addressing the angry Jews and telling his story to them, they could not bear to hear more from him, and then they raised their voices and said, "Away with such a fellow from the earth, for he is not fit to live!" So the commander ordered him to be brought into the barracks. The next day the commander commanded the chief priests and all their council to appear and brought Paul down and set him before them, because he wanted to know for certain why he was accused by the Jews, and then a dispute occurred between them, causing the commander to bring Paul into the barracks. As for the Jews, they plotted to kill Paul. When the commander knew of their plot, he sent Paul guarded to the Roman governor Felix in Caesarea and wrote to him a letter about the matter.

The governor Felix commanded the chief priests and the elders to come and brought Paul to hear from them, but they came to no conclusion. Then after two years, Festus succeeded Felix; and Felix, wanting to do the Jews a favor, left Paul bound. When Festus had come to the province, he went to Jerusalem. Then the high priest and the chief men of the Jews asked him to bring Paul to Jerusalem, while they lay in ambush along the road to kill him. But Festus ordered that Paul should be kept at Caesarea and asked the Jews who have authority to go with him and accuse Paul to see if there is any fault in him. On the next day after they had arrived at Caesarea, sitting on the judgment seat, he commanded Paul to be brought. The Jews laid many complaints against him, which Paul protested against.

Then Festus said to Paul, "Are you willing to go to Jerusalem and there be judged before me concerning these things?"

Paul said, "I appeal to Caesar."

Festus answered, "To Caesar you shall go!"

And after some days, King Agrippa came to Caesarea to greet Festus, then Festus laid Paul's case before the king.

Then Agrippa said to Festus, "I also would like to hear the man myself."

Festus answered, "Tomorrow, you shall hear him" (Acts 22–25).

So the next day, Agrippa said to Paul when was brought, "You are permitted to speak for yourself."

So Paul started to speak, and among what he said are these words:

> I myself thought that I should do everything I could against the cause of Jesus of Nazareth. That is what I did in Jerusalem. I received authority from the chief priests and put many of God's people in prison; and when they were sentenced to death, I also voted against them. Many times, I had them punished in every synagogue and tried to make them deny their faith. I was so furious with them that I even went to foreign cities to persecute them. (Acts 26:9–11)

The narrations of Paul's persecution of the followers of Christ are full of mysteries. But there is no doubt that the decision of the persecution was issued by the high priest, who has official authority over the temple and has his own forces. Paul cannot destroy the church, going from house to house, dragging out the believers, both men and women, and threw them into prison on his own; but there must be trooping to follow his command in the persecution of the followers of Christ. Therefore, for some reason, Paul was chosen by the chief priests to act on their behalf in the implementation of their plan to stop the expansion of the religion of Christ in the Jewish community and was provided with men.

Here are some important questions: Where was the authority of the Roman governor when Paul was keeping up his violent threats of murder on the followers of Christ (Acts 9:1)? Can the chief priests and their client Paul kill people while they were under the control of the Roman state? Can they enter the houses and drag people to prison and bring followers of Christ in Damascus to Jerusalem to be punished on their own? Are not the prisons under the authority of the Roman governor? Is not the Roman governor the one to approve the entering to prisons and release prisoners? And even the Jews had a custom that the Roman governor always set free prisoner for them during the Passover (John 18:39). Why suddenly did come to the mind of the young Paul the idea of cleaning Damascus, the far city, from the followers of Christ while the disciples are still in Jerusalem and the other followers are scattered in nearby Judea and Samaria? Is there still room in the prison of Jerusalem for the men and women in Damascus to be brought to Jerusalem? Was Paul equipped with enough power to bring them all bound in chains as prisoners all the way to Jerusalem? Or did he take with him only some anonymous false witnesses that he carefully selected for a purpose in himself?

Suddenly Paul announced his conversion to the religion of Christ

The story of Paul's conversion to Christianity, or "the turning point" in his life, was on the road to Damascus. It started when he went to the high priest and asked letters from him to the synagogues of Damascus, so that if he found any follower of Jesus, whether men or women, he might bring them bound to Jerusalem. (Acts 9:1–2). The story recorded in the book of Acts in three separate narrations are full of discrepancies and confusion. In any sort of investigation, the one who tells the truth keeps unchanged in his statements, even with repetitions, making it very hard for anyone to accuse him of giving false witness. But the one who pretends to be speaking the truth, surely, he will be easily exposed when he repeats the narration of his story. The narrations are as follows:

The first narration

In Acts chapter 9, as related by the author Luke.

> *As he (Saul) journeyed he came near Damascus, and suddenly a light shone around him from heaven. Then he fell to the ground, and heard a voice saying to him, "Saul, Saul, why are you persecuting me?" And he said, "Who are you, Lord?" And the lord said, "I am Jesus whom you are persecuting. It is hard for you to kick against the goads." So, he trembling and astonished, said, "Lord, what do you want me to do?" And the lord said to him, "Arise and go into the city, and you will be told what you must do." And the men who were journeyed with him stood speechless, hearing a voice but seeing no one. Then Saul arose from the ground, and when his eyes were opened, he saw no one. But they led him by the hand and brought him into Damascus. And he was three days without sight, and neither ate nor drank.* (Acts 9:3–9)

Then the author Luke wrote: *"Now there was a certain disciple at Damascus named Ananias"* (Acts 9:10). And Jesus came to him in a vision and asked him to go to the house where Paul is staying, and he gave him the address: the street called Straight, house of Judas. And he said to him, *"Inquire at the house of Judas for one called Saul of Tarsus, for behold, he is praying"* (Acts 9:11). The author also tells us that at the same time, Paul saw in a vision a man named Ananias coming in and putting his hand on him so that he might receive his sight (Acts 9:12). *"And Ananias went his way and entered the house, and laying his hands on him, he said, "Brother Saul, the lord Jesus, who appeared to you on the road as you came, has sent me that you may receive your sight and be filled with the holy spirit"* (Acts 9:17). Then Paul was baptized and spent some days with the disciples at Damascus preaching in the synagogues. Then after many days were past, the Jews plotted to kill him. But their plot became known to Paul, and he succeeded to leave Damascus and went to Jerusalem to join the disciples there (Acts 9:18–20, 23–26).

The second narration

In Acts chapter 22, the author Luke continues to write down Paul's own account as he was addressing the angry Jews who wanted to kill him. After telling the Jews about his experience of persecuting the followers of Christ, Paul began to tell them the story of his conversion to Christianity, and he said to them,

> *Now it happened, as I journeyed and came near Damascus at about noon, suddenly a great light from heaven shone around me. And I fell to the ground and heard a voice saying to me, "Saul, Saul, why are you persecuting me?" So, I answered, "Who are you Lord?" And he said to me, "I am Jesus of Nazareth, whom you are persecuting." Now those who were with me indeed saw the light and were afraid, but they did not hear the voice of him who spoke to me. So, I said, "What shall I do, Lord?" And the Lord said to me, "Arise and go into Damascus, and there you will be told all things which are appointed for you to do." And since I could not see for the glory of that light, being led by the hand of those who were with me, I came into Damascus.*

> *Then one, Ananias, a devout man according to the law, having a good testimony with all the Jews who dwelt there, came to me; and he stood and said to me, "Brother Saul, receive your sight." And at the same hour I looked up at him. Then he said, "The God of our fathers has chosen you that you should know His will, and see the Just One (Jesus), and hear the voice of his mouth. For you will be his witness to all men of what you have seen and heard. And now why are you waiting? Arise and be baptized, and wash away your sins, calling on the name of the Lord."* (Acts 22:6–16)

The third narration

In Acts chapter 26, the author Luke continues to write down Paul's own account as he was addressing King Agrippa, telling him the story of his conversion to Christianity. He said,

> *As I journeyed to Damascus with authority and commission from the chief priest. At midday, O King, along the road I saw a light from heaven, brighter than the sun, shining around me and those who journeyed with me. And when we all had fallen to the ground, I heard a voice speaking to me and saying in the Hebrew language, 'Saul, Saul why are you persecuting me? It is hard for you to kick against the goads." So I said, "Who are you, Lord?" And he said, "I am Jesus, whom you are persecuting. But rise and stand on your feet; for I have appeared to you for this purpose, to make you a minister and a witness both of the things which you have seen and of the things which I will yet reveal to you. I will deliver you from the Jewish people, as well as from the Gentiles, to whom I now send you, to open their eyes and to turn them from darkness to light,*

and from the power of Satan to God, that they may receive forgiveness of sins and an inheritance among those who are sanctified by faith in me." (Acts 26:12–18)

There is no doubt that Paul was an intellectual, enlightened, active, influential, philosopher and a skillful leader. He was well positioned to carry out his ambition, through the delegated authority of the high priest to him. He was also proficient and clever in that he did not enter Christianity through the door of the disciples. Rather, he entered from the door that Stephen had opened for him. He entered through Jesus himself and appointed himself as an apostle and Jesus's spokesman, away from the authority of the disciples. Paul thought about Stephen's claim of seeing the heavens opened and Jesus standing at the right hand of God and then calling Jesus, so he decided to practice that himself, so he chose the place and the witnesses.

If Paul's main goal was to bring the followers of Christ in Damascus to Jerusalem to be punished, why did he not follow the followers of Christ who fled from him to nearby Judea and Samaria? Why did he choose distant Damascus despite the hardship of bringing the followers of Christ to Jerusalem? He had chosen distant Damascus to formalize his journey in order to achieve a personal goal that came to his mind while he was guarding the clothes of those stoning Stephen and heard him calling Jesus, who he claimed had seen him standing at the right hand of God! He will not be able to achieve his goal once he leaves his house and declares that he has become a Christian, for Jesus appeared to him, because he knows that no one will believe him. Likewise, he could not claim that Jesus appeared to him on a personal journey because there would be no strong reason for such a claim. He was not interested in following the followers of Christ that fled from him to nearby Judea and Samaria, because he might not find anyone to play the same role that was played by a man named Ananias, whom Luke said of him that he was a disciple of Christ, while Paul issued for him a recommendation testimony from all the Jews, the enemy of the disciples, in Damascus! So in order to formalize his journey, and that it is for the sake of persecuting the followers of Christ as an acceptable reason to claim the appearance of Christ on the road, Paul himself went to the high priest and suggested that he give him letters to the synagogues of distant Damascus, claiming to bring the followers of Christ from there to be punished in Jerusalem.

Paul returned from the journey of Damascus declaring that Christ appeared to him on the road and appointed him an apostle to the Gentiles and that had a direct line with him. And through this direct line, and by his own techniques and patience, he succeeded to achieve his dream of having an ideological leadership in the society through his own church that was different from the church of the disciples and his own doctrines that were different from Jesus's doctrines. He took some items from Jesus's life such as his miraculous birth, rumor of his death and resurrection, the ascension and the returning and mixed them with some elements of the faith of the most popular, classic superstitious religions of pagan cults and created his very own new Christianity. So instead of Paul truly converting to Christianity, he converted Christianity to his own thoughts and philosophy. Paul's Christianity has remained as a great trial for nations ever since. It was the will of God that allowed Satan to use Paul to bring this great trial so it would become as a way of testing the faith of the people. The Christianity of Paul will remain so until the second coming of Jesus when all the truth about him will be clearly manifested again for all to see.

Anyone who believes that Jesus is a human messenger believes also that he cannot appear or communicate with people by inspiration from his place in heaven. The one who inspires the messengers is only God. So there is no need to look for witnesses for Paul's claim because certainly he is a liar.

Jesus already reminded people to be aware of this self-appointed apostle, who came in his own name. He said, *"I have come in my father's name, and you do not receive me; if another comes in his own name, him you will receive"* (John 5:43). Who is the person who came in his own name and had more coverage in the new testaments than Jesus, or even his disciples? The answer is Paul. Therefore, whoever the truth has been clear to him, but he remains with his inherited faith, has voluntarily chosen to fall into the trial and will be condemned. As for those whom the truth has been clear to them and hold on to it, they have passed this trial.

Discrepancies in the narrations of the alleged conversion

It is not the contradictions in the narrators that prove Paul's lie, but only one thing is with you, the reader. The reader who believes that Jesus is pure human being sent by God and not a literal Son of God, this is enough to know that Paul is a falsifier, because the human Jesus cannot possibly appear and communicate with any of the people of the earth and reveal to Paul his false gospel as well as all the messengers of God. But the one who believes that Jesus is God or a real son of God, he should first ascertain the truth about Jesus in order to see the reality of Paul. The contradictions in the narrations of Paul's alleged conversion to Christ's religion are as follows:

1. In the first narration there is a record about the men who were traveling with Paul in his journey to Damascus, thus, *"And the men who were journeyed with him stood speechless, hearing a voice but seeing no one"* (Acts 9:7). His companions here were hearing and not seeing. But in the second narration, the situation of the companions was reversed. *"Now those who were with me indeed saw the light and were afraid, but they did not hear the voice of him who spoke to me"* (Acts 22:9). His companions here were seeing and not hearing. While in the third narration, the companions did not hear or see anything, because they all fell to the ground with Paul. *"We all had fallen to the ground"* (Acts 26:14). In any regular court of law, such contradictory testimonies would be held suspect and dismissed.
2. In the first and the second narrations, only Paul fell to the ground. *"Then he fell to the ground"* (Acts 9:4). And the men who were with him remained standing. They were speechless in the first narration. *"And the men who were journeyed with him stood speechless"* (Acts 9:7) and were just

afraid in the second narration. *"Now those who were with me indeed saw the light and were afraid"* (Acts 22:9). But in the third narration, Paul and all his men had fallen to the ground. *"We all had fallen to the ground"* (Acts 26:14). Such contradictory testimonies would be thrown out of any court of law.

3. Paul fabricated two different scenarios for his alleged conversion to the religion of Christ, according to the audience speaking to them. In the scenario of the second narration, Paul was addressing angry Jews at him, so his narration of events were like this:

- The fall was only for Paul while his companions remained standing awake.
- Paul was careful that his companions don't hear the alleged dialogue of Jesus with him. And because they did not fall with him to the ground in this narration, therefore Paul did not make Jesus to talk to him about what he should do, even though he had disrupted the sense of hearing of his companions. *"Now those who were with me indeed saw the light and were afraid, but they did not hear the voice of him who spoke to me."* Rather, he claimed that Jesus had only asked him to go to Damascus and there would be told (alone) about what he should do by a mediator who Paul said that his name is Ananias, who had a devoutness testimony from Paul himself and also a testimony of goodness from all the Jews in Damascus.
- Because Paul was speaking to Jews, he did not say anything about his alleged primary mission as a messenger for non-Jews.

While in the third narration, Paul was addressing Gentiles and Roman pagans (Romans, political authority) at the auditorium. They were King Agrippa; the Roman governor Festus; the companion of the king Bernice, and the commanders and the prominent men of the city (Acts 25:23). So his narration of events was like this:

- The fall was for Paul and his companions as well.
- In this scenario, there was no need for Jesus to ask Ananias in a vision to go to a house in Damascus, where Paul dwelt, because there was no need of using this Ananias to play the role of mediator. Rather, Paul showed Jesus as if he had enough time to take charge of the whole matter by himself on the road. He claimed that Jesus asked him alone to rise and stand on his feet and delivered a direct speech to him at the site on the road, telling him what to do in detail.
- Since Paul wanted to show Jesus in this scenario speaking to him directly on the road with details about his alleged inauguration as a messenger, so he made all his companions fall to the ground with him and then claimed that he was the only one whom Jesus had awakened and addressed him directly with this speech:

> *I am Jesus, whom you are persecuting. But rise and stand on your feet; for I have appeared to you for this purpose, to make you a minister and a witness both of the things which you have seen and of the things which I will yet reveal to you. I will deliver you from the Jewish people, as well as from the Gentiles, to whom I now send you, to open their eyes and to turn them from darkness to light, and from the power of Satan to God, that they may receive forgiveness of sins and an inheritance among those who are sanctified by faith in me.* (Acts 26:15–18)

Even the pagan Festus realized that it was just a hallucination. He said with a loud voice, *"Paul, you are beside yourself! Much learning is driving you mad!"* (Acts 26:24).

- Paul did not dare to claim that Jesus also awoke his companions so that they might hear his alleged speech with him about appointing him as a messenger so that they can be eyewitnesses to the inauguration. Rather, he had disrupted the sense of hearing of his companions in the second narration because he did not make them fall to the ground with him. Not only that, but he had mentioned nothing about them after his claim that they have brought him to Damascus. He just had forgotten all about them. Luke, the author of Acts of the Apostles, also ignored them. Had the incident been true, the companions of Paul would have a role in the narration as eyewitnesses, and they would have mentioned the extent of the impact of the incident on their faith, as Jews, in Christ.

- Paul confirmed to his Roman audience the claim that Jesus had appointed him as their messenger (to the Gentiles, non-Jews).

Again, a case like this in a simple court of law would be held suspect and hence dismissed because of the contradictory statements of Paul about the place where he was informed by Jesus. Was it on the road or in Damascus?

4. The author Luke wrote in the first narration about Ananias, the man whom Paul claimed he came to him in the house where he stayed in Damascus, that he is a disciple of Christ. *"Now there was a certain disciple at Damascus named was Ananias"* (Acts 9:10). While Paul said of Ananias in the second narration, while addressing the angry Jews, *"Then one, Ananias, a devout man according to the law, having a good testimony with all the Jews who dwelt there"* (Acts 22:12). How did all the Jews in Damascus consider the disciple of Christ, Ananias, as a man who is devout according to the law and testified to him while in reality they are against Christ and his disciples? Rather, they disbelieved in the teaching of Jesus about the law that the unknown Ananias was following. Paul himself went to Damascus claiming to work with the Jews there to clean

up their city of the followers of Christ, including Ananias himself.

The truth of Ananias is related to Jesus's truth. And since the truth of Jesus is that he is a human prophet, so he cannot appear or communicate with Paul or other from his place in heaven. And at the same time, it is impossible for Jesus to speak in a vision to the alleged disciple Ananias and ask him to go to a house where Paul was staying, although he had lied to Jesus and claimed that he appeared to him on the road to Damascus. And if Ananias was not a fictitious person and had really seen a vision, then it is a diabolical vision to support Paul's alleged incident on the road to Damascus. And since Paul had already issued a devoutness testimony for Ananias and announced of a testimony of goodness for him also, from all the Jews, the enemies of Jesus's disciples in Damascus, this might indicate that the unknown Ananias was already in agreement with them and he worked in a collusion with Paul to play the role of the Baptist in his alleged conversion to the religion of Christ.

5. Luke wrote that when Jesus asked Ananias of Damascus in the vision to go to the house where Paul was staying, he answered and said, *"Lord, I have heard from many about this man, how much harm he has done to your saints in Jerusalem. And here he has authority from the chief priests to bind all who call on your name"* (Acts 9:13–14). If Ananias had heard from many how much harm Paul had done to the followers of Christ in Jerusalem and that he had come to Damascus with an authority from the chief priests to arrest all those who call on Jesus's name, so why did he remain in Damascus waiting for Paul to arrest him and bring him bound to Jerusalem? Why did he not flee with the disciples of Damascus just as the followers of Christ who were in Jerusalem fled? *"At that time a great persecution arose against the church which was at Jerusalem; and they were all scattered throughout the region of Judea and Samaria except the apostles"* (Acts 8:1).

6. The problem of Paul was not only on the road to Damascus, but also after he entered the city. To see Paul's contradictions clearly, we compare the following narrations:

The first narration

Luke wrote in his book the Acts of the Apostles about Paul, after he entered Damascus:

> *Then Saul spent some days with the disciples at Damascus. Immediately he preached the Christ in the synagogues, that he is the son of God... Now after many days were past, the Jews plotted to kill him... Then the disciples took him by night and let him down through the wall in a large basket. And when Saul had come to Jerusalem, he tried to join the disciples; but they were all afraid of him and did not believe that he was a disciple. But Barnabas took him and brought him to the apostles. And he declared to them how he had seen the Lord on the road, and that he had spoken to him, and how he had preached boldly at Damascus in the name of Jesus. So, he was with them at Jerusalem coming in and going out. And he spoke boldly in the name of the Lord Jesus and disputed against the Hellenists, but they attempted to kill him. When the brethren found out, they brought him down to Caesarea and sent him out to Tarsus.* (Acts 9:19–20, 23, 25–30).

The second narration

Speaking to King Agrippa, Paul said of what he had done after entering Damascus,

> *Therefore, King Agrippa, I was not disobedient to the heavenly vision, but declared first to those*

in Damascus and in Jerusalem, and throughout all the region of Judaea, and then to the Gentiles. (Acts 26:19–20)

The third narration

In his letter to the Galatians, Paul wrote of what he had done after entering Damascus,

> *But when it pleased God, who separated me from my mother's womb and called me through His grace, to reveal His son in me, that I might preach him among the Gentiles, I did not immediately confer with flesh and blood, nor did I go up to Jerusalem to those who were apostles before me; but I went to Arabia, and returned again to Damascus. Then after three years I went up to Jerusalem to see Peter and remained with him fifteen days. But I saw none of the other apostles except James, the Lord's brother. Now concerning the things which I write to you, indeed, before God, I do not lie. Afterward, I went into the regions of Syria and Cilicia.* (Gal. 1:15–21)

The contradictions in these narrations can be summed up as follows:

1. In the third narration, Paul claims that his itinerary after the alleged appearance of Jesus to him on the road, started from Damascus to Arabia, then back to Damascus. Then after three years he went up to Jerusalem. Finally, after fifteen days, he went into the regions of Syria and Cilicia. While in the first narration, his itinerary started from Damascus, and after many days, he went to Jerusalem, then he went down to Caesarea and was sent out to Tarsus.

2. In the third narration, Paul claims that after Jesus's alleged appearance on the road to Damascus, he did not consult anyone, and he was not in need to see the disciples in Jerusalem. Rather, he went immediately to Arabia, then returned to Damascus. Then after three years, he went to Jerusalem for the first time. While in the first narration, he went to Jerusalem, for the first time, after spending many days in Damascus, not three years.
3. In the third narration, Paul claims that he went to Jerusalem to see Peter. He met him and remained with him fifteen days. And he saw none of the other disciples except James. This means that he did not have any preaching activity in Jerusalem with the disciples during his staying with Peter. While in the first narration, when Paul had come to Jerusalem, he tried to join the disciples but they were all afraid of him. But Barnabas took him and brought him to the disciples. So he was with them at Jerusalem coming in and going out. And he spoke boldly in the name of Jesus.
4. If Paul said in Galatians, *"Now concerning the things which I write to you, indeed, before God, I do not lie"* (Gal. 1:20), so was Luke lying in what he wrote in the Acts of the Apostles?

Why did Paul change the religion of Christ?

This question comes to mind a lot, but there is no ready, short answer. It is inconceivable to think that what Paul did was a Jewish conspiracy to obliterate the religion of Christ, after the failure of the persecution efforts led by Paul. The Jews also tried to kill Paul when he came up with teachings against their law. The substitution of the religion of Christ with the religion of Paul was a personal initiative by Paul himself. His epistles were no more than an invented lie, supported by Satan. There is no doubt that there were many factors behind the main reason for Paul to have corrupted the religion of

Jesus and to have produced his own brand of Christianity and clothe it with the fake mask of the Christ. These main factors are as follows:

1. Paul considered Christ's disciples to have no superiority in scholarship, education, and leadership. This also was the same thought of the high priests and the elders of the Jews toward the disciples. About this thought toward the leader of the disciples, Peter, and his companion John, the author Luke wrote, *"The members of the Council were amazed to see how bold Peter and John were and to find out that they were ordinary men of no education"* (Acts 4:13). They were fishermen (Matt. 4:21; Luke 5:10). And at the same time, Paul saw how those ordinary fishermen of no education, as he perceived them, had an ideological leadership in their society, while he, as an intellectual, enlightened Jewish Pharisee, who received strict instruction in the law and with knowledge about the books of the Old Testaments, was characterized by leadership but without ideological leadership in the society. Rather, he was merely a leader over some uneducated soldiers of the high priest when he got his trust to lead the movement of persecuting the followers of Christ.
2. Although Paul was enjoying the favor of the high priest and was given an authority to act on his behalf on persecuting the followers of Christ and provided with men to carry out his orders, yet Paul was not a man of war but of thought, religion, and philosophy. So it would not satisfy his ambition to be merely a leader over some uneducated soldiers of the high priest. Moreover, it would not satisfy his ambition also to be merely an executor of the high priest's agenda while he was seeking an ideological leadership in the society.

Paul already realized that he could not obtain religious leadership in the Jewish society with the existence of the elders and the high priests, and he could not call to Judaism in the Gentile's world, because it is restricted to the Israelites only. And in his heart, there was no acceptance of the truth that the disciples were preaching, nor he had the psychological readiness to join the religion of Jesus through the gate of the ordinary fishermen disciples whom he despises; and he does not originally accept to be under the authority of the disciples or to learn from them. *"But from those who seemed to be something—whatever they were, it makes no different to me...for those who seemed to be something added nothing to me"* (Gal. 2:6). Rather, he thought that he was not in need to learn from any human. *"I did not immediately confer with flesh and blood, nor did I go up to Jerusalem to those who were apostles before me"* (Gal. 1:16–17). Because he did not think that he was the least bit inferior to those very special so-called apostles and thought that he was a knowledgeable man. *"For I consider that I am not at all inferior to the most eminent apostles. Even though I am untrained in speech, yet I am not in knowledge. But we have been thoroughly made manifest among you in all things"* (2 Cor. 11:5–6).

3. After Paul persecuted the followers of Christ in Jerusalem with the authority delegated to him by the high priest and after the followers of Christ scattered throughout the provinces of Judea and Samaria because of the persecuting, the combatant Paul took a warrior rest, then he saw that the results did not achieve his ambitions, especially when he perceived that all results were in favor of the name of the high priest. Paul thought and plotted. He did not think that he was the least bit inferior to the apostle Peter, as he claimed. He perceived how the ordinary fisherman man of no education, Peter, was at the head of the church in Jerusalem and his followers increasing in numbers and clinging to Christianity in spite of their being persecuted. Then he thought about his psychological obsession, obtaining an ideological leadership in the society, and he succeeded to perceive an open market for promoting himself as a leader. Yes, it is the land of the neighboring Gentile. But what could he market there? Certainly not the religion of Moses because it is not for marketing there. And he did not learn about the religion of Jesus and was not willing to

learn it from the disciples, and he would not accept Peter's church authority, whom he despised along with the rest of the disciples, so he went away from the truth and was proud. At this moment, a desire and evil thought came to him from Satan to achieve his ambition, where it reminded him of the opened door by Stephen leading to Jesus in heaven. So Paul decided to enter, and through this door, he was able to replace the earthly, materialistic authority that was delegated to him by the high priest, which did not achieve his ambition as an ideological leader, by another alleged heavenly, spiritual authority from Jesus himself, then through this alleged authority, he managed to invent another Christianity with another different Jesus that carried his own thoughts and philosophy and gave him a religious leadership outside the Israelite's race.

On the road to Damascus, Paul inaugurated the first episode of the alleged serial communications with Jesus. And by his cleverness, or the stupidity of others, people immediately accepted his claim that he had converted directly from a nonbeliever of Jesus and persecutor of his followers to an inspired messenger without even passing through the faith stage in Jesus first. And he managed to impose his illusion as Jesus's apostle, who has God's secret wisdom that was hidden from humanity.

4. In the course of history, from time to time, and from all religions, some people appear who have some kind of mental derangement or mental illness such as megalomania, schizophrenia, visions or illusions, have the desire for dominion and leadership. Some claimed prophethood and apostleship; others came out with some notional interpretations or even laws. The strength of the effect of the thoughts of such mentally deranged people depends on the type of religion they ascribe to and the surrounding circumstances. And even though they vary in time, place, and thoughts, certainly, there is one common factor that

brings them together: Satan beautifies their evil thoughts for them so they consider them as good. Jesus already reminded people to be aware of such mentally deranged people. He said,

> *Take heed that no one deceives you. For many will come in my name, saying, "I am the Christ," and will deceive many... Then many false prophets will rise up and deceive many... For false christs and false prophets will arise and show great signs and wonders, so as to deceive, if possible, even the elect. See, I have told you beforehand.* (Matt. 24:4–5, 11, 24–25)

And he also said,

> *Many will say to me in that day* (day of judgment), *"Lord, Lord, have we not prophesied in your name, cast out demons in your name, and done many wonders in your name? And then I will declare to them, I never knew you; depart from me, you who practice lawlessness!"* (Matt. 7:22–23)

And he also said, *"I have come in my Father's name, and you do not receive me; if another comes in his own name, him you will receive"* (John 5:43). And John wrote, *"Beloved, do not believe every spirit, but test the spirits, whether they are of God; because many false prophets have gone out into the world"* (1 John 4:1). What mentally deranged people say about themselves may explain some of their personality patterns and psychological behavior. So what did Paul say about himself?

- *"But when it pleased God, who separated me from my mother's womb and called me through His grace"* (Gal. 1:15).
- *"But what if my untruth serves God's glory by making his truth stand out more clearly? Why should I still be condemned as a sinner?"* (Rom. 3:7).

- *"All things are lawful for me, but I will not be brought under the power of any"* (1 Cor. 6:12).
- *"I think I also have the spirit of God"* (1 Cor. 7:40).
- *"I am acting like a fool, but you have made me do it. You are the ones who ought to show your approval of me. For even if I am nothing, I am in no way inferior to those very special apostles of yours"* (2 Cor. 12:11).
- *"Are they Hebrews? So am I. Are they Israelites? So am I. Are they Abraham's descendants? So am I. Are they Christ servants? I sound like a madman—but I am a better servant than they are! I have worked much harder. I have been in prison more times, I have been whipped much more, and I have been near death more often"* (2 Cor. 11:22–23).
- *"I repeat: no one should think that I am a fool. But if you do, at least accept me as a fool, just so I will have a little to boast of. Of course, what I am saying now is not what the Lord would have me say; in this matter of boasting I am really talking like a fool"* (2 Cor. 11:16–17).
- *"Perhaps I am an amateur* (untrained) *in speaking, but certainly not in knowledge"* (2 Cor. 11:6).
- *"You will agree, then, that I was not a burden to you. But someone will say that I was tricky and trapped you with lies"* (2 Cor. 12:16).
- *"I know that good does not live in me—that is, in my human nature. For even though the desire to do good is in me, I am not able to do it"* (Rom. 7:18).

Even the pagan Festus, realized Paul's personality pattern, and his psychological behavior. He shouted at him, *"You are mad, Paul! Your great learning is driving you mad!"* (Acts 26:24).

How did Paul carry out his plan to create his own new Christianity?

Certainly, Paul was implementing a secret critical path method to form a new religion that would achieve his dream of gaining a religious leadership. A religion that contains his own thoughts and philosophy and falsely carries the name of Christ so he can market it in the neighboring pagan areas to the Jews. Satan already had beautified the secret critical path method for Paul and helped him to implement its ten overlapping items. At the end, Paul succeeded to gain a religious leadership, but it was at the expense of the truth that was in the true religion of Jesus. The items of the critical path method are as follows:

1. Claiming that he had a heavenly authority from Jesus himself. He claimed that Jesus appeared to him from heaven as a bright shining light and spoke to him. The road to Damascus was the theater where he performed this deception alone, claiming that those who were with him had fallen to the ground and did not hear Jesus. He then gave them no role as eyewitnesses, rather be omitted in his narrations.

> *As I journeyed to Damascus with authority and commission from the chief priest. At midday, O King, along the road I saw a light from heaven, brighter than the sun, shining around me and those who journeyed with me. And when we all had fallen to the ground, I heard a voice speaking to me and saying in the Hebrew language, "Saul, Saul why are you persecuting me? It is hard for you to kick against the goads." So, I said "Who are you, Lord?" And he said, "I am Jesus, whom you are persecuting. But rise and stand on your feet; for I have appeared to you for this purpose, to make you a minister and a witness both of the things which you have seen and of the things which I will yet reveal to you. I will deliver you from the Jewish people, as well as from the Gentiles, to whom I now send you, to open their eyes and to turn them from darkness to light, and from the power of Satan to God, that they may receive forgiveness of sins and an inheritance among*

those who are sanctified by faith in me." (Acts 26:12–18)

2. Preaching about Jesus among the Jews, confirming that he is Christ the Son of God, not a real but in its metaphorical sense in Hebrew, to show them his alleged conversion to the religion of Christ.

> *Immediately he preached the Christ in the synagogues, that he is the son of God... But Saul increased all the more in strength, and confounded the Jews who dwelt in Damascus, proving that this Jesus is the Christ... So he was with them at Jerusalem, coming in and going out. And he spoke boldly in the name of the Lord Jesus.* (Acts 9:20, 22, 28).

> *"Paul was constrained by the spirit, and testified to the Jews that Jesus is the Christ"* (Acts 18:5).

3. Keeping a similar teaching as that of the disciples at the beginning of his mission, to dispel any doubts about him, focusing more on the rumor of the alleged death and resurrection of Jesus.

> *Then Paul stood up and motioning with his hand said, "Men of Israel, and you who fear God listen... From this man's seed* (David) *according to the promise, God raised up for Israel a savior—Jesus—after John had first preached, before his coming, the baptism of repentance to all the people of Israel. And as John was finishing his course, he said, 'Who do you think I am? I am not he. But behold, there comes one after me, the sandals of whose feet I am not worthy to loose.'"* And Paul did not forget to mention some of his own teaching in a flu-

ent way utilizing the rumor of the alleged death and resurrection. He continued saying, *"Men and brethren, sons of the family of Abraham, and those among you who fear God, to you the word of this salvation has been sent. For those who dwell in Jerusalem, and their rulers, because they did not know him, nor even the voice of the prophets which are read every Sabbath, have fulfilled them in condemning him. And though they found no cause for death in him, they asked Pilate that he should be put to death... But God raised him from the dead... And we declare to you glad tidings—that promise which was made to the fathers... Therefore, let it be known to you, brethren, that through this man is preached to you the forgiveness of sins; And by him everyone who believes is justified from all things from which you could not be justified by the law of Moses."* (Acts 13:16, 23–28, 30, 32, 38–39)

4. Emphasizing that he is not in need to learn from any human source because he has an alleged direct audiovisual contact with Jesus and revelation from God. He said about himself, *"Paul, a servant of Jesus Christ, called to be an apostle, separated to the gospel of God"* (Rom. 1:1).

And also, he said,

Nevertheless, brethren, I have written more boldly to you on some points, as reminding you, because of the grace given to me by God, that I might be a minister of Jesus Christ to the Gentiles, ministering the gospel of God, that the offering of the Gentiles might be acceptable, sanctified by the holy spirit. (Rom. 15:15–16)

He further said, *"And my teaching and message were not delivered with skillful words of human wisdom, but with convincing proof of the power of God's spirit"* (1 Cor. 2:4).

He also said about himself, *"Paul, whose call to be an apostle did not come from man or by means of man, but from Jesus Christ and God the Father, who raised him from death"* (Gal. 1:1).

And he also said, *"I went* (back to Jerusalem) *because God revealed to me that I should go"* (Gal. 2:2).

Rather, he had the audacity to say something about himself that no true messenger had said about himself. He said, *"But when it pleased God, who separated me from my mother's womb and called me through His grace"* (Gal. 1:15). While in the verse before this, he wrote about himself how bad and evil person he was. *"For you have heard of my former conduct in Judaism how I persecuted the church of God beyond measure and tried to destroy it"* (Gal. 1:13). What about approving of the murder of Stephen (Acts 8:1), destroying the church; going from house to house to drag out the believers, both men and women, and throwing them into prison (Acts 8:3); keeping up threats and murder against the followers of Jesus (Acts 9:1); doing everything he could against the name of Jesus; and voting against the followers of Jesus and having them punished in every synagogue, compelling them to blaspheme and persecuting them even to foreign cities (Acts 26:9–11)? If God had chosen this evil man since he was in his mother's womb, as he claimed, surely God would had protected him from all evil things and made him a good example. He even himself admitted that he is not worthy to be called an apostle because he persecuted the church of God. *"For I am the least of the apostles, who am not worthy to be called an apostle, because I persecuted the church of God"* (1 Cor. 15:9).

Paul claims that the gospel he preaches was revealed to him by Jesus. He said,

> *But I make known to you, brethren, that the gospel which was preached by me is not according to man. For I neither received it from man, nor was I*

taught it, but it came through the revelation of Jesus Christ. (Gal. 1:11–12)

He affirmed his total independence from everyone and that he was not in need for the disciples of Christ who were before him. He denied going to Jerusalem to meet the disciples, only after three years. He said,

> *But when it pleased God, who separated me from my mother's womb and called me through His grace to reveal his son to me, that I might preach him among the Gentiles, I did not immediately confer with flesh and blood, nor did I go up to Jerusalem to those who were apostles before me; but I went to Arabia and returned again to Damascus. Then after three years I went up to Jerusalem to see Peter.* (Gal. 1:15–18)

The alleged direct audiovisual contact with Jesus is as follows: The author of the book of Acts narrated,

> *Now the Lord spoke to Paul in the night by a vision, "Do not be afraid, but speak, and do not keep silent; for I am with you, and no one will attack you to hurt you, for I have many people in this city."* (Acts 18:9–10)

Another narration for the alleged communication between Jesus and Paul. He said,

> *I went back to Jerusalem, and while I was praying in the Temple, I had a vision, in which I saw the Lord, as he said to me, "Hurry and leave Jerusalem quickly, because the people here will not accept your witness about me." "Lord." I answered. "They know very well that I went to the synagogues*

> *and arrested and beat those who believe in you. And when your witness Stephen was put to death, I myself was there approving of his murder and taking care of the clothes of his murderers." "Go," Jesus said to me, "for I will send you far away to the Gentiles."* (Acts 22:17–21)

Another alleged meeting is reported here: *"But that following night the Lord stood by him and said, "Be of good cheer, Paul: for as you have testified for me in Jerusalem, so you must also bear witness at Rome"* (Acts 23:11).

The author of the book of Acts also narrated another type of alleged contact between Paul and Jesus, where he said,

> *Now when they had gone through Phrygia and the region of Galatia, they were forbidden by the Holy Spirit to preach the word in Asia. After they had come to Mysia, they tried to go into Bithynia, but the Spirit did not permit them. So, passing by Mysia, they came down to Troas. And a vision appeared to Paul in the night. A man of Macedonian stood and pleaded with him saying, "Come over Macedonia and help us." Now after he had seen the vision, immediately we sought to go to Macedonia, concluding that the Lord had called us to preach the gospel to them.* (Acts 16:6–10)

It seems that whenever Paul does not like a place for any reason, he would just claim that he had received the signal of the spirit of Jesus telling him not to go there. But when he wanted to go Macedonia, he claimed that he had received a signal from Jesus using a Macedonian citizen, standing and begging Paul to go there.

Finally, he also claimed that he communicated with heaven through an angel sometimes. He said,

> *For there stood by me this night an angel of the God to whom I belong and whom I serve, saying, "Do not be afraid, Paul; you must be brought before Caesar; and indeed God has granted you all those who sail with you."* (Acts 27:23–24)

It seems that Paul wanted to convince the people that Jesus had forgotten all about his disciples and established a direct line of contact with him instead. But Jesus, after all, was no more than a human messenger proclaiming the message of God to his people the Jews. God rescued him from those who wanted to kill him by ascending him to heaven. And since then, he had no power to communicate or to appear to any human being. All the activities of the disciples after him were through God's guidance, support, wisdom, and the blessing of Jesus's prayers for them, where he asked God,

> *Now I am no longer in the world, but these* (the disciples) *are in the world, and I come to You. Holy father, keep through Your name those whom you have given me that they may be one as we are.* (one). *While I was with them in the world, I kept them in Your name. Those whom You gave me I have kept; and none of them is lost except the son of perdition* (Judas), *that the Scripture might be fulfilled. But now I come to You, and these things I speak in the world, that they may have my joy fulfilled in themselves... I do not pray that You should take them out of the world, but that You should keep them from the evil one... Sanctify them by Your truth. Your word is truth. I do not pray for these* (disciples) *alone, but also for those who will believe in me through their words. That they all may be one, as You Father are in me, and I in You; that they also may be one in us, that the world may believe that You sent me. And the glory which You gave me*

I have given them, that they may be one just as we are one. (John 17:11–13, 15, 17, 20–22)

The strange thing was that, while the disciples in Jerusalem and the provinces were saying that they were receiving guidance from the Holy Spirit, Paul, on the other hand, was claiming to have direct guidance from Jesus and the Holy Spirit, with teachings that contradict the teachings of Jesus in which the Holy Spirit reminded the disciples! Jesus said to his disciples, *"But the helper, the Holy Spirit, whom the father will send in my name, he will teach you all things, and bring to your remembrance all things that I said to you"* (John 14:26). How does the Holy Spirit remind the disciples of the teachings of Jesus and at the same time inspire Paul with other teachings that contradict what had reminded the disciples? Was the Holy Spirit contradicting himself? Certainly no. Because the Holy Spirit, originally, was not sent to Paul. The one who inspired him was another spirit. The details of which will come later. This spirit was the one who made Paul to say about the disciples that they were false apostles, deceitful workers. Paul says,

> *But what I do, I will also continue to do, that I may cut off the opportunity from those who desire an opportunity to be regarded just as we are in the things of which they boast. For such are false apostles, deceitful workers, transforming themselves into real apostles of Christ. And no wonder! For Satan himself transforms himself into an angel of light. Therefore, it is no great thing if his ministers also transform themselves into ministers of righteousness, whose end will be according to their works.* (2 Cor. 11:12–15)

Yes, Paul was right. It is no wonder if the servants of Satan disguised themselves to look like real apostles of Jesus. Paul himself was a good example.

5. Emphasizing his alleged specialization as an apostle to the neighboring Gentiles to the Jews, appointed by Jesus directly. Paul claimed that Jesus said to him on the road to Damascus,

> *I am Jesus, whom you are persecuting… I will deliver you from the Jewish people, as well as from the Gentiles, to whom I now send you, to open their eyes and to turn them from darkness to light, and from the power of Satan to God, that they may receive forgiveness of sins and an inheritance among those who are sanctified by faith in me.* (Acts 26:15, 17–18)

Paul was a clever man. He knew that his new pagan doctrines and philosophy would not be acceptable to any sane Jew. So he prepared himself to concentrate on preaching the new pagan Christianity to the neighboring pagan nations to the Jews. And in order for the pagans to accept him, he emptied his Christianity of law and kept faith only. But it was a new brand of faith completely different from the faith that was brought by all the previous messengers of God, including Jesus himself. A faith that was coated with a layer of the alleged blood of Christ. Also, he prepared the Gentiles to accept the idea of his claim as a messenger to them, claiming that he is one of God's holy apostles and that He had singled him out with His grace for them as He revealed to him the mystery of Christ, which in other ages was not made known to the sons of men, as it has now been revealed by the Spirit to Paul, that the Gentiles share with the Jews in obtaining God's promise in Christ through the gospel of Paul himself. Notice how Paul plays with words when he said,

> *For this reason I, Paul, the prisoner of Jesus Christ for you Gentiles, if indeed you have heard of the dispensation of the grace of God which was given to me for you, how that by revelation he made known to me the mystery (as I wrote before*

in a few words, by which, when you read, you may understand my knowledge in the mystery of Christ), which in other ages was not made known to the sons of men, as it has now been revealed by the Spirit to His holy apostles and prophets: that the Gentiles should be fellow heirs, of the same body, and partakers of His promise in Christ through the gospel, of which I became a minister according to the gift of the grace of God given to me by the effective working of His power. (Eph. 3:1–7)

Here also he is emphasizing his alleged mission to the Gentiles. He said, *"For so the Lord commanded us: 'I have set you to be a light to the Gentiles, that you should be for salvation to the ends of the earth'"* (Acts 13:47).

And when the Jews opposed Paul and blasphemed, he shook his garments and said to them, *"Your blood be upon your own heads; I am clean. From now on I will go to the Gentiles"* (Acts 18:6).

And he also said to the Jews who were in Rome, *"Therefore let it be known to you that the salvation of God has been sent to the Gentiles, and they will hear it!"* (Acts 28:28).

He also said, *"I am speaking now to you Gentiles: As long as I am an apostle to the Gentiles, I will take pride in my work"* (Rom. 11:13).

He also said, *"Nevertheless, brethren, I have written more boldly to you on some points, as reminding you, because of the grace given to me by God, that I might be a minister of Jesus Christ to the Gentiles, ministering the gospel of God, that the offering of the Gentiles might be acceptable, sanctified by the Holy Spirit... For I will not dare to speak of any of those things which Christ has not accomplished through me, in word and deed to make the Gentiles obedient"* (Rom. 15:15–16, 18).

He also said, *"But when it pleased God, who separated me from my mother's womb and called me through His grace to reveal his son to me, that I might preach him among the Gentiles"* (Gal. 1:15–16).

He also said, *"The gospel, to which I was appointed a preacher an apostle, and a teacher for the Gentiles"* (2 Tim. 1:10–11).

6. Changing the prevailing concept of the term "savior" and replacing it with a new concept. While the term "savior" means the person who rescues or saves people from danger, loss, death, going astray in faith, committing sins, etc., Paul took advantage of the opportunity when the early Christians who had no certain knowledge about what had happened to Jesus when the Jews tried to kill him. But they followed conjectures and rumors about his alleged death, and he claimed that it was a sacrifice, in common with the sacrifice of the pagan Mithras cult to create a new conception for the term "Savior." And so he started teaching a faith that already existed in pagan mythology when he transformed Jesus into a "Divine Savior" who had descended to earth from heaven and experienced death for the purpose of saving mankind from their sins. And thus, Paul invented a false way to an alleged salvation, other than the way of salvation that was preached by all the messengers, including Jesus himself.

Jesus never saw himself as a savior by his blood, but rather he wanted people to accept him as a messenger of God to the Jews. He asked them to repent and keep the commandments. Also, his disciples after him never believed or preached the alleged way to salvation that was invented by Paul. We can see that from the following:

Jesus said, *"Most assuredly I say to you, he who hears my word and believe in Him who sent me has everlasting life"* (John 5:24). Also, he said, *"And this is eternal life, that they may know you, the only true God, and Jesus Christ whom you have sent"* (John 17:3). And he answered the man who asked him about the eternal life (salvation), saying, *"No one is good but One, that is God. But if you want to enter into life keep the commandments"* (Matt. 19:17).

What about the disciples, what did they say about the savior? Peter said, *"Him God has exalted to his right hand to be prince and savior, to give repentance to Israel and forgiveness of sins"* (Acts 5:31). It is clear that Jesus came to save the Jews, not by blood but by repentance and believing in his message in order for their sins to be forgiven. And Peter also said, *"Nor is there salvation* (for the Jews) *in any other, for there is no other name under heaven* (that time) *given among men by which we* (as Jews) *must be saved"* (Acts 4:12).

As for Paul, this is what he said while talking to the Jews, alongside the disciple Barnabas: *"From this man's seed* (David) *according to the promise, God raised up for Israel a savior Jesus"* (Acts 13:23).

Here, Paul was keeping to the teaching of the disciples that Jesus came to save the Jews because his audience were Jews and his companion was a disciple, Barnabas. But when he was apart from the disciples, he preached like this,

> *Not with the blood of goats and calves, but with his own blood he entered the most holy place once for all, having obtained eternal redemption. He then would have had to suffer often since the foundation of the world; but now, once at the end of the ages, he has appeared to put away sin by the sacrifice of himself.* (Heb. 9:12, 26)

And also, like this,

> *For I delivered to you first of all that which I also received: that Christ died for our sins according to the Scriptures.* (1 Cor. 15:3)

7. Giving more emphasis on claiming holiness for his own gospel, to put people under the illusion of divine sources for his own thoughts and philosophy in his gospel by which people are saved if they hold fast that word that he preaches to them.

> *Moreover, brethren, I declare to you the gospel which I preached to you, which also you received and in which you stand, by which also you are*

saved, if you hold fast that word which I preached to you. (1 Cor. 15:1–2)

Rather, he claimed that God will judge the secrets of men by Jesus according to his gospel. *"In the day when God will judge the secret of men by Jesus Christ according to my gospel"* (Rom. 2:16).

What did Paul say about his own gospel, which he wrote of himself?

- *"Our savior Jesus Christ, who has abolished death and brought life and immortality to light through the gospel, to which I was appointed a preacher, an apostle, and a teacher of the Gentiles"* (2 Tim. 1:10–11).
- *"Knowing that I am appointed for the defense of the gospel"* (Phil. 1:17)
- *"For our gospel did not come to you in word only, but also in power, and in the Holy Spirit and in much assurance, as you know what kind of men we were among you for your sake"* (1 Thess. 1:5).
- *"That I might be a minister of Jesus Christ to the Gentiles, ministering the gospel of God, that the offering of the Gentiles might be acceptable, sanctified by the Holy Spirit"* (Rom. 15:16).
- *"I was made a servant of the gospel by God's special gift, which He gave me through the working of his power"* (Eph. 3:7).

Also, he said about preaching his gospel: *"I have no right to boast gust because I preach the gospel. After all, I am under orders to do so. And how terrible it would be for me if I did not preach the gospel"* (1 Cor. 9:16).

Paul claimed that he did it as a matter of duty because God entrusted him with this task. He was willing to be anything in order to win over as many people as possible. Also, he announced that he become all things to all men, that he may save some of them by whatever means are possible. He claimed he did all this for his gospel's sake in order to share in its blessings (1 Cor. 9:17–23). And he said to the Gentiles, *"The gospel which was preached by me is not according to man. For I neither receive it from man, nor was I taught it, but it came through the revelation of Jesus Christ"* (Gal. 1:11–12).

There could not have been a greater lie than making Jesus God, the One who inspires His messengers. How could Paul make God, or even Jesus, responsible for his blasphemy, lies, and pagan polytheistic teaching that he preached to the pagan Gentiles? Jesus himself did not speak about his true Gospel the same way that Paul spoke about his vain gospel. Yes, it was a different gospel than that of Jesus. In Paul's personal gospel, there is not a single word that gives the actual teaching of Jesus, nor is there even one of his parables. Instead, he spreads his own invented teaching and his own philosophy. In fact, he was avoiding quoting the teachings of Jesus because his invented personal gospel conflicts the true Gospel of Jesus. It promotes falsehood and lawlessness.

What are the doctrines with which Paul opposed Jesus and his disciples?

The main doctrine that exposed the falsehood of Paul was his corruption of the reality of Jesus, who presented himself clearly to his people as the son of man, and no more than a human prophet. Jesus said, *"But now you seek to kill me, a man who has told you the truth which I heard from God. Abraham did not do this"* (John 8:40). Also, he said, *"Do not work for food that spoils; instead, work for the food that last for eternal life. This is the food which the Son of man will give you* (his message)*"* (John 6:27). And also, he said, *"Assuredly, I say to you, no prophet is accepted in his own country"* (Luke 4:24). And the disciple Peter said regarding Jesus, *"Jesus of Nazareth, a man attested by God to you by miracles, wonders, and signs which God did through him"* (Acts 2:22).

While Paul, the first corrupter of Jesus, said, *"My brethren, my kinsmen according to the flesh, who are Israelites…and from whom, according to the flesh, Christ came, who is over all, the eternally blessed God* (Rom. 9:3–5). *Christ is the image of God* (2 Cor. 4:4), *the image of the invisible God* (Col. 1:15) *who, being in the form of God, did not consider it robbery to be equal with God, but made himself of no reputation, taking the form of a servant, and coming in the likeness of man. And being found in appearance as a man, he humbled himself and became obedient to the point of death"* (Phil. 2:6–8).

Paul also corrupted the figurative Hebrew meaning of the term "Son of God" from the one who was sanctified by and sent from God, as Jesus himself explained when he said to the Jews, *"Do you say of him whom the Father sanctified and sent into the world, 'You are blaspheming, because I said, 'I am the son of God'?"* (John 10:36). Paul corrupted it to another real deity, as a real son of God beside his father. His primary function is based on his alleged death, as a savior washing the sins of mankind by his blood. *"The gospel of God which He promised before through His prophets in the Holy Scriptures, concerning His Son Jesus Christ our lord who was born of the seed of David according to the flesh, and declared to be the son of God with power, according to the spirit of holiness, by the resurrection from the dead"* (Rom. 1:1–4). *"When the fullness of the time had come, God sent forth His own son, born of a woman, born under the law"* (Gal. 4:4). *"God did not even keep back His own son but offered him for us all"* (Rom. 8:32). Neither Jesus Christ nor his followers ever preached such pagan mythology. But the entire gospel of Paul is centered on this mythology.

Paul opposed Jesus about the salvation formula. Jesus said to the Jews, *"Most assuredly I say to you, he who hears my word and believe in Him who sent me has everlasting life"* (John 5:24). Also, he said, *"And this is eternal life, that they may know you, the only true God, and Jesus Christ whom you have sent"* (John 17:3). And he answered the man who asked him about the eternal life (salvation), saying, *"No one is good but One, that is God. But if you want to enter into life keep the commandments"* (Matt. 19:17). While the salvation formula according to Paul is thus: *"So if you confess with your mouth the lord Jesus and believe in your heart that God has raised him from the dead, you will be saved"* (Rom. 10:9).

Paul also opposed Jesus and the disciples regarding the law. The Christ Jesus came to fulfill the law. He said,

> *Do not think that I came to destroy the Law or the prophets. I did not come to destroy but to*

> *fulfill. For assuredly I say to you, till heaven and earth pass away, one jot or one title will by no means pass from the law till all is fulfilled. Whoever therefore breaks one of the least of these commandments, and teaches men so, shall be called least in the kingdom of heaven; but whoever does and teaches them, he shall be called great in the kingdom of heaven.* (Matt. 5:17–19)

And the disciple James said regarding the law, *"What does it profit, my brethren, if someone says he has faith but does not have works? Can faith save him?"* (James 2:14). And he also said, *"But do you want to know, O foolish man, that faith without works is dead?"* (James 2:20).

While Paul was the first one who taught men to neglect the law and just keep faith only. He said, *"Now God's way of putting people right with Himself has been revealed. It has nothing to do with Law. God puts people right through their faith in Jesus"* (Rom. 3:21–22). And he also said, *"Therefore we conclude that a man is justified by faith apart from the deeds of the law"* (Rom. 3:28). And also said, *"Knowing that a man is not justified by the works of the law but by faith in Jesus Christ, even we have believed in Christ Jesus, that we might be justified by faith in Christ and not by the works of the law; for by the works of the law no flesh shall be justified"* (Gal. 2:16).

And he also said about circumcision,

> *Listen! I, Paul, tell you that if you allow yourselves to be circumcised, it means that Jesus is of no use to you at all. Once more I warn any man who allows himself to be circumcised that he is obliged to obey the whole Law. Those of you who try to be put right with God by obeying the Law have cut yourselves off from Christ. You are outside God's grace. As for us, our hope is that God will put us right with him; and this is what we wait for by the power of God's spirit working through our faith. For when*

we are in union with Christ Jesus, neither circumcision nor the lack of it makes any difference at all; what matters is faith that works through love. (Gal. 5:2–6)

Is it conceivable that Jesus would warn people about circumcision and keeping the law? Surely not.

A troubling point is that Paul was warning people not to be circumcised because circumcision means an obligation to the whole law, *"I warn any man who allows himself to be circumcised that he is obliged to obey the whole Law,"* and that the circumcised cut themselves off from Christ and they are outside God's grace. Despite this, he circumcised his non-Jewish friend Timothy when he wanted to take him along on the journey. Luke wrote in Acts, *"Paul wanted to have Timothy go on with him. And he took him and circumcised him because of the Jews who were in that region, for they all knew that his father was a Greek"* (Acts 16:3). So Paul obliged this poor Timothy to obey the whole law and cut him off from Christ and became outside God's grace (according to Paul's own theory) in order to appease the Jews.

The disciples built their beliefs on a base of Christ's direct words to them. They walked with him for more than three years and were taught directly by Jesus himself. Paul, on the other hand, no man had ever taught him Christianity; and he never walked with Jesus, and even a mere quoting from Jesus did not. But he claimed that he was given all knowledge in a momentary vision of Jesus on the road to Damascus. Then he found it necessary to claim a direct line of contact with Jesus and the Holy Spirit to give holiness for his thoughts and philosophy.

The Christ Jesus has already informed his disciples that they will be supported by a spirit from God to come after him, to teach them and remind them all that he had said to them. Jesus said, *"But the Helper, the Holy Spirit, whom the father will send in my name, he will teach you all things, and bring to your remembrance all things that I said to you"* (John 14:26). And since the apostles and Paul are in total disagreement, so who inspired Paul to go against the teaching of Christ?

Was it the same spirit that was sent by God to teach the disciples and remind them of Jesus's words? Surely, it cannot be that the one who taught the disciples as the one that inspired Paul. The disciples who followed the teaching of Jesus were supported by a spirit from God; but Paul, who followed his own thoughts and philosophy, was also supported, but by another spirit. It was an evil spirit that has made his own doctrines, thoughts, and philosophy fair-seeming to him. So are those disciples who were on a clear proof from the words of Jesus like Paul, to whom Satan beautified for him his philosophy and desires? Surely, they are not alike. There is no doubt that Paul was the first corrupter of the doctrines of Jesus. And unfortunately, these corrupted doctrines have replaced the true doctrines that were brought by Jesus, and Paul has become the founder of today's Christianity.

Just as this evil spirit inspired Paul to proclaim that Jesus is God, because of his claim that he was a real Son of God, it also inspired him to utter about God in his own gospel, with words that are extremely bad, such as the following:

Paul falsely claimed that the reason for God to give a chance of salvation for the Gentiles through him personally was just to make the Jews jealous of Gentiles. He said, *"Because they (the Jews) sinned, salvation has come to the Gentiles, to make the Jews jealous of them"* (Rom. 11:11). And he also claimed that the reason for God to have mercy on the Gentiles (through him) was because the Jews were disobedient. He said, *"As for you Gentiles, you disobeyed God in the past; but now you have received God's mercy because the Jews were disobedient"* (Rom. 11:30).

And this evil spirit inspired Paul to ascribe foolishness and weakness to God. He said, *"Because the foolishness of God is wiser than men, and the weakness of God is stronger than men"* (1 Cor. 1:25). Finally, the evil spirit inspired him to think that it really pleased God when He chose him since he was in his mother's womb and called him to serve Him, when He decided to reveal His alleged son to him (on the road to Damascus) so that he might preach him among the Gentiles. *"But when it pleased God, who separated me from my mother's womb and called me through His grace to reveal His son to me, that I might preach him among the Gentiles"* (Gal. 1:15–16).

If Paul underrated the might of God, what about Jesus? He also was not left out from the foolishness of the gospel of Paul. He already ascribed a curse to Jesus, he said, *"Christ has redeemed us from the curse of the law, having become a curse for us, for it is written, 'Cursed is everyone who hangs on a tree'"* (Gal. 3:13).

The evil spirit inspired Paul also to present Jesus as a heavenly being who chose after he had been pushed by his father to accept suicide for the sake of saving mankind. He said, *"Every Jewish priest performs his services every day and offers the same sacrifices many times; but these sacrifices can never take a way sins* (Heb. 10:11). *God did not even keep back His own son but offered him for us all* (Rom. 8:32) *so that by his sacrificial death, he should become the means by which people's sins are forgiven only through their faith in him* (Rom. 3:25–26). *Not with the blood of goats and calves, but with his own blood he entered the most holy place once for all, having obtained eternal redemption* (Heb. 9:12). *Christ, however offered one sacrifice for sins, an offering that is effective forever, and then he sat down at the right side of God"* (Heb. 10:12).

Then this evil spirit inspired him to manufacture a key for paradise from the alleged blood of Jesus and give it to anyone who would confess that Jesus is Lord and believe that God raised him from the dead, without any requirement or obedience to law. He said,

> *So if you confess with your mouth the lord Jesus and believe in your heart that God has raised him from the dead, you will be saved. There is no distinction between Jews and Greek, for the same Lord over all is rich to all who call upon Him.* (Rom. 10:9, 12)

Also, the evil spirit inspired Paul to believe that all the works and the preaching of Jesus and his disciples during his three years of ministry on earth were useless. There was no need for all of that; it was vain and a waste of time. The only beneficial point in Jesus's life was his alleged death and resurrection. Paul said, *"And if Christ is not risen, then our preaching is vain, and your faith is also vain"* (1 Cor. 15:14).

The evil spirit did not forget to inspire Paul to curse the law of God with Jesus and abolish adherence to it, because adherence to the law is not a worship for God and it has no purpose except to make man know that he has sinned. Paul said, *"Those who depend on obeying the Law live under a curse... Christ has redeemed us from the curse of the law, having become a curse for us"* (Gal. 3:10, 13). *"Now God's way of putting people right with Himself has been revealed. It has nothing to do with Law. God puts people right through their faith in Jesus"* (Rom. 3:21–22). *"For no one is put right in God's sight by doing what the Law requires; what the Law does is to make man know that he has sinned"* (Rom. 3:20). *"Law was introduced in order to increase wrongdoing; but where sin increased, God's grace increased much more* (Rom. 5:20), *"knowing that a man is not justified by the works of the law"* (Galatians 2:16). *"I refuse to reject the grace of God. But if a person is put right with God through the Law, it means that Jesus died for nothing"* (Gal. 2:21).

The evil spirit directed Paul to lie while he was telling his story to King Agrippa. He said,

> *But declared first to those in Damascus and in Jerusalem, and throughout all the region of Judaea, and then to the Gentiles, that they should repent, turn to God, and do works befitting repentance. For these reasons the Jews seized me in the temple, and they tried to kill me.* (Acts 26:20–21)

Here Paul presented himself to King Agrippa as a good man. He was almost killed by the Jews because he just asked them that they should repent, turn to God, and do works befitting repentance. This is absolutely lie. The Jews did not seize him while he was in the temple and try to kill him because he preached that they must repent of their sins and turn to God as he claimed. Rather, the Jews opposed Paul for teaching those of them residing in Gentile lands to abandon the law of Moses, telling them not to circumcise their children or follow the Jewish customs. The narration says the disciples said to Paul:

> *Brother Paul, you can see how many thousands of Jews have become believers, and how devoted they all are to the Law. They have been told that you have been teaching all the Jews who live in Gentiles countries to abandon the Law of Moses, telling them not to circumcise their children or follow the Jewish customs.* (Acts 21:20–21)

The narration continues as thus,

> *Some Jews from the province of Asia saw Paul in the temple. They stirred up the whole crowd and grabbed Paul, crying out, "Men of Israel, help! This is the man who goes everywhere teaching everyone against the people of Israel, the Law of Moses and the temple. And now he has even brought some Gentiles into the temple and defiled this holy place!" They said this because they had seen Trophimus from Ephesus with Paul in the city, and they thought that Paul had taken him into the temple. And all the city was disturbed; and the people ran together, seized Paul and dragged him out of the temple; and immediately the doors were shut. The mob was trying to kill Paul, when a report was sent up to the commander of the Roman troops that all of Jerusalem was rioting. At once the commander took some officers and soldiers and rushed down to the crowd.* (Acts 21:27–32)

The evil spirit convinced Paul to lie, where he said, *"But what if my untruth serves God's glory by making his truth stand out more clearly?*

Why should I still be condemned as a sinner?" (Rom. 3:7). It also beautified for him lies and hypocrisy so that people might share him the falsehood through his own particular gospel. He said,

> *To the Jews I became as a Jew, that I might win Jews; to those who are under the law (I became), as under the Law, that I might win those who are under the law; to those who are without law (I became), as without law, (not being without law toward God, but under law toward Christ), that I might win those who are without law; to the weak I became as weak, that I might win the weak. I have become all things to all men, that I might by all means save some. Now this I do this for the gospel's sake, that I may be partaker of it with you.* (1 Cor. 9:20–23)

The evil spirit convinced him that he was an exceptional person, and all things are lawful for him. So he said, *"All things are lawful for me, but all things are not helpful. All things are lawful for me, but I will not be brought under the power of any"* (1 Cor. 6:12). Not only that, notice how this evil spirit made the evil of his deeds fair-seeming, in a philosophical style. Paul said,

> *We know that the Law is spiritual; but I am a mortal man, sold as a slave to sin. I do not understand what I do; for I do not do what I would like to do, but instead I do what I hate. Since what I do is what I do not want to do, this shows that I agree that the Law is right. So, I am not really the one who does this thing; rather it is the sin that lives in me. I know that good does not live in me. For even though the desire to do is in me, I am not able to do it. I do not do the good I want to do; instead, I do the evil that I do not want to do. If I do what I don't want to do, this means that I am no longer the one*

> *who does it; instead, it is the sin that lives in me. So, I find that this law is at work: when I want to do what is good, what is evil is the only choice I have. My inner being delights in the law of God. But I see a different law at work in my body—a law that fights against the law which my mind approves of. It makes me a prisoner to the law of sin which is at work in my body. What an unhappy man I am! Who will rescue me from this body that is taking me to death?* (Rom. 7:14–24)

The evil spirit directed Paul to be a racist apostle and ascribed racism to God. He said,

> *It was written that Abraham had two sons: the one by a bondwoman, the other by a free-woman. But the who was of the bondwoman was born according to the flesh, and he of the free woman through promise, which things are symbolic. For these are the two covenants: the one from Mount Sinai which gives birth to bondage, which is Hagar—for this Hagar is Mount Sinai in Arabia, and corresponds to Jerusalem which now is, and is in bondage with her children—but the Jerusalem above is free, which is the mother of us all... Now we, my brothers, as Isaac was, are children of promise... Nevertheless what does the Scripture say? "Cast out the bondwoman and her son, for the son of the bondwoman shall not be heir with the son of the free-woman." So then, brethren, we are not children of the bondwoman but of the free."* (Gal. 4:22–31)

Another odd thing is that Paul used his gospel to send his greetings and the greetings of his friends to other friends and also utilized it for some personal news. All these personal things are considered as a part of his alleged inspired gospel as word of God. About his greetings, Paul wrote,

> Greet Priscilla and Aquila, my fellow workers in Christ Jesus. Greet to my beloved Epaenetus, who was the first fruits of Achaia to Christ. Greet Mary, who labored much for us. Greet Andronicus and Junias, my kinsmen and my fellow prisoners who of note among the apostles, who also were in Christ before me. Greet Amplias, my beloved in the Lord. Greet Urbanus, our fellow worker in Christ, and Stachys, my beloved. Greet Apelles, approved in Christ. Greet those who are of the household of Aristobulus. Greet Herodion my kinsmen. Greet those who are of the household of Narcissus who are in the lord. Greet Tryphaena and Tryphosa, who have labored in the Lord. Greet the beloved Persis who labored much in the Lord. Greet Rufus, chosen in the Lord, and his mother and mine. Greet Asyncritus, Phlegon, Hermes, Patrobas, Hermas, and the brethren how are with them. Greet Philologus and Julia, to Nereus and his sister, and Olympas and all the saints who are with them. (Rom. 16:3–15)

About the greetings of his friends that he wrote in his gospel to other friends, he wrote:

> Timothy, my fellow worker, and Lucius, Jason and Sosipater, my kinsmen, greet you. I, Tertius, who wrote this epistle, greet you in the Lord. Gaius my host and the host of the whole church, greets you. Erastus, the treasurer, the treasurer of the city, greets you, and Quartus, a brother. The grace of our lord Jesus Christ be with you all. Now to Him who is able to establish you according to my gospel and the

preaching of Jesus Christ, according to the revelation of the mystery which was kept secret since the world began. (Rom. 16:21–25)

About other personal news in the alleged gospel of God, Paul wrote,

Timothy, diligent to come to me quickly; for Demas has forsaken me, having loved this present world, and. has departed for Thessalonica— Crescens for Galatia, Titus for Dalmatia. Only Luke is with me. Get Mark and bring him with you, for he is useful to me for ministry And Tychicus Have sent to Ephesus. Bring the cloak that I left with Carpus at Troas when you come and the books especially the parchment. Alexander the coppersmith did me much harm. may the Lord repay him according to his work. You also must beware of him, for he has greatly resisted our words. At my first defense no one stood with me, but all forsook me. May it not be charged against them. But the Lord stood with me and strengthened me, so that the message might be preached fully through me, and that all the Gentiles might hear. And I was delivered out of the mouth of the lion. And the Lord will deliver me from every evil work and preserve me for his heavenly kingdom. Greet Prisca and Aquila, and the household of Onesiphorus. Erastus stayed in Corinth, but Trophimus I have left in Miletus sick. Do your utmost to come before winter. Eubulus greets you, as well as Pudens, Linus, Claudia, and all the brethren. (2 Tim. 4:9–21)

And he wrote to his friend Titus and said,

> *When I send Artemas to you, or Tychicus, be diligent to come to me at Nicopolis, for I have decided to spend the winter there. Send Zenas the lawyer and Apollos on their journey with haste, that they may lack nothing. All who are with me greet you. Greet those who love us in the faith.* (Titus 3:12–13, 15)

With all these problems of Paul, he insisted to think that he had God's spirit. He said, *"I think I also have the spirit of God"* (1 Cor. 7:40).

What do you think, reader? Was it a spirit from God or from Satan?

8. Working independently and away from the disciples of Christ in order to be able to spread his thoughts, philosophy, and his interpretation of Jesus's message among people, his plan was in two stages:

The first stage

Start by exalting and venerating of himself as an apostle who was chosen by God since he was in his mother's womb (Gal. 1:15). He proudly proclaimed his independence: *that he did not go to anyone for advice, nor did he go to Jerusalem to see those who were apostles before him* (Gal. 1:16–17). Rather, he totally depended on a series of alleged visions of Jesus. He claimed to have received ordination and that he was not in need to learn from any human being, not even from the disciples who preceded him. Paul said, *"I do not think that I am the least bit inferior to those very special so-called 'apostles' of yours… As the truth of Christ is in me, no one shall stop me from this boasting in the regions of Achaia"* (2 Cor. 11:5, 10). It was three years later that he went to Jerusalem to see Peter, and he stayed with him for fifteen days. He did not see any other apostles except James (Gal. 1:18–19). He proudly claimed that as Jesus appeared to the disciples after the crucifixion, he was the last one who saw Jesus, even though he was the least of the apostles, but he worked harder than any of them.

> *Last of all he appeared also to me—even though I am like someone whose birth was abnormal. For I am the least of all the apostles, I do not even deserve to be called an apostle, because I persecuted God's church. But by God's grace I am what I am, and the grace that he gave me was not without effect on the contrary, I have worked harder than any of the other apostles.* (1 Cor. 15:8–10)

The second stage

Infiltrating the ranks of the disciples to discredit them and warn his followers of them, to make the success of his satanic mission by replacing their teachings, which they received directly from Jesus, with his own teachings and interpretation of the message of Jesus. He proclaimed that, saying,

> *Fourteen years later I went back to Jerusalem with Barnabas, taking Titus along with me. I went because God revealed to me that I should go. In a private meeting with the leaders I explained the gospel that I preach to the Gentiles. I did not want my work in the past or in the present to be a failure.* (Gal. 2:1–2)

He then started speaking badly about the disciples, saying,

> *My companion Titus, even though he is Greek, was not forced to be circumcised, although some wanted it done. pretending to be fellow believers, these men slipped into our group as spies, in order to find out about the freedom we have through our union with Jesus, they wanted to make slave of*

> us, but in order to keep the truth of the gospel safe for you we did not give in to them for a minute. But those who seemed to be the leaders—I say this because it makes no difference to me what they were; God does not judge by outward appearances—those leaders, I say, made no new suggestion to me. On the contrary, they saw that God had given me the task of preaching the gospel to the Gentiles, just as He had given Peter the task of preaching the gospel to the Jews. For by God's power, I was made an apostle to the Gentiles, just as Peter was made an apostle to the Jews. (Gal. 2:3–8)

Paul continued to speak evil about the disciples, accusing some of them of hypocrisy and how they were wrong and how he was right. He said,

> But when Peter had come to Antioch, I withstood him to his face, because he was to be blamed; for before some certain men came from James, he would eat with the Gentiles; but when they came, he withdrew and separated himself, fearing those who were of the circumcision. And the rest of the Jews also played the hypocrite with him, so that even Barnabas was carried away with their hypocrisy. But when I saw that they were not straightforward about the truth of the gospel, I said to Peter before them all, "If you, being a Jew, live in the manner of Gentiles and not as the Jews, why do you compel Gentiles to live as Jews?" (Gal. 2:11–14)

Furthermore, Paul considered the disciples to be false apostles, who lie about their work and disguise themselves to look real apostles of Christ, as the ministers of Satan transforming themselves into ministers of righteousness. He said,

> *I do not think that I am the least bit inferior to those very special so-called apostles... As the truth of Christ is in me, no one shall stop me from this boasting in the regions of Achaia. Why? Because I do not love you? God knows! But what I do, I will also continue to do, that I may cut off the opportunity from those who desire an opportunity to be regarded just as we are in the things of which they boast. For such are false apostles, deceitful workers, transforming themselves into real apostles of Christ. And no wonder! For Satan himself transforms himself into an angel of light. Therefore, it is no great thing if his ministers also transform themselves into ministers of righteousness, whose end will be according to their works... Are they Hebrews? So am I. Are they Israelites? So am I. Are they Abraham's descendants? So am I. Are they Christ servants? I sound like a madman—but I am a better servant than they are! I have worked much harder. I have been in prison more times, I have been whipped much more, and I have been near death more often.* (2 Cor. 11:5, 10–15, 22–23)

He warned the Gentiles in Galatia from the true Gospel of the disciples. He wrote,

> *I marvel that you are turning away so soon from him* (Paul himself) *who called you in the grace of Christ, to a different gospel* (of the apostles), *which is not another, but there are some* (the followers of the disciples) *who trouble you and want to pervert the gospel of Christ* (Paul's gospel). *But even if we, or an angel from heaven preach any other gospel to you than what we have preached to you, let him be accursed. As we have said before, so now I say again, "If anyone preaches any other gospel to you than what you have received* (from Paul), *let him be*

> *accursed. For do I now persuade men, or God? Or do I seek to please men? For if I still pleased men I would not be a servant of Christ. But I make known to you, brethren, that the gospel which was preached by me is not according to man. For I neither receive it from man, nor was I taught it, but it came through the revelation of Jesus Christ."* (Gal. 1:6–12)

And he also warned the Gentiles in Corinth from the followers of the disciples. He said,

> *I wish you would tolerate me even when I am a bit foolish. Please do it… I am afraid that your minds will be corrupted and that you will abandon your full and pure devotion to Christ—in the same way that Eve was deceived by the snake's clever lies. For you gladly tolerate anyone* (followers of the disciples) *who comes to you and preaches a different Jesus* (true Jesus) *not the one* (fake Jesus) *we* (Paul) *preached or if you accept a spirit and a gospel completely different from the spirit and the gospel you received from us* (Paul) *you may well put with it. I do not think that I am the least bit inferior to those very special so-called apostles."* (2 Cor. 11:1, 3–5)

And thus, in a way that Paul did not perceive, gradually, God exposed him. Actually, God caused Paul to expose himself through his own words. He admitted that there was another Jesus of the disciples, Truly Jesus, who was different from Falsely Jesus of Paul, and a spirit and a gospel completely different from the spirit and the gospel he had preached to the Gentiles (2 Cor. 11:3–4).

9. Quoting the Old Testament out of context and manipulated it to match his own personal doctrines and false thoughts. Paul dared to say about Jesus that he became a curse for humanity and that the law of God brings with

it a curse. *"Christ has redeemed us from the curse of the law, having become a curse for us, for it is written, 'Cursed is everyone who hangs on a tree.'"* (Gal. 3:13). Was Jesus a curse? Certainly, not a believer would say such a horrible thing. But Paul misused the following text in the Old Testament.

If a man has committed a sin worthy of death, and he is put to death, and you hang him on a tree, his body shall not remain overnight on the tree, but you shall surely bury him that day... For he who is hanged is accursed of God. (Deut. 21:22–23)

It is clear from the context that the text here speaks of the criminal person who has a sin worthy of death. It has nothing to do with what Paul tried to attribute to Jesus when he quoted part of the text in Deuteronomy outside context to suit his false claim of the curse of Christ.

Does the law bring curses to its followers? Surely not. And no believer would say such a thing. But Paul has another view in which he opposes God's purpose in sending His law to people with his apostles. Paul said, *"Christ has redeemed us from the curse of the law"* (Gal. 3:13). *"Those who depend on obeying the Law live under a curse. For the scripture says, 'Cursed is everyone who does not continue in all things which are written in the book of the law, to do them'"* (Gal. 3:10). Paul here quoted a text from Deuteronomy in the Old Testament out of context. The text clearly says, *"Cursed is the one who does not confirm all the words of this law"* (Deut. 27:26). The words of that law were written by Moses on some large stones covered with plaster, as God had instructed him, *"And you shall write very plainly on the stones all the words of this law"* (Deut. 27:8). Then Moses asked the people of Israel, saying, *"You shall obey the voice of the Lord your God and observe His commandments and His statutes which I command you today"* (Deut. 27:10). In other words, people should live under a law that comes from God and anyone of the people of Israel who ignores or disrupts the law of God is under God's curse. Thus, the curse mentioned in the text is for those who ignore God's law or disrupt it: *"Cursed is the one who does not confirm all the words of this law,"* not for those who depend upon God's law and give obedience to it. But Paul manipulated the text of Deuteronomy 27:26 out of context in his favor, to fit his reversed thoughts: the Law brings curse, those who depend on obeying the Law live under a curse, and also Jesus became a curse for us because he accepted to be hanged on a tree to redeem us from the curse of the law (Gal. 3:13). All this in order to disrupt the law, where he claims that a person is put right with God only through faith in Jesus, never by doing what the Law requires (Gal. 2:16). Because if a person is put right with God through the law, it means that Jesus died for nothing (Gal. 2:21).

Also, in the same way in quoting some texts of the Old Testament out of context, he said, *"But that no one is justified by the law in the sight of God. For the scripture says, 'The just* (one) *shall live by faith"* (Gal. 3:11). Here, Paul wants to focus on his false doctrine that *"a man is not justified by the works of the law but by faith in Jesus Christ... For by the works of the law no flesh shall be justified"* (Gal. 2:16). And he tried to prove that by quoting a text from the Old Testament out of context and manipulated it: *"The just* (one) *shall live by faith."* He quoted this text from the book of Habakkuk in the Old Testament out of context. And the truth is that the entire text of Habakkuk says, *"Behold the proud* (one), *his soul is not upright in him. But the just* (one) *shall live by his faith. Indeed, because he transgresses by wine, he is a proud man"* (Hab. 2:4–5). This text discusses the difference between the wicked (the proud) who, because of their unbelief, have become arrogant in following God's orders and for this, they will perish, and the righteous (the just), who live by their faith, which make them steadfastly work under God's law. For *"faith without works is dead!"* (James 2:20) and *"What does it profit, if someone says he has faith but does not have works? Can faith save him?"* (James 2:14).

Here also, Paul tries to focus on his false doctrine that the law of God has nothing to do with faith. He said, *"Yet the law is not of faith, but 'The man who does them shall live by them"* (Gal. 3:12). And he tried to prove that by quoting a text from the Old Testament out of context and manipulated it: "The man who does them shall live by them." Paul quoted this text from the book of Leviticus in the Old Testament, when God spoke to Moses, saying, *"You shall therefore keep my statutes and my judgments, which if a man does, he shall live by them; I am the Lord"* (Lev. 18:5).

Surely, no one will follow the law of God without a faith urging him to follow. But Paul manipulated the last phrase of the text, *"If a man does, he shall live by them,"* out of context in his favor, to prove his false doctrine of the separation between the faith and keeping the law, where he claimed that whoever obeys the law will be left relied on it and will not be justified before God. While the text shows that life does not stand upright without keeping of God's statutes and provisions.

Another example of Paul manipulating the texts of the Old Testament out of context is narrated by Luke in his book the Acts of the Apostles, that after three days of the arrival of Paul to Rome, he called the local Jewish leaders there to a meeting in which he spoke about his relationship with the Jews of Jerusalem. After hearing from him, they set another day with him to hear again from him, and many of them came to where Paul was staying. He explained to them his message from morning till night, and he tried to convince them about Jesus by quoting from the law of Moses and the writings of the prophets. Although he completely omitted any mention of his core doctrine: that of the atonement of the cross! (Acts 28:17–23).

Some Jews were convinced of what had been said, and the others did not believe. So, when they did not agree among themselves, they went away after Paul had said to them,

> *The Holy Spirit spoke rightly through Isaiah the prophet to our fathers, saying, "Go to this people and say: 'Hearing you will hear, and shall not understand. And seeing you will see, and not perceive; for the heart of this people has grown dull. Their ears are hard of hearing, and their eyes they have closed, lest they should see with their eyes and hear with their ears, lest they should understand with their hearts and turn, so that I should heal them.' Therefore, let it be known to you that salvation of God has been sent to the Gentiles, and they will hear it."* (Acts 28:25–28)

Paul quoted this text from the Old Testament from the book of Isaiah (Isa. 6:9–10) out of context in his favor because he wanted to insult those Jews who attended his council in Rome and were not convinced of his beliefs.

Paul's conceit pushed him to consider himself as God's light to the Gentiles. He once made a speech to the Jews in Antioch, saying to them (with the disciple Barnabas by his side),

> *It was necessary that the word of God should be spoken to you first; but since you reject it, and judge yourselves unworthy of everlasting life, behold, we turn to the Gentiles. For so the Lord has commanded us, "I have set you to be a light to the Gentiles. That you should be for salvation to the ends of the earth."* (Acts 13:46–47)

Have Jesus set Paul to be a light to the Gentiles and be for salvation to the ends of the earth? Surely not. But Paul quoted a text that was given exclusively to the prophet Isaiah and attributed to himself. The text of Isaiah clearly says,

> *The Lord said to me, "I have a greater task for you, my servant* (Isaiah) *Not only will you restore to greatness the people of Israel who have survived, but I will also make you* (Isaiah) *a light to the Gentiles. That you should be my salvation to the ends of the earth."* (Isa. 49:6)

It was just a cut-and-paste job.

In his letter to the Romans chapter 3, Paul made nine cuts and pastes from Psalm 51, 14, 53, 5, 10, 140, 36 and from Isaiah 59 and from Ecclesiastes 7.

10. The final item of the critical path method of Paul to rebranding of Jesus's religion according to his own thoughts and philosophy was the marketing of the salvation formula that he

made from the alleged blood of Jesus on the cross. *"So, if you confess with your mouth the lord Jesus and believe in your heart that God has raised him from the dead, you will be saved"* (Rom. 10:9). So he limited Christianity to the cross and made salvation conditional to total dependency on Christ's alleged death on the cross. He wrote, *"And if Christ is not risen, then our preaching is vain, and your faith is also vain"* (1 Cor. 15:14).

Thus, Paul replaced the salvation formula that Jesus preached among the Israelites, which was based on believing that there is only one true God and that Jesus is His messenger and to keep the commandments. To the Israelites, Jesus said, *"Most assuredly I say to you, he who hears my word and believe in Him who sent me has everlasting life"* (John 5:24). *"And this is eternal life, that they may know you, the only true God, and Jesus Christ whom you have sent"* (John 17:3). And when a man asked Jesus, *"Good Teacher, what good things shall I do that I may have eternal life?"* So he said to him, *"Why do you call me good? No one is good but One, that is God. But if you want to enter into life keep the commandments"* (Matt. 19:16–17). Paul replaced all of that with a pagan salvation formula based on believing in the alleged sacrificial death of the alleged son of God when his father sent him to earth to commit suicide on the cross. Glorified be your Lord, the Lord of honor and power! He is free from what Paul attributed unto Him.

How did the disciples deal with Paul after he was exposed, and how was his end?

Paul and the disciple Barnabas spent some time in Antioch teaching and preaching (Acts 15:35). But since they both had different intentions, for Paul wanted to preach his own falsely Jesus and his own falsely gospel to the Gentiles, a conflict must occur between the true and false. There was a sharp argument had happened between the two, so they separated from one another! The matter was not merely a personal controversy about travel's arrangements. But it was a deep doctrine controversy, after Paul's reality was exposed for Barnabas. The author of Acts wrote:

> *Then after some days Paul said to Barnabas, "Let us now go back and visit our brethren in every city where we have preached that word of the Lord and see how they are doing." Now Barnabas was determined to take with them John called Mark. But Paul insisted that they should not take with them the one who had departed from them in Pamphylia and had not gone with them to the work. Then the contention became so sharp that they parted from one another. And Barnabas took Mark and sailed to Cyprus.* (Acts 15:36–39)

Surely, if both had the same intention and doctrine, they would not had separated from one another because of an absurd reason; rather, they would make serving of the religion above personal considerations. And after period of a long time, Paul got his things ready and left for Jerusalem where the disciples are. When he arrived there, he had a meeting with the disciple James and all the church elders. He told them about his activities among the Gentiles (Acts 21:17–19). In view of the fact that the news already reached the disciples about Paul's dissenting dubious activity, so they wanted to put him through a trial. They said to him,

> *"Brother Paul, you can see how many thousands of Jews have become believers, and how devoted they all are to the Law. They have been told that you have been teaching all the Jews who live in Gentile countries to abandon the Law of Moses, telling them not to circumcise their children or follow the Jewish customs. What then? The assembly must certainly meet, for they will hear that you have come. This is what we want you to do. There are four men here who have taken a vow. Go along with*

> *them and join them in the ceremony of purification and pay their expenses; then they will be able to shave their heads. In this way everyone will know that there is no truth in any of the things that they have been told about you, but that you yourself live in accordance with the Law of Moses. But as for the Gentiles who have become believers, we have sent them a letter telling them we decided that they must not eat any food that has been offered to idols, or any blood, or any animal that has been strangled, and that they must keep themselves from sexual immorality.* (Acts 21:20–25)

There was no other option for Paul except to obey because he had no power to face the large group of people who came together to meet for him. So the next day, Paul did as they asked him.

> *So Paul took the men and the next day performed the ceremony of purification with them. Then he went into the temple and gave notice how many days it would be until the end of the period of purification, when a sacrifice would be offered for each one of them. But just when the seven days were about to come to an end, some Jews from the province of Asia saw Paul in the temple. They stirred up the whole crowd and grabbed Paul, crying out, "Men of Israel, help! This is the man who goes everywhere teaching everyone against the people of Israel, the Law of Moses and the temple. And now he has even brought some Gentiles into the temple and defiled this holy place!" They said this because they had seen Tophimus from Ephesus with Paul in the city, and they thought that Paul had taken him into the temple. And all the city was disturbed; and the people ran together, seized Paul and dragged him out of the temple; and immediately the doors were shut. The*

> mob was trying to kill Paul, when a report was sent up to the commander of the Roman troops that all of Jerusalem was rioting. At once the commander took some officers and soldiers and rushed down to the crowd. When the people saw him with the soldiers, they stopped beating Paul. The commander went over to Paul, arrested him, and ordered him to be bound with two chains. Then he asked, "Who is this man, and what has he done?" Some in the crowd shouted one thing, others something else. There was such confusion that the commander could not find out exactly what had happened, so he ordered his men to take Paul up into the fort. (Acts 21:26–34)

As for the disciples, they were present, but they did nothing to stand up for Paul because he was not of them and they were not of him. Rather, they left him alone in facing the anger of the crowd. After this event, there is no mention for the disciples in the book of Acts because the author specialized the rest of the book for Paul alone, who again faced the anger of the Jews after the Romanian commander had gave him permission to speak to the angry Jews. When Paul started to tell the people about himself and the story of his alleged conversion to the religion of Jesus, they did not control themselves. *"Then they raised their voices and said, 'Away with such a fellow from the earth, for he is not fit to live!'"* (Acts 22:22). The commander ordered his men to take Paul into the barracks and to bring the chief priests and all their council tomorrow to meet with Paul because he wanted to know for sure what the Jews were accusing Paul of (Acts 22:30). Paul succeeded to create a dissension among the Jews themselves, so the commander brought him back into the barracks (Acts 23:6–10). Then the commander knew that the Jews were planning to kill Paul, so he sent him to Felix the governor in Caesarea (Acts 23:12–24). Paul stayed in Caesarea two years. He was under guard with some freedom, as to allow his friends to come to him (Acts 24:23–27). After Felix, came Festus as a governor, who commanded Paul to be brought to stand before the Jews who had come to him with many serious complaints against Paul; but Paul defended himself. Then the governor asked Paul, *"Are you willing to go up to Jerusalem and there be judged?"* Paul refused and said, *"I appeal to Caesar."* Then Festus, after conferring with his advisers, answered, *"You have appealed to Caesar? To Caesar you shall go!"* (Acts 25:6–12).

And after some days, King Agrippa came to Caesarea. Then Festus commanded Paul to be brought before King Agrippa, who permitted Paul to speak. Paul started to tell the audience about himself and the story of his alleged conversion to the religion of Jesus. Festus could not control himself and said with a loud voice, *"You are mad, Paul! Your great learning is driving you mad!"* (Acts 26:24). Then King Agrippa said to Festus, *"This man might have been set free if he had not appealed to Caesar"* (Acts 26:32). Then Paul was sent with some other prisoners to Rome in Italy (Acts 27:1). Now when they arrived in Rome, Paul was allowed to dwell by himself with a soldier who guarded him (Acts 28:16). Paul dwelt two whole years in his own rented house (Acts 28:30).

Here, the narration of the book of Acts is finished. It is not known exactly what had happened later to Paul. But according to tradition, Paul was beheaded, several miles out of the city of Rome, at the AD sixties. It was during the time of the Emperor Nero who issued the decree to kill him in the wake of the great fire of Rome because he accused the "Christians" of Rome of kindling the fire. Surely, Jesus did not come to rescue him as Paul himself claimed that Jesus had said to him on the road to Damascus, *"I will rescue from the Jewish people, as well as from the Gentiles, to whom I now send you"* (Acts 26:17). Or as he also claimed, *"And the lord will rescue me from all evil and take me safely into his heavenly kingdom"* (Tim. 4:18).

Unfortunately, mainstream Christianity today is the religion of Paul, not Jesus. After Paul spread his own Christianity in the pagan nations of some parts of the Middle East and some of the cities of the Roman Empire, the Roman Empire in the fourth century decided to take Paul's mainstream Christianity as the formal religion of the empire. Then this Christianity continued to spread in northern Europe and then throughout the world. There is no doubt that Paul was one of the greatest tribulations in the history of humanity. How many countless millions of people have already been misled?

CHAPTER 6

The way to God after Jesus

Illusions and realities

Any newborn anywhere in the world is born with the innate nature, a natural submission to one God and admission in monotheism. This is how God created mankind. The newborn baby is never born a Christian or a Jew or a Hindu or a Buddhist. But rather his parents have raised him to be a Christian or Jew or a follower of any other faith. So the child grows up with the faith of its environment, putting trust in its parents, teachers, priests, scholars, scriptures, and society. The difference among people around the world about this fact is this: whoever was born in a society where the innate, the upright natural true faith about God is maintained, no conflict within man would occur. But those who were born in a society where the innate nature is corrupted with myths that have been inherited, surely, as the child grows up, there will be a conflict within itself, between the faith of the innate nature and the inherited faith of the society. The depth of this conflict may vary among people, and it is especially strong with those of deep thinking. Others may be heedless about it. Those who pay attention to the conflict may start to seek the truth through contemplation and research to find the answers for the questions arising from such conflict.

The heedless ones are under the allurement of this present life and the burden of the inheritance of their parents' faith, the surrounding society, and the deceit of Satan. Thus, they are not willing to make any effort to seek the truth or even to listen. They are not willing to exert any effort to differentiate between illusions and realities. You will find them supporting each other in order to remain with their inherited faith. Surely, Satan makes it fair-seeming to them, all that which they believe and do. They would say, "We are satisfied with our faith. We do not need to search for another one." They would repeat, "We were born on the faith of our parents, and upon it we will die." But the matter-of-fact is that they were not born on that faith but on the innate monotheistic nature, then their parents brought them up on their false faith.

God gave man a long life span that whosoever would receive admonition may reflect. He should not just live to eat and enjoy while being preoccupied with a false hope and dream. He should not let the allurement of this present life deceive him and should not let Satan deceive him also away from the true way to salvation. He should not let confusion and friends pressure him from seeking the truth. He should not let the pride arising from higher education, fame, origin, and color stops him from checking the faith with him. He should think about the heathens whose efforts have been wasted in this life while they thought that they were acquiring good with their faith in their false gods. He should not gamble with his soul! It is very risky to leave his life to proceed with an inherited faith till the moment of death. He should not let the angel of death be the one to wake him up from the false dream, when all facts will begin to unfold during the agony of death that he has been avoiding. At that moment, his sight will see the arrangement of the assisting angels making the way for the angel of death to take his soul. And by their faces and the way how those angels appear and deal, he will be able to predict his final destiny before leaving this world. Certainly, it is too late then. There will be no U-turn back to this life to correct the faith and way because death is the gateway to the other stages of the life of the souls at the Barrier, which is a transitional state in a barrier place between this life and the Hereafter, where the souls of the dead go, waiting for the resurrection for the next life. See Luke 16:19–31.

How can we find the true way to salvation?

In order for a person to find the only true way to salvation, he has to make some efforts such as the following:

1. To have the true intention in his heart to seek the truth.
2. To start to check the source of his faith (scriptures). His faith should come only from true inspired Words of God.
3. He should always ask for proofs for what he has been asked to believe. It is very dangerous for him to be just a blind follower or to remain upon an inherited faith without proofs. He should not accept any text as a proof from unreliable books full of contradictions and mistakes because it is a man-made book, not God's.

The prophet to come after Jesus

There is a prophecy in the book of Deuteronomy, in the Old Testament, about a prophet to be appointed by God with the following details: he would be among the brethren of the Israelites. He would be like Moses. The words of God would be in his mouth. He speaks only what God would command him. Anyone who refuses to obey him would be punished by God. If this prophet speaks something in the name of God without His command or speaks in the name of other gods, so this prophet must die for it. Whatever this prophet speaks must come true, if not, he has spoken on his own authority; and people should not fear him. The text of the prophecy says that God said to Moses,

> *I will raise up for them a prophet like you* (Moses) *from among their brethren, and will put my words in his mouth, and he shall speak to them all that I command him. And it shall be that whoever will not hear My words, which he speaks in My name, I will require it of him. But the prophet who presumes to speak a word in My name, which*

> *I have not commanded him to speak, or who speaks in the name of other gods, that prophet shall die. And if you say in your heart, "How shall we know the word which the lord has not spoken?" When a prophet speaks in the name of the Lord, if the thing does not happen or come to pass, that is the thing which the Lord has not spoken; the prophet has spoken it presumptuously: you shall not be afraid of him.* (Deut. 18:18–22)

There are here two important points:

1. If this prophet was not among the Israelites themselves, but among their brethren, then who are the brethren of the Israelites (Abraham's descendants through his son Isaac)? The answer is the Ishmaelite (Abraham's descendants through Isaac's older brother, Ishmael).
2. This prophecy must come to pass, and this prophet had to be raised; otherwise, the text would be false.

The Jewish scholars and priests knew from their books that God would send two persons, one is a Messiah and the other is a prophet. And they also knew that all the prophets after Moses were neither the Messiah nor the promised prophet. And when God sent the Prophet John the Baptist before the Prophet Jesus, *"the Jews sent priests and Levites from Jerusalem to ask him, 'Who you are?' He confessed, and did not deny, but confessed, 'I am not the Christ.' And they asked him, 'What then? Are you Elijah?' He said, 'I am not.' 'Are you the prophet?' And he answered, 'No'"* (John 1:19–21). Even the common Jews knew that a prophet would come, and so when they witnessed the miracle of Jesus's blessing the food, they declared, *"This is truly the prophet who is to come into the world"* (John 6:14). Although Jesus had told his disciples that someone would come after him, but the disciple Peter, as Luke, author of the Acts narrated, had a different understanding as he made God's promise of sending two persons, a Christ, and a prophet, just one person, by claiming that the promised prophet who is like Moses (Deut. 18:18–22) is the Christ Jesus himself. Knowing that there is no narration in any gospel tells that Jesus had told his disciples or the Jews that he was the prophet that, like Moses, is mentioned in the prophecy in Deuteronomy. Luke narrated in his book, the Acts of the Apostles, that while Peter was calling the Jewish people in the temple, after the ascension, he asked them to believe and listen to Jesus, who was preached to them before by the mouth of God's former prophets. He said to them, *"For Moses truly said to the fathers, 'The Lord your God will raise up for you a prophet like me from your brethren. Him you shall hear in all things, whatever he says to you'"* (Acts 3:22).

The church fathers who believed that Jesus was God or his real begotten son also believed that Jesus is the prophet who is like Moses in Deuteronomy 18:18–22. How can this be? How can Jesus be God and a prophet like Moses at the same time? Actually, the church fathers found themselves compelled to direct the prophecy of the prophet who is like Moses to Jesus, even though this contradicts their belief in him as God, because they do not believe in another prophet to come after Jesus.

Surely, Jesus was a prophet for the Israelites. But the prophet who is like Moses that is mentioned in the book of Deuteronomy does not apply to Jesus for two reasons:

1. Jesus was not among the brethren of the Israelis. Rather, he was not from an Israeli father or any other human father. He is a created human by God's word (Be), then he was in the womb of an Israeli woman.
2. Jesus was not like Moses in any aspect, such as birth, family life, end of his life on earth, leadership among the Jews, and acceptance by those whom he was sent to.

And if the prophet who is like Moses that is mentioned in the book of Deuteronomy does not apply to Jesus but rather to another prophet who comes after him, then surely Jesus was aware of this prophet. So what did he say about him?

The author of the Gospel of Matthew narrated that while Jesus was teaching in the temple, the Jewish chief priests and the elders of the people came to him, then a discussion took place among them, so Jesus told them that because they rejected him, the prophethood after him would be taken from the Israelite nation and given to another nation (the Ishmaelite). Jesus said to the Jewish chief priests and elders, *"Therefore I say to you, the kingdom of God will be taken from you* (the Israelites) *and given to a nation (the Ishmaelite) bearing the fruits of it"* (Matt. 21:43).

On the last night of Jesus with his disciples, and after they ate the Passover meal (the Last Supper) in the upper room, Jesus announced about another person whom God would send after him with an immortal message. He said to them, *"And I will pray the Father, and He will give you another helper, that he may abide with you forever, even the spirit of truth"* (John 14:16–17). Then he also clearly declared to them that his message would not be any more valid when this other person comes because he would be the one to take over the guidance of people into all truth and he would bring many new teachings that Jesus did not speak before. He also specified the descriptions of this other person who would come after him and said,

> *I still have many things to say to you, but you cannot bear them now. However, when he the spirit of truth has come, he will guide you into all truth; for he will not speak on his own authority, but whatever he hears he will speak; and he will tell you things to come. He will glorify me.* (John 16:12–14)

So the descriptions that define the person who would come after Jesus are as follows:

1. He has hearing and speaking organs. *"He will not speak on his own authority, but whatever he hears he will speak."*

2. He is an obedient person, complying with commands; submissive to God's will; cannot speak on his own authority; but only speaks what he hears from God.
3. He will not come to bring to people remembrance the things that Jesus said. But rather, he will bring a new teaching from God (many things) that Jesus did not utter before, and he will guide people into all truth.
4. He will glorify Jesus.

If a Christian person had read with some consideration and pondering over Jesus's prophecy about the person who would come after him with many new teachings that Jesus had not spoken before, to take over of guiding people into all truth (John 16:12–14), then he would begin to question within himself the following:

1. Who was the person that came after Jesus?
2. What are the many new teachings that he brought that Jesus did not utter before?
3. How did he guide people into all truth?
4. Are the new teachings that were brought by this person an extension of Jesus's teachings or replacing them?
5. Is salvation now restricted only in believing and following the new teachings that were brought by that person?

Important questions for every Christian who makes salvation in the Hereafter the most important goal he seeks to achieve. If this Christian person had decided to go to the pastors or to those who have knowledge of the Bible to get an answer for the first question, Who is the person that is mentioned in (John 16:12–14) to come after Jesus, in order to believe in him and follow him? What would their answer be?

They will answer, the person who came after Jesus is the Holy Spirit. For Jesus had previously told his disciples that the Holy Spirit would be sent to them after him. He said, *"But the helper, the Holy Spirit, whom the father will send in my name, he will teach you all things, and bring to your remembrance all things that I said to you"* (John

14:26). And they will also say that this prophecy was fulfilled fifty days after the ascension of Christ when the Holy Spirit descended on the disciples in the form of divided tongues, as of fire, and one sat upon each of them.

> *Now when the day of Pentecost had fully come, they were all with one accord in one place. And suddenly there came a sound from heaven, as of rushing mighty wind, and it filled the whole house where they were sitting. Then there appeared to them divided tongues, as of fire, and one sat upon each of them. And they were all filled with the Holy Spirit.* (Acts 2:1–4)

Now this Christian questioner has two options, either to be convinced of this ready-made answer without being sure of it or to try, with a little thought, to make sure that this answer is correct, because the matter is related to his own salvation in the next life.

In fact, if this Christian questioner thinks a little, it will be clear to him that the prophecy of Jesus about the person who would come after him with many new teachings to take over of guiding people into all truth can never fit the Holy Spirit for the following reasons:

1. Jesus said of the person that would come after him that he is "the spirit of truth" *"and I will pray the Father, and He will give you another helper, that he may abide with you forever, even the spirit of truth"* (John 14:16–17). *"But when the helper comes, whom I shall send to you from the Father, the Spirit of truth who proceed from the Father, he will testify of me"* (John 15:26). *"However, when he the spirit of truth has come"* (John 16:13). And elsewhere, Jesus also spoke about the coming of the Holy Spirit after him. He said, *"But the helper, the Holy Spirit, whom the father will send in my name"* (John 14:26). So is the Spirit of Truth and the Holy Spirit one thing or two different entities?

First, we should know that the "Spirit of Truth" is a familiar spiritual phrase or title given to a person or spiritual things, such as the following:

a. The Holy Spirit is a Spirit of Truth.
b. God's revealed words to the prophets are a Spirit of Truth, such as the Gospel in which Jesus spoke as well as the books of all other prophets.
c. What the righteous experience of feelings of tranquility, enlightenment, support, and such like is a Spirit of Truth from God.
d. The human prophet sent by God is considered as a Spirit of Truth. *"Beloved, do not believe every spirit, but test the spirits, whether they are of God; because many false prophets have gone out into the world"* (1 John 4:1). Every spirit, that is, every prophet.

Jesus already prophesied about two different persons to come after him. But how to distinguish between them if each one of them can be considered as a Spirit of Truth? The difference between the two is by the type of defined task for each one of them, as follows:

a. The person would come with the task of teaching the disciples all that Jesus had recommended them and reminding them all things that he said to them. This person is the Holy Spirit, who came in the name of Christ to support the disciples after the ascension of Christ. *"But the helper, the Holy Spirit, whom the father will send in my name, he will teach you all things, and bring to your remembrance all things that I said to you"* (John 14:26). And Jesus said, *"He who believes in me, as the Scripture has said, out of his heart will flow rivers of living water"* (John 7:38). Then the author of the Gospel of John explained these words, saying, *"But this he (Jesus) spoke concerning the Spirit, whom those believ-*

ers in him would receive; for the Holy Spirit was not yet given, because Jesus was not yet glorified" (John 7:39).
b. The person would come with the task of bringing many new teachings that Jesus had not spoken before and taking over of guiding people into all truth. This person is the Spirit of Truth, i.e., prophet of truth or the true prophet, who cannot speak on his own authority, but rather what he hears from God.

I still have many things to say to you, but you cannot bear them now. However, when he the spirit of truth has come, he will guide you into all truth; for he will not speak on his own authority, but whatever he hears he will speak; and he will tell you things to come. He will glorify me. (John 16:12–14)

2. Jesus said that the reason that he did not speak the many other things was that the people would not be able to bear. *"I still have many things to say to you, but you cannot bear them now"* (John 16:12). Luke wrote in his book, the Acts of the Apostles, that the Holy Spirit came to the disciples fifty days after the ascension of Christ.

Now when the day of Pentecost (Fiftieth day) *had fully come, they* (the disciples) *were all with one accord in one place. Then there appeared to them divided tongues, as of fire, and one sat upon each of them. And they were all filled with the Holy Spirit.* (Acts 2:1–4)

Certainly, the many other things that Jesus did not speak about would not come with the Holy Spirit fifty days after his ascension because people still cannot bear them but rather come after hundreds of years have passed.

In fact, Jesus wanted to inform his disciples that his message was not the last. Rather, there is another message (the many things that he did not say) that will be brought by another prophet after him. As for him, he has only finished his part. On the last night of Jesus with his disciples, after they ate the Last Supper in the upper room, Jesus lifted up his eyes to heaven and said, *"I have glorified You on the earth. I have finished the work which You have given me to do"* (John 17:4). So the person who brought the many things that Jesus did not speak (another message) was not the Holy Spirit who came to remind the disciples of Jesus's words fifty days after his ascension but rather another prophet after hundreds of years.

3. Jesus said that there would be a person to come after him, with many things that Jesus himself did not speak about, to take over of guiding people into all truth. If this person was the Holy Spirit, so what are the many new things that the Holy Spirit brought when he descended on the disciples fifty days after the ascension of Christ? The answer is none. But he taught them and reminded them of all that Jesus had spoken to them. While the many other things that Jesus did not speak is another message that came with the Spirit of Truth, the prophet of truth after hundreds of years.
4. The Christians scholars do not believe in a prophet to come after Jesus. And they say that the Spirit of Truth who would come after Jesus with many things to guide people into all truth (John 16:12–14) is the Holy Spirit, who came to the disciples (without any new teaching, but to bring to their remembrance all things that Jesus said to them) (John 14:26).

Now, if we ask the Christians scholars who is the Holy Spirit? The scholars who believe in the Trinity, will answer and say that the Holy Spirit is God himself. One of the three coequal, coeternal hypostases, God the Holy Spirit.

This answer puts those Christians scholars in a serious dilemma in which they cannot avoid, because they believe that the Holy Spirit is God Himself and at the same time also believe that the obedient person who is complying with commands, submissive to God's will, cannot speak on his own authority, whom Jesus prophesied to come after him, is God the Holy Spirit, who is God Himself!

So could it be that the Holy Spirit is God Himself and at the same time He is the obedient person that Jesus prophesied to come after him, who cannot speak on his own authority? Certainly, it cannot be. Just as Jesus cannot be God or a real son of God and at the same time the prophet who is like Moses. So just as the prophecy about the prophet who is like Moses in Deuteronomy 18:18–22 was wrongly addressed to Jesus, we see Jesus's prophecy concerning the same prophet who would come after him was wrongly addressed to the Holy Spirit.

In my discussion with some pastors in their churches, I was asking them how they believe that the Holy Spirit is God Himself and at the same time they believe that the obedient person who is complying with commands, submissive to God's will, cannot speak on his own authority, whom Jesus prophesied to come after him (John 16:12-14) is God the Holy Spirit? One pastor said, "I have never thought about that!" While another pastor, who has a live show, tried to find a way to escape this dilemma. He said, "Imagine this big office, there is a boss in a leading position, who give orders to other two bosses." I replied and said, "With this example, you have just abolished the fake-monotheism of the three coequal Gods in one God in the Trinity. You are now just a heathen, who believes in multiple disparate deities, who are subjected to the authority of the greatest one of them." Of course, he did not like my answer. So he wanted to end the discussion by saying, "Do not put the words of God under microscope." So I told him, "You would not see any defect in the true words of God if you put them under a microscope."

Also, if we ask any Christians who believes in the Trinity and say to him, who is the prophet like Moses? He will say, "Jesus." Okay, who is Jesus? He will say, "God." Okay, who is the one to come after Jesus? He will say, "The Holy Spirit." Okay, who is the Holy Spirit? He will say, "God." Okay, who is God? He will say, "Jesus." Okay, who is Jesus? He will say, "the prophet like Moses." Okay, who will come after him? He will say, "The Holy Spirit." Okay, who is the Holy Spirit? He will say, "God." Okay, who is God? He will say, "Jesus." Okay, who is Jesus? He will say, "Son of God." Okay, who is the Son of God? He will say, "Jesus." Okay, who is Jesus? He will say, "The brother of James." Okay, who is James? He will say, "The brother of God!" Oops! Does God have a brother? As far as my knowledge, the fake Christianity of Paul is the only pagan religion that believes that their god has a brother! So he would also be "god the uncle" for the son of James! Anyway, it must be stopped. Otherwise, the questions will keep going on and on unless it can be understood and comprehended that Jesus was "God, a Prophet like Moses, the Holy Spirit, and the son of God at the same time."

Even the Christians who do not believe in the Trinitarian doctrine have also a serious dilemma, in which they cannot avoid, because they believe that the one who would come after Jesus is the Holy Spirit, and at the same time believe that the Holy Spirit is not a person or hypostasis in a Trinity, but is God's effective power, even though the text clearly used a masculine definite pronoun to indicate to an obedient person complying with commands, submissive to God's will, and having hearing and speaking organs.

No one can take the place of a person but a person. No mere power, influence, or a feeling could take the place of Jesus after him. So the prophecy about the person who would come with the many things that Jesus did not say is not the Holy Spirit but a human messenger who came with all the characteristics that were told by Moses and Jesus about him. In fact, they were applicable only to him.

Who is this prophet?

Nearly six hundred years after the Christ, a prophet who was a descendant of Ishmael, the son of Abraham, was sent by God in fulfillment of His promise to Moses and in fulfillment of the prophecy of Jesus when he told the chief priests and the elders of the people that the kingdom of God would be taken from them and given to a nation bearing the fruits of it (Matthew 21:43) and in fulfillment of his prophecy about the spirit of truth who would come after him with many new things and guide people into all truth (John 16:12–14). He was like Moses in all aspects, such as birth, family life, end of his life on earth, leadership among his people, and acceptance by those whom he was sent to. The words of God were in his mouth. He spoke only of what God had commanded him. If he had spoken something in the name of God without His command, he would have been killed for it. And whatever this prophet had said came to pass. He is the last of God's prophets, he brought the many things that Jesus did not utter, in a universal and final message to remain with humanity until the end of life on earth. This prophet glorified Jesus most, and God revealed to him the truth about Jesus after Paul had distorted it and also the truth about his mother, Mary, who was purified and chosen by God above all women. This last of the prophets is the Prophet Muhammad, peace be upon him, that God sent to all mankind. God (Allah) said in the holy Quran, *"Muhammad is not the father of any of your men, but he is the Messenger of Allah and seal* (i.e., last) *of the prophets. And Allah is Ever All-Aware of everything"* (Quran 33:40). And also, He said, *"And We* (Allah, it is a plural of respect) *have not sent you* (O Muhammad) *except as a giver of glad tidings and a Warner to all mankind, but most of men know not"* (Quran 34:28).

About 4,500 years ago, Allah commanded His prophet Abraham to take his wife, Hagar, and his infant son, Ishmael, from his place in Palestine to dwell far away in Arabia, in an uninhabited, dry, and uncultivable valley in the place of Makkah today, where the first house of worship would be established for mankind. Abraham complied, and Hagar accepted Allah's command, believing that He would not neglect them. And after Abraham left them, he invoked Allah, saying,

> *O our Lord! I have made some of my offspring to dwell in an uncultivable valley by your Sacred House, our Lord, that they may establish prayer. So, fill some hearts among men with love towards them, and provide them with fruits so that they may give thanks.* (Quran 14:37)

When the water that with Hagar had finished and became thirsty with the baby, she stood on a mountain near their place so that she might see someone. When she did not see anybody, she went down and crossed the valley to another mountain and went up on it and did not see anyone either. She repeated her seeking between the two mountains seven times. In the last time, she heard a voice from the direction where her baby Ishmael was. She went toward him and saw a great miracle! The water started to spring from the earth. This spring took the name Zamzam, and Hagar and her son lived in that place, and people started flocking to the place because of the water after they saw birds in the sky hovering around it. Zamzam water still spring till today.

Abraham was visiting his family in Makkah from time to time. In one of his visits, after his son Ishmael had grown up, Allah Almighty commanded him to raise in that place the foundations of the first house of worship that was established for mankind (the Kaaba), and Allah Almighty had shown Abraham the place of the house. Allah said, *"Indeed, the first House* (of worship) *established for mankind was that at Bakkah* (Makkah), *full of blessing, and guidance for the worlds"* (Quran 3:96). And also, He said, *"And* (remember) *when We showed Abraham the site of the* (Sacred) *House* (the Kaaba at Makkah) (saying) *'Do not associate anything with Me and purify my House for those who circumambulate it, and those who stand* (in prayer) *and those who bow and prostrate'"* (Quran 22:26). And He also said, *"And* (remember) *when Abraham and Ishmael were raising the foundations of the House* (the Kaaba at Makkah), *saying, 'Our Lord! Accept* (this service) *from us, Verily, You are the All-Hearer, the All-Knower'"* (Quran 2:127). And after Abraham and Ishmael completed the construction of the Kaaba, Allah commanded Abraham to proclaim to mankind the pilgrimage. Allah said, *"And proclaim to mankind the Hajj* (pilgrimage). *They will come to you on foot and on every lean camel, they will come from every deep and distant* (wide) *mountain highway* (to perform Hajj)*"* (Quran 22:27).

Allah blessed Ishmael with prophethood, who began spreading monotheism and worshiping of Allah in Makkah. And people started to come to the Sacred House to perform pilgrimage at its annual season. But over the centuries, the Arabs there deviated from the straight path, where they corrupted their religion and took the idols as deities. Although the Kaaba was the center of their worship and their annual pilgrimage, they filled it with idols and pictures. The ignorance age continued so until Allah sent among them the last of the prophets, Muhammad, peace be upon him, from the lineage of the prophet Ishmael, who he was born in Makkah in the year AD 571. He was an orphan, where his father died when he was a fetus in his mother's womb. And when he reached the age of six, his mother died. He lived his childhood as an orphan under the sponsorship of his grandfather, and when he reached the age of eight, his grandfather died, so his uncle sponsored him, and in his early age was working as a shepherd.

Allah was with the Prophet Muhammad, peace be upon him, in his life in the midst of that pagan society that worshiped idols in the Kaaba, and therefore, he did not invoke to any idol. Rather, he used to isolate himself from his people, worshiping God alone, and he hated alcohol and vices. He was the best of his people in manners, the truer in utterance, and the trustier; so his people called him the honest trustworthy. And when he reached the age of forty, Allah sent the Holy Spirit, Angel Gabriel, to him with the first revelation and sent him a messenger to the world. The first revelation was the first five verses of chapter 96. Allah said,

> *Read! In the Name of your Lord Who has created* (all that exists). *He has created man from a clot* (a piece of thick coagulated blood). *Read! And your Lord is the Most Generous. Who has taught* (the writing) *by the pen. He has taught man that which he knew not.* (Quran 96:1–5)

The Prophet Muhammad, peace be upon him, stayed in Makkah, calling his people for thirteen years. He and those who followed him faced troubles and difficulties from the people of Mecca. Then Allah prepared for him who will support him when he met the pilgrims from Madinah who accepted Islam and invited him to their city. So Allah Almighty authorized him to emigrate to Madinah in the year AD 622 with the people of Makkah who followed him. And he lived in Madinah for ten years, calling people to the religion of Allah until it spread in the Arabian Peninsula, starting from Makkah, which he conquered. He died in AD 632 at the age of sixty-three years old. The caliphs after him and the believers continued to this day to spread the religion of Allah, Who ensured its superiority over all religions. Allah said, *"It is He Who has sent His Messenger* (Muhammad) *with guidance and the religion of truth, to make it superior over all religions even though the polytheists hate (it)"* (Quran 9:33).

Is religion important in man's life, and what is its name with God?

Is that all in life, just trying to enjoy the time as much as possible? And even if this is achieved, is it enough to feel completely satisfied? Does life pass without a map? The humans on planet earth are on a journey, but to where? What is the goal? Is there a road map for this journey? And where is it located?

Believing in the existence of Allah, the Creator, raises an important question: why did God create man on planet earth? The Creator has not left the answer to such important question to man's guesswork, but He answered it Himself so that the people who strayed will have no argument against God after knowing God's answer to such question.

Before we know the answer of God Almighty to the question of the purpose of His creation of man, we can also ask why God created the universe. God Almighty answered this question Himself also and said, *"And We did not create the heavens and earth and that between them for mere play. We did not create them except in truth, but most of them do not know"* (Quran 44:38–39). In this answer, we have to consider two attributes of God Almighty, namely the attribute of creation and the attribute of wisdom. God is a wise Creator. He creates what He wills. It is not in vain, not for amusement and play, but of a perfect wisdom. So what is the truth for which God Almighty created the heavens and the earth and what is between them (the universe)? The truth is that, the creation of the universe is a sign, so that the creature realizes that God is the Creator, the One and Great, the One God the Regulator the Wise, the Lord of the heavens and the earth and everything between them, Lord of the worlds. Allah said, *"And among His signs is the creation of the heavens and the earth, and whatever moving* (living) *creatures He has dispersed in them both"* (Quran 42:29). And also, He said, *"And We did not create the heavens and earth and that between them for mere play"* (Quran 21:16). And also, He said, *"And We did not create the heaven and earth and that between them aimlessly"* (Quran 38:27).

Imagine if this great universe with its precise laws and creatures, from the major galaxies to the smallest microscopic creature, without intelligent sane creatures such as the human and the jinn (an intelligent spirit of lower rank than the angels, able to appear in human and animal forms and to possess humans). Who then will realize this truth for which God created the universe, death and life? The wisdom of God Almighty required to create two types of creation (man and jinn) with minds that enable them to contemplate the creation of God and His cosmic signs so that they realize the truth in the creation of the universe: that its Creator is One, there is nothing like Him, and He alone has the divinity. At the same time, their minds enable them to realize their limits as weak creatures submissive to this One Creator God.

God has commanded man to use his mind and think deeply about the creation of the heavens, the earth, and the souls and how He originated the creation. Allah said, *"Say, 'Travel in the land and see how* (Allah) *originated the creation, and then Allah will bring forth the creation of the Hereafter. Verily, Allah is able to do all things'"* (Quran 29:20). And He said, *"Say, 'Observe what is in the heavens and the earth.' But of no avail will be signs or warners to a people who do not believe"* (Quran 10:101). And He said, *"Have not those who disbelieved known that the heavens and the earth were joined together as one united piece, then We* (Allah) *parted them?"* (Quran 21:30). And He said, *"And among His Signs is the creation of the heavens and the earth, and the difference of your language and colours. Verily, in that are indeed signs for men of sound knowledge"* (Quran 30:22). And He said,

Verily, in the creation of the heavens and the earth, and in the alternation of night and day, and

> *the ships which sail through the sea with that which is of use to mankind, and what Allah has sent down from the sky of rain, giving life thereby to the earth after its lifelessness and dispersing therein every* (kind of) *moving creature, and* (His) *directing of the winds and the clouds which are held between the sky and the earth, are indeed signs for people of understanding.* (Quran 2:164)

And He said,

> *Verily, in the creation of the heavens and the earth, and in the alternation of night and day, there are indeed signs for men of understanding. Those who remember Allah while standing, sitting, and lying down on their side, and think deeply about the creation of the heavens and the earth,* (saying): *"Our Lord! You have not created* (all) *this without purpose, glory to You! Give us salvation from the torment of the Fire."* (Quran 3:190–191)

And He said,

> *And on the earth are signs for those who have Faith with certainty. And also in your own-selves. Will you not then see?* (Quran 51:20–21)

God Almighty has sent messengers to people to inform them that they were not created in vain, Allah said, *"Did you think that We had created you in vain, and that you would not be brought back to Us?"* (Quran 23:115), and to announce to them the wisdom and the goal for which God created the rational human on planet earth, which is the realization and the acknowledging God's Oneness in worship. Allah said, *"And I* (Allah) *have not created the jinn and mankind except that they should worship Me* (Alone)*"* (Quran 51:56). God has made human with an innate nature that would make him to surrender to one God and submission in monotheism. Allah said,

> *Therefore stand firm in your devotion to the true faith, the upright nature with which Allah has endowed man. Allah's creation cannot be changed. This is surely the true religion, although most men do not know it.* (Quran 30:30)

However, a questioner may ask, Does God need the belief and worship of man and jinn?

Certainly, God does not need any of his creatures on earth or in the heavens and does not take any one of his creation as an ally to help him, for He is the Rich (Free of all needs) Worthy of all praise. Allah said, *"And say, "All praises be to Allah, Who has not begotten a son, and Who has not partner in* (His) *Dominion, nor He is low to have a protector. And glorify Him with* (great) *glorification"* (Quran 17:111). And He said, *"O mankind! It is you who stand in need of Allah. But Allah is Rich* (Free of all needs) *Worthy of all praise"* (Quran 35:15). And God Almighty has made it clear to people that He stands not in need of their belief and their worship, but He will not approve that the jinn and mankind disbelieving in Him and His existence, and He will not approve that they take another deity besides Him, because everything other than God is a creature that does not deserve to be worshiped besides God. Allah said, *"If you disbelieve, then verily, Allah is not in need of you; He likes not disbelief for His slaves* (human and jinn)*"* (Quran 39:7). And He said, *"But whoever disbelieves then indeed, Allah is free from need of the worlds"* (Quran 3:97). Therefore, God did not compel man to believe but rather gave him a free will and a choice between faith and unbelief. And in accordance with the justice and wisdom of God Almighty, He explained to us that this worldly life is short so that He may test us as to which of us is best in performing of worshiping Him alone, and that real life is the life of the Hereafter, where the price of eternal happiness there is the monotheism of God, by worshiping Him alone in this worldly life according to His teachings, while the eternal misery in the Hereafter is a price for not following the way of the appointed messenger by God for us. Also, according to God's justice, He will not make the believers equal to the nonbelievers in their present life and after their death.

In order for this sane creature to last on the planet earth, God created him with instincts and desires that make him multiply and coexist, because this rational human cannot live isolated alone on the planet earth but needs different relationships with others. Yet the creator of man is sufficient to organize and guide all human relationships, and this is the religion of God that came to address minds. The function of religion is the guidance and indication of how to practice these various relationships: the relationship of the created human with his Creator and his relationship with himself and his instincts; with his family and with his community; with the whole world and with the environment and other creatures; and with life itself, with clarification of the criteria of right and wrong in practicing these different relationships. And the more a person's relationship with God is guided by God, the more his other relationships will be straightened. Indeed, he succeeded who works to straighten the path of the instincts and desires of himself in accordance with God's teachings. And indeed, he failed and lost who follows his whims and desires. And based on this, is it not the one who his innate nature has been distorted by inherited myths, and worships the creature instead of the One God, the Creator, who begets not, nor was He begotten and there is none coequal or comparable unto Him, more astray than other creatures that have no mind? Indeed, Allah said,

> *And surely, We have destined many of the jinn and mankind for Hell. They have hearts wherewith they understand not, and they have eyes wherewith they see not, and they have ears wherewith they hear not* (the truth). *They are like cattle, nay even more astray; Those! They are the heedless ones.* (Quran 7:179)

The religion that God chose for man is not just an item in his identification card, but a comprehensive way of life according to the laws that came from the Creator of mankind. All the religions of all the messengers were united in one name, one essential faith that was never revised since Adam. As for the laws and patterns of worship, they were however revised from time to time, and from one messenger to another through the history of prophethood, till the messages was sealed by the final revision that came with the final messenger, Muhammad, to all mankind.

God Himself has given His religion, since Adam's descent and the spread of his descendants on earth, the name Islam. The word "Islam" means surrendering to the One true God. And the surrendering means obedience to God in his monotheism in accordance with the guidance that came by all the messengers. So Islam is the name of the religion of all the messengers and prophets that God sent. And the followers of each messenger are Muslims. The religion of God is not labeled with a name of a prophet, a geographical area, or of a scholar but rather the surrendering to God. Allah said, *"Truly, the religion with Allah is Islam"* (Quran 3:19).

God sent Jesus with a new version of Islam to the people of Israel, in which he fulfilled and confirmed the Torah and to make lawful to them part of what was forbidden to them. This is considered a partial invalidation of Moses's law. It was a local message, limited to the people of Israel only, and was limited with a time, till the time when Prophet Muhammad was appointed with the final universal revision of Islam, to invalidate all previous revisions and to abide with all mankind forever. So Prophet Muhammad became the only way to God for all mankind. No one on the surface of the earth, who knew the reality of Islam by proofs, can come to God except by following Prophet Muhammad, peace be upon him. Allah said, *"And whoever seeks a religion other than Islam, it will never be accepted of him, and in the Hereafter, he will be one of the losers"* (Quran 3:85).

It is all over, and the matter is already determined and finalized. "There is no God but Allah, and Muhammad is His messenger." This is already the only accepted faith, and this is the final formula of salvation. There is no other choice. Therefore, a person should search for proven truth and not just rely on what he has been inherited from his parents, environment, and pupilage. He should not accept anything without proofs because it is very risky just to let one's life go on with an inherited faith till the death moment, then find out the truth about this later on at that moment, then later on the day of judgment. It will be too late then.

The Quran is the final book of God. It was revealed to Prophet Muhammad during a twenty-three year-period through the Holy Spirit, Angel Gabriel. Allah said, *"And indeed, it* (the Quran) *is revealed by the Lord of the worlds. The Trustworthy Spirit* (Gabriel) *has brought it down upon your heart* (O Muhammad) *that you may be of the warners, in plain Arabic language"* (Quran 26:192–195). Then the Prophet Muhammad would dictate it literally to the scribes of the revelation, and many of the prophet's companions would memorize it. The Quran has been protected by God himself. Allah said, *"Indeed, it is We who sent down the Dhikr* (i.e., the Quran) *and surely We will guard it"* (from corruption)*"* (Quran 15:9). And He said, *"And We have sent down to you* (O Muhammad) *the Book* (this Quran) *in truth, confirming the Scriptures that came before it and stands as a guardian over them"* (Quran 5:48). Meaning, the Quran testifies the truth of the books that came before it (i.e., the Torah and the Gospel) and stands as a quality control over them, confirming the truth in them, showing the change and the corruption and invalidating their laws.

The Quran essentially is a book of legislation and law, and it is a living miracle for all generations, which they can be sure was revealed from Allah and was guarded by Himself from any corruption. Read the following proofs:

1. The Quran constituted an open challenge to every nation or individual who do not believe in the Quran to consider the Quran carefully, with deep pondering over it, to look for even one mistake, and they will not find one. Allah said, *"Do they* (the non-Muslim) *not then consider the Quran carefully? Had it been from other than Allah they would surely have Found therein many discrepancies"* (Quran 4:82).

Who can speak such a certain language about his book? Only Allah Almighty does.

2. Also, the Quran constituted an open challenge to them to produce a discourse like the Quran, or even a chapter of the like thereof, and they can never do, because if anyone at any time can do that, then this means that the Quran was composed by a human being, but if no one can do that, then this means that the Quran was revealed by Allah Almighty. Allah said,

> *And if you* (non-Muslim) *are in doubt concerning that which We have sent down* (The Quran) *to Our slave* (Muhammad), *then bring a chapter of the like thereof and call your witnesses* (supporters and helpers) *beside Allah, if you are truthful. But if you do it not, and you can never do it, then fear the Fire* (Hell) *whose fuel is men and stones, prepared for the disbelievers.* (Quran 2:23–24)

And He said,

> *Or do they* (non-Muslim) *say: "He* (Muhammad) *has forged it* (The Quran)?" *Say, "Bring then a chapter like it, and call upon whomsoever you can beside Allah, if you are truthful."* (Quran 10:38)

And He said,

> *Or do they say* (non-Muslim): *'He* (Muhammad) *has forged it* (The Quran)?" *Nay! They believe not! Let them then produce a discourse like it* (The Quran) *if they are truthful.* (Quran 52:33–34)

And He said, *"Falsehood cannot come to it* (The Quran) *from before it or behind it; (it is) sent down by the All-Wise, Worthy of all praise"* (Quran 41:42).

Who can challenge people to the day of resurrection and say to them, "You can never bring a chapter of the like thereof my book, even if you would call your helpers?" Only Allah Almighty does. In fact, the Quran constituted an open challenge to both mankind and jinn together to cooperate with each other and produce a discourse like the Quran, and they will never do. Allah said,

> *Say: "If the mankind and the jinn* (the unseen creatures) *were together to produce the like of this Quran, they could not produce the like thereof, even if they help one another."* (Quran 17:88)

Even the most ingenious and talented human or jinn cannot speak about his book with such strong and challenging language. Only Allah Almighty does.

3. Allah said about the Prophet Muhammad, peace be upon him, and the Quran,

   > *Neither did you* (O Muhammad) *read any book before it* (this Quran), *nor did you write any book* (whatsoever) *with your right hand. In that case, indeed, the followers of falsehood might have doubted. Rather, it* (the Quran) *is distinct verses are preserved in the breasts of those who have been given knowledge. And none reject Our signs except the wrongdoers.* (Quran 29:48–49)

4. Allah said,

   > *Perish the two hands of Abu Lahab* (an uncle of Prophet Muhammad) *and perish he! His wealth and his children well not benefit him! He will be*

burnt in a Fire of blazing flames! And his wife too, who carries wood (thorns which she used to put on the way of Prophet Muhammad). *In her neck is a twisted rope of palm fiber.* (Quran 111:1–5)

The miracle of this chapter is that it speaks clearly about the final destiny of the uncle of the Prophet and his wife, that it will be the hellfire in the Hereafter. In other words, the chapter was a ten-year challenge for both the uncle and his wife that by no means they would accept Islam, and they will die on disbelief and then to the torment of hell. Both failed to go against this chapter, and even by pretending the acceptance of Islam in order to put the Prophet into a critical situation. Both died not believing after more than ten years since this challenge chapter was revealed. Who can challenge about what is in the breasts of men? And who can tell about the final destiny of a human being? The One who revealed this Quran, Allah the All-Knowing.

5. Allah said,

And because of their (the Jews) *saying* (in boast), *"We killed the Messiah Jesus, son of Mary, the Messenger of Allah." but they killed him not, nor crucified him, but it was made to appear so to them, and those who differ in the matter are full of doubts. They have no* (certain) *knowledge, they follow nothing but conjecture. For surely, they killed him not. But Allah raised him up unto Him. And Allah is Ever All-Powerful, All-Wise.* (Quran 4:157–158)

Who can disprove, with such strong language, the rumor of crucifying Jesus that was spread by the Jews and accepted by many people for six hundred years, upon which Paul built his fake Christianity? Surely, only the One who rescued Jesus, Allah. It is only one short verse in the Quran that challenges all those who believe that Jesus was crucified, with all their sciences, technology, and communication skills to prove the crucifixion of Jesus. It is an open challenge to all mankind and jinn (the unseen creatures) till Jesus's second coming!

6. The Islamic doctrines, the certainties, the just laws, the high moral standards, the high decencies that are good for every era, for everywhere and nation, since the descending of the Quran.
7. The promise of Allah for those who disbelieve in the Quran that He will show them His signs in the universe, and in their own selves, until it becomes manifest to them that the Quran is the truth. Allah said,

> Say: "Have you considered: if it (the Quran) is from Allah, and you disbelieve in it, who would be more astray than one who is in opposition far away. We will show them Our signs in the universe, and in their own selves, until it becomes manifest to them that this (the Quran) is the truth. (Quran 41:52–53)

The scientific miracles in the Quran are signs that prove that it is the literal word of God was revealed by Him to His final prophet, Muhammad. It is just a living miracle for all generations, and therein is indeed a reminder for him who has a heart or gives ear while he is heedful. These scientific miracles in the Quran are some facts that were mentioned before almost fifteen centuries ago and only recently were discovered by scientists, which prove the true prophethood of Muhammad, such as the following:

- *Human embryonic development*

Allah said,

> *And indeed We* (Allah) *created man* (Adam) *out of an extract of clay. Then We made him* (the offspring of Adam) *as a drop of sperm in a safe*

lodging (the womb) *Firmly fixed. Then We made the sperm into a clot of congealed blood; then We made the clot into a little lump of flesh, then We made out of that little lump of flesh bones, then We clothed the bones with flesh, then We brought it forth as another creation. So, blessed be to Allah the Best to create!* (Quran 23:12–14)

- *The origin of the universe*

    Allah said, *"Have not those who disbelieved known that the heavens and the earth were joined together as one united piece, then We* (Allah) *parted them?"* (Quran 21:30). And He said, *"Then He* (Allah) *turned towards the heaven when it was smoke"* (Quran 41:11).

- *The reality of the mountains*

    Allah said, *"And He* (Allah) *has set firm mountains into the earth so that it would not shake with you"* (Quran 16:15). And He said, *"Have We not made the earth as a resting place, and the mountains as pegs?"* (Quran 78:6–7).

- *About seas*

    Allah said, *"He* (Allah) *has let free the two seas meeting together. Between them is a barrier which none of them can transgress"* (Quran 55:19–20).

- *About estuary of rivers in the seas*

    Allah said, *"And it is He* (Allah) *Who has let free the two seas* (kinds of water). *One is palatable and sweet, and the other is salty and bitter. And*

He has set a barrier and complete partition between them" (Quran 25:53).

The Quran contains 114 chapters. It was not revealed to Prophet Muhammad all at once, or even in sequence or complete chapters, but it was revealed in dispersed parts according to dispersed events, during twenty-three years. And then he dictated any inspiration of the Quran to the assigned scribes, for he neither read any book before the Quran nor did he write any book by his hand. But even though Prophet Muhammad was illiterate, and the Quran was sent down in dispersed parts over a long period, it came out in the end as a whole, without any single mistake. *"Falsehood cannot come to it* (The Quran) *from before it or behind it;* (it is) *sent down by the All-Wise, Worthy of all praise"* (Quran 41:42).

The question now is, can an illiterate man produce a book by himself, a book of 114 chapters with detailed explanations to mankind of every kind of similitude, of all aspects of life and the Hereafter, the past and the future, the unseen world and the creation, while it was dictated to the scribes in dispersed parts within twenty-three years and with an open challenge to all mankind and the jinn to put his book under a microscope in order to find even one single mistake or to produce the like of his book, or even one chapter? Certainly, no man can do that, not even from the jinn. Even the most ingenious and talented human or jinn with the use of high technology cannot challenge all mankind and the jinn. Only Allah with his final preserved revelation (the Quran) does. Allah said,

> *So I* (Allah) *swear by the setting of the stars. And verily, that is indeed a mighty oath, if you but know that indeed, it is a noble Quran. In a book well-guarded* (the Preserved Tablet with Allah in the heaven) *which none can touch but the purified* (the angels) (it is) *a revelation from the Lord of the worlds.* (Quran 56:75–80)

And whoever reads the Quran with the intention of seeking truth, surely, he will be able to see and feel the difference between the words of Allah and the word of man and to see and feel a language that is so powerful, so eloquent, and at the same time very precise and direct to the point. Allah said,

> *O mankind! Verily, there has come to you a convincing proof* (Prophet Muhammad) *from your Lord; and We* (Allah) *sent down to you a manifest light* (this Quran). *So, as for those who believed in Allah and held fast to Him, He will admit them to His Mercy and Grace, and guide them to Himself by a Straight Path.* (Quran 4:174–175)

And also, Allah said,

> *Say: O you mankind! Now truth* (The Quran and Prophet Muhammad) *has come to you from your Lord. So, whosoever receives guidance, he does so for the good of his own self; and whosoever goes astray, he does so to his own loss; and I am not* (set) *over you as disposer of affairs to oblige you for guidance.* (Quran 10:108)

Christianity and Christians

God never called any religion that was brought by any one of his messengers at anytime, anywhere with the name of that messenger. And that is because all the religions of all the messengers were united in one name, Islam, surrendering to the One true God. Allah said,

> *Truly, the religion with Allah is Islam. Those who were given the Scripture* (Jews and Christians) *did not differ except, out of mutual jealousy, after knowledge had come to them. And whoever disbe-*

lieve in the verses of Allah, then surely, Allah is Swift in taking account. (Quran 3:19)

So Jesus Christ did not bring a new name for a new faith, but with the same faith's name that all the prophets before him had brought, that may his people, the Israelites, submit themselves to none but Allah alone and that they associate no partners with Him (i.e., Islamic monotheism). But Jesus observed the disbelief among the majority of the Jews, with the exception of a few of his followers who believed in him and asked him to bear witness that they have surrendered themselves to God (i.e., Muslims).

People themselves may create a name for a prophet and his followers. So what was the first given name to Jesus and his followers concerning his religion? The answer is with the author of Matthew. He said,

> *So Joseph got up, took the child* (Jesus) *and his mother, and went back to Israel… He was given more instruction in a dream, so he went to the province of Galilee and made his home in a town named Nazareth. And so, what the prophets had said came true: "He will be called a Nazarene."* (Matt. 2:21–23)

Also, Matthew narrated that when a girl saw Peter, she said, *"This fellow also was with Jesus of Nazareth"* (Matt. 26:71). Mark and Luke narrated that a man with unclean spirit cried out, *"Let us alone! what have we to do with you, Jesus of Nazareth?"* (Mark 1:24; Luke 4:34). See also John 18:5 and Acts 2:22.

What about the followers of Jesus? What was the first given name to them concerning their religion? The author of the book of Acts gives us the answer. He wrote about a Jewish orator named Tertullus, who spoke before the governor Felix against Paul, saying, *"We found this man* (Paul) *to be a dangerous nuisance; he starts riots among the Jews all over the world and is a leader of the party of the Nazarenes"* (Acts 24:5).

So the term Nazarenes designates the followers of Jesus as a first given name to them. But what about the term "Christian," how did it originate?

The answer is also in Acts. *"It was at Antioch that the believers were first called Christians"* (Acts 11:26).

Therefore, "Christian" was a Greek term that was first coined in Antioch by Greco-Romans Gentiles before it later became the dominant label. So Christianity is a late-given label by people to the religion brought by Jesus. It was not given by God, nor by the Christ himself. And the fact is that the Jews who believed in Jesus were considered Israelite Muslims while those Jews who rejected Jesus were non-Muslim Israelites.

What about Christianity and those who are known today as Christians?

Well, if Christianity means the genuine teaching of the Christ and a Christian means the one who has the complete and genuine image of Jesus inside his heart, then such a people are no longer in existence. Because, as the Islamic way of Moses was revised by the Islamic way of Jesus in the Israelite world, so the Islamic way of Jesus was already revised by the final Islamic, universal revision brought by the final universal messenger, Muhammad.

So those people who keep the belief in Jesus as God, or son of God, or as a savior who died to save mankind (i.e., Jesus, whom Paul falsified), they will remain with a fake label. Surely, he is not a Christian, the one who keeps in his heart the Christ of Paul. It is an insult to Jesus himself that such a person is labeled a Christian while Jesus is innocent of everything Paul wrote about him. But rather, they ought to be called Pauline or even polytheists due to their associating Jesus with God in His divinity and lordship. We should not call them Christians, even if they are identified as such. The matter has been determined and finalized by God when He has addressed them, saying, *"Surely, they have disbelieved who say: 'Allah is the Messiah Jesus'"* (Quran 5:72).

He also said, *"Surely, disbelievers are those who said: Allah is the third of the three (in a Trinity)"* (Quran 5:73).

And He also said,

> *And to warn those who say, "Allah has begotten a son." No knowledge have they of such a thing, nor had their fathers. Mighty is the word that comes out of their mouths* (i.e. He begot a son). *They utter nothing but a lie.* (Quran 18:4–5)

And He also said,

> *And they say: "The Most Gracious* (Allah) *has begotten a son. Indeed, you have brought forth* (said) *a terrible evil thing. Whereby the heavens are almost torn, and the earth is split asunder, and the mountains fall in ruins, that they ascribe a son to the Most Gracious* (Allah). *But it is not suitable for* (the Majesty of) *the Most Gracious* (Allah) *that He should beget a son. There is none in the heavens and the earth but comes unto the Most Gracious* (Allah) *as a slave."* (Quran 19:88–93)

And He also said,

> Say: *"He is Allah,* (the) *One. Allah is the Self-Sufficient Master. He begets not, nor was He begotten. And there is none co-equal or comparable to Him."* (Quran 112:1–4)

And He also said,

> *They have said, "Allah has begotten a son" Glory is to Him! He is free of all needs. To Him belongs whatever is in the heavens and whatever is in the earth. You have no authority for this* (claim). *Do you say against Allah what you know not. Say: "Verily, those who invent falsehood against Allah*

will never be successful." (For them is brief) *enjoyment in this world; then to Us is their return; then We will make them taste the severest torment because they used to disbelieve.* (Quran 10:68–70)

And He also said,

> *Indeed, Allah does not forgive association with Him, but He forgives what is less than that for whom He wills; and whoever sets up partners with Allah, he has indeed invented a tremendous sin.* (Quran 4:48)

And He also said,

> *And because of their* (the Jews) *saying* (in boast) *"We killed the Messiah Jesus, son of Mary, the Messenger of Allah," but they killed him not, nor crucified him, but it was made to appear so to them, and those who differ in the matter are full of doubts. They have no* (certain) *knowledge, they follow nothing but conjecture. For surely; they killed him not. But Allah raised him up unto Him. And Allah is Ever All-Powerful, All-Wise.* (Quran 4:157–158)

Therefore, what has been called Christianity today is no more a valid way to God for two reasons:

1. The true Christianity of Jesus had been abrogated and updated by the final message brought by the final prophet, Muhammad, as Jesus had abrogated Judaism when he was appointed some two thousand years ago in the Israelite world.
2. Today's Christianity does not possess the genuine image of Jesus but the fake forgery of Paul.

The religion of Jesus, as well as all other previous religions, were local religions to certain people and for a limited time. And that is why the true religion of the Christ and the Gospel were not preserved by God because it was not the final message, but a message for the Israelites only and for a limited time, almost six hundred years, when the final universal messenger, Muhammad, was appointed with the final revision of God's religion, Islam, to all mankind.

Conditions of salvation

Salvation can never be through a savior or deeds but only by the mercy of God that embraces all things. He shall ordain that mercy to those with true faith who performed their good deeds in accordance with His true revelation to his true prophets. So only you can save yourself through the mercy of God by seeking, then accepting, the only true faith and performing good deeds as directed by God. There is only one way to salvation because there is only one truth. That truth is from your Lord, then whosoever wills, let him believe and whosoever wills, let him disbelieve, and whoever disbelieve no salvation for him.

There are two conditions in order to attain salvation by the mercy of God.

1. To have the true faith. And your faith would not be true unless you maintain the six pillars of the true faith.
2. To do good deeds. God will not accept a good deed of you unless you maintain the two pillars of the good deeds.

The true faith and its Six Pillars

Faith is the acknowledging of the heart, which is the belief of the heart, its confirmation, and its acting by obeying the commands. And this must be followed by the utterance of the tongue and acts in the body (the practice of actual and verbal acts of worship), and these parts are interrelated, each part of which is indispensable to the other. Faith in the heart does not steady on a fixed level but rather increases and decreases. The more a person chooses to practice more acts of obedience, the more his faith increases, and the more his faith increases, the more he obeys. And the more he chooses to disobey, the more his faith decreases, and the more his faith decreases, the more his sins increase. Thinking about the greatness of Allah and His signs and remembering Him a lot strengthens and increases faith.

As for the six pillars of true faith, they are as follows:

1. To believe in Allah
2. To believe in angels
3. To believe in the books of Allah
4. To believe in His messengers
5. To believe in the Last Day (the Hereafter)
6. To believe in fate (predestination), the good of it and the bad of it

Allah said, *"And whosoever disbelieve in Allah, His Angels, His Books, His Messengers, and the Last Day, then indeed he has strayed far away"* (Quran 4:136). *"Indeed, all things We created with predestination"* (Quran 54:49). And Prophet Muhammad, peace be upon him, asked Angel Gabriel, "Then tell me about the faith?" Angel Gabriel answered, "To believe in Allah, His angels, His books, His messengers, and the Last Day, and to believe in fate (predestination) the good of it and the bad of it."

I. Believing in Allah

It means believing in His existence and in all that He has said about Himself in the Quran and what His prophet Muhammad, peace be upon him, has said about Him. Believing in Allah is the origin of the religion, and knowing Allah is the basis for monotheism and the first thing that a person is religiously required to know.

Giving deep thought to Allah's creations and cosmic signs lead to belief in His existence. And no matter how much atheists pretend to deny the existence of the Creator, Allah; however, their inner selves are convinced of the existence of something that started everything. And if we ask them how the universe began and what is it made of. They will say that the big bang is the beginning of everything, and at the same time, they say that the big bang was a reaction to something else. This means that something must have come before. Therefore, the big bang was not the beginning, but there was something prior to that.

If the big bang was a reaction to something else that was prior to it, as it should be, this means that the rules of the universe were in place before the universe existed, and that there was He Who preceded those rules in existence, because He is the One Who enacted them and decided them, and He is the One Who Has no beginning and began everything. And He certainly cannot be created by anyone because if He was created, then He was not the First, and since He was not created by anyone else, did He create Himself? This is not possible, for how does He decide to create himself when He was not existed before the decision? This means that He existed without a creator, and His existence was not preceded by Nothingness, and He did not create Himself. And that is Allah, the Only Creator.

Allah is the name of the Lord, the Creator of the universe and all that exists, the Regulator of every affair, Who destine of all events and destinies. He is the infinite One and Who Has all the attributes of absolute perfection that do not change, neither increase nor decrease. He is the First without beginning, and nothing is before Him. And He is the Last without end, and nothing is after Him, and all things shall perish except Allah. He is the Most High, and nothing is above Him, and the Most Near, and nothing is nearer than Him. No vision can grasp Him, and He is beyond human comprehension. He is the Ever living, the One Who sustains and protects all that exists. Neither slumber nor sleep overtakes Him, and He grabs all vision. He is the Only existed, to whom the material's rules and space-time do not apply.

Allah creates what He wills, and He is over all things competent, when He decrees a matter, He only says to it, "Be—" and it is. He is the Owner and the Sustainer of all creatures. The God of angels, jinn, and mankind. He Who gave to each thing its form and nature, then guided it aright. He created us for monotheistic in worshipping Him, and He is the Only One Who deserves the worshipping, humiliation, and submission. One and Only, the Self-Sufficient Master, Whom all creatures need. He begets not, nor was He begotten. There is nothing like Him, nor Has similar, nor an equal to Him. Allah has never begotten a son, and how can He have a son when He has no wife? Nor has there ever been with Him any deity. If there had been other deities, then each deity would have taken away what he had created, and some would have tried to overcome others, and had there been in heaven and earth other deities besides Allah, both heaven and earth would have been ruined.

Allah is the Most Merciful. He forgives sins. He rejoices at the repentance of the believer, and He does not tire of repeating repentance. He is the Greatest in which all minds cannot realize His Greatness, and He is the justice in which He made oppression is forbidden for Himself and for His servants, so He will not punish anyone unless a clear proof is made before him, and He burdens not a person beyond his scope. Nothing vanishes from His sight, hear, and knowledge. He hears and knows the secret and that which is yet more hidden. Nothing occupies Him about another thing, and no voice about another voice, and no creation about another creation, and He Which is indispensable for any exist.

Allah is Beautiful in Essence, Beautiful in Attributes, Beautiful in Deeds, and Beautiful in Names. Allah Almighty said,

> "He is Allah, besides Whom there is no other god, the King, the Holy One, the One Free from all defects, the Giver of security, the Watcher over His creatures, the All-mighty, the Compeller, the Supreme. Glory be to Allah above all that they associate as partner with Him. He is Allah, the Creator, the Inventor of all things, the Bestower of forms. To him belong the best Names. All that is in the heavens and the earth glorify Him. And He is the All-mighty, the All-Wise. (Quran 59:23–24)

Where is Allah?

Every place, space, and time is a creature with a beginning, a scope, extent, bounds, and outer edge. And every existed in a place is also a creature having a specified size. And Allah exists before the creation of every place, space, and time. He encompasses of everything, and nothing encompasses of Him. So when we ask where is Allah? We are not asking about a finite created whereabouts in which Allah is, and Allah forbid it, to be restricted in size or be encompassed with a place, because every place is created from nothing, while Allah was and had nothing with Him, neither space nor time. And Allah is not subject to the laws of space and time; but, rather those laws are subject to Him, because He is the Creator of space and time and its laws. The existence of Allah Almighty is transcendent on the concepts of time and space that we perceive with our senses because our awareness is subject to the laws of space and time.

Allah Almighty told us that he is in heaven. The Almighty said, *"Do you feel secure that He Who is over the heaven* (Allah) *will not cause the earth to cave in beneath you?"* (Quran 67:16). Heaven here means the height, and the highest and greatest of Allah's creatures is the Throne that surrounds all creatures, and no creature is above it. And if Allah is in absolute height, then Allah Almighty rises above the Throne and above all the creatures, and that is why Allah Almighty said, *"The Most Gracious* (Allah) *rose over* (Istawa) *the Throne* (in a manner that suite His Majesty)*"* (Quran 20:5). Al-Istiwa is the perfect of a state, and the state here is the height and rising, i.e., the perfection of Allah's absolute height and rising over all his creatures surrounded by the Throne, a rising that suite His majesty. And if the Throne is the highest of Allah's creations, which is carried by angels, then Allah is greater than to be carried by a creature; rather, He is transcendent over the Throne. He does not mix or tangent to any creature, with the belief that He is not in a place, because Allah was before He created the Throne and the place, and He is now as He was before the creation of the Throne and the place. And since the heavens surround the earth, so they are high on it, and since the Kursi (literally a footstool or chair. It is not the Throne) extends over the heavens and the earth, so it is high on them, and since the Throne (which Allah rose over it in a manner that suits His Majesty) surrounds the Kursi, so it is high on it, and Allah Almighty has the absolute high on all sides and nothing above Him.

The human being and all earthly creatures compared to the earth are nothing, the earth compared to the galaxy is nothing, and the galaxy compared to the universe is nothing, and the universe compared to the Kursi is nothing, and the Kursi compared to the Throne is nothing, and the Throne compared to Allah is nothing. Therefore, the entire universe and all the creatures that inside and outside it compared to Allah are nothing. He is the Highest above all the creatures, and none of Allah's creatures deserves to be glorified or worshiped beside Allah Almighty. Allah said,

> *They have not appraised Allah with true appraisal. And on the Day of Resurrection the whole of the earth will be grasped by His Hand and the heavens will be rolled up in His Right Hand. Exalted is He and high above what they associate as partners with Him.* (Quran 39:67)

Some people when you ask them where is God? They say, "He is everywhere" This is a mistake, because Allah Almighty exists where no place. He is the Most High, above the Throne and all the creatures. Nothing is above Him, and not mixing by Himself with the world, dispensing with all His creatures; but He is with them with His knowledge, vision, hearing, and regulating.

Allah's names and attributes

The names of Allah Almighty are every name that He called Himself with in his book or named by His prophet Muhammad, peace be upon him, and they are beautiful names that have no flaw. Allah said, *"And to Allah belong the best names, so call on Him by them and keep away from those that pervert them. They will be recompensed for what they have been doing"* (Quran 7:180). It is not permissible for a person to call Allah with a name that Allah has not named for Himself.

As for the attributes of Allah Almighty, they are all attributes of perfection in which He described Himself in His book, or in the words of His messenger Muhammad, peace be upon him, that are not similar and not compared to the attributes of the creatures, whether this attribute is one of the self-attributes, which are inherent in the essence of Allah, such as life, knowledge, hearing, seeing, power, and others, or one of the acting attributes that relates to the will of Allah. He does it whenever He wills according to His wisdom, such as creating, forgiveness, mercy, and others.

There are attributes that Allah Almighty has negated about Himself in his book or in the words of His prophet Muhammad, peace be upon him, which are attributes of imperfection, such as death, sleep, impotence, laziness, fatigue, forgetfulness, boredom, sickness, miserliness, fear, failure, and other attributes of imperfection.

Dealing with the attributes of Allah

The believer must confirm every attribute that Allah has confirmed for Himself or His prophet Muhammad, peace be upon him, has confirmed for Him, without describing in what way or resembling, in the sense that a person knows the meanings of Allah's attributes, but he does not know how and is not permissible at all to ask about how, nor it is permissible for him to represent the attributes of Allah or to resemble them with something, because Allah Almighty says, *"There is nothing like Him, and He is the All-Hearer, the All-seer"* (Quran 42:11). And because man also knows by reason, that there is a great difference between the Creator and the creature in essence, attributes, and actions. Therefore, he must believe that Allah's attributes are in a way that suits His Majesty not known to man and inconceivable how they are, for Allah Almighty is Greater than any how it comes to the human's mind, and even it is not for man, originally, to speak or ask about them, because "There is nothing, whatever, like Him."

And the believer must also negate every attribute that Allah has negated about Himself in His book or is negated by His prophet Muhammad, peace be upon him, and not to describe Allah with an attribute that is not mentioned by Allah or His prophet Muhammad, peace be upon him:

Monotheism.

Every person on the surface of this earth must confirm the Oneness of Allah Almighty with his heart, tongue, and worship; so he firmly believes that only Allah Almighty is the Lord Creator the Possessor of the kingdom, the Regulator of every affair and that Allah Almighty is the only true God who deserves to be worshiped, and that no one shares Allah the perfection of His attributes and names. The worshipping is all that Allah loves and pleases with the apparent and hidden words and deeds, and there are many kinds of them, such as prayer, charity, fasting, pilgrimage, supplication, remembrance of Allah, fear of Him, hope, love, trust, seeking help, sacrificing, repentance, and others.

II. Believing in angels

It means believing in their existence. They are great, severe creatures that Allah Almighty created them from light, before the jinn who were created from the fire and before mankind who were created from clay; and they are good by nature, worshiping, obedient, glorifying Allah and never are they tired. They were created with a creation that differs from the jinn and mankind. Although they have male names, they are without desires as they do not eat, drink or reproduce and have the ability to manifest in different bodies. They are noble and pious and are with wings. They are many that their number is known only to Allah Almighty Who has chosen messengers from them for missions related to the universe and creatures' affairs. They do not disobey Allah in what He commands them but do what they are commanded. Among their missions are the following:

- Bringing down the revelation from Allah to His messengers and supporting them, and this is the function of Angel Gabriel, who is called the Spirit, the Spirit of God, and the Holy Spirit. Allah said, *"Say,* (O Muhammad) *'The Holy Spirit brought it* (the Quran) *down from your Lord in truth"* (Quran 16:102). And He said, *"And We gave Jesus the son of Mary clear signs and supported him with Holy Spirit"* (Quran 2:87).
- Hell keepers. There are nineteen angels. One of them his name is Malik. Allah said, *"Over it* (Hell) *are nineteen* (angels as keepers of Hell). *And We have set none but angels as guardians of the Fire"* (Quran 74:30–31). And He said, *"And they* (Who are in Hell) *will cry: 'O Malik! Let your Lord make an end of us.' He will say: 'Verily, you shall abide forever'"* (Quran 43:77).
- Throne bearers. Allah said, *"Those* (angels) *who bear the Throne* (of Allah)*"* (Quran 40:7).
- Angels entrusted to write the deeds of the people. Allah said, *"And indeed* (appointed) *over you are keepers to watch you. Noble writing down* (your deeds). *They know whatever you do"* (Quran 82:10–12).
- Angels entrusted to guard humans from evil. Allah said, *"Each person has guardian angels before him and behind him, who watch him by Allah's command"* (Quran 13:11).
- Angels entrusted with breathing souls into the bodies in the wombs.
- Angels entrusted with the preparation for separating the soul from the body during death, and then the angel of death gets the soul out of the body. Allah said, *"Until when death comes to one of you, Our messengers* (angel of death and his assistants) *take his soul, and they never neglect their duty"* (Quran 6:61). And He said, *"Say: The angel of death, who*

has been entrusted with you, will take your soul. Then to your Lord you will be returned" (Quran 32:11).
- Angels ask for forgiveness for the believers and for those on the earth. Allah said, *"Those* (angels) *who bear the Throne.* (of Allah) *and those around it glorify the praises of their Lord, and believe in Him, and ask forgiveness for those who believe"* (Quran 40:7). And He said, *"And the angels glorify the praises of their Lord and ask for forgiveness for those on the earth"* (Quran 42:5).
- An angel entrusted with blowing the Trumpet to end life in the universe, then blowing it again for the resurrection. His name is Israfil. Allah said, *"And the Trumpet will be blown, and all who are in the heavens and all who are on the earth will swoon away, except him whom Allah wills. Then it will be blown a second time, and behold they will be standing, looking on* (waiting)*"* (Quran 39:68).
- Angels entrusted to the rain, one of them is Michal.
- Angels entrusted with the arrangement of the affairs from heaven to earth with the command and will of Allah Almighty.

III. Believing in the books of Allah

It means believing, in general, in all of the heavenly books that Allah revealed to the prophets and messengers. They are books whose number and names are known only to Allah, Who said,

> *Mankind were once one nation* (of one religion) *then Allah sent the prophets with glad tidings and warnings, and with them He sent down the Scripture in truth to judge between people in matters wherein they differed.* (Quran 2:213)

And He said,

> *O you who believe! Believe in Allah, and His Messenger* (Muhammad), *and the book* (the

Quran) *which He has sent down to His Messenger, and the Scripture which He sent down to those before* (him); *and whosoever disbelieve in Allah, His Angels, His Books, His Messengers, and the Last Day, then indeed he has strayed far away.* (4:136)

As for the books that have been mentioned in the Quran, we believe in them specifically, namely:

1. The Torah was revealed by Allah to Moses, peace be upon him.
2. The Gospel was revealed by Allah to Jesus, peace be upon him.
3. Al Zabour (Psalms) Allah revealed it to David, peace be upon him.
4. The Scriptures of Ibrahim, peace be upon him.
5. The Quran was revealed by Allah to Muhammad, peace be upon him.

The Quran is the only book that Allah has guarded it from corruption because it is the last book that is directed to all generations of successive humanity. Allah Almighty said, *"Indeed, it is We who sent down the Dhikr* (i.e., the Quran) *and surely We will guard it"* (from corruption)*"* (Quran 15:9). And at the same time, it stands as a censor over the scriptures that came before it, showing what has been changed in them and confirming the truth therein, because Allah Almighty did not guard the Torah and the Zabur (Psalms) and the Gospel because they were directed to a specific nation (the people of Israel) and for a specified period. Therefore, not all of what the Bible contains are the original texts that Allah revealed to his prophets but rather contain books were produced through purely human efforts, fallible endeavors that relied upon undocumented narrations, rumors, and hearsay. Allah Almighty said, *"And We have sent down to you* (O Muhammad) *the Book* (this Quran) *in truth, confirming the Scriptures that came before it and stands as a guardian over them"* (Quran 5:48).

IV. Believing in Allah's messengers

It is to believe that Allah Almighty sent a messenger to every nation, calling them to worship Allah alone, Who has no partner and avoid worshipping of others. Allah said, *"And verily, We have sent among every nation a messenger (proclaiming): 'Worship Allah (alone) and avoid all false deities'"* (Quran 16:36). And all of them are honest, pious, trustworthy, and were supported by miracles, and signs that showing their truthfulness; and they have conveyed the message. Allah has shown the wisdom of sending the messengers. He said, *"Messengers who brought good news as well as of warning in order that mankind should have no plea against Allah after the (coming of) Messengers. And Allah is Ever All-powerful, All-Wise"* (Quran 4:165).

We believe in every messenger and prophet that Allah has mentioned in the Quran, and we also believe that Allah has sent other messengers and prophets whose names and number are known only to Allah. Almighty said, *"And (We sent) messengers about whom We have related* (their stories) *to you (O Muhammad) before and messengers about whom We have not related to you"* (Quran 4:164). And He said, *"And, indeed We have sent messengers before you (O Muhammad), of some of them We have related to you their story. And of some We have not related to you their story"* (Quran 40:78).

The messengers and prophets that Allah has mentioned in the Quran are twenty-five: Adam, Noah, Idris, Hood, Saleh, Shu'aib, Abraham, Lot, Ishmael, Isaac, Jacob, Joseph, Moses, Aaron, David, Solomon, Job, Elias, Elisha, Isaiah, Jonah, Zachariah, John, Jesus, and Muhammad, peace be upon them all. Whoever disbelieves in one of the messengers or the prophets, he has disbelieved in Allah Almighty. Allah said,

> *Verily, those who disbelieve in Allah and His Messengers and wish to make distinction between Allah and His Messengers* (by believing in Allah and disbelieving in His Messengers) *saying, "We believe in some but reject others," and wish to adopt a way in between. They are in truth disbelievers.*

And We have prepared for the disbelievers a humiliating torment. And those who believe in Allah and His Messengers and make no distinction between any of them, We shall give them their rewards; and Allah is Ever Oft-Forgiving, Most Merciful." (Quran 4:150–152)

Those messengers, Allah has preferred some of them to others, and He raised some of them in degrees in dignity and status. Allah said, *"Those Messengers! We preferred some of them to others; to some of them Allah spoke* (directly); *others He raised to degrees"* (Quran 2:253). All the messengers agree in their call to the origin of religion, which is monotheism and unifying Allah in worshipping. As for the branches of religion, which are the laws and rulings, they differ among themselves according to the wisdom of Allah Almighty in testing of nations according to the difference in their times and conditions, until it was sealed with the final Message that was came with the final prophet, Muhammad, peace be upon him. Allah said, *"To each among you, We have prescribed a law and a clear way. If Allah had willed, He would have made you one nation* (united in religion), *but that* (He) *may test you in what He has given you"* (Quran 5:48).

V. Believing in the Last Day (the Hereafter)

The last day is the day of resurrection, and it begins when all mankind will emerge from the graves to stand before Allah for judgment and ends directing them to ultimate destiny and eternal immortality, either in paradise or hell. Believing in the Last Day is related to the belief in the unseen, for it is of the knowledge of the unseen, there is no physical evidence or eyewitnesses for it, except what Allah Almighty has said in his books and by the tongues of his prophets.

This vast and great universe, with all its creatures it, will end one day. Allah said, *"When the heaven is cleft asunder. And when the stars have fallen and scattered. And when the seas are burst forth. And when the* (contents of) *graves are scattered* (i.e., exposed). (Then) *each soul shall know what it has done and what it has failed to do"* (Quran 82:1–5). And He said, *"Whatsoever is on it* (the earth) *will perish"* (Quran 55:26). Then another metaphysical life beyond human comprehension begins, a life that completely different in all its details from our short earthly life. Allah said, *"Allah originates the creation, then He will repeat it, then to Him you will be returned"* (Quran 30:11). And He said, *"Every soul will taste death. Then to Us will you be returned"* (Quran 29:57). All the prophets spoke with a clear statement from Allah as well as some parables about the next life so that people may believe. It is easier for Allah to return people back to life again after they have been perished. Allah said, *"And it is He who originates the creation, then He will repeat it; and this is easier for Him"* (Quran 30:27).

When the sound human intellect meditates two of Allah's attributes of wisdom and justice, he will realize the necessity of recreating creation for another life, where they are judged, and so does logic. This realization occurs when meditating on the following question:

Did Allah create the human race in vain (without any purpose)? Of course not. Because Allah created this sane human in order to realize that there is no God but Allah and worship Him alone. Allah said, *"Did you think that We had created you in vain, and that you would not be brought back to Us?"* (Quran 23:115). And since the justice of Allah Almighty is the most perfect, it certainly that He will not treat those who rejected his message, after it has clearly reached them, like those who accepted it. Allah said, *"Or do those who commit evil deeds think that We shall make them equal with those who believe* (Islamic Monotheism) *and do righteous deeds, in their present life and after their death? Worst is the judgement that they make"* (Quran 45:21).

Allah's dealings with people, after their resurrection, will take place after facing a fair judgment for how far their achievement was in worshipping Him alone on earth. Certainly, it is a different treatment, according to His perfect wisdom and justice. Those who believed and worshiped Allah alone properly will differ in the ranks of their eternal bliss according to the degree of their achievements in the task of worship in their worldly life. As for those who knew the true message of Allah clearly but did not accept it and they continued their false religion or did not believe in Allah, all their deeds will be in vain and will differ in the level of Allah's eternal punishment. Every human will face his own record, and those who have committed crimes in this life and succeeded in escaping the prescribed punishment they deserve will face Allah's full justice in the next life.

The journey to the next life begins with the moment of death when the angels of death come to the person to take out his soul. The man's vision at this time can see all the arrangements of angels to get his soul out of his body while those around him see not. Allah said,

> *Then why do you not* (intervene) *when* (the soul of a dying person) *reaches the throat? And you at the moment are looking on. But We* (i.e., Our angels who take the soul) *are nearer to him than you, but you see not.* (Quran 56:83–85)

And when the soul reaches the throat, it will be snatched by the angel of death. The body will be buried in the earth and turns into dust. As for the soul, it will continue the journey to the next life, where the beginning is from the Barrier, which is a transitional state in a barrier place between this life and the Hereafter, where the souls of the dead go, waiting for the resurrection for the next life. Allah said,

> *Until when death comes to one of them* (those who join partners with Allah), *he says: "My Lord! send me back, so that I may do good works in the world I have left behind!" No! It is but a word that he speaks; and behind them there shall stand a barrier until the Day when they will be resurrected.* (Quran 23:99–100)

The souls of the dead will remain there in different situations of happiness or suffering without feeling the time until the beginning of the next life, when all people are resurrected from their graves.

Luke mentioned in his gospel something about the life of the Barrier (Luke 16:19-31).

Before the end of the life on the planet earth, small and then major signs will appear indicating the proximity of the date, such as the great smoke, the coming of the impostor Christ, the second coming of Jesus, and the last sign is sunrise from the west. Then, at the appointed time, Allah commands the angel Israfil to blow the trumpet. It is a single shout, then every creature on earth and in heaven will swoon away, except what Allah wills from some angels. Allah said, *"And the Trumpet will be blown, and all who are in the heavens and all who are on the earth will swoon away, except whom Allah wills"* (Quran 39:68). Then they would die successively, and the last of them would be the angel of death, so only Allah Almighty remains. Allah said, *"All things shall perish except Himself"* (Quran 28:88).

After a while, Allah knows best, Allah will raise angel Israfil from the dead, then he will blow the trumpet a second time, then by Allah's power, every soul will join a new physical body that Allah will create it from the coccyx (a small bone in the base of the spine) wherever it is buried in a grave or scattered on the surface of the earth or at the bottom of the sea. All people, the first and the last will be resurrected from the graves with bodies and souls. Allah said, *"Then it will be blown a second time, and behold they will be standing, looking on* (waiting)*"* (Quran 39:68). And He said, *"And the Trumpet will be blown and behold from the graves they will come out quickly to their Lord"* (Quran 36:51). And He said, *"Wheresoever you may be, Allah will bring you together* (on the Day of Resurrection)*"* (Quran 2:148). Then they are all directed to the gathering land. It is a new flat earth that differs in its features from this existing earth, waiting for the coming of Allah Almighty for the judgment. Allah said, *"On the day when the earth will be changed into a different earth and so will the heavens, and they* (all creatures) *will come out before Allah, the One the Irresistible"* (Quran 14:48). Everyone will be judged in a day its length is fifty thousand years, which is called the Last Day. Allah said,

> *And We have fastened every man's deeds to his neck, and on the Day of Resurrection, We shall bring out for him a book* (record) *which he will find wide open.* (It will be said to him) *"Read your book* (record). *Sufficient is yourself against you this Day accountant.* (Quran 17:13–14)

And He said,

> *Then as for him who will be given his Record in his right hand, he surely, will receive an easy reckoning* (Quran 84:7–8). *But whosoever is given his Record behind his back, he will cry out for his destruction, and he shall enter a blazing Fire, and made to taste its burning.* (Quran 84:10–12)

And He said,

> *And We shall set up Scales of justice for the Day of Resurrection so no soul will be dealt unjustly at all. And if there be the weight of a mustard seed, We will bring it. And Sufficient are We to take account.* (Quran 21:47)

And He said,

> *And the earth will shine with the light of its Lord* (Allah, when He will come to judge among people), *and the Book* (record of deeds) *will be placed, and the prophets and the witnesses will be brought forward, and it will be judged between them in truth, and they will not be wronged. And each person will be paid in full of what he did; and He is Best Aware of what they do.* (Quran 39:69–70)

And He said,

> *And the Book* (one's Record of deeds) *will be placed* (in the right hand for a believer, and in the left hand for a disbeliever), *and you will see the criminals fearful of that within it, and they will say, "Oh, woe to us! What sort of Book is this that leaves neither a small thing nor a big thing but has recorded it with numbers!" And they will find all that they did, placed before them, and your Lord treats no one with injustice.* (Quran 18:49)

And those who never receive the true message of Allah clearly will be sorted and gathered together and then tested. Some of them will pass the test, and some of them will fail.

After reckoning, those who deserve paradise will be led to it in groups. Allah said,

> *And those who kept their duty to their Lord will be led to Paradise in groups till when they reach it, and its gates will be opened and its keepers will say: "peace be upon you! you have done well, so enter here to abide therein.* (Quran 39:73)

And all those who deserve hell will be driven in groups to it. Allah said,

> *And those who disbelieved will be driven to Hell in groups till when they reach it the gates thereof will be opened. And its keepers will say: "Did not the Messengers come to you from yourselves, reciting to you the Verses of your Lord, and warning you of the Meeting of this Day of yours?" They will say: "Yes," but the Word of torment has been justified against the disbelievers.* (Quran 39:71–72)

And He said,

> *And on the Day when the Hour will be established, that Day shall* (all people) *be separated. Then as for those who believed and did righteous good deeds, such shall be honored and made to enjoy luxurious life in a Garden of Delight* (Paradise). *And as for those who disbelieved and denied our verses and the Meeting of the Hereafter, such shall be brought forth to the torment.* (Quran 30:14–16)

It is a completely different life in the Hereafter. It is not in this existing universe that will perish and end, but elsewhere with another settings and laws, as well as the souls of people will be in bodies created in another shape. Allah said, *"We have decreed death to you all, and We are not outstripped in that We will change your likenesses and create you in* (shape) *that you know not"* (Quran 56:60–61). No soul knows what is kept hidden for them of joy and happiness in paradise and the torment of hell cannot be imagined, and there is no death but eternal immortality.

VI. Believing in Fate (Predestination), the Good of It and the Bad of It

Fate is one of the pillars of faith, that a person's faith is only complete with believing in all of them. Understanding fate strengthens believing in it and is the basis for understanding the occurrence of life events, because he who understands the fate (predestination) understands life and vice versa. And since predestination is connected to the human's life and his final destiny, so entering the topic will be from the door of the life itself.

The simple definition of human life on earth is a series of different events that start from birth and end at death moment. There is no life without events, nor events without life. The main fact in a person's life is that it proceeds according to events that were predetermined for him in advance (predestined) by the will of Allah before he comes to life. In other words, when a human comes into the world, the written plan of his life has preceded him. He will live every minute of his life according to this plan, and there is no way to change. Certainly, it will come to mind several questions about this fact, such as the following:

- On what basis has the man's life plan being written as well as his final destiny in the Hereafter before he came to this world?
- Does the human have any choice in his life plan?
- How can the human be held accountable for events written in his life plan before he comes into the world?
- Why is there no room to change the plan to better?

Whoever does not understand the truth of fate, it is natural for such questions to come to mind, and vice versa. In order to understand fate, we begin with the following solid facts and then build upon them the details of the research.

1. *First fact*: Allah Almighty is the Lord, the Creator of everything. He is alone the Regulator of every affair, who destine of all events and destinies, the Omnipotent, who Reigns supreme over all creatures, and in His hand is the dominion of all things. He is not questioned about what He does, while people will be questioned. Allah said, "*And He is the Supreme above His servants*" (Quran 6:18). And He said, "*So exalted is He in whose hand is the dominion of all things*" (36:83). And He said, "*He is not questioned about what He does, but they will be questioned*" (21:23). Man is a creature that cannot be independent in himself, free of the need for his Lord, and get out of the authority of his Creator and Owner.

2. *The second fact*: No movement or action of any creature, from the greatest creature to the smallest microscopic creature, inside and outside the universe, can occur except by the will and permission of the Creator of the universe. Man

cannot do what he wants unless his Lord Creator wills and permits. Allah said, *"Yet you cannot will unless that Allah wills—the Lord of the worlds"* (Quran 81:29). And even thoughts, ideas, and evil whispers do not come to a person's mind unless Allah Almighty wills, for He is the Lord, the possessor of dominion, Who manages and regulates all affairs.

3. *The third fact*: Allah Almighty does not will any movement inside and outside the universe by any creature except for a perfect wisdom. He does not will anything amusement and play or in vain or without meaning, wisdom, and goodness. Allah said, *"And to Him (Alone) belongs the supremacy in the heavens and the earth; and He is the All-mighty, the All-Wise"* (Quran 45:37). And He is the Almighty, the Creator of all events.

4. *The fourth fact*: Allah Almighty has made for man a free will where he can choose the field of good or the field of evil. Allah said, *"And by the soul and He who proportioned it. And inspired it its wickedness and its righteousness"* (Quran 91:7-8). And He said, *"And say, 'The truth is from your Lord, so whoever wills—let him believe; and whoever wills—let him disbelieve'"* (Quran 18:29). And He said, *"To any of you that chooses to go forward, or to remain behind"* (Quran 74:37). And He said, *"Then whoever wills will remember it"* (Quran 74:55). And He said, *"Verily, this is an admonition, so whosoever wills, let him take a path to his Lord (Allah)"* (Quran 76:29).

Therefore, all of man's behaviors and actions happen by the will of Allah according to the choice and will of man himself, and every human being is responsible for his behaviors and actions because Allah does not compel him to do so.

5. *The fifth fact*: All the events that the human being is exposed to without his will and choice, whether beloved or hated events, they fall upon him by the will of Allah according

to his perfect wisdom. Allah said, *"It is He Who gives life and causes death. And when He decrees a matter, He but says to it 'Be,' and it is"* (Quran 40:68). And the human is not responsible for the events that fall upon him.

Thus, we can say that fate (predestination) is all that Allah wills and permits, according to His perfect wisdom, to happen to the creature and to happen from it.

The human desire (wanting) and will

If we discuss the predestination of the human only among the creatures who have a will, Allah has made for the human a desire, which is the wanting, intention, tendency, and choice. These meanings of the desire represent the theoretical aspect of the human psyche. Allah said, *"And by the soul and He who proportioned it. And inspired it its wickedness and its righteousness"* (Quran 91:7–8). Likewise, Allah has made for the human a will that represents the practical aspect of man, when he makes the decision to put his desire, intention, and choice into action. But it is a will that associated with the will and permission of Allah, the Omnipotent Lord of creatures, as a person cannot do what he wants and desires unless Allah wills that for him that is, He permits it to happen. Allah said, *"Yet you cannot will unless that Allah wills—the Lord of the worlds"* (Quran 81:29). And He said, *"And never say of anything, 'Indeed, I will do that tomorrow,' except* (with the saying), *'If Allah wills!'"* (18:23–24). And we know with certainty that all what Allah wills of our actions will be in accordance with His perfect wisdom. Allah has indicated this and said, *"But you cannot will, unless Allah wills. Verily, Allah is Ever All-Knowing, All-Wise"* (Quran 76:30). And as much as the willpower of a person is, the strength of determination on initiating the action will be.

Man knows of what he wants to do tomorrow, for example, but he does not know whether he will be able to do that or not, because this is associated with the will of Allah Almighty (his permission). Allah said, *"No person knows what he will earn* (achieve) *tomorrow"* (Quran 31:34). And if Allah wills and permits a person to do what he wants, He will make it easy for him; and if He does not will, He will create, according to his wisdom, the necessary obstacles. Allah said, *"And never say of anything, 'Indeed, I will do that tomorrow,' except (with the saying), 'If Allah wills!'"* (18:23–24). Therefore, when a person wants to do an obedience (worship), he will not practice it unless Allah Almighty wills for him to do so, bearing in mind that he will be rewarded for the intention to do the obedience, in the case that the obstacle is beyond his control. The messenger of Allah, peace be upon him, said, "Whoever determines on initiating a good deed, but he could not do it, Allah will write it for him as a completed good deed." And when a person wants to commit a sin, he will not commit it unless Allah Almighty wills for him to do so, and likewise, when he wants to practice a normal deed (nondevotional), it will not be done unless Allah wills that for him.

Man's life plan

Every human soul has a written life plan according to Allah's eternal knowledge and wisdom, before He created the universe. And when the soul is born with the physical body, it lives its determined age according to this written plan, which contains events that Allah permits them to occur at their appointed times. The written events in the human life plan are of two types:

1. Actions (events) that will fall upon the human by the Creator and the creature, whether beloved or hated events. With this type of events, man has neither will nor choice. Rather, Allah, in his perfect wisdom, permits them to fall upon the human; and man is not responsible for them. The beloved actions (events) of the Creator that fall upon the human may be as a bounty and favor from Him, or as a test and a trial, or as a reward for good deeds that the human has done. As for the hated actions (events) of the Creator that fall upon the human, they may be as a test and a trial or as a punishment for bad deeds that the human has done, perhaps he may turn to Allah's obedience. Examples of Allah's

actions that fall according to His perfect wisdom on man: the bodily shape of a person, his age, his health status and family status, his livelihood, his skills and abilities, the areas of joy and sadness in his life, the calamities that he afflicts, the gains he gets, and other beloved and hated events.

As for the actions (events) that fall upon the human by the creature, they include all acts of good and abuse that Allah permits with His perfect wisdom to come from a creature (a person or animal, for example) and fall upon another.

2. Actions (events) that occur by the person himself by choice, whether they are good devotional deeds, bad, or ordinary (nondevotional), as man has a will and choice in all his actions; but no action takes place unless Allah wills so.

Allah has already known (eternally without a beginning) all the events that will take place in a person's whole life, from birth to death, which are events that Allah is going to will to fall upon the person without his choice, and events (actions) that Allah is going to will for the person to do them with his own choice; and He wrote that in the person's life plan. Thus, according to the supreme wisdom of Allah, a person's life plan is predetermined in advance (predestined). Allah's eternal knowledge of what a person will choose to do and what Allah is going to will to fulfill of the person's choices of actions and writing that down does not mean that Allah Almighty has compelled the person to do his actions, but rather every person is responsible for his own actions.

SALEH ALI AS-SUBAYIL

The known aspect of fate (predestination)

The known aspect of fate is the manner or mechanism by which events were destined, as each destined passes through four stages, which are as follows:

1. The stage of the eternal knowledge of Allah. The knowledge of Allah is eternal, not preceded by ignorance. It is surrounding everything wholly and in details. Allah Almighty said, *"Indeed Allah is, of all things, Knowing"* (Quran 29:62). And He said, *"Allah surrounds all things in His knowledge"* (Quran 65:12). Allah knows the unseen and knows what will be before it occurs and after it was. He knows that it has been and knows what is being occurring, and He knows how to be if what was not would be, and He knows all that the breasts conceal. Allah already knew eternally what every person will choose to do, to say, and to believe, and knows all the deeds that He will permit for a person to do and what He would not. And He knows what He will permit to fall upon a person of events and what He would not.

2. The stage of writing. Before creating the universe, Allah created the Pen and the Preserved Tablet (the Mother of the Book). Then Allah decreed to write His knowledge of what will happen until the day of resurrection, so He said to this matter, "Be," and it was so. Allah said, *"Do you not know that Allah knows all that is in the heaven and on the earth? Verily, it is (all) in the book. Verily, that is easy for Allah"* (Quran 22:70). And He said, *"Those who disbelieve say: "The Hour will not come to us." Say: "Yes, by my Lord, the All Knower of the Unseen, it will come to you, not even the weight of an atom or less than that or greater escapes His knowledge in the heavens or in the earth but it is in a Clear Book"* (Quran 34:3). And He said, *"And with Him are the keys of the unseen, none knows them but He. And He knows whatever there is in the land and in the sea; not a leaf falls,*

but He knows it. There is not a grain in the darkness of the earth nor anything fresh or dry but is written in a Clear Book" (Quran 6:59). Thus, all our actions that Allah wills us to do are already written in the Preserved Tablet, before the creation of this universe, as well as all the events that He wills to fall upon us. And so our lives proceed accordingly.

3. The stage of Allah's will (His permission) preceding the event. Every event inside and outside the universe is preceded by Allah's will, and nothing will happen from any creature except with the will of Allah. Therefore, when the appointed time comes for any act that a person chooses to do or any event that to fall upon him, as it exists eternally in the knowledge of Allah, and is written in the preserved tablet, then the will of Allah precedes it in order for it to happen. Allah said, *"The Originator of the heavens and the earth. When He decrees a matter, He only says to it: 'Be'—and it is"* (Quran 2:117). And He said, *"Yet you cannot will unless that Allah wills—the Lord of the worlds"* (Quran 81:29). And He said, *"And never say of anything, 'Indeed, I will do that tomorrow,' except* (with the saying), *'If Allah wills!'"* (18:23–24).

4. The stage of creating the event (action). This means bringing the event into existence on its time, whether the events that fall upon the human or the actions (events) that occur by the person himself by choice. Allah knows the event when it occurs, just as He knew it eternally before it occurred. Allah will not hold us accountable for our good and bad deeds with His eternal knowledge written in the Preserved Tablet, but He will judge us according to the final version of the Records of our devotional deeds. Allah said, *"While Allah created you and that which you do"* (Quran 37:96). And He said, *"Say: 'Allah is the Creator of all things; and He is the One, the Irresistible'"* (Quran 13:16).

The unknown aspect of fate (predestination)

As for the unknown aspect of fate (predestination), it is that a person does not know what Allah has destined for him until it happens, and likewise, he does not know the secret of Allah and His wisdom in what He wills and chooses of different fates for him and the timing of their occurrence. To Allah belongs the choice of fates as He chooses the fittest and appropriate, and He is the most knowledgeable in what therein of wisdom. Man may not be able to perceive Allah's wisdom in fate, and Allah may show some of His wisdoms to man. But man must believe that Allah Almighty never be unjust to anyone nor wills or does anything in vain or without meaning, wisdom, and goodness. Allah said, *"And it may be that you dislike a thing which is good for you and that you like a thing which is bad for you. Allah knows but you do not know"* (Quran 2:216). And He said, *"It may be you dislike a thing and Allah brings through it a great deal of good"* (Quran 4:19). Allah has made this present life with its destinies a home of test and trial. Will we have patience on the hated fates as an obedience to Him, or will we get angry and object? Will we thank Him for the beloved fates in recognition of his grace, or will we transgress and disregard His grace? Allah tests us with evil and with good as trial. And He tests us with something of fear, hunger, loss of wealth, lives and fruits. And He tests some of us by means of others and has raised us in ranks, some above others that He may try us in that which He has bestowed on us and has favored some of us over others in wealth and properties; and all the bounty is in the Hand of Allah alone, He grants it to whom He wills, and He selects for His mercy whom He wills. And every human is a facilitated for all what have been written for him in the Preserved Tablet.

Tape of life (movie of life)

Each person has his own diverse destinies that are eternally present in the knowledge of Allah Almighty, then they were written in the Preserved Tablet before the universe was created. The series of occurrence of human destinies begins from the mother's womb, where Allah wills (permits) the destinies of this stage to occur inside the womb. Allah said, *"It is He Who shapes you in the wombs as He wills"* (Quran 3:6). Then the destinies of the stage of the present life start to appear from birth to death. And then the destinies of man's soul at the stage of the Barrier (a transitional state in a barrier place between this life and the Hereafter, where the souls of the dead go) will be hidden from the eyes of the living. And then the destinies of the stage of the Hereafter appear from the resurrection until the final destiny in paradise or hell.

Therefore, every person's life goes according to a plan in which is written all the actions that Allah knows that the person will choose by himself to do with Allah's permission as well as the events that Allah will permit to fall upon him, at a specific time for each act and event according to Allah's wisdom. The closest depiction of the human's relationship to fate (destiny) in this present life is the kinescope (movie), for events were recorded by a camera, and just as the film contains several scenes (snapshots) of pictures, and when the film is shown, the images (pictures) pass successively through the projector, and each image has a specific time of passage to appear a moving picture, likewise is the destinies of man in his worldly life, where all scenes of his destinies are written and take their way to happen by the will of Allah Almighty according to their specified time in the show that begins with birth and ends with death. Also, man will not be able to see any scene of a future fate before it has been created (happening).

Fate and causes

The causes of the predestinations are also written predestinations that Allah Almighty willed to occur, whether they are by Allah's action or by the action of man. And since the causes are written predestinations, they also have their causes, and so on. Therefore, causes and predestinations are interrelated and intertwined. To clarify this, Allah has destined monetary sustenance for a person, and the cause for this sustenance was inheriting his relative who died, and the cause of the death of his relative was a predestined accident that occurred to him, and the cause of the accident was that he chose to speed, and the cause of his choice of speed was his desire to reach his destination early. Thus, Allah Almighty wills, with His knowledge and wisdom, to facilitate apparent or hidden causes (reasons) for the occurrence of predestinations. And when the predestinations occur by Allah's action without an apparent cause, they do not fall in vain but for a cause hidden by Allah with a wisdom. And what happens to any person of good conditions in his religion and worldly life, it is a blessing, grace, and generosity from Allah Almighty; and in that there is more than one wisdom. The trial (test) may be one of them. Also, the bad conditions that happen to him in his religion and worldly life may be due to his sins or as a trial as well. Allah said, *"What comes to you of good is from Allah, but what comes to you of evil, (O man), is from yourself"* (Quran 4:79). And Allah said, *"Everyone is going to taste death, and We shall make a trial of you with evil and with good. And to Us you will be returned"* (Quran 21:35).

As for the causes that make a person chooses his own actions, every person has his will, his intention, and his own reasons that make him choose his actions that Allah Almighty has willed to occur from him. For example, a person performs obedience due to the strength of his faith; and he may disobey due to the weakness of his faith, work of Satan, following his lusts, or due to his ignorance. And he practices ordinary (nondevotional) actions for various reasons such as desire or need for them or because of affection, emotion, interaction, striving, love of possession, etc.

Everything that happens is because Allah has predestined it. This saying does not mean not to search for the cause of the occurrence of fate, because the cause (which is also written predestination) may be without the will and choice of the person but it is an act of Allah Almighty or an act of a creature that fell on the person or the cause of fate may be the act of the person himself and within his will and choice, such as negligence and lack of caution or recklessness and exposing himself and others to destruction or criminal motives.

Not every cause that a person does leads to a desired result except what Allah Almighty wills to be a cause for the occurrence of what is desired. Allah Almighty wills for wisdom, and He wills not for wisdom either, for not every bullet is fatal, nor every recklessness leads to death, nor every disaster is lethal, nor is every suicide attempt is successful, nor every supplication is answered, nor every striving that brings sustenance, nor does every marriage produce offspring. If this is the case, then the person has no choice but to work and strive, perhaps Allah has willed this work and effort as a cause for achieving what is desired. Allah said, *"And your Lord said, 'Call upon Me; I will respond to you.' Indeed, those who disdain My worship will enter Hell contemptible"* (Quran 40:60). And Prophet Muhammad, peace be upon him, said, "Do deeds. Everyone is facilitated for what it is created for Him," i.e., for what it is written and destined for him. The command "Do deeds" is the password in every person's life because he does not know about the causes that Allah has written that lead to what is desired.

Examples of causes and destinies from life and the Quran

    A. When fate and cause are by Allah's action.
        1. A fate by Allah's action that fell upon a person (he was burned, for example) and the cause was a fate by Allah's action that fell upon the same person, when Allah sent a thunderbolt at him.
        2. A fate by Allah's action that fell upon a person (he inherited money, for example) and the cause was a fate by Allah's action that fell upon another person, as the heir's relative died.
    B. When fate is by Allah's action and the cause is a fate by man's action.
        1. A fate by Allah's action that fell upon a person (Allah healed him from a disease, for example) and the cause was a fate by the act of the same person where he used to pray to Allah to heal him or used a medicine as well as the one who Allah provided him because of his striving. Also, the one who Allah raised his degrees because of his educational attainment and whoever is afflicted with calamity due to throwing himself into

destruction or because of his insistent of committing sins. Allah said, *"What comes to you of good is from Allah, but what comes to you of evil,* (O man), *is from yourself"* (Quran 4:79).

    2. A fate by Allah's action that fell upon a person (his success, for example) and the cause was a fate by the act of another person where his parents used to pray to Allah for his success. The same applies to the one who won elections because most of the voters voted for him.

C. When fate is by man's action and the cause is a fate by Allah's action
    1. A fate by man's action (making a banquet, for example) and the cause was a fate by Allah's action that fell upon the same person, for Allah made him a successful person. And likewise, those who praise and pray to Allah because of their distress.
    2. A fate by man's action (having a graduation party, for example) and the cause was a fate by Allah's action that fell upon another person where Allah helped his son to graduate.

D. When fate and cause are by man's action
    1. A fate by man's action (he went on a hunting trip, for example) and the cause was a fate by the act of the same person, as he bought a hunting rifle.
    2. A fate by man's action (taking revenge on his aggressor, for example) and the cause was a fate by the act of another person that fell upon the same person, where the aggressor struck him.
    3. A fate by man's action (he triumphed for the oppressed from his oppressor, for example) and the cause was a fate by the act of another person that fell upon another person, where someone wronged another person.

Another illustrative example from life for fate and causes: Friends who wanted to travel and have several choices of places, and they sat to choose between them. They were discussing and convincing each other, and Allah knows from eternity about the place that He will permit (will) their agreement on it and wrote that. And when they decide to start preparing, they will not travel unless Allah wills, at the appointed time. Certainly, Allah wills for them to travel to the agreed-upon place for wisdom that may appear to them, and they may not know it. Perhaps that Allah willed them to travel to that place, to be a cause for the fate of others, such as the livelihood of the owners of the shops from which they will shop, the livelihood of the birds and animals of that place that will eat their food leftovers, and it may be the death of one of them is predestined there, or there may be a poor person that Allah willed to provide him from their alms, or something else.

Another example: When you go to the market and find what you want in more than one shop, Allah Almighty knows from eternity the shop you want to go to and the reasons for that, but your desire will not be transformed into action unless Allah wills that for you, for He facilitates for you the causes and make it easy for you to go to the owner of the shop that was destined for him to have a provision through you.

The examples from the Quran are as follows:

A. *When fate and cause are by Allah's action*
   A fate by Allah's action, that fell upon a person (the pregnancy of Mary, for example) and the cause was a fate by Allah's action that fell upon the same person (blowing into her). Allah said, *"And Mary, the daughter of Imran who guarded her chastity. And We blew into* (her garment) *through Our angel* (i.e., Gabriel)*"* (Quran 66:12). Likewise, giving birth to Mary, the cause was an act of Allah to make Jesus a sign to the people and an example for the Israelis. Allah said,

> *He said, "Thus* (it will be)*; your Lord says, 'It is easy for me, and We will make him* (Jesus) *a*

sign to the people and a mercy from Us. And it is a matter (already) *decreed.'"* (Quran 19:21)

And Allah said about Jesus, *"He* (Jesus) *was not more than a servant upon whom We bestowed favor, and We made him an example for the Children of Israel"* (Quran 43:59).

B. *When fate is by Allah's action and the cause is a fate by man's action*

A fate by Allah's action, that fell upon a person (giving a birth of a son for Zachariah) and the cause was a fate by the act of the same person, where Zachariah called his Lord. Allah said, *"At that time Zachariah invoked his Lord, saying, 'O my Lord! Grant me from You, a good offspring. You are indeed the All-Hearer of invocation'"* (Quran 3:38). Likewise, the cause of Jonah's survival in the belly of the whale was a fate by his action, where he praised Allah and called Him. Allah said,

And (remember) *the man of the fish* (Jonah) *when he went off in anger and thought that We would not decree* (anything) *upon him. And he called out within the darkness, "There is no deity except You* (O Allah)*; exalted are You. Indeed, I have been of the wrongdoers."* (Quran 21:87–88)

C. *When fate is by man's action and the cause is a fate by Allah's action*

A fate by man's action (the supplication of the people to Allah Almighty if they embark on a ship and a wave covers them, making their invocations for Him only) and the cause was a fate by Allah's action that fell upon the same person (they were overwhelmed by the wave). Allah said, *"And when a wave covers them like shades, they invoke Allah, making their invocations for Him only"* (Quran 31:32). As well as the despair of people, because of bad conditions that afflicted them. Allah said, *"But if evil afflicts them (the people) because of (evil deeds and sins) that their hands have put forth, immediately they despair"* (Quran 30:36).

D. *When fate and cause are by man's action*
A fate by man's action (Moses struck the Egyptian) and the cause was a fate by the same person, (Moses's racism for his own party, under the influence of Satan). Allah said, *"The man of his party asked him for help against his enemy, so Moses struck him with his fist and (unintentionally) killed him. (Moses) said, 'This is from the work of Satan. Indeed, he is a plain misleading enemy'"* (Quran 28:15). As well as the transgresses of Pharaoh, caused by his arrogance and being a tyrant on earth. Allah said, *"Indeed, Pharaoh exalted himself in the land and made its people into factions, oppressing a sector among them, slaughtering their (newborn) sons and keeping their females alive. Indeed, he was of the corrupters"* (Quran 28:4).

Questions in fate (predestination)

Q 1: Does a person have a choice in his written life plan?
A1: Yes, because he is the one who chooses all his actions that he performs, and Allah was aware of his choice for them from eternity, so He wrote them and willed them for him and facilitated their happening from him.
Q 2: Can a person do anything in order that may Allah change or erase some of what has been written in his life plan in the Preserved Tablet?
A2: The Preserved Tablet is with Allah Almighty. There is no room for change or erasure, because the pens were lifted, and the Written Pages have dried up. But a person can do the causes that by Allah's will erase his sins that were written by the angels in the Records of his devotional deeds or change them into good deeds, by repenting and seeking forgiveness and doing

more obedience. And any action that Allah Almighty wills in the Records of the devotional deeds of a person is known to Him and is written in the Preserved Tablet. Man will be held accountable on the day of judgment according to the final version of the Records of his devotional deeds, where it shall be brought out for him, and he will find it wide open. Allah said, *"Allah erases what He wills and confirms, (what He wills) And with him is the mother of the book* (the Preserved Tablet)*"* (Quran 13:39). And He said, *"Except those who repent, believe, and do righteous deeds; for those, Allah will change their sins into good deeds, and Allah is Oft-Forgiving, Most Merciful"* (Quran 25:70). And He said, *"And perform prayer at the two ends of the day and in some hours of the night. Verily, the good deeds remove the evil deeds. That is a reminder for those who remember"* (Quran 11:114).

Q3: What about supplication, does it not prevent the occurrence of fate, or in other words, changes the fate to another fate? As it was narrated on the authority of the Prophet Muhammad, peace be upon him.

A3: First, the scholars of hadith weakened the narration of the hadith of singling out supplication, with the preventing of the occurrence of a written fate. However, there is no doubt that supplication is one of the causes that Allah Almighty may have willed, at the initial writing that was before the creation of the universe, to make the supplication a cause for writing a desirable fate for the person which Allah knew that he would choose to supplicate and He would answer him. Because if it were not for his supplication and Allah's answering, would have been another (undesirable) fate instead. Like the prayer of Jonah in the belly of the great fish, Allah willed to proceed with it, the fate of saving him, instead of the fate of staying in its belly. Allah said, *"Had he not been of them who glorify Allah, he would have indeed remained inside its belly till the Day of Resurrection"* (Quran 37:143–144).

To clarify this, if a person supplicates, and Allah wills that his supplication be answered, does this mean erasing a previous written fate, during supplication, and then writing the answer to the supplication in its place as a new destiny? This certainly does not happen. Because there is no room for change or erasure in the Preserved Tablet, after the initial writing that was before the creation of the universe, because the pens were lifted and the Written Pages have dried up. And the Messenger of Allah, peace be upon him, made it clear to his wife, Um Habiba, that Allah Almighty will not advance anything before its time or delay something until after its time, in the fixed deadlines, the numbered days, and the divided livelihood.

So, a person's act of supplication is a cause and a fate, like other causes that a person does. And when a person supplicates and Allah answers him, Allah Almighty knew from eternity that this person will choose to supplicate, and He will permit him to do it and will answer him and make his supplication a cause for the occurrence of the desired destiny, so Allah wrote it and then willed for this person to make the supplication at its time and willed to fulfill for him his desired destiny on its time as well. Therefore, man makes supplication and other causes, perhaps that Allah Almighty has written it as a cause for the occurrence of the desired fate.

Allah says, *"And no moving* (living) *creature is there on earth but that upon Allah is its provision, and He knows its place of dwelling and place of storage. All is in a clear book"* (Quran 11:6). There are livelihoods and gains that Allah has written for all living creatures on earth, including people, regardless of their beliefs. And he who worships a false god and calls him is written for him all his livelihood and gains. And his supplication to his false god may coincide with the near time of his obtaining his predestined livelihood and earnings, so he thinks that the false god has answered him, so his faith in his false god strengthens, and here is the trial.

Q4: Why has Allah destined for the disbeliever to be an infidel and for a Muslim to be a Muslim?

A4: Guiding and misguiding are among the deeds of Allah and his decrees, for Allah guides whom He wills and leaves in astray whom He wills. While conversion (accepting guidance) and going astray are among the deeds of the human.

Allah Almighty has sent to all mankind a guidance through His revelation to His prophets and His books, about what they should believe and do. Allah does not punish any person until after it came into being that the guidance has been clearly reached him and the motives and causes for accepting the guidance were not prevented from him but rather were available for him. And the human being, in the end, is the one who desires guidance or blindness, as what happened to the Pharaoh, despite the eternal knowledge of Allah Almighty that Pharaoh will not accept guidance. He instructed Moses and Aaron to give him the motive for accepting the guidance by speaking to him mildly and gave Moses the power to perform miracles before him. Therefore, the Pharaoh will have no excuse at the Judgment Day, for not accepting the guidance brought by Moses.

Allah has destined for the disbeliever to be an infidel because it is already there in the eternal Knowledge of Allah that the infidel would choose blindness, not the guidance that had reached him with proofs, so Allah willed to fulfill for the infidel, his desire of choosing blindness. But if Allah had known that the infidel hates of being infidel, this hatred would have been, by Allah's will, a cause that Allah guides him. Likewise, if Allah knows that the infidel has the intention to search for the truth and transform that intention into a practical will of searching, then Allah Almighty will facilitate for him the ways that help him to see the truth.

And Allah has destined for the Muslim to be a Muslim because it is already there in the eternal Knowledge of Allah that the Muslim would choose the proven guidance, not the blindness, so Allah willed to fulfill for the Muslim his desire of choosing proven guidance. No creature can control another heart or prevent it from believing without its consent. Allah said, *"Except for one who is forced* (to renounce his religion) *while his heart is secure in faith"* (Quran 16:106). One of the tyranny and transgress of Pharaoh is that he was angry with the magicians that they believed without his permission, but he could not change their hearts by severe torture.

Q5: Why did Allah help the Muslim till he was a Muslim, and he did not help the disbeliever, so he became an infidel?

A5: Allah helped the Muslim till he was a Muslim because the Muslim thought deeply of the proofs, the motives, and causes of the guidance that Allah has established for him, then he preferred guidance to blindness. Therefore, Allah granted him guidance and made easy for him what is destined for him, rather He rewarded him for the guidance by increasing his guidance. Allah said, *"While as for those who accept guidance, He increases their guidance and bestows on them their piety"* (Quran 47:17).

And Allah did not help the disbeliever, so he became an infidel because the infidel knew about the guidance and he did not take into account the proofs, the motives, and causes of the guidance that Allah has established for him and preferred blindness to guidance and closed the door of guidance against himself. Therefore, Allah cut off His help from him and permitted to leave him in his error that he had chosen by himself and did not prevent him from what is destined for him. Rather, He punished him for preferring blindness to guidance by extending him into error. Allah said, *"Whoever Allah sends astray, none can guide him; and He leaves them in their transgression, wandering blindly"* (Quran 7:186). And He said, *"Whoever is in error, the Most Gracious* (Allah) *will extend to him"* (Quran 19:75). And He said, *"But We leave those who do not expect the meeting with Us, in their transgression, wandering blindly"* (Quran 10:11). And Allah Almighty knows whether this stray human will continue to choose to remain astray or will he choose to convert to guidance before his death. What he will choose is already known to Allah from eternity and written in the Preserved Tablet.

Q6: Allah Almighty says, *"And We did not send any messenger except in the language of his people to state clearly for them, and Allah sends astray whom He wills and guides whom He wills. And He is the Exalted in Might, the Wise"* (Quran14:4). Someone may say, why does Allah punish those whom He willed to send astray?

A6: Allah willed to create us to worship Him alone by choice and not by compulsion, so He made our soul capable of inclining toward guidance or error. He also created a will in us which is the ability or the willingness to transform our choices and our tendencies toward guidance or error into actions and practices. Allah Almighty said, *"And say: 'The truth is from your Lord.' Then whosoever wills, let him believe; and whosoever wills, let him disbelieve"* (Quran18:29). But it is a will that is associated with Allah's will because He is the Lord of the creatures, Who reigns supreme over them, and nothing happens in the universe except with His will and His permission. Allah Almighty said, *"Yet you cannot will unless that Allah wills—the Lord of the worlds"* (Quran 81:29). Neither the messengers nor the strength of their statement makes people be guided, but Allah alone is He who wills that the will of the one who chooses going astray come to pass and the will of the one who chooses conversion (accepting guidance). Allah said, *"Verily, you* (O Muhammad) *guide not whom you love, but Allah guides whom He wills"* (Quran 28:56). And He said, *"(This is) a Book* (the Quran) *which We have revealed unto you* (O Muhammad) *in order that you might lead mankind out of darkness into the light by permission of their Lord to the path of the All-Mighty, the Owner of all praise"* (Quran 14:1). And He said, *"And it is not for any person to believe except by permission of Allah, and He will put the wrath on those who are heedless"* (Quran 10:100). And Allah has revealed the consequence of guidance and going astray. He said, *"Verily, We have sent down to you* (O Muhammad) *the Book* (the Quran) *for mankind in truth. So, whosoever accept the guidance, it is only for* (the benefit of) *his soul; and whosoever goes astray, he goes astray only for his* (own) *loss. And you* (O Muhammad) *are not guardian over them"* (Quran 39:41).

Thus, guiding and misguiding are among the deeds of Allah and his decrees. And when Allah wills misguidance to a person, this does not mean that Allah forced him to astray, but it means that Allah permits the fulfillment of the desire of the person who chose to go astray and preferred blindness to guidance, even though that Allah had established for him the proofs, the motives, and causes of the guidance. Allah said, *"And as for Thamud, We guided them, but they preferred blindness to guidance"* (Quran 41:17). God's will for misguidance means leaving the one who prefers the astray to the guidance, in his error that he had chosen by himself. Rather, He punishes the one who has deviated, by causing his heart to deviate. Allah said about the people of Moses, *"And when they deviated, Allah caused their hearts to deviate"* (Quran 61:5). And He extends for the stray person in his astray that he had chosen by himself to death or sees in his heart the sincere desire for converting, then He opens his breast to the guidance. Allah said, *"Whoever is in error, the Most Gracious* (Allah) *will extend to him"* (Quran 19:75). He also guides whom He wills, meaning that Allah permits the fulfillment of the desire of the person who preferred guidance to astray after Allah had established for him the proofs, the motives, and causes of the guidance. And Allah leaves astray and guides in accordance with His perfect knowledge and perfect wisdom, not in vain, in foolishness, or in compulsion. And Allah knows from eternity of what people will choose of guidance or astray. Allah said, *"Truly, your Lord knows best who has gone astray from His path, and He is the best Aware of those who are guided"* (Quran 16:125).

Allah Almighty has mentioned those who He wills for them the guidance. He said, *"Say,* (O Muhammad) *'Indeed, Allah leaves astray whom He wills and guides to Himself whoever turns to Him in repentance'"* (Quran 13:27). And He said, *"Allah chooses for Himself whom He wills, and guides unto Himself who returns to Him"* (Quran 42:13). Allah will guide he who turns to Him, rather increases his guidance. *"While as for those who accept guidance, He increases their guidance and bestows on them their piety"* (Quran 47:17). Allah also has mentioned those who He wills for them the astray, i.e., leaves them astray and not guides them until they choose to change what is wrong that in themselves, and they are the following:

- The lying, doubting transgressor: Allah said, *"Indeed, Allah does not guide one who is a transgressor and a liar"* (Quran 40:28). And He said, *"Thus Allah leaves astray he who is a transgressor and skeptic"* (Quran 40:34).
- The wrongdoers: Allah said, *"And Allah sends astray the wrongdoers. And Allah does what He wills"* (Quran 14:27).
- Those who Satan made their evil deeds seem fair to them: Allah said, *"Then is one to whom the evil of his deeds has been made fair-seeming, so he considers it good* (like one rightly guided)? *For indeed, Allah sends astray whom He wills and guide whom He wills"* (Quran 35:8).
- The disbelievers: Allah said, *"And Allah does not guide the disbelieving people"* (Quran 2:264). And He said, *"Truly, Allah guides not him who is a liar, and a disbeliever."* (Quran 39:3).
- The rebellious, disobedient: Allah said, *"And Allah guides not those people who are rebellious, disobedient to Allah"* (Quran 9:80).

Q7: What about the existence of evil in the world? Does the perfection of Allah Almighty Himself and His attributes require that there be no evil in the world? Why does evil exist, and who brought it into existence?

A7: The fact that Allah is perfect in His Essence and Attributes does not necessitate that everything He creates should be perfect and free from defects as well, because Allah Almighty created every creature, in the state it is in, for a wisdom and goodness. And everything that Allah has not created, the wisdom and goodness will be by being not existed. And if we know that Allah's wisdom in creating man in this world's life is not to make him happy, but rather to worship Allah alone and test his commitment to it, while granting him the free will and the ability to do right and wrong, then we will understand why evil, mistake, suffering, and tiredness exist in life. For Allah has not created the life of this world to be the home of permanent settlement, rather He created it to be, with all the good and evil in it, a home of trial for all people. Allah Almighty said, *"Do people think that they will be left alone because they say: 'We believe,' and will not be tested?"* (Quran 29:2). A home of passage to the home of the Hereafter. Whoever successfully overcomes the difficulties of the trial of good and evil in it, by committing to the sincerity of loyalty to the true faith for which he was created for, he will not find any evil in the Hereafter, but rather the ultimate in happiness, pleasure, bliss, and eternal enjoyment. Allah Almighty said, *"And therein is whatever the souls desire and what delights the eyes, and you will abide therein eternally"* (Quran 43:71). And He said, *"And this worldly life is not but diversion and amusement. And indeed, the home of the Hereafter that is the eternal life, if only they know"* (Quran 29:64).

Evil is an effect (attribute) and not a material being (essence), meaning that evil is an attribute of a situation or action, and it is a relative matter. In other words, there is no evil except that it has a good on the other side. Evil has not existed in vain or does not lead, somehow, to an objective, wisdom, and goodness greater than the existence of evil itself and greater than the harm resulting from it, whether the evil that emanates from people or the evil that comes from nonpeople, and whether our minds comprehend the extreme wisdom and goodness behind the existence of evil or not.

Exposing people to the trials of the good and evil has the wisdom of examining the sincerity of loyalty to the true faith for which people were created for, and it is not logical that Allah tests people without suffering from evil, because if there was no evil, there would be no difference between the patient the diligent and the impatient and lazy one. Allah Almighty said, *"And We shall make a trial of you with evil and with good. And to Us you will be returned"* (Quran 21:35). Also, in the existence of evil, the wisdom of granting human the freedom of the will is manifest, which there will be people who choose evil as others choose good. And in the struggle and resistance to temptation and being patient over its pain, it helps the self-discipline. And in addition to the wisdom of testing people with evil, there is also the wisdom of punishing unrepentant sinners with evil. Allah Almighty said, *"And whatever strikes you of disaster—it is because of what your hands have earned. And He* (Allah) *pardons much"* (Quran 42:30). And also, the wisdom of warning them to return to their Lord before meeting Him on the day of resurrection. Allah Almighty said, *"And verily, We will make them taste of the near torment* (i.e. the torment in the life of this world, i.e. disasters, calamities) *prior to the supreme torment* (in the Hereafter), *in order that they may* (repent and) *return* (to Allah)*"* (Quran 32:21). And He said, *"And We tried them with good* (blessings) *and evil* (calamities) *in order that they might turn* (to Allah's obedience)*"* (Quran 7:168). And in evil, there is also the wisdom of expiating the sins of man because whatever afflicts the believer, whether fatigue, illness, anxiety, sadness, or harm, even a thorn pricks him, is that Allah expiates his sins through it, as the Prophet Muhammad, peace be upon him, told. And other extreme wisdom.

Who brought evil into existence? Since evil is not a material being (essence) but rather an attribute of a situation or an act that comes from Allah's creatures, whether rational creatures or irrational, so it is not correct to attribute evil to Allah Almighty, because Allah only wants good for the outcome of His actions and He only wants good for His servants and what Allah wills to do, doing it is better than not doing it, and what He does not do, its existence is evil, therefore, He did not do it. The existence of evil in the world and the painful predestination that people hate does not mean that Allah wants it out of love and contentment with it, for Allah's command and approval can never be directed to evil but only to good. Allah Almighty said, *"Say, 'Indeed, Allah does not order immorality. Do you say about Allah that which you do not know?"* (Quran 7:28). And He said, *"If you disbelieve, then verily, Allah is not in need of you; He likes not disbelief for His slaves* (people)*"* (Quran 39:7). Rather, it means that Allah wills and permits, with great wisdom and goodness, for evil to fall on His creatures or to emanate from His creatures who have the free will, depending on the degree of the integrity of their hearts and the goodness of their intentions. *"And by the soul and He who proportioned it. And inspired it its wickedness and its righteousness"* (Quran 91:7–8). Therefore, people are the ones who may choose other than the good that Allah wanted for them, and in this case, evil is due to the misuse of the free will that Allah granted them, as it is not possible for a person to be a free creature that has a free will, but he cannot do evil, because preventing evil emanating from him means canceling his free will, and then he would become a directed creature without a will; rather, it becomes a meaningless that Allah grants people the will and at the same time prevents evil to emanate from them and always pushing them to choose what is right.

As for the evil that emanates from Allah's irrational creatures according to the laws that Allah has spread in the universe, it is evil in one aspect, not in all aspects, just as it has a harm in one aspect, it has a benefit in another aspect; and it is a harm emanating from those irrational creatures in unusual circumstances. So evil is one of its manifestations and not an act of Allah because all Allah's actions are good, wise, and beneficial, and there is no evil in them in any aspect. Therefore, evil is not attributed to Allah, neither in action, nor in description; but rather, it is in His creatures. See how the Qur'an attributes goodness to Allah without evil. Allah Almighty said, *"Say, 'I seek refuge with* (Allah), *the Lord of the daybreak, from the evil of what He has created* (i.e., the evil of His creatures)*'"* (Qur'an 113:1–2). And Allah Almighty said about Abraham, who said about Allah, *"Who has created me, and it is He Who guides me. And it is He Who feeds me and gives me to drink. And when I am ill, it is He Who cures me. And Who will cause me to die, and then will bring me to life* (again)*"* (Quran 26:78–81). Abraham attributed to Allah the creation, guidance, feeding, watering, causing death and resurrection, but he did not attribute disease (evil) to Allah. And Allah said about the righteous man whom Moses asked to accompany him, *"As for the ship, it belonged to poor people working in the sea. So, I* (the righteous man) *intended to make a defective damage in it, as there was a king behind them who seized every* (good) *ship by force"* (Quran 18:79). The righteous man did not attribute the intention of making a defective damage (evil) in the ship to Allah; rather, he attributed it to himself. But he attributed the will of reaching the age of maturity to Allah. The Almighty Allah said, *"So your Lord intended that they reach maturity"* (Quran 18:82). And Allah said about the believers of the jinn, who said, *"And we know not whether evil is intended for those on earth, or whether their Lord intends for them a Right Path"* (Quran 72:10). Evil was not attributed here to Allah, but goodness (the right path) was attributed to Him.

Q8: What about Satan? Isn't he the evil itself and there is no good in his existence? And why does Allah permit Satan to seduce?

A8: Allah did not create Satan as evil one who leads people to evil. Rather, he is one of the jinn, just like humans, created to worship Allah alone. Allah said, *"Except Iblis* (Satan). *He was one of the jinn"* (Quran 18:50). And He said, *"And I* (Allah) *have not created the jinn and mankind except that they should worship Me (Alone)"* (Quran 51:56). The Satan, who was not created a Satan, worshiped Allah voluntarily; and Allah raised him to heaven, for his good worship, to be with the angels, but he differed from them in the origin of creation, for he is a jinn created from fire. Allah said, *"He created man* (Adam) *from sounding clay like the clay of pottery. And the jinn He created from a smokeless flame of fire"* (Quran 55:14–15). He has a free will to do good and evil within the limits of his ability. As for the angels, they were created from light and have no will. Allah said about angels, *"They do not disobey Allah in what He commands them but do what they are commanded"* (Quran 66:6).

Allah does not leave alone any believer from among the jinn and mankind to say, "I believe," and will not be tested. And after Allah created Adam, He willed to test the faith of that genie in heaven (Iblis who is from the jinn), so He commanded him to prostrate with the angels to Adam. The angels that Allah created do not disobey Him and do what they are commanded. They prostrated. As for that worshiper genie (Iblis), who has free will, he could not control the envy and arrogance that clouded his heart; so he chose, of his own free will to reject Allah's direct order for him to prostrate to Adam. Allah said,

> (Remember) *when your Lord said to the angels: "Truly, I am going to create man from clay. So, when I have fashioned him and breathed into him* (his) *soul created by Me, then you fall down prostrate to him." So, the angels prostrated themselves, all of them, except Iblis* (Satan), *he was proud and was one of the disbelievers.* (Quran 38:71–74)

And then when Allah asked him (He knew) about the reason that prevented him from prostrating to Adam, instead of asking forgiveness, repenting and complying, he insisted on his disobedience, and even arguing with Allah, protesting that the origin of his fiery creation is superior to the origin of Adam's clay creation. Allah said,

> (Allah) *said: "O Iblis* (Satan)*! What prevents you from prostrating yourself to one whom I have created with Both My Hands. Are you too proud* (to fall prostrate to Adam) *or are you one of the high exalted?" [Iblis (Satan)] said: "I am better than he. You created me from fire, and You created him from clay."* (Quran 38:75–76)

At that time, and for his insistence on disobedience, Allah expelled him from His mercy and cursed him. Allah said, "(Allah) *said: 'Then get out from here; for verily you are outcast. And verily, My curse is on you till the Day of Recompense'"* (Quran 38:77–78). The matter is over, and this genie realized that he had fallen into a trial, and that he would not be included with

Allah's mercy, but rather to the hellfire in the Hereafter, and worst indeed is that destination. And since then, this genie (Iblis) has chosen to become a Satan and held a grudge against Adam and his offspring after him, then asked Allah to keep him alive till the day of resurrection. Allah said, *"[Iblis (Satan)] said: 'My Lord, reprieve me till the Day the (dead) are resurrected.'"* (Quran 38:79). Allah Almighty knows from eternity that this genie will choose not to remain steadfast in faith, and he will choose not to repent but to insist on arrogance and transforming to Satan. Also, Allah knew about Satan's purpose behind his request of keeping him alive. Therefore, Allah, the All-Wise, the All, just willed to pay that genie, who had become a devil, his due for his previous good deeds in this worldly life by fulfilling his request of keeping him alive but until the Day of the time well-known. Allah said, "(Allah) *said: 'Verily, you are of those reprieved till the Day of the time appointed.'"* (Quran 38:80–81). After Satan got his request of keeping him alive guaranteed, he declared his enmity to humanity and his striving to seduce them so they share him his inevitable destiny in the Hereafter. Allah said, *"[Iblis (Satan)] said: 'By Your Might, then I will surely, mislead them all, except Your chosen slaves amongst them'"* (Quran 38:82–83). And Allah said, "(Iblis) *said: 'See this one* (Adam) *whom You have honoured above me, if You keep me alive to the Day of Resurrection, I will surely, seize and mislead his offspring* (by sending them astray) *all but a few!'"* (Quran 17:62). And Allah said, "(Iblis) *said: 'Because You have sent me astray, surely, I will sit in wait against them* (human beings) *on Your straight path. Then I will come to them from before them and behind them, from their right and from their left, and You will not find most of them as thankful ones* (i.e., they will not be dutiful to You)'" (Quran 7:16–17). And Allah Almighty has willed to fulfill Satan's will of tempting people in their worldly life because it is a home of testing and trial. And Allah decreed that whosoever follows Satan, he will mislead him and will have power over him and drive him to the torment of the fire. But he has no power over those who believe and put their trust only in Allah.

Allah said, "(Allah) *said: 'Go, and whosoever of them* (Adam's offspring) *follows you, surely, Hell will be the recompense of you* (all) *an ample recompense. And befool them gradually those whom you can among them with your voice, make assaults on them with your cavalry and your infantry, share with them wealth and children, and make promises to them.'" But Satan promises them nothing but deceit. "Verily, My servants you have no authority over them. And All-Sufficient is your Lord as a Guardian"* (Quran 17:63–65). And Allah said, *"And among mankind is he who disputes concerning Allah, without knowledge, and follows every rebellious devil. For him (the devil) it is decreed that whosoever follows him, he will mislead him, and will drive him to the torment of the Fire"* (Quran 22:3–4). And Allah said, *"So when you want to recite the Quran seek refuge with Allah from Satan, the outcast* (the cursed one). *Verily, he has no power over those who believe and put their trust only in their Lord* (Allah). *His power is only over those who obey and follow him* (Satan), *and those who join partners with Him* (Allah)*"* (Quran 16:98–100). And Allah said, *"Verily, We* (Allah) *made the devils protectors and helpers for those who believe not"* (Quran 7:27). And Allah said, *"And whoever takes Satan as protector or helper instead of Allah, has surely, suffered a manifest loss"* (Quran 4:119).

Therefore, Allah Almighty has told us that Satan is an enemy to us and that we should take him as an enemy, and He warned us against him and guided us on how to guard against him. Allah said, *"O mankind! Verily, the promise of Allah is true. So let not this present life deceive you and let not the chief deceiver* (Satan) *deceive you about Allah. Surely, Satan is an enemy to you, so take* (treat) *him as an enemy. He only invites his followers that they may become the dwellers of the blazing Fire."* (Quran 35:5–6). And Allah said, *"And say to My servants that they should say those words that are the best* (because) *Satan Verily, sows a state of conflict and disagreements among them. Surely, Satan is to man a plain enemy"* (Quran 17:53). And Allah said, *"And follow not the footsteps of Satan. Verily, he is to you an open enemy. He commands you only what is evil and sinful, and that you should say against Allah what you know not"* (Quran 2:168–169). And Allah said, *"Did I not command you, O Children of Adam, that you should not worship Satan. Verily, he is a plain enemy to you. And that you should worship Me alone. That is the Straight Path"* (Quran 36:60–61). And Allah said, *"Satan wants only to excite enmity and hatred between you with intoxicants and gambling and hinder you from the remembrance of Allah and from the prayer. So, will you not then abstain?"* (Quran 5:91). And Allah said, *"And if an evil whisper comes to you from Satan, then seek refuge with Allah. Verily, He is All-Hearer, All-Knower. Verily, those who are pious, when an evil thought comes to them from Satan, they remember (Allah), and indeed they then see* (aright)*"* (Quran 7:200–201). And Allah said, *"And say: 'My Lord! I seek refuge with You from the whisperings of the devils. And I seek refuge with You, My Lord! Lest they should come near me'"* (Quran 23:97–98).

In the end, Allah Almighty tells us about the speech that Satan will deliver in the Hereafter, amidst hell, to those who followed him in this worldly life. A tragic depiction in which there is a lesson and a reminder for him who has a heart or gives ear while he is heedful. Allah said,

> *And Satan will say when the matter has been decided: "Verily, Allah promised you a promise of truth. And I too promised you, but I betrayed you. I had no authority over you except that I called you, and you responded to me. so blame me not, but blame yourselves. I cannot help you, nor can you help me. I deny your former act in associating me as a partner with Allah" (by obeying me in the life of the world). Verily, there is a painful torment for the polytheists and wrong-doers.* (Quran 14:22)

It is not possible to deny the perfect wisdom in the existence of Satan. Do we not resort to Allah to seek refuge from Satan? Is not Allah will not leave us alone to say, "We believe," without being tested? Our struggle against Satan's seduction and his commands to us to do evil and immorality elevates the level of our worship of Allah and distinguishes the one with weak faith from the strong.

Q9: Does Allah predestine sins on a person and then hold him accountable for them?

A9: Yes. But predestining of sins on a person does not mean that Allah oblige or compel this person to sin. Rather, it means that Allah, with His eternal knowledge, has known that this person would choose on his own to commit the sin at a certain time, so He wrote the will of this person and willed to be fulfilled by creating its occurrence at its time. So predestining of sins on a person is based on two things:

1. The eternal knowing of Allah about the choosing of this person to commit the sin on a certain time and wrote that.
2. The will of Allah Almighty that the will of this person of committing the sin be fulfilled at its time.

Therefore, every sin that Allah willed (permitted) to occur from you, you are responsible for it because it occurred according to your choice and will. And any will (desire) of sin that was not fulfilled, it is for a wisdom that Allah did not will it to occur. Allah wills to fulfill the desire (will) of a person in committing sins for a wisdom, and He does not will for a wisdom either. There is a person whose disobedience became a cause for his repentance, and a person whose the punishment of his disobedience became a cause for his righteousness, and a person whose disobedience became a cause for his persistence in disobedience like Satan, and a person who, when it is said to him, "Fear Allah," he is led by arrogance to more sin, and a person whom Allah have mercy on him, so He does not will him to fall into sin. And if Allah wills to fulfill the desire (choice) of the criminal or the oppressor in committing a crime, then the matter does not end when the criminal or the oppressor is imprisoned, for example, but rather, Allah

Almighty will take revenge for the oppressed from the oppressor on the judgment day. Allah Almighty said, *"And let not the disbelievers think that Our postponing of their punishment is good for them. We postpone the punishment only so that they may increase in sinfulness. And for them is a disgracing torment"* (Quran 3:178).

Q10: Can a person argue using the predestination as reasoning for his sins?

A10: No. He has no right to argue using the predestination as reasoning for his transgression, nor negligence, because all of these are his own choices and his own will to act. But he may argue using the predestination as an excuse in the calamities that fall upon him and says, "It is predestined," because what had fallen upon him is one of the actions (deeds) of Allah in which there is neither will nor choice for the human.

Q11: Is it a must that a person accepts the fate (destiny) of the sin he committed?

A11: Yes. A person must accept the fate (destiny) of the sin and not be angry because Allah willed for him the fulfilling of his desire to sin. But a person should not be pleased with his own will of committing it, using Allah's will for its happening as an excuse. And if he is indignant, it should be against himself, which was defeated before its desires. He can repent, and if he did that, we know that it is written as well.

Q 12: What does a person who has fallen upon him a hated fate say?

A 12: He should say, "It is destined by Allah, and He did what He willed."

Q13: Is the will of acting of a person consistent with what is written, or what is written is consistent with the will of the person?

A13: Both of them. For Allah Almighty eternally knows of what a person will choose in terms of actions, and He also knows what He wills for him to do from his choices and what He wills not, then He wrote that. Therefore, a person finds himself facilitated to do what Allah wills for him to do of his written choices.

Q14: If we assume that Allah revealed to a person in a dream some of what He had written for him, for example a calamity, what can he do to avoid it?

A14: He cannot do anything other than what is written for him, for it is not possible for a person to go differently than what has been written for him even if he saw it. Therefore, since a person cannot see or know what is written for him, he has no choice but to do what he thinks that may be a cause for obtaining what he wants, hoping that it has been written that Allah is willing to make his act as a cause for obtaining what he strives for. Prophet Muhammad, peace be upon him, said, "Do deeds. Everyone is facilitated for what it is created for Him." (i.e., for what it is written and destined for him). So whoever complied and chose to do the causes, we know that his action was predestined and written, and whoever did not comply and did not choose to do the causes, we know that Allah has known from eternity that this person would not choose to do the causes, so He has not destined and written for him doing the causes.

The benefit of understanding fate (predestination)

Many people avoid talking about fate, even though it is one of the important pillars of the faith of the Muslim and the basis on which human life and behavior are based. A person may not be required to know all the details, but he is obligated to know the essential knowledge about destiny that makes his belief in predestination free of doubts and suspicions.

The Quran tells us about fate as well as the Sunnah. Allah said, *"Indeed, all things We created with predestination"* (Quran 54:49). And He said, *"Verily, Allah will accomplish His purpose. Indeed, Allah has already set a measure for all things"* (Quran 65:3). And He said, *"Verily, Allah does what He wills"* (Quran 22:18). And He said, *"No calamity befalls on the earth or in yourselves but is inscribed in the Book of Decree (the Preserved Tablet) before We bring it into existence. Verily, that is easy for Allah. In order that you may not grieve at the things over that you fail to get, nor rejoice over that which has been given to you.*

And Allah likes not prideful boasters" (Quran 57:22–23). And He said, *"No calamity befalls, but by the permission of Allah"* (Quran 64:11). And He said, *"What comes to you of good is from Allah, but what comes to you of evil, (O man), is from yourself. And We have sent you, (O Muhammad), as a messenger to mankind, and sufficient is Allah as a Witness"* (Quran 4:79). And He said, *"Say: 'Nothing shall ever happen to us except what Allah has decreed for us.'"* (Quran 9:51). And He said, *"Is it they who would portion out the Mercy of your Lord? It is We Who portion out between them their livelihood in this world, and We raised some of them above others in ranks, so that some may employ others in their work. But the mercy* (paradise) *of your Lord is better than whatever they accumulate"* (Quran 43:32). And He said, *"And it is He who has made you successors upon the earth and has raised in ranks, some above others that He may try you in that which He has given you. Indeed, your Lord is swift in retribution, and certainly He is Forgiving, Most Merciful"* (Quran 6:165). And He said, *"Do people think that they will be left alone because the say: "We believe," and will not be tested?"* (Quran 29:2). And He said, *"Everyone is going to taste death, and We shall make a trial of you with evil and with good. And to Us you will be returned"* (Quran 21:35). And He said, *"Do they not see that Allah enlarge provision for whom He wills and restricts it. Verily, in that are indeed signs for a people who believe"* (Quran 30:37). And He said, *"And Allah has given some of you more than to others in wealth and properties"* (Quran 16:71). And Allah said, *"And no moving* (living) *creature is there on earth but that upon Allah is its provision, and He knows its place of dwelling and place of storage. All is in a clear book"* (Quran 11:6). And Allah said, *"We raise whom we will in degrees. Certainly, your Lord is All-Wise, All-Knowing"* (Quran 6:83). And Allah said, *"And if Allah touches you with harm, there is none who can remove it but He; and if He intends any good for you, there is none who can repel His Favor which He causes it to reach whomsoever of His servants He wills. And He is the Oft-Forgiving, the Most Merciful"* (Quran 10:107). And He said, *"Whatever Allah grants to people of mercy* (i.e. of good), *none can withhold it; and whatever He withholds, none can release it thereafter. And He is the Exalted in Might, the wise"* (Quran 35:2). And He said, *"In whatever form He willed has He assembled you"* (Quran 82:8). And He said, *"To Allah belongs the dominion of the heavens and the earth; He creates what He wills. He gives to whom He wills female* (children), *and He gives to whom He wills males* (children). *Or He makes them* (both) *males and females, and He renders whom He wills barren. Indeed, He is the All-Knower and is able to do all things"* (Quran 42:49–50). And He said, *"And no aged man is granted a length of life nor is a part cut off from his life but is in a book. Surely, that is easy for Allah"* (Quran 35:11). And He said, *"And Allah has created you and then He will cause you to die; and of you there are some who are sent back to senility, so that they know nothing after having known* (much). *Truly, Allah is All-Knowing, All-Powerful"* (Quran 16:70). And He said, *"And it is not* (possible) *for one to die except by permission of Allah at a decree determined"* (Quran 3:145).

The Messenger of Allah, peace be upon him, said, "What missed you would not have befallen you, and what befallen you, it would not have missed you." And he said, "And know that if the nation gathered together to benefit you with something, they will not benefit you except with something that Allah had written for you. And if they gathered together to harm you with something, they will not harm you except with something that Allah had written for you; pens were lifted, and the Written Pages have dried up." And he said, "No one of you, but his place in Hell or Paradise is already written." They said, "Shall we just rely on this?" Prophet said, "Do deeds. Everyone is facilitated for what it is created for Him" (i.e., for what it is written and destined for him), then he read the verse (from Quran) "As for he who gives and fears Allah and believes in the best (reward), We will make smooth for him the path of ease (goodness). But he who is greedy miser and thinks himself self-sufficient and denies the best (reward), We will make smooth for him the path toward difficulty (evil)."

Whoever understands the fate (destiny) will realize that Allah has created death and life that He may test us as to which of us is best in deed and has made this present life with its destinies a home of test and trial; and portioning out the livelihood among people according to His wisdom; and has favored some of us over others in wealth and properties; and has raised us in ranks, some above others that He may try us in that which He has bestowed on us. And Allah Almighty does not oppress people with His destiny in this present life, the home of test and trial, but rather tests them; for Allah Almighty is not unjust to the servants and He does not want an injustice to us and treats no one with injustice and does not oppress even a weight of an atom, but the people oppress themselves. Therefore, whoever understands fate and believes in it firmly in his heart will not envy anyone for what Allah has given him of his bounty, because of his certainty that all livelihoods have been portioned out by Allah Almighty Himself among people and has favored some of them over others in types of livelihood according to his wisdom, and that envy is something of objection to the wisdom of Allah, and who is wiser than Allah? And he will not be preoccupied psychologically in comparing his condition with others but praises Allah for his condition and strives to do legitimate causes, which Allah, may facilitate for him to change his condition for the better, if that is destined for him and written. And if an evil thought comes to him from Satan and found some envy in his heart toward another whom Allah has blessed with his bounty, he remembers Allah's wisdom in portioning out all kinds of livelihoods. And at once, he has insight, praising Allah for the provision that He has portioned out for him, and nothing will be diminished from it.

He who understands the fate (destiny) will realize that he is only to be patient and have recourse to Allah toward the painful destinies that fall upon him so that he may obtain the good news of Allah's blessings, forgiveness, and mercy.

> Allah said, *"Give glad tiding to the patient who, when afflicted with calamity, say, 'Truly to Allah we belong and truly, to Him we shall return.' Those are the ones upon whom are blessing from their Lord and mercy. And it is they who are the guided ones.* (Quran 2:155–157)

Indignation and complaining will change nothing of the matter, but rather he may lose, because of this, both this present life and the Hereafter. Preoccupation with others may lead the person to some objecting questions to the wisdom of Allah, such as the following: Why does Allah extend the provision for some people and restrict it for others? Why does He grant success to some and does not grant it to others? Why some are healthy, and others are sick? Why do some people get longer lives so that they may have more chance to be guided, and others get shorter lives so that they may have less chance to be guided? And other objecting questions. Note that acceptance of guidance has nothing to do with longevity. Rather, adherence to the truth whenever it reaches a person till the death, whether it is long-lived or short-lived. Allah said, *"Did We not give you lives long enough, so that whosoever would receive admonition could receive it? And the warner came to you"* (Quran 35:37).

When a person believes that all his actions that he did were done by his own will and own choice and that they were written in the Preserved Tablet based on the eternal knowledge of Allah and that Allah did not compel him to do them but rather He willed and permitted according to His wisdom to fulfill for him his desire and choice and also when a person believes that all the beloved and hated events that fall upon him are known to Allah and were written in the Preserved Tablet and are subject to Allah's will and that they do not fall upon him in vain or for no meaning, no wisdom, and no goodness and that Allah does whatever He wills and does not oppress the weight of an atom, his belief in all this, his satisfaction, and his acceptance of what Allah has willed for him brings him contentment and happiness, increases his dependence on Allah, and urges him to do the causes for what is good of his life and his Hereafter and removes envy and discontent.

The Messenger of Allah, peace be upon him, said, "Wonder of the matter of the believer. His matter is all good, and that is not for anyone but the believer. If good befell him, he thanks, so it was good for him. And if bad befell him, he is Patient, so it was good for him."

Testing of faith

It is easy for a person to say "I believed." Therefore, Allah will not leave man to say, "I have believed" without testing his faith. Allah Almighty said,

> *Do people think that they will be left alone because they say, "We believe," and will not be tested? And We indeed tested those who were before them. And Allah will certainly make* (it) *known* (the truth of) *those who are true and will certainly make* (it) *known* (the falsehood of) *those who are liars,* (although Allah knows all that before putting them to test). (Quran 29:2–3)

Perhaps the story of Moses and the sorcerers (magicians) of Pharaoh is the clearest example of the sincerity of the heart's acknowledging of faith and the utterance of it with the tongue. When Pharaoh gathered the sorcerers to defeat Moses with their sorcery, *"Moses said to them, 'Throw what you are going to throw!'" So they threw their ropes and their sticks and said, "By the might of Pharaoh, it is we who will certainly win!" Then Moses threw his stick, and behold, it swallowed up all that they falsely showed! And the sorcerers fell down prostrate, saying, "We believe in the Lord of the worlds, the Lord of Moses and Aaron." Pharaoh said, "You have believed in him before I give you permission. Surely, he indeed is your chief, who has taught you magic! So verily, you shall come to know. Verily, I will cut off your hands and your feet on opposite sides, and I will crucify you all." They said, "No harm! Surely, to our Lord we are to return. Verily, we really hope that our Lord will forgive us our sins, as we are the first of the believers"* (Quran 26:43–51).

And among the people is he who has a weak faith, who did not delve deep into religion but worships Allah on the edge of the religion. If his life goes on well, he is content with that goodness and not with his weak faith. But if a trial befalls him, he turns back (revert to disbelief) due to the weakness of his faith. He loses both this world and the Hereafter. Allah Almighty said,

> *And among people is he who worships Allah on an edge. If good befalls him, he is content therewith; but if a trial befalls him, he turns back on his face* (revert to disbelief after embracing Islam). *He loses both this world and the Hereafter. That is the evident loss.* (Quran 22:11)

One of Allah's perfect justice is that He will not call to account for disbelieving the one who was forced to disbelieve while his heart is secure in faith. Allah said,

> *Whoever disbelieves in Allah After his belief, except for one who is forced* (to disbelieve) *while his heart is secure in faith. But those who* (willingly) *open their breasts to disbelief, upon them is wrath from Allah and for them is great punishment.* (Quran 16:106)

The two pillars of accepting good deeds (devotional deeds)

1. The devotional deeds should be performed sincerely for the sake of Allah only. Allah said, "*Verily, We have sent down the Book to you* (O Muhammad) *in truth. So, worship Allah* (Alone) *by doing religious deed sincerely for Allah's sake only*" (Quran 39:2). And He said, "*Say* (O Muhammad): *'Verily, I am commanded to worship Allah* (Alone) *by obeying Him and doing religious deed sincerely for His sake only*" (Quran 39:11). And He said, "*Say* (O Muhammad): *'Allah Alone I worship by doing religious deed sincerely for His sake only.'*" (Quran 39:14). And He said, "*He is the Ever-Living; there is no deity except Him, so call upon Him,* (being) *sincere to Him in religion*" (Quran 40:65).
2. The devotional deeds should be performed in the same way as the Prophet Muhammad reported. Allah said, "*Say* (O Muhammad): *'O mankind! Verily, I am sent to you all as the Messenger of Allah to Whom belongs the dominion of the*

heavens and the earth. There is no deity except Him; He gives life and causes death.' So, believe in Allah and His Messenger (Muhammad), *the unlettered prophet, who believes in Allah and His words, and follow him that you may be guided"* (Quran 7:158). And He said, *"Say* (O Muhammad): *'If you* (really) *love Allah, then follow me,* (so) *Allah will love you and forgive you your sins. And Allah is Oft-Forgiving, Most Merciful'"*(Quran 3:31). And He said, *"He who obeys the Messenger* (Muhammad), *has indeed obeyed Allah"* (Quran 4:80).

But what about the deeds of geniuses and great scientists who devoted themselves to research and discoveries to provide great services to humanity and those who contemplated what in the universe and contributed to progress and civilization? Do these deeds of them benefit them in the Hereafter?

Every scientist and discoverer who helped humanity and other creatures with spirits, if he was a believer as Allah commanded and intended the rewarded from Allah, his deeds will benefit him in the Hereafter. And if he was among those who rejected the true Islam that has reached him with proofs and insisted on a false belief, his deeds will not benefit him in the Hereafter, even if he did them for Allah's sake, but Allah will reward him for these deeds in the life of this world only, as well as those who did such deeds for the sake of this world in terms of money and fame. Allah said,

> *Whosoever desires the life of this world and its glitter, to them We shall pay in full* (the wages of) *their deeds therein, and they will have no diminution therein. They are those for whom there is nothing in the Hereafter but Fire, and vain are the deeds they did therein. And of no effect is that which they used to do.* (Quran 11:15–16)

And He said,

> *The example of those who disbelieve in their Lord is that their deeds are like ashes, on which the wind blows forcefully on a stormy day; they shall not be able to get aught of what they have earned. That is the straying, far away* (from the Right path). (Quran 14:18)

And He said,

> *As for those who disbelieved, their deeds are like a mirage in a desert. The thirsty one thinks it to be water, until he comes up to it, he finds it to be nothing; but he finds Allah with him, Who will pay him in full his due* (Hell). *And Allah is Swift in taking account.* (Quran 24:39)

And He said,

> *Say, "Shall We tell you the greatest loser in respect of* (their) *deeds? Those whose effort have been wasted in this life while they thought that they were acquiring good by their deeds. They are those who deny the signs* (proofs, evidences, verses, revelations, etc.) *of their Lord and the Meeting with Him* (in the Hereafter). *So, their deeds are in vain, and on the Day of Resurrection, We shall no weight for them. That shall be their recompense, Hell; because they disbelieved and took My signs* (proofs, evidences, verses, revelations, etc.) *and My Messengers by way of jest and mockery.* (Quran 18:103–106)

The return of Jesus Christ to earth

Before talking about the second coming of Christ, let us read what Allah Almighty said about the first coming of Christ to this world.

The Quran tells us about Jesus's grandmother and her husband, and even the birth of his mother, Mary. Allah told us how He had chosen the family of Imran (Mary's father), saying,

> *Allah chose Adam, Noah, the family of Abraham and the family of Imran above mankind and jinn* (of their times). *Offspring, one of the other, and Allah is All-Hearer, All-Knower.* (Remember) *when the wife of Imran said: "O My Lord! I have vowed to You what* (the child that) *is in my womb to be dedicated for Your service* (free from all worldly work; to serve Your place of worship, the temple), *so accept this from me. Verily, You are the All-Hearer, the All-Knower." Then when she gave birth to her child,* (Mary), *she said: "O my Lord! I have given birth to a female child." And Allah knew better what she brought forth. "And the male is not like the female, and I have named her Mary, and I seek refuge with You* (Allah) *for her and for her offspring from Satan, the outcast." So, her Lord* (Allah) *accepted her with goodly acceptance. He made her grow in a good manner and put her under the care of Zechariah.* (Quran 3:33–37)

Then Allah told us that He had chosen Mary.

> *And* (remember) *when the angels said, "O Mary! Verily Allah has chosen you, purified you, and chosen you above the women of mankind and jinn* (of her lifetime)." (Quran 3:42)

Then we are told of the Good News of Jesus. Allah said,

> (Remember) *when the angels said, "O Mary! Verily, Allah gives you the glad tidings of a Word from Him, his name will be the Messiah Jesus, the*

son of Mary, held in honor in this world and in the Hereafter, and will be one of those who are near to Allah." (Quran 3:45)

(Jesus was a word from Allah, meaning that Allah created him with the word "Be." So Jesus was a fetus in his mother's womb without a father, just as Adam was without a father or mother but with the word "Be.")

Then Almighty Allah tells us how Mary conceived Jesus with no father and how he was born. He said,

> *When Mary withdrew in seclusion from her family to a place facing East. She placed a screen* (to screen herself) *from them; then We* (Allah) *sent to her Our Spirit* (angel Gabriel), *and he appeared before her in the form of a man in all respects. She said: "Verily, I seek refuge with the Most Gracious* (Allah) *from you, if you do fear Allah."* (The angel) *said: "I am only a messenger from your Lord,* (to announce) *to you the gift of a righteous son." She said: "How can I have a son when no man has touched me, nor am I unchaste?" He said: "So* (it will be), *your Lord said: "That is easy for Me and We* (Allah) *will appoint him as a sign to mankind and a mercy from Us* (Allah), *and it is a matter* (already) *decreed." So, she conceived him, and she withdrew with him to a far place* (i.e. Bethlehem). (Quran 19:16–22)

Allah also said,

> *And she* (Mary) *who guarded her chastity We* (Allah) *breathed into* (the sleeves of) *her* (shirt or garment) *through Our spirit* (angel Gabriel) *and We* (Allah) *made her and her son a sign for the mankind and jinn.* (Quran 21:91)

About Jesus's birth, Allah said,

> *And the pains of childbirth drove her* (Mary) *to the trunk of a date-palm. She said: "Would that I had died before this and had been forgotten and out of sight!" Then* (a voice) *cried to her from below her, saying: "Grieve not: your Lord has provided a water stream under you." And shake the trunk of the date-palm towards you; it will let fall fresh ripe-dates upon you. Then she brought him* (the baby) *to her people, carrying him. They Said: "O Mary! Indeed, you have brought a mighty thing. O sister* (i.e., the like) *of Aaron* (a pious man at her time) *your father was not a man who used to commit adultery, nor your mother was an unchaste woman."* (Quran 19:23–28)

Then Allah tells us about the first miracle of Jesus:

> *Then she pointed to him* (the baby, Jesus). *They said: "How can we talk to one who is a child in the cradle? He* (Jesus) *said: "Verily, I am a slave of Allah; He has given me the Scripture and made me a Prophet. And He has made me blessed wheresoever I be, and has enjoined on me prayer and charity, as long as I live. And dutiful to my mother, and made me not arrogant, rebellious. And peace be upon me the day I was born, and the day I die, and the day I shall be raised alive!"* (in the Hereafter). (Quran 19:29–33)

Then Allah confirmed the reality of Jesus, saying,

> *Such is Jesus, son of Mary.* (It is) *a statement of truth. About which they doubt* (or dispute). *It befits not* (the majesty of) *Allah that He should beget a*

son (this refers to the slander of the Christians against Allah, by saying that Jesus is the son of Allah). *Glorified* (and Exalted) *is He* (above all that they associate with Him). *When He decrees a thing, He only says to it: "Be" and it is.* (Quran 19:34–35)

And Allah also said about the reality of Jesus:

Verily, the similitude of Jesus before Allah is as that of Adam. He created him from dust, then he said to him: "Be"—and he was. (Quran 3:59).

About Jesus's mission and miracles, Allah said,

And He (Allah) *will teach him* (Jesus) *the Book and wisdom and the Torah and the Gospel. And will make him a messenger to the Children of Israel* (saying), *"I have come to you with a sign from your Lord, that I design for you out of clay, a figure like that of a bird, and breathe into it, and it becomes a bird by Allah's Leave; and I heal him who was born blind, and the leper, and I bring the dead to life by Allah's Leave. And I inform you of what you eat, and what you store in your houses. Surely, in that is a sign for you, if you are believers. And I have come confirming that which was before me of the Torah, and to make lawful to you part of what was forbidden to you, and I have come to you with a proof from your Lord. So, fear Allah and obey me. Truly! Allah is my Lord and your Lord, so worship Him* (Alone). *This is a Straight Path."* (Quran 3:48–51)

About the rescue of Jesus from the plot of the Jews to crucify him, Allah said,

> *And because of their* (the Jews) *saying* (in boast), *"We killed the Messiah Jesus, son of Mary, the Messenger of Allah." but they killed him not, nor crucified him, but it was made to appear so to them, and those who differ in the matter are full of doubts. They have no* (certain) *knowledge, they follow nothing but conjecture. For surely; they killed him not. But Allah raised him up unto Him. And Allah is Ever All-Powerful, All-Wise.* (Quran 4:157–158)

What happened after Jesus's ascension? Allah tells us,

> *Then the sects differed* (i.e. the Christians about Jesus), *so woe to the disbelievers* (those who gave false witness by saying that Jesus is the son of Allah) *from the meeting of a great Day* (the Day of Resurrection). *How clearly will they see and hear the Day when they will appear before Us!* (Allah)*! But the Polytheists and wrong doers today are in plain error. And warn them of the day of grief and regrets, they are in a state of carelessness, and they believe not.* (Quran 19:37–39)

And He also said,

> *O people of the Scripture* (Christians)*! Do not exceed the limits in your religion, nor say of Allah aught but the truth. The Messiah Jesus, son of Mary, was* (no more than) *a Messenger of Allah and His word* ("Be"—and he was) *which He bestowed on Mary and a spirit created by Him; so, believe in Allah and His Messengers. Say not: "Three* (trinity)*!" Cease!* (it is) *better for you. For Allah is* (the only) *One God, glorified is He above having a son. To Him belongs all that is in the heavens and all*

that is in the earth. And Allah is All-Sufficient as a Disposer of affairs." (Quran 4:171)

And He, Most High, also said,

> *Surely, they have disbelieved who say: "Allah is the Messiah Jesus, son of Mary." But the Messiah said: "O Children of Israel! Worship Allah my Lord and your Lord." Verily whosoever sets up partners with Allah, then Allah has forbidden Paradise to him, and the Fire will be his abode. And for the polytheists and wrong doers there are no helpers. Surely, disbelievers are those who said: "Allah is the third of the three* (in a Trinity).*" But there is no God but One God, Allah. And if they cease not from what they say, verily, a painful torment will befall on the disbelievers among them. Will they not turn with repentance to Allah and ask His Forgiveness? For Allah is Oft-Forgiving, Most Merciful. The Messiah, son of Mary, was no more than a messenger; many were the Messengers that passed away before him. His mother* (Mary) *was a woman of truth. They both used to eat food* (as any other human being, while God does not eat). *Look how We* (Allah) *make the signs clear to them; yet look how they are deluded away from the truth. Say: "How do you worship besides Allah something which has no power either to harm or to benefit you? But it is Allah Who is the All-Hearer, the All-Knower." Say: "O people of the Scripture!* (the Christians), *Exceed not the limits in your religion* (by believing in something) *other than the truth, and do not follow the vain desires of a people who went astray before and who misled many, and strayed* (themselves) *from the right path."* (Quran 5:72–77)

And to those who say that God has begotten a son, He, the Almighty, responds,

> *And they say:* "*The Most Gracious* (Allah) *has begotten a son. Indeed, you have brought forth* (said) *a terrible evil thing. Whereby the heavens are almost torn, and the earth is split asunder, and the mountains fall in ruins, that they ascribe a son to the Most Gracious* (Allah). *But it is not suitable for* (the Majesty of) *the Most Gracious* (Allah) *that He should beget a son. There is none in the heavens and the earth but comes to the Most Gracious* (Allah) *as a slave. Verily, He knows each one of them, and has counted them a full counting. And every one of them will come to Him alone on the Day of Resurrection.*" (Quran 19:88–95)

And He also said,

> *And to warn those who say,* "*Allah has begotten a son.*" *No knowledge have they of such a thing, nor had their fathers. Mighty is the word that comes out of their mouths* (i.e. He begot a son). *They utter nothing but a lie.* (Quran 18:4–5)

And He also said,

> *And say,* "*Praise to Allah, Who has not begotten a son, and Who has no partner in* (His) *Dominion and has no* (need of a) *protector out of weakness; and magnify Him with all magnificence.*" (Quran 17:111)

As regards the return of Jesus Christ to earth, Allah said,

> *And he (Jesus), son of Mary shall be a known sign for* (the coming of) *the Hour* (Day of Resurrection). *Therefore, have no doubt concerning it. And follow Me* (Allah)*! This is the Straight Path."* (of Islamic Monotheism, leading to Allah and to His Paradise). (Quran 43:61)

And Allah also said,

> *And there is none of the people of the Scripture* (Christians) *but must believe in him* (Jesus, son of Mary, as only a Messenger of Allah and a human being) *before his death. And on the Day of Resurrection, he* (Jesus) *will be a witness against them.* (Quran 4:159)

The phrase in the above verse, "before his death," has two interpretations:

1) Before Jesus's death after his second coming, or
2) A Christian's or a Jew's death, at the time of the appearance of the angel of death when he will realize that Jesus was only a messenger of Allah and had no share in divinity.

Why and how will Jesus come back?

Jesus must return to earth because, as a human being, he must die and be buried in the earth as all mortals must. Allah said, *"Thereof* (the earth) *We* (Allah) *created you, and into it we shall return you, and from it we shall bring you out once again.* (On the resurrection Day)*"* (Quran 20:55). And He said, *"Therein* (the earth) *you shall live, and therein you shall die, and from it you shall be brought out* (i.e., resurrected)*"* (Quran 7:25).

So Jesus will return when his appointed death is near in order to die upon earth. This second coming of Jesus will correspond with the time of the appearance of the trial of the False Messiah, the

Antichrist, on earth. This Antichrist is a nonbelieving human being to whom Allah will give power as a trail for humanity. His power will be such that he will bring life to a dead person, similar to the power that Allah granted the true Messiah, Jesus. The Antichrist is a young man of ruddy complexion, curly haired, and one-eyed. Every messenger warned his people from this Antichrist, including Jesus himself. This could be what the author of Mark wrote about Jesus, when describing this trial, saying,

> *How terrible it will be in those days… For the trouble of those days will be far worse than the world has ever known from the very beginning when God created the world until the present time. Nor will there ever be anything like it again.* (Mark 13:17–19)

Then the true Messiah, Jesus, will kill the false messiah near Jerusalem.

Jesus will come down from heaven wearing colored garments. His descent will be on the white minaret, east Damascus, putting his hands on the wings of two angels. He will not bring a new religion nor will he rule with his previous religion, because it was abrogated by the final Islamic, universal revision brought by the final, universal messenger, Muhammad. So Jesus will be a follower of the final Islamic message, and he will rule people justly by the law of the Quran as a just ruler. He will break the cross. At his time, money will be in abundance so that nobody will accept it. He will live on earth seven years, then die and be buried like the other messengers and mankind in general. So his total life on earth would be forty years. His first coming was for thirty-three and his second coming will be for seven years. And on the day of resurrection, he will be resurrected from death like the rest of mankind and the jinn. And he will give testimony before Allah and reject all of those who put divinity in him and his mother.

The messenger of mercy

Allah the Almighty said about Prophet Muhammad, peace be upon him, *"And We have not sent you,* (O Muhammad) *except as a mercy to the worlds"* (Quran 21:107).

To anyone who believes in Allah, Creator, possessor of the kingdom, Regulator of the affairs of all things, and God.

To anyone who believes in the messengers of Allah, Abraham, Moses, and Jesus.

To anyone who believes in the books of Allah, the scriptures of Abraham, Torah, and the Gospel.

To all of those, Allah says, *"Say: O people of the Scripture come to a word that is just between us and you, that we worship none but Allah alone, and that we associate no partners with Him, and that none of us shall take others as lords besides Allah"* (Quran 3:64).

It is a call to believe in Allah alone, who has not begotten a son and who has no partner in His dominion nor is He is in need of a helper or supporter. He rose over His throne above all His creations. He never manifested in a human form, never came down to earth, never died to redeem mankind. And it is a call not to make another deity with Allah. The Almighty Allah says, *"And do not make with Allah another deity. Verily, I* (Muhammad) *am a plain warner to you from Him"* (Quran 51:51).

It is a call to believe in all the books of Allah that He revealed to his messengers. Only the final book of Allah, the Quran, is the one that is still preserved by Allah. Previous Allah's books such as the Torah of Moses and the Gospel of Jesus were not. The extant Bible is a collection of many books were produced by anonymous authors through purely human efforts. These books themselves contain words of Allah, words of the prophets, and words of men. And as such, they are not reliable as sources for true belief.

It is a call to believe in all the messengers of Allah from Noah to the last one, Muhammad, peace be up on them all. Prophet Muhammad was sent to all mankind as the final messenger. Read about the biography of this great messenger, and you will come to know that he was sent as a mercy from Allah to the worlds.

It is a call to believe in the next life, the Hereafter. Allah will raise us from the dead for judgment. He will judge our faith and deeds. Then we will be driven to our final eternal destiny: paradise for those who died on the true faith and performed their good deeds in accordance with Allah's instructions or to the eternal suffering in the fire of hell for those who died disbelieving, or those who have gone astray with false faith, or who have associated partners with Allah, despite that the clear message of Allah has reached to all of them.

On the day of judgment, while there are billions of people who believed in Jesus as God waiting for their turn for the judgment, Allah will ask Jesus, saying,

> *O Jesus son of Mary! Did you say to men: "Worship me and my mother as two gods besides Allah?" Then Jesus will say, "Glorified are You! It was not for me to say what I had no right* (to say). *Had I said such a thing, You would surely have known it. You know what is in my inner self though I do not know what is in Yours; truly, You, only You, are the All-knower of all that is hidden* (and unseen). *Never did I say to them aught except what You did command me to say: 'Worship Allah, my Lord and your Lord.' And I was a witness over them while I dwelt amongst them, but when You took me up, You were the Watcher over them; and You are a witness to all things. If You punish them, they are Your slaves, and if You forgive them, verily You, only You, are the All-Mighty, the All-Wise."* (Quran 5:116–118)

Then Allah will say,

> *This is a Day on which the truthful will profit from their truth: theirs are Gardens under which rivers flow* (in Paradise). *They shall abide therein*

forever. Allah is pleased with them and they with Him. That is the great success. (Quran 5:119)

It is a call to be among those truthful who will profit from their truth by not believing in Jesus as God or a literal son of God who died to save mankind and practicing their deeds according to the final message from Allah. For Allah said, *"And whoever seeks a religion other than Islam, it will never be accepted of him, and in the Hereafter, he will be one of the losers"* (Quran 3:85).

It is a call to salvation. Seek the truth with true intention, and Allah will guide you to the truth. Do not give your mind to another to manufacture a belief that will not benefit you on the day of judgment.

It is a call for you, Christian reader, to start to know that Jesus never preached the faith that you have in your heart about him, that he was God or the literal son of God who died as a savior for mankind. Try to think deeply about this. How is it that a Muslim can prove his faith in Jesus from Jesus's words in the Bible, while the Christian cannot bring even one proof for his faith in Jesus from Jesus's words. Is it not something amazing? And that should encourage you to start seeking the truth.

It is a call for you, Christian reader, to check your inherited faith. Do not let your life go on with the dream of the god who killed himself for you and believing that this dream is your ticket to paradise. Do not let the angel of death be the one to wake you up from this dream when he comes to you to take your soul. It is very bad for a person to discover, at that very late moment, that the ticket of this false dream is to the other place. No father or mother or brother or friend or society will benefit you. So save your soul. You will have no excuse on the day of judgment. You cannot say to Allah, "Nobody informed me." Here the call of truth has now reached you. Do not miss it. And do not make a way for Satan to drive you away from it, because his aim is to keep you as you are, in order to share with him the price that he had paid for his sin that caused him to go to hell in the Hereafter. And let not a friend hinder you from this reminder after it came to you. Allah Almighty said about the situation on the day of resurrection of those who were misled by their friends after they knew the truth:

> *And* (remember) *the Day when the wrong-doer will bite at his hands, he will say: "Oh! Would that I had taken a path with the Messenger (Muhammad). Ah! Woe to me! would that I had never taken so-and-so as an intimate friend! He indeed led me astray from the Reminder after it had come to me. and Satan is to man ever a deserter in the hour of need."* (Quran 25:27–29)

How can you join the only way to salvation?

Whenever you decide to accept the fact that the true path to salvation is only in the final message, Islam. And you have decided to join this only way to salvation, you should declare the first pillar of Islam (in Arabic), saying, "Ash-hadu an la ilaha illa Allah, wa ash-hadu anna Muhammad rasool Allah," meaning: "I testify that there is no God but Allah. And I testify that Muhammad is His messenger."

Upon declaration of these two testimonies with believing in them in your heart, you are at once a Muslim. You should then have a shower for purification. Then you should start to learn and practice the second pillar of Islam, which is to pray five times a day, on their times. The third pillar is to pay a charity to the needy believing people. There are certain rules and regulations concerning this pillar. The fourth pillar is to fast the whole month of Ramadan. And the fifth pillar is to perform pilgrimage to Makkah once in your lifetime, if you can afford to do so.

It is your duty to start learning how to properly worship Allah. Don't just wait for others to come to teach you. But you need to get help and advice from knowledgeable and reliable Muslims. Should you visit any Islamic center near you, they will be more than happy to help you. But remember to always seek proof from the Quran or Prophet's Sunna (way). May Allah grant you success and confirm you on the true way.

CHAPTER 7

Consideration and pondering over the gospels

Putting gospels under microscope

Any book containing contradictions and mistakes cannot, by necessity, have come from God. Moreover, relying upon such a book for one's salvation would lead to disastrous consequences. We have already seen the reality of Paul's personal gospel, which he claimed that he received and learned it through revelation from Jesus Christ. His personal gospel does not contain the words of Jesus that give his actual teaching; instead, he spreads his own invented teaching and his own philosophy that conflicts with the true Gospel of Jesus and the teaching of his disciples. More than half of the New Testament is written by Paul (fourteen books). In his personal gospel, we saw how Paul uttered against God, Jesus, the disciples, and the law with utterly terrible words. We also saw how he allowed for himself untruths and fickleness.

Surely, any book that without divine sources is fallible. The claim of Stephen in the Acts of the Apostles is one of the examples. He claimed that he saw heaven open and the Son of Man standing at the right hand of God (i.e., he saw two distinct personages next to each other, which means that he already individualized each one with his own limited magnitude, space, and direction!) Surely, this claim of Stephen is incredible and inconceivable, simply because it exceeded all bounds, and it is just against the natural way in which God has created mankind—that is, no vision can encompass Him!

The Quran on the other hand challenges all mankind and the jinn (the unseen creatures) with an open challenge to put the Quran under the microscope of examination and consideration so that they search for one mistake and they will not find, or to bring a chapter of the like thereof and call their supporters and helpers, but they can never do it or to produce the like of this Quran, which they could not produce the like thereof, even if they help one another. Who can speak about his book with such a strong, challenging language to the day of resurrection? Only Allah Almighty. And the challenge is to mankind and the jinn together.

What about the authenticity of the four gospels and to what extent they are reliable? To determine that, we need first a careful checking and pondering over them. As it is well-known, the oldest dated copy of the New Testament was written in common Greek, and as we saw before in the dialogue with the four authors of the gospels, they were not inspired while they were writing but produced them through their own efforts. These four gospels are not from the "One Gospel" of which God had revealed to Jesus and commanded us to believe in as with His other true books, but they are biographical books of Jesus produced through purely human efforts that relied upon undocumented narrations, rumors, hearsay, and copying from previous human books. And since this is the reality of these four books, it is not surprising that they contain a mixture of words of God, words of men, and some inherited traditions. The attribution to their authors is pure speculation because the original authors were anonymous.

The picture will be much clearer, if we suppose that the four authors themselves have gathered to apply the system on how to put their gospels under the microscope of consideration and pondering:

MARK: Matthew, what is your source for the list of genealogies that you mentioned at the beginning of your gospel and which you claimed to be the lineage of Jesus?

MATTHEW: First Chronicles, one of the books of the Old Testament. Why are you asking?

MARK: You cannot make a genealogy of Jesus, simply because he does not have a human father. Did you not know that you committed many mistakes when you wrote the first paragraph in your gospel that says, *"The book of the genealogy of Jesus Christ, the son of David, the son of Abraham"* (Matt. 1:1). Then you copied the genealogy list that was mentioned in 1 Chronicles?

MATTHEW: What are these mistakes?

MARK: First, how do you claim that this list of names that you copied is a genealogy of Jesus while the list ends with Joseph (the carpenter), the husband of Mary, of whom was born Jesus? *"And Jacob begot Joseph the husband of Mary, of whom was born Jesus who is called Christ"* (Matt. 1:16). What is the relationship of Joseph with Jesus, who was born without a father? It is a genealogical list of Mary's husband, Joseph, with which Jesus had nothing to do. And if we compare the list of genealogies mentioned in 1 Chronicles with the list that you copied in your gospel and claimed to be the genealogy of Jesus, we see that you have eliminated three sequent generations of the descendants of the prophet Solomon. You wrote from father to son like this, *"And Joram begot Uzziah. Uzziah begot Jotham, Jotham begot Ahaz"* (Matt. 1:8–9). While your source, 1 Chronicles, from father to son like this, *"Joram his son, Ahaziah his son, Joash his son, Amaziah his son, Azariah his son, Jotham his son, Ahaz his son"* (1 Chron. 3:11–13). You have eliminated Ahaziah, Joash, and Amaziah!

Also, you have eliminated another generation from the same line of prophet Solomon's descendants. You have written from father to son like this, *"And Amon begot Josiah. Josiah begot Jeconiah and his brothers. Jeconiah begot Shealtile"* (Matt. 1:10–12). While your source, 1 Chronicles from father to son like this, *"Amon his son, and Josiah his son. The sons of Josiah were Johanan the firstborn, the second Jehoiakim… The sons of Jehoiakim were Jeconiah and Zedekiah. And the sons of Jeconiah were Assir, Shealtile his son"* (1 Chron. 3:14–17). You made

Grandpa (Josiah) give birth to his grandson (Jeconiah). Oh, Matthew!

MATTHEW: I was compelled to make Jesus a descendant of David. But since there is no link between them, I used the genealogical list of Joseph, the husband of his mother.

MARK: This is illogical, Matthew. Jesus cannot belong to any recorded lineage as he was not descended from any human father. What about your elimination of three sequent generations from the list of the descendants of the prophet Solomon? And why did you delete Jehoiakim also from the list and showed the Grandpa (Josiah) give birth to his grandson (Jeconiah)?

MATTHEW: About the three generations Ahaziah, Joash, and Amaziah, it was a mistake of copying. But Jehoiakim, I intentionally canceled him.

MARK: But why?

MATTHEW: Because Jehoiakim was a very bad king. Have you not read about him in the Old Testament, in the book of Jeremiah (Jer. 36:20–31)? He burned the words of God in the scroll that Baruch had written at the instruction of Jeremiah, so God warned him. The text says, *"Therefore thus says the Lord concerning Jehoiakim king of Judah: "He shall have no one to sit on the throne of David, and his dead body shall be cast out to the heat of the day and the first of the night"* (Jer. 36:30). So how do you want me to display Jesus as a descendant of a blacklisted man? How does Jesus sit on the throne of David while the text says, *"He shall have no one to sit on the throne of David"*? He is blocking the way. I cannot connect Jesus to the throne of David if this bad man is in the list of the lineage. So I saw that the solution would be to delete him from the list and making the grandfather a direct father of his grandson, and nobody will notice.

MARK: There was absolutely no need for all of the alleged lineage series of Jesus. I already told you that it is not possible to make a genealogical list of a man who did not descend from any human father.

LUKE: But I wrote in my gospel about the angel who spoke to Mary, saying, *"And shall call his name Jesus. He will be great and will be called the Son of the Highest; and the Lord God will give him the throne of his father David. And he will reign over the house of Jacob forever, and of his kingdom there will be no end"* (Luke 1:31–33).

MATTHEW: Have you heard this, Mark? It would be a problem if I had put Jehoiakim in the list of the lineage, although God had threatened him. If I had not deleted him from the list of the lineage, the prophecy of giving Jesus the throne of David, which Luke mentioned (1:32) would be false. Or the threatening of God to Jehoiakim in (Jer. 36:30), it would be false. And in both cases, it is a problem.

JOHN: I am sure that what Luke mentioned (1:32) is wrong.

LUKE: How is that?

JOHN: I will tell you later.

LUKE: Oh, Matthew, you made a mistake by making Jesus belong to the house of David through his son Solomon, where there is Jehoiakim in this way. As for me, I know that I cannot make Jesus belong to David because he has no father. But I have made Jesus to be a son of Joseph, as was supposed, so that I could use the lineage list of Joseph to link Jesus with David. *"Now Jesus himself began his ministry at about thirty years of age, being as was supposed the son of Joseph, the son of Heli"* (Luke 3:23). But I did not use Solomon's way to connect Jesus with David. Instead, I used another way with another lineage list that differed from the lineage list that you copied. Oh, Matthew! I have linked Jesus to David through his other son, Nathan, as there are no obstacles.

MATTHEW: But the way of Nathan is very long, forty-one generations, while the way of Solomon is a shorter way to David, only twenty-six generations. There is no problem with Jehoiakim. He was deleted from the list.

MARK: But both of you included a son of fornication in the alleged genealogy of Jesus!

JOHN: He was a son of incest adultery!

LUKE: Who was that?

JOHN: Perez, the son of Judah, the son of Jacob, the son of Isaac. He is in your Gospel, Luke (3:33–34) as well as in your Gospel,

Matthew (1:2–3). And you even mentioned his mother, Tamar. Do you know who Tamar was, Matthew?

MATTHEW: Yes, I know. Is she not she the wife of Er, the son of Judah? Then when Er was killed, she married his brother Onan. Then when Onan was also killed, her father in-law, Judah, asked her to remain a widow in her father's house until his third young son, Shelah, was grown. She went to her father's house and waited and waited for Shelah. But her father in-law, Judah, already had forgotten all about her.

JOHN: That is right. But the problem was that she had her son, Perez, from her father-in-law, Judah. It was incest adultery with him. And she delivered twins, Perez and Zerah.

MATTHEW: Yes. But Judah, her father-in-law, did not recognized her because she was disguised. And she wanted to remind him that she had a long waiting for his son, Shelah, who was already old. But really, I do not know what the wisdom behind this story is to be included in a book of God (Gen. 38). There is no objective, or purpose, or even advice out of this story. In fact, it simplifies incest adultery.

JOHN: Yes. But do you know that you and Luke are both in trouble for putting this Perez in your lists of the alleged genealogy of Jesus?

MATTHEW AND LUKE: How?

JOHN: Have you not read this text in Deuteronomy? *"One of illegitimate birth shall not enter the congregation of the Lord; even to the tenth generation none of his descendants shall enter the congregation of the Lord"* (Deut. 23:2). So in this case with Perez, David cannot enter to the congregation of God, because he is the tenth generation starting from Perez! What do you think of this problem?

MARK: There must be something wrong, either the story of Judah and Tamar or the text of Deuteronomy. By the way, Matthew, why did you not delete Perez from your list as you did with Jehoiakim?

MATTHEW: According to the text of Deuteronomy, it is the problem of David and not Jesus!

LUKE: Even you, John, you have also written something wrong!
JOHN: Where is that?
LUKE: You have reported that Jesus said, *"No one has ascended to heaven but he who came down from heaven, that is the son of man who is in heaven"* (John 3:13).
JOHN: How is it wrong?
LUKE: Have not you read this text in Genesis? *"And Enoch walked with God; and he was not, for God took him"* (Gen. 5:24). And in 2 Kings, it says, *"And it came to pass, when the Lord was about to take up Elijah into heaven by a whirlwind"* (2 Kings 2:1). And also, this text—*"Then it happened, as they continued on and talked that suddenly a chariot of fir appeared with horses of fire and separated the two of them; and Elijah went up by a whirlwind into heaven"* (2 Kings 2:11). Here are Enoch and Elijah, who also ascended to heaven.
JOHN: Perhaps I haven't noticed these two.
LUKE: Not only this, John! You wrote that Jesus said to the Jews, *"And I, if I am lifted up from the earth"* (John 12:32). Then after only one verse, you have forgotten all about what you had written. Then you wrote that the Jews asked Jesus, *"How can you say, 'The son of man must be lifted up? Who is this son of man?"* (John 12:34). In his discussion with the Jews this time, Jesus did not mention the term "son of man," but he said, *"If I am lifted up."* So why did you make the people questioning Jesus with the term "son of man"?
John: Yes, what is this? How could I do such a thing? I think that I have mixed up between two different dialogues of Jesus with the Jews. Maybe I just let myself go on writing without thinking. So my thoughts jumped so fast, then they came out this way. Anyway, all of us make mistakes, nobody is perfect. Ask Matthew.
MATTHEW: Why me? I do not write false things. Okay, I may have corrupted historical facts, but I do not write false things.
JOHN: What about your false report? You wrote, *"Jesus, when he cried out again with a loud voice. Then the curtain hanging in the Temple was torn in two from top to bottom. The earth shook,*

and the rocks split apart, and the graves were opened; and many bodies of the saints who had died were raised to life. They left the graves, and after Jesus rose from death, they went into the holy city and appeared to many"* (Matt. 27:50–53). You were the only one who reported this event.

MATTHEW: When I copied the Gospel of Mark, I saw that he narrated a cosmic event that occurred during the crucifixion, saying, *"Now when the sixth hour had come, there was darkness over the whole land until the ninth hour"* (Mark 15:33). Then he wrote that after Jesus breathed his last, a local event occurred. *"The veil of the temple was torn in two from top to bottom"* (Mark 15:38). Mark wanted by those events, which he wrote from his imagination, to add an intense feeling of horror and fear to the crucifixion incident. But I saw that it was not enough to feel frightened, so I imagined other events that would give the crucifixion more horror and fear.

I know that there are some people who will ask, "Why only Matthew does the Holy Spirit concern him with such exciting news?" But all of us know that the Holy Spirit has nothing to do with our writing. All of our writings are based on our skills and pure efforts, without any connection with heaven. But I admit that I am in trouble now because of this scoop! I have written elsewhere, *"On the next day, the chief priests and Pharisees went to Pilate saying, 'Sir, we remember, while he* (Jesus) *was still alive, how that deceiver said, "After three days I will rise."'"* (Matt. 27:62–63). Surely, the chief priests and Pharisees would not dare to go to Pilate and called Jesus as a deceiver if it was true that the earth shook, and the rocks split apart, and the graves were opened, and many bodies of the saints who had died were raised to life, and they left the graves and went into the holy city and appeared to many. Rather, those Jews may believe in Jesus, and perhaps maybe the pagan Pilate as well. I wish I did as Luke did.

JOHN: What did Luke do?

LUKE: I copied the text of Mark without any additions. *"And it was about the sixth hour, and there was darkness over all the earth until the ninth hour. Then the sun was darkened, and the veil of the temple was torn in two"* (Luke 23:44–45).

MATTHEW: But whoever reads what I have written and what you have written, oh, Luke, in the introduction of your gospel knows that one of us is not telling the truth.

JOHN: How is this?

MATTHEW: Luke wrote in the introduction telling us why he wrote his gospel, saying, *"Because I have carefully studied all these matters from their beginning"* (Luke 1:3). And when the reader sees that Luke, who claims to have carefully studied all matters from their beginning, has not written anything about the events that I mentioned in my gospel of earth shaking, cracking of rocks, opening of the graves, and the resurrection of those who died and entering the city and appearing to many. This means that they were events in my imagination only or that Luke did not studied carefully all matters from their beginning as he claimed. But the good thing was that nobody has asked me about those who got out of the graves and went into the holy city whether they were naked or wearing clothes!

JOHN: I realized before the reader that what you wrote, Matthew, as well as what Mark invented, then copied by Luke, were delusions that did not happen. And therefore, I did not write anything about these things. And if what you all wrote was true, it will be transmitted through generations to this day. Anyway, you have many other problems with your gospel, oh, Matthew! You wrote that the chief priests and elders took counsel about the thirty pieces of silver that Judas returned to them. *"And bought with them the potter's field, to bury strangers in... Then was fulfilled what was spoken by Jeremiah the prophet, saying, 'And they took the thirty pieces of silver, the value of him who was priced, whom they of the children of Israel priced, and gave them for the potter's field, as the Lord directed me'"* (Matt. 27:7, 9–10). Do you know who said these words, Matthew?

MATTHEW: Was not prophet Jeremiah?

JOHN: No, it was not Jeremiah, but Zechariah. You are misleading the readers, Matthew! Read this text in Zechariah, *"So they weighed out for my wages thirty pieces of silver. And the Lord said to me, "Throw it to the potter" that princely price they set on me. So, I took the thirty pieces of silver and threw them into the house of the Lord for the potter"* (Zech. 11:12–13).

MATTHEW: How did this happen? I was sure of my writing. It seems that I was under an illusion. Yes. Read the text in Jeremiah. It is totally different. *"So, I bought the field from Hanameel, the son of my uncle who was in Anathoth, and weighed out to him the money, seventeen shekels of silver"* (Jer. 32:9). I cannot correct this mistake now. It is too late.

JOHN: So do not say that "I do not write false things." You also have this problem that Peter asked Jesus, *"See, we have left all and followed you. Therefore, what shall we have?" So Jesus said to them, "You who have followed me will also sit on twelve thrones, judging the twelve tribes of Israel"* (Matt. 19:27–28). So you already included Judas with them, Matthew!

MATTHEW: Yes, I admit. I should not have written this. I forget about Judas. I should have done like Luke when he just copied from Mark. I wanted to say something new, different from Mark, but unfortunately Judas was there.

JOHN: What have you written, Luke?

LUKE: When Peter said to Jesus, *"See, we have left all and followed you," Jesus said to them, "I assure you that anyone who leaves home or wife or brothers or parents or children for the sake of the kingdom of God, will receive much more in this present age and eternal life in the age to come"* (Luke 18:28–30).

JOHN: Thank you, Luke. But you, Matthew, your problems are not finish yet. You also wrote this—*"Josiah begot Jeconiah and his brothers about the time they were carried away to Babylon"* (Matt. 1:11). As we discussed before, Josiah did not begot Jeconiah, but he begot Jehoiakim the one you have deleted from the lists of the alleged genealogy of Jesus. And Jehoiakim is the one who begot Jeconiah, as it was stated in 1 Chronicles. *"The sons of Josiah were Johanan the firstborn, the second Jehoiakim… The sons of Jehoiakim were Jeconiah his son and Zedekiah his son"* (1 Chron. 3:15–16). But the problem now is that you made

Grandpa Josiah give birth to his grandson Jeconiah at the captivity of Babylon, while in fact, Josiah was dead before the Babylonian captivity. The captivity took place during the reign of grandson Jeconiah. Read this text from the book of 2 Kings, *"So Jehoiakim rested with his fathers. Then Jehoiachin*(Jeconiah) *his son reigned in his place... Jehoiachin* (Jeconiah) *was eighteen years old when he became king, and he reigned in Jerusalem three months... And Nebuchadnezzar, king of Babylon came against the city, as his servants were besieging it. Then Jehoiachin* (Jeconiah) *king of Judah, his mother, his servants, his princes, and his officers went out to the king of Babylon; and the king of Babylon, in the eighth year of his reign, took him prisoner... Also he carried into captivity all Jerusalem... Ten thousand captives...and carried Jehoiachin* (Jeconiah) *captive to Babylon"* (2 King 24:6, 8, 11–12, 14–15).

The funny thing, Matthew, is that you made Jeconiah (Jehoiachin) to be born after he became a king at age eighteen! How could it be, Matthew? And how come you say, "I do not write false things"?

LUKE: He he he!

JOHN: Why are you laughing at him, Luke? You also did the same.

LUKE: Who? Me? No way. It is impossible for me to write such a thing as him.

JOHN: You wrote, *"The son of Joannas, the son of Rhesa, the son of Zerubbabel, the son of Shealtiel, the son of Neri"* (Luke 3:27). And that is absolutely wrong. Read this text in 1 Chronicles, *"And the sons of Jeconiah were Assir, Shealtiel his son, and Malchiram, Pedaiah, Shenazzar, Jecamiah, Hoshama, and Nedabiah. The son Pedaiah were Zerubbabel and Shimei. The sons of Zerubbabel were Meshullam, Hananiah"* (1 Chron. 3:17–19). You have mixed up this family, Luke! You made Zerubbabel a son for Shealtiel, but the book of 1 Chronicles in the Old Testament makes Zerubbabel a son for Pedaiah, and Shealtiel would be his uncle, not his father! Also, you made Shealtiel a son for Neri, but 1 Chronicles says that Shealtiel is a son for Jeconiah!

MATTHEW: He he he!

JOHN: Do not laugh, Matthew! You also have the same problem. You wrote, *"Jeconiah begot Shealtiel and Shealtiel begot Zerubbabel. And Zerubbabel begot Abiud"* (Matt. 1:12–13). Here you also make Zerubbabel a son for Shealtiel, while the book of 1 Chronicles makes him a son for Pedaiah and makes Shealtiel his uncle, not his father! Also, you have invented a new son for Zerubbabel and named him Abiud, while the sons of Zerubbabel, as stipulated in the book of the 1 Chronicles, are *"The sons of Zerubbabel were Meshullam, Hananiah…and Hashubah, Ohel, Berechiah, Hasadiah, and Jushab-Hesed—five in all"* (1 Chron. 3:19–20). Really, both of you were mixing those families. You, Luke, wrote, *"The son of Shelah, the son of Cainan, the son of Arphaxad"* (Luke 3:35–36). While 1 Chronicles says, *"Arphaxad begot Shelah, and Shelah begot Eber"* (1 Chron. 1:18). You have invented a new father for Shelah, and you named him Cainan! You already made Shelah the grandson of Arphaxad, not his direct son. And the problem with you, Luke, is you already claimed, saying, *"Because I have carefully studied all these matters from their beginning"* (Luke 1:3). What type of careful study is this, Luke?

MATTHEW AND LUKE: What about Mark? Does that mean he has no mistakes at all?

JOHN: He also has his own mistakes.

MARK: It is impossible.

JOHN: Do not say, "Impossible" You wrote that Jesus said to the Pharisees who protested against the work of the disciples on the Sabbath, *"Have you never read what David did that time when he needed something to eat? He and those with him, so he went into the house of God and ate the bread offered to God. This happened when Abiathar was the High priest"* (Mark 2:24–26). But if we read 1 Samuel about the same story, it says, *"Now David came to Nob, to Ahimelech the priest… David said to Ahimelech, 'What have you on hand? Give me five loaves of bread in my hand, or whatever can be found.' And the priest answer David and said, 'There is no common bread on hand; but there is holy bread…' So the priest gave him holy bread; for there was no bread there but the showbread which had been taken from before the Lord"* (1 Sam. 21:1, 3–4, 6). Oh, Mark, the high priest was Ahimelech, not Abiathar!

LUKE (whispering in Matthew's ear): Thank God that we did not copy the priest's name Abiathar when we copied the text from Mark. Where did Mark get this name Abiathar from?

MARK: Luke, what have you whispered to Matthew? Are you happy with the problems that are in the beginning of your gospel?

LUKE: Like what?

MARK: You wrote, *"And it came to pass in those days that a decree went out from Caesar Augustus that all the world should be registered. This census first took place while Quirinius was governing Syria. So, all went to be registered, everyone to his own city. And Joseph also went up from Galilee, out of the city of Nazareth, into Judea, to the city of David, which is called Bethlehem, because he was of the house and lineage of David, to be registered with Mary, his betrothed wife, who was with child. So it was, that while they were there, the days were completed for her to be delivered"* (Luke 2:1–6). But Luke, you may have forgotten that you wrote before, *"There was in the days of Herod, the king of Judea… Now after those days the wife of Zachariah conceived a baby* (John the Baptist). *In the sixth month of this pregnancy, the Angel Gabriel was sent by God to a city of Galilee named Nazareth, to a virgin betrothed to a man whose name was Joseph… The angel said to here, "You will conceive a son, and shall call his name Jesus"* (Luke 1:5, 24, 26–27, 31). Here, you showed the birth of Jesus take place during the reign of Herod, not Quirinius, as you have previously mentioned! Note that Matthew states that Jesus was born during the reign of Herod, then his son Archelaus succeeded him. He wrote, *"Now, after Jesus was born in Bethlehem of Judea in the days of Herod the king… But when Herod was dead… Archelaus reigned over Judea after his father Herod"* (Matt. 2:1, 19, 22).

No one can help you with this plight, Luke! Unless you want to say that Mary became pregnant with her son Jesus during the reign of Archelaus, and the pregnancy continued until the reign of Quirinius came! Where is your careful study for all matters from their beginning, Luke? What type of careful study is this? A big difference in two consecutive chapters!

JOHN: He he he! Okay, since you have talked about the birth of Jesus, do you remember that I said before, "I'm sure what Luke mentioned was wrong"? Because he said something about the angel who talked to Mary and said to her, *"He will be great, a will be called the son of the Highest; and the Lord God will give him the throne of his father David. And he will reign over the house of Jacob forever, and of his kingdom there will be no end"* (Luke 1:32–33). We all know that Jesus did not sit on the throne of David even for one hour! And he never reigned over the Jews. In fact, they rejected him and plotted to kill him. And he used to escape and hide from them, and you want us, oh, Luke, to believe that he sat on the throne of David and reigned over the Jews? I have said in my gospel, *"Therefore when Jesus perceived that they were about to come and take him by force to make him king, he departed again to a mountain by himself alone"* (John 6:15). How would he escape and hide from a promised kingdom by the angel? Also, I wrote *"He came to his own, but his own received him not"* (John 1:11).

MARK: Yes, John, please show them their countless problems.

JOHN: These are the problems of all of you. And I will start with you, Mark! Because you are the one who wrote first, then these two came later and copied from you and added. You, Mark, wrote that Jesus said, *"And when you hear of wars and rumors of wars, do not be troubled; for such things must happen, but the end is not yet. For nation will rise against nation, and kingdom against kingdom. And there will be earthquakes in various places, and there will be famines and troubles. These are the beginning of the sorrows"* (Mark 13:7–8). Also, you wrote, *"But in those days, after that tribulation, the sun will be darkened, and the moon will not give its light; the stars of heaven will fall, and the powers in heaven will be shaken. Then they will see the son of man coming in the clouds with great power and glory"* (Mark 13:24–26). And also, you wrote that Jesus said, *"Assuredly; I say to you, this gen-*

eration will by no means pass away till all these things take place" (Mark 13:30).

Oh, Mark, it takes centuries for nation to rise against nation and kingdom against kingdom, not in just a few years, until that generation which existed more than two thousand years ago to passes away. Now how many years and how many generations have already passed since you wrote such a thing? And yet Jesus still has not come back. Not only that, Mark, but you also wrote that Jesus said, *"Of him the son of man also will be ashamed when he comes in the glory of his father with the holy angels"* (Mark 8:38). And he also said to them, *"Assuredly I say to you that there are some standing here who will not taste death till they see the kingdom of God come with power"* (Mark 9:1). Those people who were standing there had enough death, but Jesus has not come yet, Mark!

Also, you, Luke, you have copied the same words of Mark about Jesus's second coming before those who were standing there taste death (Luke 9:26–27). But why have you added two days in (9:28) more than what Mark wrote in (9:2)? He wrote after six days, and you wrote after eight days. You know, Luke, I do not trust your careful study anymore! But the good thing about you is that in your second account about the return of Christ, you made the return ticket open. You did not book him with a certain generation who were there some two thousand years ago! (Luke 17:22–37).

You have put yourself in trouble, Matthew! You were very sure that Jesus would have come before two thousand years! You've confirmed this matter three times! One time was by your own words, and twice, you have copied from Mark! Why did you not do it only two times, as Luke did? One with a booking date and the other is open, to give yourself a chance? Why did you confirm all those three times? Were you really sure of the story? Or were you just copying from Mark without thinking about it? You wrote that Jesus said to his disciples, *"When they persecute you in one town, run away to another one. I assure you that you will not finish your work in all the towns of Israel before the son of man comes"* (Matt. 10:23). Only you Matthew who has written such thing! And you have copied from Mark about the second coming of Jesus before those who were standing there tasted death (Matt. 16:27–28). And also, you have copied from him that the generation who was there at that time will by no means pass away till Jesus comes back (Matt. 24:6–34), even though Jesus has said that nation will rise against nation, and kingdom against kingdom before he comes back.

MATTHEW: What do you think, John? Why has he not come back yet?

LUKE: Maybe the disciples have not finished their work in all the towns of Israel yet. Or the generation you and Mark have mentioned has not died yet!

JOHN: He he he! Are you making fun of them, Luke, because you did not book a return date in your second narration? Don't forget that you also copied Mark's account that Jesus would come back before those who were standing there taste death. Those people who were standing there had now enough death, but Jesus has not come back yet, Luke! Anyway, they waited for him at the year 1000 but he did not show up, so they gave him a chance till the year 2000 and still did not show up. So they had to give him another chance till the year 3000!

MATTHEW: I see. I really thought that Jesus would go up to heaven for some certain years and then come back soon, as Paul claimed. *"The Lord* (Jesus) *himself will descend from heaven with a shout, with the voice of an archangel, and with the trumpet of God. And the dead in Christ will rise first. Then we who are alive and remain shall be caught up together with them in the clouds to meet the Lord in the air. And thus, we shall always be with the Lord. Therefore comfort one another with these words"* (1 Thess. 4:16–18). Now more than two thousand years have passed since the prophecy, but nothing happened as Paul had prophesied. Now it seems just doubling by thousands of years. I was narrow-minded.

MARK: Let's just stop this. Our problems seem endless.

JOHN: Not before you tell us why did you make it difficult for the people and put a horrible test for them?

MARK: Where is that?

JOHN: You wrote that after Jesus had appeared to the eleven disciples, he told them about the signs that would follow those who believe in him. And among the signs he said, *"If they pick up snakes or drink any poison, they will not be harmed"* (Mark 16:17–18). I will start with you, Mark! If you are a true believer of Christ, can you drink any poison or anything deadly now?

MARK: No way.

JOHN: So why did you lie? And said that Jesus had said such thing? Perhaps the hospitals now have the records for the nonbelievers in Jesus. Those who died because they accidentally drank a poison, their names are listed in those records!

LUKE: He he he!

MARK: Do not laugh, Luke! I have not written such thing. My gospel ends at (16:8). I do not know who wrote 9–20. So I am not responsible for anyone who became rash and drank a poison to test his faith in Jesus! Anyway, let us just change the subject and have question and answers instead.

MATTHEW: Yes. It is a good idea. I will start. What did Jesus say to identify the disciple who would betray him (Judas)?

MARK: *"Who dips with me in the dish"* (Mark 14:20).

MATTHEW: I copied from Mark (Matt. 26:23).

JOHN: *"It is he to whom I shall give a piece of bread when I have dipped it"* (John 13:26).

LUKE: *"The hand of my betrayer is with me on the table"* (Luke 22:21). Okay, it is now my turn to ask. What was the signal of Judas to identify Jesus?

Mark: The kiss. And Judas kissed Jesus (Mark 14:44–45).

MATTHEW: I copied from Mark (Matt. 26:48–49).

LUKE: The kiss. And Judas drew near to Jesus to kiss him (Luke 22:47).

JOHN: No signal, no kiss. (John 18:4–5). It is my turn now. What happened to the troops and officers who came to arrest Jesus?

MARK: Nothing (Mark 14:43–49).

MATTHEW: If Mark said, "Nothing," me too. (Matt. 26:47–52).

LUKE: Nothing. (Luke 22:47–53).

JOHN: *"They drew back and fell to the ground"* (John 18:6). Didn't you say that you have carefully studied all matters from their beginning, Luke? Have you not heard about this? Okay, I will ask again. With whom was Peter when he denied Jesus three times?

MATTHEW: With a servant girl, then with another servant girl, then with those who stood by (Matt. 26:69–74).

JOHN: With a servant girl, then with those who stood by, then with one of the servant men (John 18:17–26).

LUKE: With a certain servant girl, then with another man, then with another man (Luke 22:56–60).

MARK: With a servant girl two times, then with those who stood by (Mark 14:66–71). Now my turn to ask. Who carried the cross?

JOHN: Jesus himself (John 19:17).

MARK: Simon, a Cyrenian (Mark 15:21).

LUKE: Simon, a Cyrenian (Luke 23:26).

MATTHEW: I copied from Mark (Matt. 27:32). Now it is my turn to ask. What are the last words of Jesus?

MARK: *"Eloi, Eloi, lama sabachthani?"* Meaning *"My God, My God why have you forsaken me?"* (Mark 15:34).

MATTHEW: I copied from Mark (Matt. 27:46).

JOHN: *"It is finished"* (John 19:30).

LUKE: *"Father, into your hands I commend my spirit"* (Luke 23:46). Okay, I will ask now. Who went to the tomb first early Sunday morning?

MARK: Three women—Mary Magdalene, Mary, the mother of James; and Salome (Mark 16:1).

MATTHEW: Two women—Mary Magdalene and other Mary (Matt. 28:1).

LUKE: Many women—Mary Magdalene; Joanna; Mary, the mother of James; and the other women with them (Luke 24:10).

JOHN: Only one woman—Mary Magdalene (John 20:1). My question now is this, To whom did Jesus appear first?

MARK: To Mary Magdalene (Mark 16:9).

JOHN: To Mary Magdalene (John 20:14).

LUKE: To two of his followers (Luke 24:15).

MATTHEW: To Mary Magdalene and other Mary (Matt. 28:9). I will ask. On which part of Jesus's body did the woman pour the costly oil, and when was that and where?

MARK: On his head. Two days before the Passover, at the house of Simon the leper (Mark 14:1, 3).

MATTHEW: Same as Mark (Matt. 26:1–7).

LUKE: No idea!

JOHN: On his feet. Six days before the Passover, at the house of Lazarus (John 12:1–3). Okay, I have a question for Matthew only. Did John the Baptist know Jesus?

MATTHEW: Well, I have two answers. During the baptism, it seemed that John already knew Jesus even before the spirit of God had descended on Jesus, because he said to him, *"I have need to be baptized by you. And after the baptism the spirit of God descended on Jesus"* (Matt. 3:13–16). The other answer is that it seemed he did not know him, because while John was in the prison, he sent two of his men to Jesus and said to him, *"Are you the coming One, or do we look for another?"* (Matt. 11:2–3).

JOHN: John recognized Jesus only when he had seen the spirit of God descended on him (John 1:31–33).

MARK: Okay, John. We also have questions, but we will not include you with us because you do not know the answers. They are not in your gospel!

JOHN: I know. Because our gospel is totally different than yours. We did not copy your gospel like Matthew and Luke. We depended on our own efforts. Anyway, I will watch you, and I may put my comments.

MARK: Okay, here is the question. When Jesus had departed from Jericho, how many blind men asked Jesus for help?

MATTHEW: Two blind men (Matt. 20:29–30).

MARK: One blind man (Mark 10:46).

JOHN: Who do you think his answer is correct, Luke?

LUKE: I think it is Mark, because he gave the name of that blind man. He was Bartimaeus, the son of Timaeus. Matthew added one extra blind man to prove that he did not depend on Mark!

Matthew: Okay. When Jesus came to the other side, to the country of the Gergesenes, how many demon-possessed men met him?

MARK: One man (Mark 5:2).

MATTHEW: Two men (Matt. 8:28).

LUKE: One man, same as Mark. (Luke 8:27). Here is my question, Did the centurion request Jesus directly by himself to heal his servant? Or did he send Jews to Jesus to ask him to heal?

MATTHEW: It was direct request by the centurion himself to Jesus (Matt. 8:5–8).

LUKE: No, the centurion sent elders of the Jews to Jesus to beg him to come and heal his servant (Luke 7:2–4).

MATTHEW: Okay. What was the race of the woman that Jesus refused to heal her daughter?

MARK: The woman was a Greek, born in the region of Phoenicia in Syria (Mark 7:26).

MATTHEW: She was a woman of Canaan (Matt. 15:22).

JOHN: What about you, Luke? What race have you given her?

LUKE: I have not copied this story.

JOHN: Why? What was your reason?

LUKE: Because both Mark and Matthew have narrated about Jesus that he was a racist, speaking to the woman in a bad manner! Both have narrated about him that he insulted and humiliated the woman, when he considered her and her nation as dogs! Both reported that Jesus said to her, *"Let us first feed the children. It is not right to take the children's food and throw it to the dogs"* (Mark 7:27; Matt. 15:26). Oh, John, can you imagine Jesus, the humble great messenger who have not spoken on his own authority but the one who sent him gave him a command what he should say, talking to the woman in such bad manner?

John: No, I cannot imagine. But, Luke, you already copied, as well as Matthew from Mark, about Jesus that he spoke in a nasty way toward his mother! All of you narrated about the mother of Jesus and his brothers, when they stood outside the house where Jesus was still talking to the people and sent in a message asking to speak with him, when one of the people said to him, *"Look, your mother and your brothers are standing outside, and they want to speak with you."* Jesus answered, *"Who is my mother? Who are my brothers?"* Then he pointed to his disciples and said, *"Look! Here are my mother and my brothers!"* All of you have shown this great messenger not respecting his mother (Mark 3:31–34; Matt. 12:46–49; Luke 8:19–21).

MATTHEW: Hey, John! You are the last one to talk about respect. You are the only one to have narrated the most insolent answer by Jesus to his mother. You have written that Jesus called his mother "Woman" instead of mother! This is in your gospel at a wedding party, when the people ran out of wine, then Jesus's mother said to him, *"They have no wine."* Jesus said to her, *"Woman, what does your concern have to do with me?"* (John 2:1–4).

MARK: Just stop it. Surely God would have made Jesus kind to his mother, but the problem is with us. Because we write without checking the narrations. Anyway, this is the last question. I am bored! But you are not included John! When Jesus sent his disciples, what did he command them to take with them?

MATTHEW: He commanded them to take nothing at all (Matt. 10:9–10).

LUKE: Same as Matthew (Luke 9:3).

MARK: No, he allowed taking a stick with them (Mark 6:8–9).

To the Christian reader

What do you think? Can we say that our God was a God of confusion because of the previous problems that we saw with the four gospels? Can we say that the mix-up that we have seen in the four gospels was an inspiration from God and the true Gospel of Jesus? Surely not. Can we say that the four gospels were corrupted? Surely not also! Because these four gospels never were the inspired Gospel of Jesus but were biographical books of Jesus produced through purely human efforts, which depend on undocumented narrations, rumors and hearsay, copying from other previous man-made scriptures. Since there was neither inspiration involved nor eyewitnesses when they were produced, it is natural to have mixture of the truth with falsehood. The words of God with words of man, rumors, hearsay, and some inherited traditions and folklore. The risk with these gospels is when they become the source of the faith! Remember that the true holy book is the one that God challenge all mankind and the jinn with an open challenge to put it under the microscope of consideration and pondering, but they will not find even a single mistake, or even to produce a discourse like the Quran, they cannot produce the like thereof. This book only is the one deserving to be called "the words of God," and it should become the source of one's faith of one who puts salvation his goal.

Conclusion

I am Jesus

A human prophet was sent by God with a doctrine was not of my own making, but from God who sent me, exclusively to the people of Israel. I already showed them the true path to their salvation, that they may know Allah is the only true God, and to know me as his messenger to them. My miracles were performed by the will of God alone—not by my own power, for I was powerless, unable to do anything of myself, neither could I speak from my own authority, but from the authority of the true God Who commanded me all that I should say. Thus, what the people heard from me were not my words, but the words of God Who sent me. I never said to men, "I was God or worship me." I did not say to them except what God had command me to say, "Worship God, my Lord and your Lord." On the day of judgment, I will say to those who believed that I was God *"I never knew you, depart from me."* And what had been reported of me that I had called myself "son of God" and called God as "my father." This was a Hebrew expression for honoring and tribute, not to meant to be taken literally. I had never claimed that I was a real son of God or the only begotten son. And when the Jews corrupted the figurative meaning of "the son" while arguing with me in the Temple to accuse me of blasphemy, then to stone me, I cornered them using their Old Testament (Psalms). I asked them how would they accuse me of blasphemy because I had used the figurative meaning of the term "son of God" while Psalms had called their judges "gods"? I reminded those Jews about the figurative meaning of the term "son of God," that it referred to one who was sanctified by and sent from God. And I also reminded them of the term "gods" that was directed to their old judges in Psalms, that was also free of any immortal connotations. It was the figurative meaning, those to whom the message of God was given.

I already finished my work that God gave me to do with the Jewish people, but also, I announced about the remaining final message to be brought by the final prophet to come after me to guide people into all truth. This prophet would be with specific descriptions such: his teachings will stay forever. He would be under commands. He cannot speak on his own authority, but only of what he hears from God. He will glorify me. And he will not come until I leave.

The Jews did not accept me. They even sought to kill me. But God thwarted their plot. I even told those Jews and challenged them that when they look for me, they will not find me, and where I go, they cannot come. I even gave them a sign for how God would rescue me. I told them, "As the Prophet Jonah was three days in the belly of the great fish, so I also will be three days in the heart of their land." And I also said to them, "As the Prophet Jonah became by his miraculous rescue a sign to the Ninevites. So, in the same way, I too would be rescued like Jonah by God. Then I would become by the miraculous rescue a sign for the people of my generation." And this sign would be the proof for those Jews that I was the true Messiah. And before the feast of the Passover, God already foretold me through His divine inspiration that He would raise me up to heaven. And while the Jews were on their way to arrest me, I made my prayers and requests with loud cries and tears to God to save me. He answered me and an angel appeared to me from heaven to strengthen me so I was able to leave the place before they came. And after the betrayer, Judas was killed, I appeared to my disciples so that they would know that I am he, the alive Christ. Then I ascended to heaven.

This was Truly Jesus presented by Jesus himself. He came in God's name, and he already prophesied of another who would come in his own name.

Yes, I am Paul

The one who came in his own name. Self-appointed apostle. I wish you would tolerate me even when I am a bit foolish. Please do it. I am jealous for you. You are like a pure virgin whom I have promised in marriage to one man only, Jesus. Not Jesus of those very special so-called apostles, but to my Jesus, the one that I have manufactured and preached to you, through my own ideas. Yes, I would go on doing what I was doing, in order to keep those other "apostles" from having any reason for boasting and saying that they work in the same way that I do. Those men are not true apostles; they were false apostles who lie about their work and disguised themselves to look like real apostles of Christ. Well, no wonder! Even Satan can disguise himself to look like an angel of light! So I am afraid that your minds will be corrupted and that you will abandon your full and pure devotion to Christ, in the same way that Eve was deceived by the serpent's lies. For you gladly tolerate any one of those so-called apostles who comes to you and preaches their Jesus, who is totally different from my Jesus! Because I already came up with an invented Jesus who is, over all, the eternally blessed God. He is the image of God, the image of the invisible God. Who, being in the form of God, did not consider it robbery to be equal with God but made himself of no reputation, taking the form of a servant, and coming in the likeness of man. And being found in appearance as a man, he humbled himself and became obedient to the point of death. For there is one mediator between God and men, the man Christ Jesus, who was born of the seed of David according to the flesh. I am the first to change the figurative meaning of the term "son of God" to the literal meaning and made Jesus a real son of God with power, according to the spirit of holiness, by the resurrection from the dead. But God was not compassionate to His own son. He delivered him to redeem those who were under the Law. He was offered by God so that by his sacrificial death he should become the means by which people's sins are forgiven only through their faith in him. Jesus became a curse for us, but by becoming a curse, he has redeemed us from the curse that the Law brings. He did not take the blood of goats and bulls to offer as a sacrifice; rather, he took his own blood and died to obtained eternal salvation for us. We were God's enemies, but He made us His friends through the death of His son. And if Jesus has not been raised from death, then we have nothing to preach and you have nothing to believe. So if you confess that Jesus is Lord and believe that God raised him from death, you will be saved. This includes everyone, because there is no difference between Jews and Gentiles. God is the same Lord of all.

So this is Falsely Jesus, who was a product of a personal initiative and an invented lie by Paul himself, and Satan has helped him at it. A pure personal hallucinatory initiative. It started from him, and grew, like a snowball, bigger and bigger as it went down through his fake churches. He spread Falsely Jesus through history. But this snowball will melt down when the sun of the truth of Truly Jesus shines upon with his return.

We have seen two completely contradictory images for Jesus in the same Bible. One was by the paintbrush of Jesus himself; the other one was rendered with the paintbrush of Paul. Both images cannot meet in one heart; both cannot be surrounded with the same frame; and both cannot meet in any point, because each of the two painters opposes the other.

Upon reading this book, there will be three cases concerning the image of Jesus inside the hearts of the readers. They are as follows:

1. Keep the fake image of Jesus that was painted by Paul, such as the belief in Jesus as God, or a real son of God, or as a savior who died to save mankind. To those I say, if the Jews at the time of Paul were not deceived with the hallucinatory initiative of Paul's alleged conversion to the religion of Jesus, rather they raised their voices and said, *"Away with such a fellow from the earth, for he is not fit to live!"* (Acts 22:22), as well as the Romanian governor Festus, who said to Paul with a loud voice, after he had heard him talking about how he converted, *"You are mad, Paul! Much learning*

is driving you mad!" (Acts 26:24), so will you let Paul to fool you today? It is risky to keep the fake Jesus of Paul inside your heart, till the time of the appearance of the angel of death to take your soul. For a surety, you will believe in the true Jesus at that moment, but I am afraid that it will be too late then! And on the day of resurrection, Jesus will be a witness against you. And if you go to him, he will say to you: *"I never knew you, depart from me"* (Matt. 7:23).

2. Keep the true image of Jesus, though incomplete. For it is stained with some touches of Paul's brush. To those readers, I say, this type of image that you have in your heart has been wasted in this life, while you thought that you were acquiring good by hanging such image of Jesus in your heart. And on the day of judgment, this type of image that you have will be just like a mirage in a desert. The thirsty one thinks it to be water, until you come up to it. You find it to be nothing, but you will find God with you, who will pay you your due!

3. Keep to the true image of Jesus in its entirety. To those readers who started to realize the truth about Jesus, I say, you have become a true Christian who follows Jesus since you opposed Paul. And to follow Jesus means to join the final religion of God, Islam. By doing this, you are putting your feet on the true path to salvation.

Allah said, *"Is he whose breast Allah has opened to Islam, so that he is in light from His Lord* (as he who is a non-Muslim)*? So, woe to those whose hearts are hardened against remembrance of Allah! they are in plain error!"* (Quran 39:22).

And He said, *"But warn by the Quran him who fears My threat"* (Quran 50:45).

And He, Most High, also said about those who did not accept the true religion of Allah, when they see the unbelievers heading to Hell, and Muslims to heaven, *"How much would those who disbelieved wish that they had been Muslims"* (Quran 15:2).

And finally, Allah said, *"This day, those who disbelieved have given up all hope of your religion; so, fear them not, but fear Me. This day, I have perfected your religion for you, completed My Favour upon you, and have chosen for you Islam as your religion"* (Quran 5:3).

Indeed, this book is a reminder. So whoever wills, let him pay attention to it, and whoever wills not, let him ignore it. But those who ignore the proofs therein will have no excuse on the day of judgment. Lest they say, "There came to us no reminder." Yes! Verily, there came to them this book as a reminder with proofs and evidence. But they denied them and kept Paul's pagan doctrines. To those, Allah said,

> *And turn in repentance to your Lord and submit to Him* (in Islam) *before the torment comes upon you, then you will not be helped. And follow the best of what was revealed to you from your Lord* (i.e., the Quran), *before the torment comes on you suddenly while you perceive not! Lest a person should say: "Oh* (how great is) *my regret over what I neglected in regard to Allah and that I was among the mockers." Or* (lest) *he should say: "If only Allah had guided me, I should indeed have been among the pious. Or* (lest) *he should say when he see the torment: "If only I had another chance* (to return to the world), *then I should indeed be among the good-doers. Yes! Verily, there came to you My verses, but you denied them, and were arrogant and were among the disbelievers."* (Quran 39:54–59)

References

Good News Bible. Today's English Version (American Bible Society)
The New King James Version Bible (Thomas Nelson, 1986)
The Interpretation of the Meaning of the Noble Quran

www.ingramcontent.com/pod-product-compliance
Lightning Source LLC
Chambersburg PA
CBHW031611160426
43196CB00006B/97